The Poems of
THOMAS SHERIDAN

Thomas Sheridan

The Poems of
THOMAS SHERIDAN

Edited by

Robert Hogan

DELAWARE

Newark: University of Delaware Press
London and Toronto: Associated University Presses

Associated University Presses
440 Forsgate Drive
Cranbury, NJ 08512

Associated University Presses
25 Sicilian Avenue
London WC1A 2QH, England

Associated University Presses
P.O. Box 338, Port Credit
Mississauga, Ontario
Canada L5G 4L8

The paper used in this publication meets the requirements
of the American National Standard for Permanence of Paper
for Printed Library Materials Z39.48-1984.

Library of Congress Cataloging-in-Publication Data

Sheridan, Thomas, 1687–1738.
    [Poems]
    The poems of Thomas Sheridan / edited by Robert Hogan.
       p.   cm.
    Includes bibliographical references (p.) and index.
    ISBN 0-87413-495-1
    I. Hogan, Robert Goode, 1930– . II. Title.
PR3687.S147A17   1994
821'.5—dc20   94-8797
                                           CIP

PRINTED IN THE UNITED STATES OF AMERICA

To the Memory of John O'Donovan
Playwright, Scholar, and Wit

Jove smiling heard, and thus replies
"You'll have more labor when he dies;
Whenever I immortal make him,
You never can, nor shall forsake him."

Contents

Contents

10   Contents

Contents

Preface

As with Swift, it will always be an impossibility to establish a definitive canon of Sheridan's poetic work. I have, however, attempted to include every poem that can definitely or plausibly be attributed to Sheridan. Among these are some pieces published for the first time, and some not previously attributed to him. In attempting to collect all of the poems that can be regarded as Sheridan's, I have included not only major poems but also every scrap or fragment of even minor doggerel that has come to my attention.[1] This practice, I am aware, has imparted a somewhat uneven texture to the book. To mitigate this problem, I have relegated some specimens of Sheridan's prolific translating and also some specimens of his pedagogical verse to appendices. Nevertheless, in the main body of the text a witty major work, like "A New Simile for the Ladies," appears in close proximity to a piece of mock-Latin or some hasty doggerel from a letter. In defense, I would note that Sheridan's work has never been collected, makes most sense when read chronologically, and seems to me the work of a very important Irish poet. Hence, it seemed preferable to put him forward in his various entirety, rather than merely by his best metrical foot.

Probably more than most poets, Sheridan used poetry as personal communication. His best work was not written to celebrate a public occasion, or to describe nature, or to reflect generally about art or love or death. In his best work, he wrote to his friends or about his enemies. To his friends, he made jokes that were sometimes whimsical and sometimes ferocious, and they often replied in kind. In his more genial vein, as in the "Patrick Reyly" letters or the "George-Nim-Dan-Dean" sequence, he loved to develop, elaborate, and top his friends' jokes. To Swift, his chief poetical correspondent, he wrote verse letters, birthday poems, and even witty invitations to dinner, and Swift usually responded. Consequently, many of Sheridan's poems can only be fully understood by seeing how they initiate or answer other poems by other poets.

Originally I had planned to include poems to and about Sheridan in a separate appendix. As this arrangement would have entailed much to-ing and fro-ing in the book for the reader, it seemed better to include the poems by Sheridan's friends in their appropriate chronological position among Sheridan's own pieces. By that arrangement, the sequences of verse warfare, the attacks and ripostes and apologies, can be more easily followed. Also, into such an arrangement Sheridan's occasional collaborations, such as "An Elegy on the Much Lamented Death of Mr. Damer" or "The Humble Petition of Stella's Friends," would easily fit. For such a social poet, this arrangement seemed particularly appropriate.

Of the many poems by Sheridan's friends, such as Delany, Helsham, George Rochfort, and possibly Henry Brooke, there is one major omission, and that is a large number of poems by Swift. The Swift poems that I have included are not always Swift's ablest remarks about or to Sheridan, but rather those which most usefully introduce facts, attitudes, or Sheridan's own poems. Thus, Swift's superb "Mary the Cook-Maid's Letter to Dr. Sheridan" is most regretfully omitted, for the material is contained with more relevance to several Sheridan pieces in other Swift poems of the period. To have included all of Swift's Sheridan poems would have considerably increased the bulk of this volume, and these poems are widely available in the modern editions of Swift by Williams, Davis, and Rogers.

As a very notable character on the Dublin scene, Sheridan occasioned much comment. His crotchets, actions, publications, play productions, and even his relations with his wife were the subject of frequent pamphlets and broadsides by acquaintances and enemies as well as by friends. One whole sequence, for instance, celebrates his fictional death, much as Swift had earlier celebrated the presumed death of John Partridge, the London astrologer. A venomous attack by William Tisdall brought forth a fusillade of counterattacks from Sheridan and two poems of commentary by onlookers. Consequently, as Sheridan found himself so frequently attacked or attacking, I have also included among his poems the many poetic pieces about him by enemies and acquaintances. This arrangement too may entail the danger of slightly submerging his own work, but that possibility seems outweighed by the value of demonstrating how a most socially engaged poet responded to his world.

In Appendix I, Verse Translations, I have included any short piece that I have discovered and all of the illustrative fragments. Several of the fragments that appear in *The Art of Punning* I have been unable to discover in the Latin authors to whom Sheridan attributed them, and I suspect that he composed the Latin lines as well as the English translation; I have, however, included them anyhow. Of Sheridan's book-length translations, I have included two specimens from his long out-of-print *Philoctetes,* but I have not included any excerpts from his translation of *Il Pastor Fido,* as it has been recently published. Rather inconsistently, I have included his translation of Tasso's "Amore Fuggitivo," which is contained as an appendix in the recent *Il Pastor Fido* volume for the poem is not only short but also a fine example of the fluency and grace which Sheridan brought to the task of translation.

To Appendix II, Educational Verses upon Latin Grammar, Prosody, and Rhetoric, I have relegated specimens of Sheridan's pedagogical verse. These originally appeared in his *An Easy Introduction of Grammar in English for the Understanding of the Latin Tongue* and his accompanying anthology *A Method to Improve the Fancy.* Although written in meter and rhyme, these verses were intended not as poetry, but as mnemonic devices to aid students to retain facts. Some of them are very deft, but would seem incongruous in the main corpus of Sheridan's poetry. Nevertheless, it would seem equally inappropriate to omit them entirely, for they illustrate Sheridan's incorrigible propensity to burst into verse for any reason, on any subject, at any moment. I have, however, omitted a number of dry illustrative lists of Latin words that he has cast into rhyme and meter.

In Appendix III, Poems of Doubtful Attribution, I have, for the sake of completeness, included some poems that have been assigned to Sheridan by previous authorities, but that seem to me highly dubious if not demonstrably wrong; again I have set forth my reasoning in the Notes. I have also included here several poems that seem to me to be very plausibly by Sheridan, and for which some case can be made, but for which I am unable to advance definitive proofs. Quite a number of other poems, which seem equally plausible as Sheridan's, I have omitted, as a case for them would be entirely speculative. For instance, just among the broadsides of the middle 1720s contained in the Trinity College Library, there is some reason to suspect that "A Poem on the Drapier's Birth-Day. Being November the 30th" and "An Express from Parnassus, To the Reverend Jonathan Swift, Dean of St. Patrick's" might be Sheridan's; he did write several birthday poems for Swift, and his one for 1737 is similar in content to "An Express from Parnassus." "The Satyr Satirrised, an Answer to a Satyr on the Reverend D——n S——t" seems suspiciously Sheridanish. So also does "A Letter from a Cobbler in Patrick-street to the P[rovost] of T. C. D.," for Sheridan is known to have written the "Letter from a Cobbler in Patrick's Street to Jet Black." For these pieces, however, and a number of others, there is no hard evidence.

In editing Sheridan's poems, I have attempted to present a text that would most closely reflect his meaning in the clearest and least distracting form. The choice of a copy-text, then, was an attempt to discover that version of a poem which seemed most accurately to reflect the author's matured and considered intentions. In instances where only one version has survived, there was, of course, no problem. Often, however, there was. Several Sheridan poems exist in his own hand, but some, such as those in the manuscript anthology *The Whimsical Medley,* were transcribed by others. Further, various versions of poems were often published. Sometimes the differences were insignificant variations of spelling or punctuation or minor changes in wording, and may well be attributed to a printer's mistakes or to unauthorized corrections. Sometimes, however, the differences were substantial. Also, some printed versions seem plausibly or definitely to have had the author's imprimatur, but others are more dubious and some he decidedly resented.

In deciding upon a copy-text, then, the choice has often been inevitable, but perhaps just as often it has been determined by the, I hope, informed guesswork of deciding what was closest to Sheridan's final intention. In a small handful of instances, the evidence was so inconclusive that I have arbitrarily chosen what seemed to me the most correct copy-text, but have incorporated a few more factually or metrically correct phrases or lines from another version. A notable instance would be the important poem "Tom Punsibi's Letter to Dean Swift," about which authorities, with good reason on both sides, firmly differ. Such compromises have been held to a minimum, and the problems behind them are detailed in the Notes to the particular poem.

When an alternative version of a poem has some plausible claim to authority, I have recorded all of its substantive variants from the copy-text. In such cases as Barrett's first publication of several poems in 1808, I have usually not recorded the variants, as he was merely transcribing from *The Whimsical Medley* and hence has no independent authority. In other cases, such as the 1828 reprinting of "A True and Faithful Inventory of the Goods Belonging to Dr. Swift, Vicar of Laracor" in *The Cheltenham Journal,* the variants seem mistakes of much later transcribers, and I have ignored them.

The printing history of the Sheridan poems is decidedly complicated. Many of the earliest pieces, as well as some by Swift and other friends, were first transcribed in the manuscript collection, *The Whimsical Medley.* Some of these were later included in collections of Swift's verse, and have been accepted as authentic. Other pieces from *The Whimsical Medley* were first printed by John Barrett in his *Essay on the Earlier Part of the Life of Swift* in 1808. A number of poems appeared in contemporary collections, such as Mathew Concanen's *Miscellaneous Poems, Original and Translated, By Several Hands* of 1724, *Fraud Detected* of 1725, *Whartoniana* of 1727, *Gulliveriana* of 1728, the fourth volume of Samuel Fairbrother's *Miscellanies in Prose and Verse* of 1735, *The Hibernian Patriot* of 1730, Concanen's The *Flower-Piece* of 1731, *The Drapier's Miscellany* of 1733, and *Poems Written Occasionally by the late John Winstanley* of 1751. Many of the Sheridan poems in these collections were taken from broadsides that Sheridan himself had probably caused to be published. However, the poems in the Samuel Fairbrother collection were printed from manuscripts that Fairbrother had somehow obtained, and this unauthorized printing so irritated Sheridan that he wrote a vitriolic poem against "Foulbrother." Nevertheless, the Fairbrother poems, whether they fully reflect Sheridan's final intentions or not, have certainly some authenticity. During his lifetime, some of Sheridan's poems appeared in his books and pamphlets such as *Ars Pun-ica* or *A Letter from a Dissenting Teacher to Jet Black*. Some appeared in periodical publications such as Faulkner's *The Dublin Journal,* in Sheridan's and Swift's *The Intelligencer,* or in *The Gentleman's Magazine*. Many were issued as Dublin broadsides, several appeared in private letters to Swift, and several were written on stray leaves of his manuscript collection of *Apothegms,* now contained in the Gilbert Collection. After Sheridan's death, his papers were acquired by his second son, Thomas, who failed in his attempt to publish a collection of his father's work by subscription and then made some manuscripts available to the English printer Dodsley for the 1745 *Miscellanies*. Other posthumous publications occurred in various Swift editions, such as Faulkner's of 1762, Deane Swift's of 1765, and Sir Walter Scott's of 1814. Some doubtful pieces were printed by Henry Wilson in his *Brookiana* and *The Polyanthea* of 1804. There are details in these volumes as well as in Wilson's *Swiftiana* that are persuasive. However, the evidence was gathered years after the deaths of the principles and yet is sometimes related with a specificity, particularly in the matter of quotation, that seems improbable. In certain other allegations, such as the close attachment of Sheridan for his wife, Wilson flatly runs counter to the evidence of many people, including Sheridan himself. For these reasons, the poems attributed to Sheridan in Wilson would need to be regarded with some skepticism.

In editing Sheridan's poems, I have attempted to present a text which would present his meaning in the clearest and least distracting form. A thoroughly academic approach would have required that the poems be printed exactly as they looked in their first authenticated appearance in either manuscript or print. However, in their various manuscript and printed versions, the poems have little consistency in spelling, capitalization, abbreviation, the use of italics, and, particularly and most confusingly, in punctuation. If Sheridan were a poet only for the academic historian, a faithful reproduction of the conventions and vagaries of eighteenth-century style would have been indeed appropriate. He seems to me, however, not a dead poet but a living one, whose wit and whimsy and invective still vitally speak to us; consequently, I have not hesitated to present him, as Pat Rogers did Swift, in modern dress.

For instance, a poem whose earliest extant handwritten version is either by Sheridan or by the scribe of *The Whimsical Medley* will often be most loosely punctuated, with even occasional stops omitted. As James Woolley points out, eighteenth-century punctuation

> . . . is not necessarily used to mark grammatical units, as is common today, but rather to signal the length of pause if the text were being read aloud—the comma marking the shortest pause, the period the longest. Illogical commas, such as those between subject and verb, often mark an emphatic pause and thus convey meaning.[2]

I know, nevertheless, of no eighteenth-century document entirely written in this fashion. Those which use punctuation to convey meaning by length of pause also use punctuation to convey grammatical relationships. Further, it is a highly subjective judgment for a modern editor to assume that the original punctuation thoroughly reflected the author's intentions, when it may well have reflected the errors of a careless copyist, or, as in Sarah Harding's case, a careless printer.

Subsequent editors, who have printed some of these Sheridan poems in Swift collections, have supplied what punctuation seemed to them most appropriate. Sometimes their versions considerably conflict, and sometimes even seem to obscure the meaning. In the original versions, the colon, for instance, is often used in a manner either misleading or meaningless to the modern reader. Or sometimes equal and parallel parts of a sentence are illogically divided by a semicolon here and a comma there. So, although I have adhered as much as possible to the original punctuation, wherever the sense would be otherwise obscured, I have not hesitated to introduce marks of punctuation as they are conventionally understood today. Occasionally also I have eliminated the comma that is merely pedantic and in no way aids an already sufficient clarity.

Some poems contain direct quotation, and some editors have used in such instances quotation marks while others have not. Thus, the first Sheridan poem in this collection, the 1718 piece, which begins "Dean Dean, since in cruxes and puns you and I deal," has two lines that appear in *The Whimsical Medley* as:

> This I told you before; do you know what I mean, sir?
> Not I, by my troth, sir. —Then read it again, sir.

Which appear in Faulkner and Williams as:

> This I told you before, do you know what I mean, Sir?
> *Not I, by my troth, Sir.* —Then read it again, Sir.

And which appear in Scott as:

This I told you before; do you know what I mean, sir.
"Not I, by my troth, sir." —Then read it again, sir.

I have consistently added quotation marks for direct quotation, feeling that they most clearly and least distractingly aid apprehension for the modern reader.

Italics seem occasionally to have been used by Sheridan, but may often have been added by a printer. A poem such as "The Original of Punning" from *Ars Pun-ica* may even be printed with several italicized words in each line, and, as the italics add only a quaint archaic quality and nothing whatsoever to the meaning, I have eliminated them, and have consistently retained italics only when, as with modern practice, the use affected the connotation of a word.

The eighteenth century made much use of capitalization, particularly in the initial letters of nouns or other significant words, no matter where they appeared in a sentence. I have conformed to modern practice and have thus usually eliminated initial capitals. In the occasional instance, however, of a common noun being raised to a personification, I have, of course, retained the initial capital letter. In a very few instances, an entire word was capitalized in the first extant printing of a poem; and, whenever I suspected that this was the printer's practice rather than the author's, I have reverted to lower case.

In spelling, Sheridan often, but far from always, abbreviated certain words, such as "shou'd" and "wou'd" for "should" and "would," or "thro'" for "through." Also, as was the custom of his time, he frequently omitted the final "e" in the past tense or past participle, so that "display'd" stands for "displayed" or "pick'd" for "picked." In such instances, I have reverted to modern practice. Occasionally, however, Sheridan abbreviated to drop a syllable from a word in order to retain his meter; thus, "Heaven" became "Heav'n" or "power" became "pow'r." In such cases, I have always retained his spelling. And, of course, in such an extraordinary case as "A Copy of a Copy of Verses from Thomas Sheridan, Clerk, to George Nim-Dan-Dean, Esq." which depends on abbreviation for its basic humor, I have scrupulously followed his practice. Also, I have inserted modern American spelling for the English eighteenth-century forms, so that "critick" becomes "critic," or "sawcy" becomes "saucy," or "scull" becomes "skull."

Finally, in the case of untitled poems, as a rule I have used the first line of the poem as the title.

It may be argued that by all of these changes a certain charming flavor is thus lost, and I would not disagree with that point. However, it seems to me that the intrinsic charm of the poems does not reside in such superficial matters, but in their basic and still vital meaning. Hence, I have modernized consistently for clarity.

The two best accounts of Sheridan's life are the twenty pages in his son Thomas's Life of Swift[3] and James Woolley's excellently researched essay, "Thomas Sheridan and Swift" in *Studies in Eighteenth Century Culture,* IX (Madison: University of Wisconsin for the American Society for Eighteenth-Century Studies, 1979), pp. 93–114. However, much information about Sheridan's life and character is to be gleaned from Swift—from many poems and from the prose pieces "The History of the Second Solomon," "Character of Dr. Sheridan," and "A Vindication of His Excellency John, Lord Carteret." Of particular value are Sheridan's letters to Swift, Swift's letters to Sheridan, and a number of joint letters to Mrs. Whiteway, which are contained in the two great modern collections of Swift's correspondence. The more usefully annotated is that by F. Elrington Ball, six volumes, 1910–14, and the more recent is that by Harold Williams, five volumes, 1963–65. There is also a published letter attributed to Sheridan in "A Pilgrimage to Quilca," *Dublin University Magazine,* 40 (1852), pp. 509–26, and there are a couple of letters in George Sherburn's *The Correspondence of Alexander Pope,* five volumes, 1956. In addition, there are some unpublished letters to Thomas Carte in the Bodleian Library and some unpublished letters to Jane Oughton in the Osborn Collection at Yale. There is also one small fragment of Anglo-Latino, possibly intended for Swift in Volume I of Sheridan's *Apothegms* in the Gilbert Collection of the Dublin Central Library, and a fragment of a letter apparently from Sheridan to Swift in the National Library of Ireland.

Many of Sheridan's poems, as has been noted above, were published, during his lifetime and since, in various editions of Swift. The fullest and most accessible such collection is Harold Williams's *The Poems of Johnathan Swift,* three volumes, 2d edition, 1958. I have also made much use of the third volume of the early eighteenth-century manuscript collection, *The Whimsical Medley,* contained in the library of Trinity College, Dublin. This volume contains the first extant transcription of many Sheridan poems. There are also individual Sheridan poems in manuscript in the Huntington Library, the Gilbert Collection of the Dublin Central Library, the National Library of Ireland, and the Royal Irish Academy. Various broadsides of uncollected poems are widely scattered—in the Trinity College Library, the National Library of Ireland, the Gilbert Collection, the British Library, the Bodleian, the Rothschild Collection at Cambridge, the Huntington Library, the Newberry Library, Yale, Texas, and elsewhere. Some important broadsides have unfortunately disappeared from the Gilbert Collection, having been cut out of their bound volumes. Other individual poems appear in various journals of the day, such as *The Gentleman's Magazine* in London, and in various Dublin journals, especially those published by George Faulkner. Unfortunately, there are no complete files of Dublin journals, and some Sheridan poems may be presumed lost. Also probably irretrievable are a number of poems, in both broadsides and journals, which were published anonymously or pseudonymously.

The most important of the Sheridan manuscripts are eleven small volumes contained in the Gilbert Collection. Nine of these volumes contain Sheridan's collection of *Apothegms* as well as a handful of unpublished poems and also a translation of Tasso's "Amore Fuggitivo." All of these appear to be in Sheridan's hand. The two other manuscript volumes contain Sheridan's translation of Guarini's *Il Pastor Fido*. The first volume appears to be in Sheridan's hand, but the second is not, and unfortunately there is a largish hiatus between the two volumes. To hazard a guess about the discrepency, one might surmise that Sheridan made a copy of the translation in two volumes, that the second scribe made another copy in two volumes, and that the first volume of Sheridan was unfortunately paired with the second volume of the second scribe. *Il Pastor Fido* and "Amore Fuggitivo," edited by the present writer and Edward A. Nickerson, were published by the University of Delaware Press in 1989.

As my own grasp of Latin has faded into the most dim remembrance of things past, I must warmly acknowledge the great help of Dwight Peterson in providing me with prose translations of several Latin poems by Sheridan and Swift, and in adding invaluable commentary. I am indebted for various assistance and kindnesses to Mark Amsler, Jerry C. Beasley, Terence Brown, Andrew Carpenter, Maurice Craig, Peter Drewniany, Nicholas Grene, David Hayton, Donald Mell, Edward A. Nickerson, John J. O'Meara, Niall Rudd, and especially to Mervyn Wall and the late Sven Eric Molin and the late John O'Donovan. In addition, the librarians of Trinity College, Dublin, the National Library of Ireland, and the Royal Irish Academy have been, as always, unfailingly helpful, as has Paula Howard of the Gilbert Collection in the Dublin Central Library. Without the previous labors of a small army of Swift editors and scholars, this work could hardly have been brought to completion; and the enormous extent of my indebtedness is, I hope, abundantly clear in the Notes. My greatest debt, however, is to Professor James Woolley of Lafayette College who gave two earlier drafts of this volume the benefit of a most informed and meticulous scrutiny. His general suggestions constituted, in effect, a much needed seminar on textual scholarship, and his specific comments have saved me from innumerable embarrassments. Despite, however, the wise counsel of so many people, whatever blemishes remain in this work must be laid at my own door.

Finally, I am indebted to the following libraries for permission to print material in their collections: the British Library for "A Prologue Spoke by Mr. Elrington," "To his Excellency our Lord Carteret," "Tom Punsibi's Farewell to the Muses," "The Humble Petition of Stella's Friends," "An Ode to be Performed at the Castle of Dublin," "A Letter of Advice to the Reverend Dr. D-la-y" and "A Trip to Temple-Oge, Stephen's Green and the Bason"; the Master and Fellows of Trinity College Cambridge for "Sheridan's Masterpiece," "The Inivitation," "Mr. Sheridan's Prologue to the Greek Play of Phaedra and Hyppolitus," "A Letter of Advice to the Reverend Dr. D-La-y" and "A Letter from a Cobbler in Patrick's-Street"; the Folger Shakespeare Library for "A Prologue to *Julius Caesar*"; the Dublin Corporation Gilbert Library for eleven manuscript poems by Sheridan and for his translation of Tasso's "Amore Fuggitivo" as well as for Samuel Owens's "A Poem"; the Huntington Library, San Marino, California, for Sheridan's holograph poem "A New Year's Gift for the Dean of St. Patrick's" (HM 14369) and for his holograph poem which begins "I'd have you to know, as sure as your're Dean" (HM 14335); the National Library of Ireland for MSS. 1494, 5913, and 8718, and for various printed broadsides; the Newberry Library for "A Letter to Tom Punsibi, Occasioned by Reading his Excellent Farce, Called Alexander's Overthrow, or, The Downfall of Babylon"; the Manuscripts Division, Department of Rare Books and Special Collections, Princeton University Libraries for Swift's three-line verse which begins "Although a great Dunce I be"; the Royal Irish Academy for the untitled manuscript poem that begins "I send this at nine"; the Board of Trinity College Dublin for various poems contained in *The Whimsical Medley* (TCD MS 879/3) and for various printed broadsides; and to the Beinecke Rare Book and Manuscript Library of Yale University Library for "A Poem on Tom Punsibi" (Beinecke General Collection BRS By 6 1722), for quotations from Sheridan's letters to Jane Oughton of January 5, 1734 (Beinecke, Osborn Files 35,186) and of November 3, 1736 (Beinecke, Osborn Files 35,189), and for the Latin Poem to Sir Richard Bulstrode (Beinecke, Osborn Files 5,271).

Notes

1. With one exception, a piece contained in one of the Sheridan volumes housed in the Gilbert Collection. It is written in pencil in Sheridan's hand, but the writing is so faint that I have been able to decipher no more than half of it.

2. James Woolley, ed., *The Intelligencer* (Oxford: Clarendon Press, 1992), p. 41.

3. Much in the younger Sheridan's life of Swift has been admired. Thus, Kathleen Williams in *Swift, The Critical Heritage* (London, 1970), p. 19 remarks that his point of view about *Gulliver's Travels* "obvious though it seems now, is an insight of genuine importance and originality in its own day." Thus, Irvin Ehrenpreis in Swift's fullest modern biography, *Swift, the Man, His Works, and His*

Age (London, 1983), Vol. III, p. 358, acknowledges that the younger Sheridan's attack on Orrery's *Observations* was well founded. Thus, also, have many of the younger Sheridan's accounts of Swift been accepted by various biographers. Nevertheless, his accuracy has frequently been doubted. As Ehrenpreis puts the case against him:

> A number of his statements and stories about Swift can be disproved. Often when they cannot, Sheridan himself traces them to questionable sources. Though he made a general claim to receive anecdotes from his father . . . , he attributes few of them explicitly to him, and few seem derived from his own recollection. He was no more than nineteen, and perhaps only sixteen, when Dr Sheridan died; and he had spent the five preceding years living in Westminster School or in Trinity College, Dublin. . . . During those years he would have talked little with a father who did not give his leisure to domestic conversation.
>
> Dr Sheridan moved to Cavan in 1735; and after that change, the son had few opportunities to observe the friendship of his father and the dean except when Swift, at the age of sixty-eight, visited Cavan. The language of Swift's references to the younger Sheridan in his own memoir of the father (written in 1738) suggests to me that the dean, though interested in the lad, was not then in touch with him. . . . Finally, the younger Sheridan wrote his life of Swift about forty-five years after his father died, and I am struck by the thinness of the few anecdotes which he specifically traces to his own encounters with the dean.
>
> Therefore, and because much of the material strikes me as prima-facie improbable, I distrust his concrete details. Nevertheless, he was Swift's godson and did receive first-hand impressions. He must also have heard enough to know how other people responded to Swift. I am therefore inclined to accept his broad view of the friendship between his father and the dean. (iii, 358)

Some of these points, such as the fact that Sheridan wrote the biography many years later, are well taken. Others strike me as distinctly more speculative or dubious, and the closing comment about the Swift-Sheridan friendship seems a strangely grudging testimony to the well attested. The younger Sheridan was born in 1719, which would have made him nineteen, and not sixteen, when his father died. We know that Swift took an interest in his godson, and we know that Swift frequently visited Sheridan's school, and sometimes asked for papers from the students to correct. It scarcely seems implausible that he would have taken a particular interest in those of the younger Thomas and that they would have helped to form his good opinion of the boy. Further, the short account that the younger Thomas gives of Swift's last visit to Cavan seems to me most plausible in its description of the Dean's difficult character at that time, and simultaneously of the Dean's unfailing kindness to an earnest and promising boy and for its description of the Dean's particular hobbyhorse about the proper pronunciation of the language. Indeed, this particular attitude strongly influenced the younger Sheridan's own subsequent career as well as those of several of his descendants, such as Richard Brinsley Sheridan, James Knowles, and James Sheridan Knowles. In the younger Thomas Sheridan's case, Swift's most notable influence was the publication of the first pronouncing dictionary in the language, in which the notion of "correctness" was derived from the most cultivated speakers, among them Swift, of the age of Queen Anne.

Also, in favor of Sheridan's reliability is his own and his father's overwhelming admiration for Swift. It must be assumed that he gleaned much of his information from his father; it should definitely not be assumed, as Ehrenpreis does, that Doctor Sheridan did not talk to the boy. On the contrary, his fondness for this favorite son may be seen in the pride with which he describes him, as well as the care he takes for him, in his letters to Thomas Carte. Finally what must particularly be taken into consideration is the characters of the father and the son. Doctor Sheridan was certainly thoughtless and foolish, and his son in his maturity was certainly, in public and in private, irascible and intractable. But my reading of their lives also suggests that both were deeply religious and profoundly honest. In sum, I would tend to read the younger Sheridan's life of Swift as probably containing errors of fact or memory, but fundamentally as an attempt to tell the unvarnished truth, as he saw it.

My own feeling about the criticisms of the younger Sheridan's reliability is that he strongly makes a point, earlier made by Delany, which many modern Swiftians do not accept—that Swift and Stella went through the ceremony of marriage. Indeed, the younger Sheridan relates one particularly touching scene that he could only have heard from his father. This is the scene shortly before Stella's death in which only she, Sheridan, and Swift were present, and in which she begs Swift to recognize her as his wife, and he turns on his heel and leaves without a word. If the usual modern view about the relations of Swift and Stella are to be accepted, obviously this account and the younger Sheridan's account generally must be discredited.

A Bibliographical Summary

The following lists represent the chief sources upon which I have relied, but many others are cited in the Notes to particular poems. I have not listed here the individual publication of particular poems in broadsides or journals, as that information is also provided in the Notes.

Major Manuscript Sources

Trinity College, Dublin. Ms. 879, *The Whimsical Medley,* Vol. III. Transcripts of recent and contemporary verse, made for Theophilus, first Lord Newtown-Butler, around 1720, containing several Sheridan poems.

Gilbert Collection, Dublin Central Library. Eleven small octavo volumes, nine containing Sheridan's Collection of *Apothegms* and two containing his translation of Guarini's *Il Pastor Fido.* Several previously unpublished poems are contained in the *Apothegm* volumes, as well as the translation of Tasso's "Amore Fuggitivo."

Major Published Works by Sheridan

An Easy Introduction of Grammar in English for the Understanding of the Latin Tongue. Dublin: D. Tompson, 1714. Contains also the anthology *A Method to Improve the Fancy.*

Ars Pun-ica, Sive Flos Linguarum: the Art of Punning; or the Flower of Languages; in Seventy-Nine Rules: For the Farther Improvement of Conversation and the Help of Memory. Dublin: James Carson, 1719.

The Philoctetes of Sophocles. Dublin: R. Owen, 1725.

The Satires of Persius. Dublin: George Grierson, 1728.

The Intelligencer. With Swift, and originally published periodically from May 11, 1728 to around May 10, 1729, in Dublin, by Sarah Harding. The first collected London edition was published by A. Moor in 1729, a second by Francis Cogan in 1730, and a modern edition edited by James Woolley by Oxford in 1992.

A Poem on the Immortality of the Soul, by Sir John Davis, to which is prefixed An essay upon the same subject. . . . Dublin: S. Hyde, 1733.

The Faithful Shepherd. A Translation of Battista Guarini's Il Pastor Fido. . . . Edited and completed by Robert Hogan and Edward A. Nickerson. Newark: University of Delaware Press, 1989.

Collections Containing Poems by or Relating to Sheridan

Miscellanies in Prose and Verse. The Fourth Edition. . . . Dublin: S. Fairbrother, 1721.

Miscellanies, Written By Jonathan Swift, D.D. . . . *The Fourth Edition.* London, 1722.

Miscellaneous Poems, Original and Translated, By Several Hands . . . *Published by Mr. Concanen.* London: J. Peele, 1724.

Fraud Detected. Or, The Hibernian Patriot. Dublin: George Faulkner, 1725.

Whartoniana: Or Miscellanies, In Verse and Prose. By the Wharton Family . . . 1727. Two volumes.

Gulliveriana: Or, A Fourth Volume of Miscellanies. . . . London: J. Roberts, 1728.

Miscellanies in Prose and Verse. Four volumes. London and Dublin: Samuel Fairbrother, 1728–35.

The Hibernian Patriot. London: A. Moor, 1730.

The Flower-Piece: A Collection of Miscellany Poems. By Several Hands. London: J. Walthoe and H. Walthoe, 1731.

The Drapier's Miscellany. Dublin: James Hoey, 1733.

The Works of J. S, D. D, D. S. P. D. in Four Volumes. Dublin: George Faulkner, 1735. Volume II contains the Poems. By 1772, this work had increased to twenty volumes with various poems added.

The Entertainer, Vol. I. London: F. Cogan, 1746.

A Supplement To the Works of The Most celebrated Minor Poets. . . . London: F. Cogan, 1750.

Poems Written Occasionally by the Late John Winstanley . . . Interspers'd with Many Others by Several Ingenious Hands. Vol. II. Dublin: S. Powell, 1751.

A Supplement to the Works of Dr. Swift. London: F. Cogan, 1752.

The Works of Jonathan Swift, D. D. . . . *Accurately revised In Six Volumes.* . . . London: C. Bathurst, 1755. Edited by Hawksworth and gradually expanded, notably by Bowyer in 1762–64, by Deane Swift in 1765, and by J. Nichols in his *A Supplement to Dr. Swift's Work: Being a Collection of Miscellanies in Prose and Verse, by the Dean; Dr. Delany, Dr. Sheridan, and others, his Intimate Friends. Vol. XXIV of the Works.* London: W. Bowyer and J. Nichols, 1776. This was the basis for the younger Sheridan's 1784 edition.

Swift, Deane, ed. *Letters, Written by the Late Jonathan Swift, D. D. . . .* Three volumes. Dublin: J. Williams, 1768.

Additions to the Works of Alexander Pope, Esq. Together with Many Original Poems and Letters, Of Contemporary Writers, Never Before Published. In Two Volumes. . . . London: H. Baldwin, 1776.

Sheridan, Thomas, ed. *The Works of the Rev. Dr. Jonathan Swift.* Seventeen volumes. London: C. Bathurst, 1784. Contains Sheridan's Life of Swift.

Miscellaneous Pieces, In Prose and Verse. By the Rev. Dr. Jonathan Swift, . . . Not Inserted in Mr. Sheridan's Edition of the Dean's Works. London: C. Dilly, 1789.

Barrett, John. *An Essay on the Earlier Part of the Life of Swift.* London: J. Johnson, J. Nichols and Son, 1808.

Scott, Sir Walter, ed. *The Works of Jonathan Swift.* Nineteen volumes. Edinburgh: Archibald Constable, 1814; rev. ed., 1824.

Roscoe, Thomas, ed. *The Works of Jonathan Swift, D. D.* Two volumes. London: Henry Washbourne, 1841.

Browning, William Ernest, ed. *The Poems of Jonathan Swift, D. D.* Two volumes. London: G. Bell and Sons, 1910.

Ball, F. Elrington, ed. *The Correspondence of Jonathan Swift, D. D.* Six volumes. London: G. Bell and Sons, 1910–14.

Ball, F. Elrington. *Swift's Verse. An Essay.* London: John Murray, 1929.

Williams, Harold, ed. *The Poems of Jonathan Swift.* Three volumes. Oxford at the Clarendon Press, 1937; rev. ed., 1958.

Horrell, Joseph, ed. *Collected Poems of Jonathan Swift.* Two volumes. London: Routledge and Kegan Paul, 1958.

Williams, Harold, ed. *The Correspondence of Jonathan Swift.* Five volumes. Oxford at the Clarendon Press, 1963–65.

Davis, Herbert, ed. *Swift: Poetical Works.* London: Oxford University Press, 1967.

Rogers, Pat, ed. *Jonathan Swift, The Complete Poems.* Harmondsworth, Middlesex: Penguin Books, 1983.

Biography and Background

Ball, F. Elrington. *A History of the County Dublin: The People, Parishes and Antiquities from the Earliest Times to the Close of the Eighteenth Century.* Dublin: Thom, 1902–6; Dublin: University Press, 1917–20.

Burtchaell, G. D., and T. U. Sadleir, eds. *Alumni Dublinenses.* Dublin: Alex. Thom, 1935.

Davis, Herbert, et al., eds. *The Prose Works of Jonathan Swift.* Fourteen volumes. Oxford: Basil Blackwood, 1939–68.

Delany, Patrick. *Observations upon Lord Orrery's Remarks.* . . . Dublin: Robert Main, 1754.

Ehrenpreis, Irvin. *Swift, the Man, His Works, and the Age.* Vol. III. London: Methuen, 1983.

Foxon, D. F. *English Verse 1701–1750: A Catalogue.* . . . Two volumes. Cambridge: Cambridge University Press, 1975.

Gilbert, Sir John. *A History of the City of Dublin.* Three volumes. Dublin: McGlashan and Gill; London: John Russell Smith, 1859.

Orrery, John Boyle, Earl of. *Remarks on the Life and Writings of Dr. Jonathan Swift.* London: A. Millar, 1752.

Sherburn, George, ed. *The Correspondence of Alexander Pope.* Five volumes. Oxford at the Clarendon Press, 1956.

Smith, David Nichol, ed. *The Letters of Jonathan Swift to Charles Ford.* Oxford at the Clarendon Press, 1956.

Swift, Deane. *An Essay upon the Life, Writings, and Character of Dr. Jonathan Swift.* London: Charles Bathurst, 1755.

Welcher, Jeanne K., and George E. Bush Jr., eds. *Gulliveriana VI.* Delmar N.Y.: Scholars' Facsimiles & Reprints, 1976.

Wilde, W. R. *The Closing Years of Dean Swift's Life.* Dublin: Hodges and Smith, 1849.

Wilson, Henry. *Brookiana, Vol. I.* London: Richard Phillips, 1804.

———. *Swiftiania, Vol. I.* London: Richard Phillips, 1804.

———. *The Polyanthea, Vol. I.* London: J. Budd, 1804.

Introduction

Although a great Dunce I be,
Happy if once I be
With my friend Punsiby.[1]
                                           —Jonathan Swift

Tom Pun-sibi, or Tom the Punster,[2] was the pseudonym of Dr. Thomas Sheridan, schoolmaster, clergyman, poet, scholar, wit, linguist, translator, and for about twenty years, the boon companion of Jonathan Swift. Sheridan is all but forgotten today, saved by Swift scholars, and his many brilliant descendants, particularly his grandson Richard Brinsley Sheridan and his great-great grandson Joseph Sheridan LeFanu, have quite overshadowed him. Even today, two hundred and fifty years after his death, his lineal descendants continue to command attention—Caroline Blackwood for her novels, for instance, or Nicola LeFanu for her music.

Nevertheless, Thomas Sheridan is important for more than being the direct ancestor of perhaps two dozen prominent writers, musicians, actors, scholars, and politicians. He is important in himself, and his chief claim upon our interest is as a poet. Curiously, he has never had a collected edition, and he is not represented in any of the notable anthologies of eighteenth-century poetry. Indeed, those of his poems which have remained in print appear only in collections of Swift's verse, and appear there mainly because they provided the occasions for poetic ripostes by Swift. Some of Swift's Sheridan poems, such as "Mary the Cook-Maid's Letter to Dr. Sheridan," are among the Dean's most adroit comic pieces. Nevertheless, Swift's editors and critics have generally deplored the rhyming riddles, the versified banter, and the playful poetic warfare that passed between the two men. Swift's most meticulous modern biographer, Irvin Ehrenpreis, describes these "Trifles" as but "laborious fun" that "can amuse few readers today." Such casual dismissals were Sheridan's lot even in his own day, and even by his own friends.

Sheridan was such a feckless man and had finally such an unsuccessful career that it was easy enough for sober judges to dismiss his poetic jokes as trivial, and to dismiss him as merely the Dean's jester. Successful

jokes, however, can hardly be fashioned by anyone who writes badly, and
Sheridan handled words, both in verse and in prose, with a facility that
often rivaled Swift's. Swift did not keep Sheridan by him for easy amuse-
ment in an idle hour, as William Tisdall and Lord Orrery charged. Swift
kept Sheridan as friend for the delight he took in Sheridan's wit. It was
a delight that could change to irritation, for in their poetic jousts the issue
was ever in doubt, and the greater writer sometimes took the greater
blow. Each partner, in fact, scored knockdowns. Each partner won bat-
tles. Indeed, Swift would hardly have engaged in a poetic contest in which
each man agreed to write the other a poem for 365 successive days if the
poems he received had not been a spur to his own increased efforts.
Certainly, the friendship was partly therapy on Swift's part to chase away
the depression of living in that "wretched, dirty Dog-hole and Prison" of
Ireland, but partly it was the joyous intellectual stimulation that he re-
ceived from the man whom he described as "Deliciae Sheridan musarum,
dulcis amice."

With such testimony from such a source, little further apology should
be needed for retrieving from the crumbling broadsides, the dusty pamph-
lets, and the faded manuscripts of the past a body of work that has a long
overdue claim on our attention.

The Sheridans were an Irish family long established in County Cavan.
Two generations before Dr. Thomas, the Reverend Denis Sheridan, a
native Irish speaker, had helped Bishop Bedell translate the Old Testa-
ment into Irish. Three of Denis's sons were themselves eminent: William,
the Bishop of Kilmore, who lost his see when he would not take the oath
of allegiance to William of Orange; Patrick, the Bishop of Cloyne; and
Thomas, the historian, who followed the fortunes of the Stuarts and is
said to have married a natural daughter of James II. A fourth brother,
James, is sometimes mentioned as the father of Dr. Thomas. However,
Trinity College records indicate that Thomas's father was Patrick Sheri-
dan of Kilmore who is listed as "colonus" or farmer. Perhaps the best,
then, that can be said is that, as Percy Fitzgerald remarked, Dr. Thomas
was a "near relation" of Denis Sheridan.

Drawing upon Trinity College documents, Burtchaell and Sadleir in
Alumni Dublinenses note that Thomas was born in County Cavan and
entered Trinity as a Pensioner or tuition-paying student on October 18,
1707, at the age of twenty. This age would put his birth in 1687, and that
date seems confirmed by Sheridan himself, who wrote in a letter of
January 5, 1734 to Jane Oughton that he was in his forty-seventh year.[3]

He was an eminently able student, and in his third year at Trinity he
received one of the "Native" scholarships. He thoroughly mastered Latin

and Greek, was fluent in French and Spanish, and had more than a nod-
ding acquaintance with several other languages.

On February 9, 1710/11, he received his B.A., and around this time he
married. His wife was Elizabeth MacFadden of Quilca, near Virginia in
County Cavan. Elizabeth was her father's sole heir, and on his death the
small property passed into Sheridan's hands. What also passed into his
hands, according to Swift, were debts and relatives that had to be sup-
ported for years.

Sheridan's marriage was a disaster from the very beginning, and Swift
described his wife as "the worst wife" he ever saw, "as cross as the devil,
and as lazy as any of her sister sows, and as nasty," and as "the most
disagreeable beast in Europe":

> He lets his wife (whom he pretends to hate as she deserves) govern, insult,
> and ruin him, as she pleases. Her character is this: Her person is detestably
> disagreeable; a most filthy slut; lazy, slothful, and luxurious, ill-natured, envi-
> ous, suspicious; a scold, expensive on herself, covetous to others: She takes
> thieves and whores, for cheapness, to be her servants, and turns them off every
> week: Positive, insolent, and ignorant, prating, overweening fool; a lover of the
> dirtiest, meanest company. An abominable tatler, affecting to be jealous of her
> husband with ladies of the best rank and merit, and merely out of affectation
> for perfect vanity.

This ferocious catalog was echoed by Sheridan himself as late as 1735,
when he wrote to Swift:

> Thus have I been linked to the Devil for twenty-four years, with a coal in my
> heart, which was kindled in the first week I married her, and could never by
> all my industry be extinguished since. For this cause I have often been charged
> with peevishness and absence among my best friends. When my soul was
> uneasy every little thing hurt it, and therefore I could not help such wrong
> behaviour. You were the only one who had an indulgence for me.

Or, as Sheridan mourned in 1736 to his friend Jane Oughton, "How terri-
ble a thing it is y^t a man Should Suffer all his life, for the phrenzy of
Youth. I was in the mad years of life when I marryed & mad to marry,
& almost mad after I had marryd."

Despite "this hell," as he once described his unhappy domestic life,
Sheridan contrived to remain for much of the time the gayest of compan-
ions and the blithest of spirits. He also had a large family. In a Latin
letter to Swift, written possibly about 1732, Sheridan remarked, "Habeo
novem infantes et uxor." Of these nine children, two were particularly
interesting. His second son Thomas became an eminent actor, theatrical
manager, lexicographer, and educational theorist, who married the play-

wright and novelist Frances Chamberlaine, and whose most notable child was the playwright Richard Brinsley. His daughter Hester, who was named after Swift's Stella, married John Knowles and her grandson was James Sheridan Knowles, the once eminent nineteenth-century dramatist and actor.

Swift found much to criticize in Sheridan's raising of his children:

> Instead of breeding up his daughters to housewifery and plain clothes, he got them, at a great expense, to be clad like ladies who had plentiful fortunes; made them only learn to sing and dance, to draw and design, to give them rich silks and other fopperies; and his two eldest were married, without his consent, to young lads who had nothing to settle on them.

Nevertheless, Swift was godfather to Sheridan's favorite and most promising son, Thomas, and relates that Sheridan sent Thomas to Westminster School in London where the boy did well. However, "the doctor was then so poor, that he could not add fourteen pounds to enable the boy to finish the year," and so he was recalled to Dublin and matriculated at Trinity.

In the account of his father which the younger Thomas wrote in his life of Swift, there is no allusion to his father's relations with his mother, but there are other indications that Sheridan was not entirely faithful. In "On the Five Ladies at Sot's Hole, with the Doctor at Their Head," a poem written about 1728, Swift gibes at Sheridan for regaling himself at a Dublin tavern among prostitutes:

> Fair ladies, number five,
>   Who in your merry freaks,
> With little Tom contrive
>   To feast on ales and steaks.
> While he sits by a-grinning,
>   To see you safe in Sot's Hole,
> Set up with greasy linen,
>   And neither mugs nor pots whole.
> Alas! I never thought
>   A priest would please your palate;
> Besides, I'll hold a groat,
>   He'll put you in a ballad. . . .

Also, in "The History of the Second Solomon," a caustic criticism of Sheridan that Swift wrote in 1729, appear the remarks:

> He is allured as easily by every new acquaintance, especially among women, as a child is by a new plaything; and is led at will by them to suspect and quarrel with his best friends. . . .

Solomon had published a humorous ballad, called "Ballyspellin," whither he had gone to drink the waters, with a new favourite lady. The ballad was in the manner of Mr. Gay's on Molly Mog, pretending to contain all the rhymes of Ballyspellin. His friend, the person so often mentioned [Swift himself], being at a gentleman's house in the neighbourhood, and merry over Solomon's ballad, they agreed to make another, in dispraise of Ballyspellin Wells, which Solomon had celebrated, and with all new rhymes not made use of in Solomon's. The thing was done, and all in a mere jest and innocent merriment. Yet Solomon was prevailed upon by the lady he went with, to resent this as an affront on her and himself; which he did accordingly, against all the rules of reason, taste, good-nature, judgment, gratitude, or common manners.

Whatever his attractions to other women, Sheridan's aversion to his wife remained constant, and he left his "unkind spouse" and one of his daughters who had married against his wishes only five shillings in his will. (To his other children, he left £50 each. However, in a lease registered in the Deeds Office on July 26, 1746, Sheridan's surviving sons, Richard and Thomas, allowed their mother to enjoy Quilca during her life and to receive all rents and profits from it.)

Yet if Sheridan was not a good husband, he was an extremely good teacher. He was ordained by Archbishop King in January 1711/12, and James Woolley remarks that:

A bishop's license was required in order to teach, and it may be that Sheridan sought this license in 1713, since a testimonium of his B.A. was issued to him on May 25, 1713. Before taking his M.A. in 1714, he seems to have begun his career as a teacher, in what were known as classical schools—schools which emphasized the Latin classics and prepared boys to be gentlemen.

Swift called Sheridan "doubtless the best instructor of youth in these kingdoms, or perhaps in Europe," and certainly he was for some years extremely successful in Dublin. Both Swift and Sheridan made jokes about Sheridan's use of the birch, but these really seem generic jokes about schoolmastering. In actuality, Sheridan seems to have been no Thwackum or Squeers, but to have based his teaching upon sound insight into the minds of young boys. He wrote:

. . . being much fretted with the unsual Restraints of a School, who before liv'd in a manner Unconfin'd, it cannot be expected their Application to their business shou'd be the Result of a willing Mind, but much less so, while they are at first presented with a Heap of Rules, which are almost equally difficult both in English and Latin. And what is as great an Obstacle as any to their being reconcil'd to such a Life, is the unmerciful Tyranny of some Masters, who unreasonably attempt to Improve their Understanding, by frightening them out of their Wits. All which taken together, we shou'd not wonder to find Boys have genrally such an Aversion for School, and such a cool Indifference for Books.

This insight is embodied in Sheridan's textbook, *An Easy Introduction of Grammar in English for the Understanding of the Latin Tongue,* which he published in 1714. In his Preface he deplored the dullness with which Latin was traditionally taught, and attributed the dullness to the teaching of the rules of Latin in Latin. His grammar, then, not merely explained the rules in plain English, but even printed many of them in verse which could act as a mnemonic aid. His intention was to tempt and coax by making dry material pleasant. "There is a great difference," he wrote, "between leading a Person in at an easy Gate to survey some pleasant Fields, and dragging him through entangled *Bushes* and *Thorns* to come at them."

The technique of making study a pleasure is also the rationale for the second part of his volume, which is a little anthology called *A Method to Improve the Fancy.* In his short Preface to *A Method,* Sheridan explains that the pieces of poetry are intended for "the Improvement of youthful fancy," and adds "Nor is this the only Advantage intended, the Peevish Boy is by them courted to Love and Admire those books, which otherwise he must be compell'd to read." The snippets of verse are in both English and Latin, and contain much from Virgil, Horace, Ovid, Shakespeare, Milton, and Cowley. And again Sheridan could not resist writing out his own definitions of various figures of speech in verse.

One would scarcely have thought that the publication of two such useful and quite innocuous works would have occasioned difficulty. However, for the perennially unlucky Sheridan, it did. Shortly after their publication, Sheridan received a letter from a fellow schoolmaster named John Greer who complained that his students were being abused by Sheridan's. If, Greer continued, the abuse did not cease, he would seek redress "in a more publick Manner." The redress, he seemed to imply, would be the exposure of Sheridan as a plagiarist.

Despite a mollifying postscript, Sheridan's letter of reply[4] contained some satire of Greer's own prose, and so in 1718 the irritated Greer produced a pamphlet entitled *Bathyllus Redivivus: An Essay Proving that the Grammar, call'd* Sheridan's, *is a Transcript from the* Royal-Grammar: *and, That his Additions are* Erroneous, Impertinent, *and* Insufficient. Greer described Bathyllus as "A Poetaster, Humourist and Mimic, in the Reign of Augustus," who claimed some work of Virgil as his own. Then in the body of the pamphlet, Greer meticulously demonstrated that Sheridan, in his lists, his prose explanations, and even in his mistakes, slavishly and with but slight verbal changes, followed the work of the sixteenth-century grammarian William Lily in *A Short Introduction of Grammar,* the so-called "Royal Grammar." Greer's pamphlet is an irrefutable and thoroughly documented establishment of Sheridan's plagiarism. Its manner is pedantic and its tone heavily ironic, but its content is completely convincing.

Shortly after Greer's attack, there appeared an anonymous eight-page pamphlet entitled *An ESSAY, Proving, That an ESSAY Proving That The GRAMMAR call'd* Sheridan's, *is a Transscript from the* Royal Grammar, *is a learned, judicious, and candid Treatise, and plainly proves Mr.* Sheridan *to be no better than he shou'd be.* Obviously by Sheridan, this ironic refutation was one of his drollest prose productions, and it effectively salvaged his reputation. The "author" of this treatise is described as "a Person of some Condition and Letters," who emerges as a reasonable man sympathetic to Greer, and one who thinks Sheridan a wild eccentric:

> Perhaps Sir you don't know, That the Man you have to deal with is the most harden'd, incorrigible Wretch in Nature. If he were not so, how is it possible, either that so many *Lashes of pointed Satyr* shou'd not make him once cry out, or at least bring him to some Sense of his Folly. Whereas I profess Sir he is as *Giddy* and *Unthinking as ever.* Sometimes he laughs and is as merry as a Madman, presently he's in the Dumps, and *Makes his Will just as he us'd to do.* And, such a will it is, as I am confident none but the mad *Earl of Pembroke* ever thought of any Thing like it. At one time he's as proud as the *Prancer in the Fable Huffs* and *Dings,* and *Pretends,* he does not care a Fig for you, and all your Satyrs, and then again he's as humble as the Ass, and wou'd give the World you were Friends with him.

Sheridan's real defense is that all Grammarians have of necessity used each other's work, and that it is no great or unusual fault to have "put one Word for another, that was like it." Then the "author" remarks:

> Now Sir you see what a cringing Submission here is. Nay I dare say you never saw any thing like it in your Life; and yet, Sir, you must not think to depend upon it; by no Means; for in Two Minutes Time *Whip* he's upon his *High Horse* again, and he says *He'll transcribe and transcribe,* and *He does not care who knows it,* and *He'll give no Body Thanks.* What, says he, *Didn't all the Grammarians that ever wrote (except the First) Transcribe and Build upon the Plan of those that went before 'em?* An impudent Dog! . . . And he farther adds upon his Honour, That if you shou'd in the mean Time set out a Grammar, and there shou'd be one Paragraph worth taking, That he will *Totidem Verbis* Transcribe and publish it. Nay more, he'll call it his own Grammar after all this. Well, but Sir, says I, pray how is this consistent? Don't you pretend in your Preface, that you have Printed a new Grammar? Pretend says he, what do you mean by that? my Words are these: *I have compil'd the following* English Grammar *for the Attainment of the* Latin Tongue. *And pray Sir is not* COMPILO *to take by Extortion or Wrong, to Rob, to Pill, to Plunder.* . . .

In short, Sir, he's the most obstinate Person you ever met with; and I am almost afraid you'll never do any Good with him; but however, if I were you, I'd try once more; 'tis ten thousand Pities such a Spirit as yours should be discouraged.

Greer was certainly a man of learning and ability, with some talent of his own for irony, and he had utterly proved his case against Sheridan. In this exchange, however, Sheridan easily won by a characteristic ebullience of fancy that made his opponent's quite sound case appear pedantic and ridiculous. It was a talent for comic writing that was to stand Sheridan in good stead as the mock-serious opponent of probably the greatest ironist in the language, Swift.

Yet, in constructing a persona of clever irresponsibility, Sheridan inadvertently laid a pitfall for himself. It was a pitfall that was deepened the next year when, in his *Art of Punning,* he solidified the public perception of his character, and even gave that character a name, Tom Pun-sibi or Tom the Punster. Bernard Shaw also had much fun in constructing the public mask that he called G.B.S. G.B.S., like Tom Pun-sibi, contained some of his creator's own characteristics, but there was much more to both Shaw and Sheridan than the mischievous prankster. Unfortunately, both creators had done their jobs so well that in the minds of many the mask became the face. The mask of Tom Pun-sibi symbolized cleverness and high spirits, but it also carried an onus of fecklessness and irresponsibility.

It was, however, responsibility allied to cleverness that characterized Sheridan as a schoolmaster. One attractive feature of his school was the production shortly before the Christmas holidays of a play. His boys took the parts, and their relatives and notable friends of the school, such as the Lord Lieutenant and the Archbishop of Dublin, were invited to see a performance either of a play in English or of one of the Greek or Latin classics in the original language. In 1720, the play was Euripides's *Hippolytus,* and for this occasion Sheridan wrote a prologue to be spoken by the youngest child in his school. His friend, the jovial Dr. Richard Helsham, was connected with the child's family and persuaded the boy to speak an alternative prologue of his own which was rather gibing at Sheridan. This was one of the rare occasions on which Sheridan lost his temper, and he almost refused to let the performance proceed. After the play, Archbishop King and the boy's father both attempted, without success, to persuade the lad to recite the original. Both Sheridan's prologue and Helsham's were published as broadsides, and, indeed, as Helsham's piece was attributed to Swift, one might wonder if Swift had not himself a hand in it.

Swift, we may certainly assume, was at many of these performances, for he took a great interest in Sheridan's school and often visited it either to hear recitations or to dine with the master. Once Swift wrote Sheridan, "Play send me a large Bundle of Exercises, bad as well as good, for I want something to read." In an obituary of Sheridan, Swift summed him up as a schoolmaster:

> His chief shining quality was that of a schoolmaster; here he shone in his proper element. He had so much skill and practice in the physiognomy of boys that he rarely mistook at the first view. His scholars loved and feared him. He often rather chose to shame the stupid, but punished the idle, and exposed them to all the lads, which was more severe than lashing. Among the gentlemen in this kingdom who have any share of education, the scholars of Dr. Sheridan infinitely excel, in number and knowledge, all their brethren sent from other schools.

James Woolley remarks that "By far the greatest portion of Sheridan's income seems always to have come from his teaching; during his best years—the middle 1720s—he earned £800 per year from his school alone." This sum, with £40 a year that his wife had inherited, and with occasionally as much as £400 from rents, should have supported even Sheridan's large family in some comfort. However, like many of his notable descendants, Sheridan was ever generous and improvident and always pressed for money. His convivial nature delighted in society, and he entertained too often and too lavishly.

Among his closest and cleverest cronies were two men he had met at Trinity, Richard Helsham and Patrick Delany. These learned and able men could also turn a witty verse, and by 1718 they formed the core of a clique that centered around Swift and that included the Rochforts of Gaulstown, and, of course, the admirable Stella who was quite capable of holding her own, either in versifying or in repartee, with any of the men. In a short piece called "Bons Mots de Stella," Swift described a couple of her remarks about Sheridan:

> Dr. Sheridan, who squandered more than he could afford, took out his purse as he sat by the fire, and found it was very hot; she said the reason was, that his money burned in his pocket. . . .
> Dr. Sheridan, famous for punning, intending to sell a bargain, said, he had made a very good pun. Somebody asked, what it was? He answered, My a——. The other taking offence, she insisted the doctor was in the right, for everybody knew that punning was his blind side.

From 1718 through the early 1720s, this group met frequently, dined and amused each other with a barrage of verse that was as clever in content as it was ingenious in form. Many of their productions were verse riddles and epigrams, and many have been jumbled together by various of Swift's editors under the heading of "Trifles." That is, as too ephemeral and trivial to warrant serious contemplation. Granted, their separate and sometimes joint productions were only intended as light verse, and many were doubtless hasty impromptus. However, if the lightness of light verse demands a carefree attitude, it also requires a considerable care for form. Indeed, the wit of the best of these pieces—among them Sheridan's circular verses and vowelless verses—depends upon as complete a command of form as do the most serious productions of the most serious poets. Even, perhaps, more so. A Wordsworth or a Yeats may include a flaccid line or a banal phrase in a serious poem without significantly impairing its cumulative impact. If, however, a writer of witty light verse once loses control, he courts complete failure.

Sheridan's delight in the tricks and quirks of language was nowhere more charmingly evident than in his popular booklet of 1719, *The Art of Punning*—or, to give it its full title, *Ars-Punica, Sive Flos Linguarum: The Art of Punning: or the Flower of Languages; in Seventy-Nine Rules: For the Farther Improvement of Conversation and Help of Memory*. This droll and frivolous work had two editions in Dublin, was published in one of Swift's collections in England (where, indeed, it was attributed to Swift), and occasioned a number of verse ripostes and pseudoencomia to its author, "Tom Pun-sibi."

Much of the humor of the booklet resides in its mock academic approach, in which the introductory matter—including dedications, congratulatory poems, and prefaces—is quite as long as the body of the work.

When Sheridan finally does turn to his subject, he first, with tongue in cheek and many misapplied quotations from classical authors, attempts to establish hoary precedents and a worthy provenance for the pun. Then he offers various definitions of punning, some sound and some silly. The Moral Definition is "Punning is a Virtue that most effectively promotes the End of Good Fellowship, which is Laughing." The Physical Definition, however, is a mock-pompous pedantry: "Punning is an Art of Harmonious Jingling upon Words, which Passing in at the Ears, and falling upon the Diaphragma, excites a titillary Motion in those Parts; and thus being conveyed by the Animal Spirits into the Muscles of the Face, raises the Cockles of the Heart."

Although Sheridan's title promises seventy-nine rules, there are actually only thirty-four. Most are charmingly absurd, but Rule XXII is particularly interesting because it obviously contains a bit of repartee from real life:

RULE XXII. *The Rule of Inoculating,* is when a Person makes an excellent

PUN, upon it, as Dean S——t one Day said to a Gentleman, who had a very little *Bob Wig,* Sir, *The Dam of your Wig is a Whisker;* upon which I came in very *a propos* and said, Sir, *That cannot be, for it is but an Earwig.*

For the unlucky Sheridan, even such an entertaining little volume evoked criticism. A 1719 rejoinder entitled "The Folly of Puns, or, False Witt Disclosed" actually concluded that "nothing has been published in this Age more prejudicial to Learning and Society than that Pamphlet."

Possibly because of his growing family, Sheridan decided to supplement his income by becoming a practicing clergyman as well as a schoolmaster. In 1724, he took his degree of Bachelor of Divinity, and two years later of Doctor of Divinity. In the meantime, Swift had decided that his friend needed help. On April 17, 1725, shortly before leaving for an extended visit to Sheridan's country place in Cavan, Swift wrote to Lord Carteret, the Lord Lieutenant of Ireland, setting forth Sheridan's merits and requesting for him "some church living to the value of 150£ per annum."

The first living to become available was Rincurran in County Cork, and Carteret immediately bestowed it upon Sheridan. Swift, well aware of his friend's faults of character, wrote him a couple of letters full of practical advice about how to comport himself. Among his strictures were: "pray act like a man of the world. . . . Pray take my advice for once, and be very busy while you are there. . . . Pray show yourself a man of abilities." A day later, a worried Swift wrote again, mentioning that it had occurred separately to him, to Stella and to Sheridan's mother-in-law that Sheridan should "make a great appearance of temperance." And of particular importance: "pray do not employ your time in lolling a-bed till noon to read Homer."

Of course, minding his business effectually was what Sheridan never did. He stopped over in Cork where his friend Archdeacon Russell asked him to preach the Sunday sermon on August 1. On Sunday morning, Sheridan, who was, as his son relates:

> . . . a very absent man, had forgot his engagement, and was sitting quietly at his lodging *en deshabille,* when a message from the Parish Clerk, who saw no preacher arrive after the service had begun, roused him from his reverie. He dressed himself with all speed, and of two sermons that he had brought with him, took the first that came to hand, without looking at it.

The text of the sermon was "Sufficient unto the day is the evil thereof," but unhappily the day was the anniversary of the Hanoverian succession to the throne. There was no political reference in the sermon, but, as Sheridan's son wrote: "Such a text on such a day, excited a general murmur through the whole congregation, to the great surprise of the preacher, who was the only person ignorant of the cause; of which he was not enformed till after he had descended from the pulpit, when the affair was past remedy." The Sheridans were, of course, a well-known Jacobite family, and everyone took the sermon as a premeditated slur. In the congregation was one Richard Tighe, a member of the Privy Council and, as the younger Thomas described him:

> . . . a furious Whig, and one of the most violent party-men of the times. He immediately took post for Dublin, where, by his representation of the matter, as Swift has observed in giving an account of this transaction, "such a clamour was raised by the zeal of one man, of no large dimensions either of body or mind, that we in Dublin could apprehend no less than an invasion by the Pretender, who must be landed in the South."

Subsequently, both Swift and Sheridan paid Tighe back in various ferocious verses that they printed, but for Sheridan the damage had been done. Carteret, a Whig appointee, had no choice but to remove Sheridan from the list of chaplains and to forbid him the Castle.

On September 11, Swift commiserated with him in a letter from Quilca, and offered some sound advice:

> Therefore sit down and be quiet, and mind your business as you should do, and contract your friendships, and expect no more from man than such an animal is capable of, and you will everyday find my description of yahoos more resembling. You should think and deal with every man as a villain, without calling him so, or flying from him, or valuing him less. This is an old lesson.

Then, after further sensible admonitions to live quietly at Quilca, to cease entertaining, to lead a regular life, and definitely not to publish his sermon, Swift concluded, "You think all the world has now nothing to do but to pull Mr. Sheridan down; whereas it is nothing but a slap in your turn, and away."

Although Sheridan's hope for preferment in the church was now dashed, some immediate good did emerge from the fiasco. Archdeacon Russell, feeling conscience-stricken about the matter, made over to Sheridan the manor of Drumlane in Cavan which produced an annual rent of £250. However, like his profligate grandson Richard Brinsley, Thomas never found any amount of money to be enough, and there were to be difficult days ahead.

Sheridan continued to find time, however, not only for conviviality and for teaching, but also for serious work. In the same year as his Cork sermon, 1725, he published a translation of Sophocles's *Philoctetes*. The translation is written in blank verse for the dialogue, but the Choruses are in various rhyme schemes and varieties of two, three, and four stress lines. All of the language is direct and easily apprehensible on the stage, as Sheridan was perhaps bearing in mind that the play might be spoken by his schoolboys. He remarked in his dedication that he made it into "plain English . . . as close as the Propriety of our language will admit."

This exemplary production was followed in 1728 by *The Satyrs of Persius,* a translation of the Latin verses of Aulus Persius Flaccus into English prose. The book is dedicated to Sheridan's former student, Lord Viscount Mountcashel, and in an introductory note Sheridan remarks that his choice of Persius was dictated in part by the six satires offering an appropriate "System of Morality" for a young man. He also says that his design was "to give as much Light, as I could, into the Meaning of a very obscure Author," and that he has striven for "Easiness of Style rather than Elegance." Sheridan achieves really more than easiness, for he seems always reaching for a vivid English equivalent rather than for a dry exactness. Thus, Persius's lines from Satyr III:

> . . . Verum-ne? Ita-ne? Ocyus adsit
> Huc aliquis. Nemon'? Turgescit vitrea bilis:
> Findor, ut Arcadiae pecuaria rudere credas.

These lines Sheridan vigorously translates as:

> Is it true? Is it so indeed: Let one of the Servants come quickly. Here. Who's there? What! will no body answer? I swell with Anger, and grow as hoarse as an Arcadian Ass.

To his translation, Sheridan allowed his schoolmaster self to append copious footnotes derived from his vast reading. Indeed, most of the pages devote more space to footnotes than to text, and this was one of the points upon which Sheridan was twitted in the poem "To My Worthy Friend TS——. D.D. On his Incomparable Translation of and Notes on Persius." Even as a scholar, he did not escape censure.

Finally, in a serious vein, Sheridan published in 1733 an edition of *A Poem on the Immortality of the Soul* by the Elizabethan poet Sir John Davis. Probably hoping for preferment, he dedicated it to the Earl of Orrery, and prefaced it with his own "An Essay upon the Immortality of the Soul." Toward the end, there is a lengthy dissection of Man, which reads in part:

> To sum up all; we see, that Childhood is vain and trifling; Youth tormented by it self, and others; Manhood racked with Ambition, Avarice, numberless Passions of Body and Mind; exposed to Calumny, Treachery, Disappointments, Fears, beside the natural Sufferings of Hunger, Thirst, Heat and Cold; teized with Sollicitudes for Family; Grief for the Loss of Children and of Friends, by Death or otherwise; and often coming to the Catastrophe of Life, behold a

greater Load laid upon him, at a Time when he is least able to bear it, I mean
all the Infirmities of old Age; ridiculed from his nearest Friends to his Servants,
for what he cannot help, the Imperfections of every Sense, which oblige him
to be an universal Dependant upon the Compassionate; and thus he totters off
the Stage, as much forgotten, and unlamented in a few Days, as if he had never
had a Being among us.

This diagnosis is used to prove the point that there must be an immortal
soul, as God would not have created man for a life so pointless and
painful. It is also interesting for the profound sincerity of its tone and as
evidence of a private individual much deeper than the social prankster.

Nevertheless, it was Sheridan's sociability and irrepressible sense of
fun that particularly endeared him to Swift. Their friendship, however,
was not always unruffled. In a witty exchange of verses possibly ten
months or so after they had met, during September and October 1718,
what had begun as raillery became, especially on Sheridan's part, more
heated. In some short poems, he lamented that Swift's Muse was dead,
and this theme he developed in a long poem called "The Funeral," which
he passed to their mutual acquaintances, and which was a fable that
showed asses and owls attending the funeral of Swift's poetic talent. This
apparently funny poem was too much for Swift, and in a letter of November 10, he complained to Delany, "I have long thought several of his
papers, and practicularly that of the Funeral, to be out of all the rules of
raillery I ever understood; and if you think the same, you ought to tell
him so in the manner you like best, without bringing me into the question,
else I may be thought a man who will not take a jest." With the same
letter he enclosed a dignified poem to Delany, in which he generalized
upon wit and humor and the type of raillery permissible in friendly social
discourse, and then critically applied his strictures to Sheridan. This
poem, of course, Delany was meant to show to Sheridan, and it had
the desired effect. Sheridan seems to have recalled and destroyed "The
Funeral," and then composed his "Palinodia" or Recantation; and so the
breach was healed.

After this, except for Sheridan's irritation over Swift's reply to his
Ballyspellin ballad, the men remained basically friends and also literary
allies until their final quarrel in 1738.[5] After 1718, Swift could still not
resist an occasional barb at his friend, such as the poem "On the Five
Ladies at Sot's Hole, with the Doctor at Their Head," to which Sheridan
would reply more or less in kind. Or Swift would write an even more
cutting piece, like "The History of the Second Solomon" of 1729. However, if Swift's view of his friend was always tempered by criticism, Sheridan's view of Swift became ever more eulogistic. In any event, by the
1718 letter to Delany, Swift definitely established the tacit rules of the

friendship, the chief being that Swift would be the captain and Sheridan his lieutenant. Indeed, in a letter of July 17, 1735 to Orrery Swift referred to "My Viceroy Trifler, Sheridan."

One or two writers not particularly well disposed to Sheridan were to accuse him of toadying and of playing the court jester. However, the tone of the Swift-Sheridan letters does not at all suggest toadying, but the mutual affection of a distinguished older man and a brilliant younger one. And Sheridan would have been a jester no matter what his company.

One aspect of Sheridan's life that afforded Swift both pleasure and exasperation was Sheridan's estate, Quilca, in County Cavan. Quilca might really be taken as a symbol of Sheridan's conduct of his own life, for he sought constantly and ineffectually to improve the place into a kind of gentility and even an appearance of grandeur. However, there was never enough money, and the usual manner of life there was makeshift and slovenly. Nevertheless, Swift visited Quilca perhaps half a dozen times, and in 1725 he, Stella, and Dingley spent several months there while he worked on *Gulliver's Travels*.

Among Swift's devastating remarks about Sheridan's estate was the short prose piece "The Blunders, Deficiencies, Distresses, and Misfortunes of Quilca." This list was begun on April 20, 1725, and was proposed to be continued weekly and to contain 21 volumes in quarto. Part of the first week's list noted:

But one lock and a half in the whole house.
The key of the garden door lost.
The empty bottles all uncleanable.
The vessels for drink very few and leaky.
The new house all going to ruin before it is finished.
One hinge of the street-door broke off, and the people forced to go out and come in at the back-door.
The door of the dean's bedchamber full of large chinks.
The beaufet letting in so much wind that it almost blows out the candles.
The dean's bed threatening every night to fall under him. . . .
Bottles stopped with bits of wood and tow, instead of corks.

Today, Quilca is allotted a half a page in the Irish Tourist Board's pamphlet on Cavan, but there are no signposts to direct one to it, and the pilgrim must depend upon a faint local memory to find his way. Nothing remains of the land-proud Sheridan's improvements, except perhaps part of a wall against which pigs huddle. However, there is still the handsome small lake and the tree-covered knoll still called "Stella's Bower" upon which Swift may have contemplated the final changes to *Gulliver's Trav-*

els, or have chortled over how appropriate Sheridan would be for, as Ehrenpreis has suggested, the model for the vague and feckless King of Laputa.

The most extended collaborative effort of Swift and Sheridan was a journal called *The Intelligencer,* which began in 1728, ran for twenty occasional numbers, and then appeared in collected editions in London in 1729 and 1730. Each man wrote about half of the contents, which were both in prose and verse, and which ranged from serious discussions of the state of Ireland, to literary matters, to attacks on their joint enemies, Richard Tighe and Dean Smedley.

Sometimes strong, sometimes scathingly amusing and sometimes, as in Sheridan's poem "The Tale of the T——d," drolly scabrous, *The Intelligencer* had no really defined character, and its readers hardly knew what to expect, either in tone or in content, from one issue to the next. Had there been more issues and had the enterprise not been carried on with the left hands of the collaborators, the paper might have grown into something more impressive. However, Sheridan, upon whose shoulders most of the business of the enterprise fell, was not always in town, and could not persuade Swift to continue. As Swift wrote Sheridan on September 18, "I told you I would think no more of it, neither do I conceive the World deserves so much trouble from you or me."

And certainly Sheridan had enough private troubles to cope with. Like his son Thomas and his grandson Richard Brinsley, he earned considerable sums of money and yet was always hardpressed for cash. As his son wrote:

> . . . his expences kept pace with his income, and increased in the same proportion. Indulging his natural disposition, he made frequent costly entertainments, and on certain days when he was freed from the afternoon attendance on school, his table was open to all *bons vivans,* jovial companions, &c. And where mirth and good wine circulated so briskly, it is to be supposed there was no lack of guests.

Swift often lectured Sheridan about his improvidence. For instance, on June 29, 1725, Swift wrote:

> I must desire that you will not think of enlarging your expenses, no not for some years to come, much less at present; but rather retrench them. You might have lain destitute till Antichrist came, for anything you could have got from those you used to treat; neither let me hear of one rag of better clothes for your wife or brats, but rather plainer than ever. This is positively Stella's advice as well as mine. She says now you need not be ashamed to be thought poor.

Ten years later the same sermon might still have been preached, but

Sheridan was still as heedless and still as buoyantly optimistic. "Belturbet fair will make me an Emperor," he wrote on August 13, 1735. And he was still as impoverished: "My purse, God help me, is grown as slender as a famished weasel," he wrote on September 17. The thrifty and businesslike Swift did try to help, both by accepting a mortgage on some of Sheridan's land and by remembering Sheridan in his will.[6]

Many of the documents that might have helped to chart Sheridan's financial affairs were destroyed by the burning of the Four Courts during the Irish Civil War; however, in the Public Records Office in Dublin is a book of extracts, compiled from 1912 to 1914 by Henry C. S. Torney, of some of the documents relating to the Sheridan family that were registered in the Deeds Office. A perusal of these sales and leases and mortgages gives a picture of Sheridan constantly juggling with property in order to raise money for his immediate expenses.

He was also juggling possibilities about changing the course of his own career in order to achieve some finally secure level of income. One such opportunity, and probably a sound one, was arranged by Swift. Worried by Sheridan's extravagant style of living in Dublin, Swift sought to find him a job in, as the younger Sheridan put it, "a distant part of the kingdom, where he would have no such temptation to indulge the extravagance of his dispostion." When the schoolmaster of Armagh died, Swift quickly applied to Primate Lindsay, who offered Sheridan the position, a lucrative enough one that would have brought in £400 in rents alone. Sheridan, however, hesitated and thought to consult his Trinity friends. According to the younger Sheridan, Swift's response was:

> Your friends, said Swift, you will ever be a blockhead as to the world: because they are pleased with your company, and gratify themselves in passing many happy hours with you in social mirth, you suppose them to be your friends. . . . Take my advice; consult none of them; but accept without hesitation of an offer which will secure you a handsome income for life, independent of casualties.

But Sheridan, as he wrote about himself in 1736, was "famous for giving the best advice and following the worst." Accordingly, he consulted his friends, among whom were probably Helsham and Delany, and he certainly also consulted his own inclinations. The upshot was that he refused the Armagh school and remained in Dublin.

He did make various attempts to better his fortunes by seeking patronage. He dedicated his Persius to young Lord Mountcashel, he dedicated his edition of Davis to Lord Orrery, and he even composed a birthday ode to Queen Caroline. None of these attempts was really successful, and during the early 1730s even his school was much less successful than before. A chief reason was that a new school, supported by Delany and some of Sheridan's other friends, had been set up in Dublin, and its success was cutting into Sheridan's. On March 27, 1733, Swift remarked about the matter:

> I own you have too much Reason to complain of some Friends, who next to yourself have done you most hurt, whom still I esteem, and frequent, though I confess I cannot heartily forgive. Yet certainly the Case was not meerly personal Malice to you, (although it had the same Effects) but a kind I know not what Job, which one of them hath often heartily repented.

Sheridan's resentment was not to be assuaged, and as late as January 17, 1735/36, he wrote to Swift:

> As for my *Quondam* friends, as you stile them, *Quon-dam*[7] them all. It is the most decent way I can curse them; for they lulled me asleep till they stole my school into the hands of a blockhead, and have driven me towards the latter end of my life to a disagreeable solitude, where I have the misery to reflect upon my folly in making such a perfidious choice at a time when it was not in my nature to suspect any soul upon earth.

In 1730, Sheridan attempted to mend matters by exchanging his living in Rincurran for one much closer to Dublin in Dunboyne, County Meath. But even this exchange worked out badly, for the income from the Meath living turned out to be considerably less than that from Cork.

Several of Sheridan's letters of 1732 and 1733 to his friend Thomas Carte survive, and, although much in them has to do with sending his son Tom to Westminster School in London and putting him under Carte's wing, Sheridan also alludes to a scheme of setting up a school of his own in London to prepare very young boys for such a school as Westminster. This project came to nothing, but some of Sheridan's remarks show how disillusioned he had become with Ireland and with his career there. On November 28, 1732, he wrote:

> I wish with all my Soul, as well as I love my country, that I were settled some where near you and London. To speak the truth I would rather be a flea-catcher to a dog in England than a privy-counsellour here.

And on June 21, 1733, he wrote:

> ... I cannot help wishing to be ... out of a country, wch every native of common reason ought to exchange for Lapland, for there they have poverty and innocent diversions, but here we have the former attended with malice & calumny. Why will you not have some compassion on a suffering soul, & get me an exchange at any rate whilst I have a little remains of life & spirit, to

begin the world again in a way of drudgery where the labourer cannot fail of his hier. Be assured that without any pretenses to prophecy, I can foresee this nation will proceed to ruin in a Geometrick proportion, & although I would not leave it like a rat, only upon the foresight of danger, yet I think my self obliged to do it for the sake of others, from whom I have a greater tenderness, than to let them live here to such an age, as to feel like my self.

By 1735, Sheridan had decided finally to remove himself from Dublin, and he exchanged his living in Dunboyne for the Mastership of the Free School in Cavan.[8] When he was closing up his old school in Dublin, the younger Sheridan tells us that Swift came to call:

He happened to call in just at the time that the workmen were taking down the pictures and other furniture in the parlour: that parlour where for such a number of years, he had passed so many happy hours; struck with the sight he burst into tears, and rushed into a dark closet, where he continued a quarter of an hour before he could compose himself.

The Cavan school was not really successful either, and Sheridan found himself again mortgaging and selling lands and attempting to collect rents. As he wrote dispiritedly to Swift on February 23, 1735/36:

My school only supplies me with present food, without which I cannot live. I hope, if I have any friends left, it may encrease, and once more put me out of a miserable dependance upon the caprice of friendship. This year has been to me like steering through the *Cyclades* in a storm without a rudder; . . . I pray God you may never feel a dun to the end of your life; for it is too shocking to an honest heart.

But dejected and harassed by problems as he was, Sheridan was able to write some of his jolliest letters to Swift in this dreariest period of his own life. His punning letters probably provided the one saving outlet for his natural high spirits, his fancy, and his cleverness. For instance, in a letter of October 5, 1735, he held forth on "jogg Ralph I":

First, with submission, you should have begun with the Poles Are Tick Ann Tar Tick, next the May read dye Ann, the Eak water, the whore Eyes on, the Eak lip Tick, the Trow Pick of can sir, the Trow pick of Cap rye corn, or Cap Rick horn, the twelve signes Aare I ease, Tower us, Jay me knee, Can Sir, lay O, Veer goe, lye braw (quoth the *Scotchman*), Sage it are eye us, Cap wrye corn us, hack weary us, and piss is, together with Cull ewers, Zounds, and Climb bats, etc., etc. In order to give you a full idea of the chief towns in Europe, I shall only mention some of Lord Peterborough's rambles. He had like to break al *Lisb on* in Portugal: he *Mad rid* through Spain; he could not find *Room* in Italy: he was *Constant in a pull* among the Turks: he met with

> his name sake *Peter's burgh,* in Musk O vye: he had like to *Crack O* in Poland: when he came to *Vye any,* he did there *jeer many:* in France he declared the King of Great Britain, with its King upon the *Par is:* in a certain northern country he took a frolic to put on a friar's cope; and then he was in *Cope in Hag in.* Pray, *Dean mark* that. In Holland he met with a G-*amster,*———*Dam* you, said he in a passion, for a cheat: he was there poxt by a whore; and he cried out, *Rot her dam* her.

Shem the Penman could have done no better.

Toward the end of his life, Sheridan worked on two lengthy projects. One was the translation of Battista Guarini's *Il Pastor Fido.* Until the publication of this version in 1989, Sir Richard Fanshawe's *The Faithful Shepherd* of 1647 was the only easily available version of Guarini's important pastoral drama. Although Bruce Penman in the Penguin *Five Italian Renaissance Comedies* calls Fanshawe "the best English translator that any Italian poet has ever had," Fanshawe often settles only for an approximation of the sense in order to fit the content into his rigid heroic couplets. Further, he reduces Guarini's admittedly extraordinary length by about a fifth. In contrast, Sheridan's use of blank verse for ordinary dialogue and of various forms of rhymed verse for the songs is more faithful to Guarini's original form, and his translation more closely approximates Guarini's length. Also, as in Sheridan's other translations, there is a clarity, ease, and suppleness of style that make his rendering more modern than Fanshawe's, and, to my mind, that retain more of the charm of the original.

Sheridan's other late project was a lengthy collection of striking or humorous anecdotes gleaned from his voluminous reading in Greek, Latin, French, Spanish, and English. He apparently first mentioned the project to Swift in 1733, for Swift wrote him on March 27:

> I am confident your Collection of *Bons mots,* and *Contes à rire* will be much the best extant; but you are apt to be terribly Sanguine about the Profits of Publishing: However it shall have all the Pushing I can give.

It was not, however, until June 22, 1737, that Sheridan wrote Swift in a Latin letter that he had now transcribed three books and was sending them over to London. There may have been as many as thirty small octavo volumes, but the nine that survive attest to an enormous expenditure of time and energy. Although the books are pleasant as a browsing read, they are a sort of academic Joe Miller's Jest Book, and one would have wished that Sheridan instead had applied himself to further translation or, better, to his own original work. In any event, the huge project came to nothing.

For twenty years, Swift and Sheridan were friends. They derived both delight and benefit from their friendship. The frivolous fun they created together would occasionally exacerbate one or the other, but only occasionally. Nor was the fun entirely frivolous, for their joking poems and their mutual playfulness with words had really the effect of forcing each to utilize his wit at its fullest stretch, and of making both to experiment with technique and with language. They extended each other's potentialities; they forced each other to become better writers and fuller men.

And so it is sad to record that at the end of their lives they became estranged. As Sheridan's son reported:

> Dr. Sheridan, finding himself disappointed in all his expectations on his removal, continued at Cavan but little more than two years; when he sold his school and returned to Dublin. While a house was preparing for him, he took up his abode as usual at the Deanery, where he was seized with a fit of illness, which confined him for some weeks to his chamber. The Dean was not in a condition at that time to afford him any consolation, nor in a disposition of mind to be troubled with a sick guest. A longer fit than usual of his old complaint, had deprived him of all society, and left him a prey to the horror of his own thoughts. He had long been weary of the world, and all that was in it. He had no prospect of relief but from death, for which he most ardently wished, even when his state was not so bad. For some years before, he never took leave of a friend in an evening, but he constantly added, "Well, God bless you, and I hope I shall never see you again." In this hopeless state, deprived of all the comforts of life, no wonder if he was dead also to the feelings of friendship. When the Doctor had sufficiently recovered to be able to go abroad, he was apologising to the Dean for the trouble he had given him; saying, "I fear, Mr. Dean, I have been an expensive lodger to you this bout." Upon which Mrs. W[hiteway], a relation of the Dean's, who then chiefly managed his affairs, and who happened to be present, briskly said, it is in your power, Doctor, easily to remedy this, by removing to another lodging. Swift was silent. The poor Doctor was quite thunderstruck. As this lady had always professed great friendship for him, and lay under considerable obligations to him, he quickly saw that this must have been done by Swift's direction; in which he was confirmed by his silence on the occasion. He immediately left the house, in all that anguish of mind, which a heart possessed of the warmest friendship must feel, upon the abrupt breach of one of so long a standing, and so sincere on his part; nor did he ever enter it again.

Sheridan did not live long after this incident, and after his death, Swift wrote an account of his character and life. In its general outlines, its facts, and judgments, the account accords with other appraisals of Sheridan by those who knew him. Nevertheless, my own feeling about the "Character of Dr. Sheridan" is exactly that of Sir Walter Scott, who wrote:

> As Swift advanced in years and infirmities, it became more difficult to please

him, or even to soothe his habitual irritation. . . . The present Character retains some traces of friendship become cold and broken. The defects of imprudence are more strongly insisted upon, than is consistent with the respect due to the memory of a departed friend; nor has the praise that affectionate warmth which the long and revered attachment of the deceased so particularly deserved.

In 1729, Swift had written an even more caustic piece about Sheridan called "The History of the Second Solomon." What Scott said of it seems equally applicable to the "Character": "This is one of the pieces in which Swift has indulged his irritable temperament, at the expense of his head and heart."

After Sheridan's death, Swift's infirmities increased apace. He was a very different man—"his understanding was gone, and his memory failed." Nevertheless, as Sheridan's son relates, "some former feelings of the heart . . . remained":

> I had a strong instance given me by his servant William, how deep an impression the Doctor had made there; who told me that when he was in this state, the Dean, every day, for a long time, constantly asked him the same question—"William, did you know Doctor Sheridan?" Yes, Sir, very well—and then, with a heavy sigh, Oh I lost my right hand when I lost him.

Sheridan's illness was far advanced when he left the Deanery, and his old friend Helsham, who died a few weeks before him, had diagnosed his illness as heart disease. Accordingly, Sheridan made his will and retired to a house in Rathfarnham owned by a Mr. O'Callaghan, the brother of one of his former students. On October 10, 1738, as Sheridan's son relates:

> Soon after dinner, the conversation happened to turn on the weather, and one of them observed, that the wind was easterly. The Doctor upon this, said, "Let it blow East, West, North, or South, the immortal soul will take its flight to the destined point." These were the last words he ever spoke, for he immediately sunk back in his chair, and expired without a groan, or the smallest struggle. His friends thought he had fallen asleep, and in that belief retired to the garden, that they might not disturb his repose; but on their return, after an hours walk, to their great astonishment, they found he was dead. Upon opening the body, Doctor Helsham's sagacious prognostic was discovered to be the immediate cause of his death. I know not whether it is worth mentioning, that the surgeon said, he never saw so large a heart in any human body.

After Sheridan's death, his son Thomas bought his papers from the estate for £50. He made several attempts to get him into print, the most ambitious attempt being a proposed multivolume edition to be issued by subscription. Unfortunately that project came to nothing, and so the bulk of Sheridan's work has never been printed. This misfortune must be particularly felt in the matter of the poems, for his son would have been the best person to establish an authoritative canon.

A modern editor in assembling Sheridan's poems, which quite constitute his finest work, faces an ultimately insoluble task. Many of the Swift-related poems were transcribed in the eighteeth-century collection called *A Whimsical Medley,* and have been printed in various collections of Swift's work. However, most of the poems in *A Whimsical Medley* were not attributed to an author, and I suspect that there is more of Sheridan's work contained in it, particularly among the many riddles, than can ever be identified. Other pieces, which were sometimes attributed to Sheridan, appeared in unauthorized contemporary collections such as those by Concanen or Fairbrother, but many others are either difficult or impossible to identify because poems published as broadsides or in journals were often either unsigned or signed by initials or by a pseudonym. The difficulty is further compounded by the penchant Sheridan shared with Swift of often writing in the guise of another character or person.

In any event, in the two hundred and fifty years since Sheridan's death, no one has published such a collection, and perhaps the reason may partly be that readers of the Sheridan poems included in editions of Swift would probably be disposed to regard him mainly as an inventive writer of trivial light verse, to compare him to the towering Swift, and to accept Swift's occasional denigrations of him.

Indeed, even in his own time, Sheridan was not all that highly regarded as a poet by his friends and contemporaries. The magisterial Swift in his poem to Delany of November 10, 1718, recommended that Sheridan improve his comic verse by studying Delany. In a 1732 letter to Pope, Swift denigrated a quatrain Sheridan had added to "Tim and the Fables" as "slovenly." In 1726, the anonymous author of "An Epistle in Behalf of Our Irish Poets to the Right Hon. Lady C——t" wrote that the wife of the Lord Lieutenant could take "punning Tom Sh——r————d—— n" and whatever other Irish poets she desired off to London with her, but that Dublin "would be perfectly undone" without Swift and Delany. Delany himself did not take Sheridan's poetic powers too seriously. In "The Pheasant and the Lark," he dismissed one Sheridan poem with the line "Tom-*tit* cou'd write, and so he *writ.*" In his *Observations upon Lord Orrery's Remarks,* he wrote that Sheridan was "a fidler, and a poet: and most certainly understood more of each, than he could execute." Orrery too had remarked that Sheridan's "pen and fiddlestick were in constant motion; and yet to little or no purpose." In his witty poem on Sheridan's circular verses, George Rochfort had Sheridan saying that "the Dean and Delany transcendently shine," but "My verse is neglected, my tunes thrown away." Doctor Helsham attacked one of the comic prologues that

Sheridan wrote for his school plays as "scurvy stuff." Even Sheridan's son dismissed one of his father's finest poems as "negligently written." And it was not merely Sheridan's versifying and fiddling that came under attack. His grammar, his book on punning, his plays, and his translation of Persius all had their more or less vehement detractors. With such a chorus of criticism in his own time, it was predictable enough that Sheridan's poetry should have been so generally dismissed and largely ignored ever since.

One cannot but feel, nevertheless, that a principal reason for Sheridan's bad press must be laid not to the quality of his work but to the nature of his own character. Both physically and intellectually, he was a highly visible and highly individual inhabitant of Dublin. He was ever in the public eye, promulgating eccentric jokes like his puppet show play or ebulliently tilting in verse broadside or prose pamphlet at his enemies. As a schoolmaster, he was original and admired, but as a wit, polemicist or "punster base," he was probably not only much too quirky but also much too prolific to be thoroughly appreciated. As Delany in a basically critical passage admitted, "He had a faculty, and indeed, a felicity of throwing out hints, and materials of mirth and humour, beyond any man I ever knew." Nevertheless, a constant shower of wit, sometimes whimsical but sometimes barbed, can often cause as much resentment as it does delight. Swift's 1718 letter to Delany was written because Sheridan was getting too funny at Swift's expense; Delany's remarks may be seen as a response to Sheridan's criticism of Delany's begging verse letter to Carteret; Helsham's prologue, written possibly with Swift's help, was a rather cruel attempt to make Sheridan look foolish on a public occasion; Swift's and his friends' retort to the carefree Ballyspellin ballad was both rather harsh and a trifle nasty. These and the many other poetic attacks upon Sheridan contained in this book are, of course, somewhat balanced by a number of tributes, even by some of the attackers, to his warmth and gaiety and good fellowship. Nevertheless, there were few tributes to his Muse; and his character, his absentmindedness, and fecklessness were easy and tempting marks to attack. Given his character, the wit could easily be seen as the fool.

Two hundred and fifty years on, however, the wit has long been dead, and the work does not at all look foolish. In a collection like this, which attempts to print the poet as completely as possible, there is some obvious unevenness. The verse squibs that Sheridan dashed down in his letters of the 1730s to Swift were not intended as considered work. A public piece meant to be sung, such as the 1728/29 Ode for the Queen's birthday, is conventional and imitative. But when Sheridan was at the top of his form—as he was in the short verse letters to Swift of 1718, or in the Dan Jackson's nose sequence of the same year, or in the George-Nim-Dan-

Dean sequence of 1721—he was brilliant. "Tom Punsibi's Letter to Dean Swift" of 1720 is as gently humorous, and as accurate, a depiction of Swift's grumpiness as one is likely to get. "A Description of Doctor Delany's Villa" has lost none of its fanciful exaggeration and sweetly chiding whimsy.

It is easy to dismiss such achievements as light verse, and light verse is doubtless the center of Sheridan's poetic achievement. It is, however, difficult simultaneously to dismiss Sheridan as a hasty or careless writer, for the success of such pieces as those cited above depends on firm and precise control. Indeed, Sheridan's control is attested also by the inventive variety of forms he successfully worked in. His technical whimsies include not only his punning, his crambos, and his deft trisyllabic rhyming, but such playful inventions as his circular verse, his vowelless verse, and his stuttering verse. In all such japes there is not merely originality, but also a formal command and a verbal fluency that result in pure wit. As he writes in his "To the Dean" of September 12, 1718:

Don't think these few lines which I send a reproach,
From my Muse on a car to your Muse in a coach.
The great god of poems delights in a car,
Which makes him so bright that we see him from far;
For were he mewed up in a coach 'tis allowed
We'd see him no more than we see through a cloud.

The formal neatness, tightness, and deftness of innumerable passages like this are heightened by Sheridan's sprightly fancy, his frequent wordplay, and his effervescent sense of fun. In his comic verse, he is a lively, droll, companionable, and most quotable poet.

As an eighteenth-century poet, however, he has also some didactic pieces, some formal poems for public occasions, and a good deal of caustic journalism and polemics. As a friend of Swift, he has also, as might be expected, a good deal of ironic verse and a couple of scabrous ones.

Also, much of Sheridan's poetic work, as was Dryden's and Pope's, was in translating. His Persius, his *Philoctetes,* and his *Pastor Fido* impressively wed scholarly correctness to his usual fluency and ease, and these qualities are strikingly evident in his short translation from the French, "On a Fountain."

The "On a Fountain" poem occurs with a few other manuscript pieces in Sheridan's notebooks in the Gilbert Collection in the Dublin Central Library. These poems are mainly love lyrics and very different in tone from his typical pieces. They are graceful and adroit, if less individual than his comic writing, but they add a romantic facet to his character that one would hardly have expected from so accomplished a comedian.

Without then making extravagant claims for Sheridan as a poet, I think
that he is an important minor writer with a range of work much wider
than that of many cf his better remembered contemporaries, and with
the comic best of it as witty, as individual, and as alive today as it was
two hundred and fifty years ago when that witty individual Tom the Pun-
man was alive and wrote it.

Notes

1. This triplet is contained in the John Wild autograph collection, Vol. I, fol.
89, in Princeton University Library.
2. James Woolley adds a more complicated interpretation of Pun-sibi:

> There is evidence that by 1732, *pun-sibi* simply meant a punster: in the *Universal Specta-
> tor* the writer of a punning letter signs himself "Joseph Punsibi" (4 March). These misuses
> of the term only show that its origin and meaning were not understood, for *pun-sibi,* which
> I take to mean "a pun on himself", refers to the surname *Sheridan*. It was interpreted to
> mean, in Irish, one who is "still [constantly] Rhyming." The (humorous?) supposition
> was evidently that the name—commonly spelled *Siridan* in this period was from the Irish
> *(go)* sir (always) and *dan* (poetry, poem), *sir* being pronounced approximately like English
> *sheer. (The Intelligencer.* Oxford, 1992, p. 17).

3. Sheridan's letters to Jane Oughton are housed in the Beinecke Rare Book
and Manuscript Library of Yale University Library.
4. Sheridan included Greer's original letter and his own letter of reply in his
1718 pamphlet, *An Essay Proving That an Essay. . . .*
5. There are possibly one or two other instances in which Swift and Sheridan
were at odds. Both are recounted in the younger Sheridan's Life of Swift, and
one of them which is generally accepted as plausible concerns

> . . . a conversation that had passed between Swift and Doctor Sheridan as they were
> riding together on the Strand, some years before the Doctor left Dublin. The topic hap-
> pened to be that of old age, which Swift said he found coming fast upon him, and he
> supposed he should not be exempt from its attendant infirmities. "But there is one vice
> its usual concomitant, the most detestable of all others, and which therefore I would
> most endeavour to guard against, I mean avarice: I do not know any way so effectual
> for this purpose, as to engage some true friend to give me warning when he sees any
> approaches of that sort, and thus put me on my guard. This office I expect from you,
> and hope you will give me a solemn assurance that you will most punctually fulfil it."
> The Doctor very readily entered into the engagement; and now thought himself bound
> to discharge it. With this view, in one of his vacations passed at the Deanery, he set down
> daily in a journal kept for that purpose, all the instances he could perceive of the Dean's
> parsimony; which in a fortnight arose to a considerable amount. Armed with these proofs,
> he one day took an opportunity of asking the Dean, Whether he recollected a discourse
> which had passed between them on the Strand, relative to old age and avarice, and the
> solemn engagement he had made him enter into upon that occasion. Swift, as one sud-
> denly alarmed, answered with precipitation, "Yes, I remember it very well—Why—do

you perceive any thing of that sort in me?" You shall be judge yourself, said the Doctor—read over that paper, and see whether it is not high time I should now perform my promise. The Dean read over the articles with a countenance in which shame and despondency were blended. When he had done, he leaned his head upon his hand, with his eyes cast to the ground, and remained for some time buried in profound thought; at last he just lifted up his eyes, without changing his posture, and casting a side glance at the Doctor, with a most significant look, asked him—"Doctor—did you never read Gil Blas?" alluding to the famous story of a similar conduct of his towards the Archbishop, when he was his Secretary, which lost him his post. After such a scene, the reader will easily conclude, that the disease was past remedy; and that the Doctor, like poor Gil Blas, would probably not continue long in favour.

The other instance relates to the death of Stella and has, I feel, been given too little weight by Swift's later biographers:

> A short time before her death a scene passed between the Dean and her, an account of which I had from my father, and which I shall relate with reluctance, as it seems to bear more hard on Swift's humanity than any other part of his conduct in life. As she found her final dissolution approach, a few days before it happened, in the presence of Doctor Sheridan, she addressed Swift in the most earnest and pathetic terms to grant her dying request. That as the ceremony of marriage had passed between them, though for sundry considerations they had not cohabited in that state, in order to put it out of the power of slander to be busy with her fame after death, she adjured him by their friendship to let her have the satisfaction of dying at least, though she had not lived, his acknowledged wife. Swift made no reply, but turning on his heel, walked silently out of the room, nor ever saw her afterwards during the few days she lived. This behaviour threw Mrs. Johnson into unspeakable agonies, and for a time she sunk under the weight of so cruel a disappointment. But soon after, roused by indignation, she inveighed against his cruelty in the bitterest terms; and sending for a lawyer made her will, bequeathing her fortune by her own name to charitable uses. This was done in the presence of Doctor Sheridan, whom she appointed one of her executors. Upon this occasion the Doctor gave an instance of his disinterested spirit; for when Mrs. Johnson mentioned his name to the lawyer, annexing a very handsome legacy to it, the Doctor immediately interposed, and would not suffer it to be put down, saying, that as she disposed of her fortune to such pious uses, he should think he defrauded the charity if he accepted any part of it. During the few days she lived after this, Doctor Sheridan gave her constant attendance, and was in the chamber when she breathed her last. His grief for her loss was not perhaps inferior to the Dean's. He admired her above all human beings, and loved her with a devotion as pure as that which we would pay to Angels. She, on her part, had early singled him out from all the Dean's acquaintance, as her confidential friend. There grew up the closest amity between them, which subsisted, without interruption, to the time of her death. During her long illness, he never passed an hour from her which could be spared from business; and his conversation, in the Dean's absence, was the chief cordial to support her drooping spirits. Of her great regard for him Swift bears testimony, in the close of one of his letters to him from London, where he says, "I fear while you are reading this, you will be shedding tears at her funeral: she loved you well, and a great share of the little merit I have with you, is owing to her solicitation." No wonder, if the Doctor's humanity was shocked at the last scene which he saw pass between her and the Dean, and which affected him so much, that it was a long time before he could be thoroughly reconciled to him.

6. In a letter of April 9, 1737, Swift wrote to Sheridan:

I have finished my will for the last time, wherein I left some little legacy which you are not to receive till you shall be entirely out of my debt, and paid all you owe to my executors. And I have made very honourable mention of you in the will as the consideration of my leaving these legacies to you. (*Correspondence,* ed. Harold Williams, Vol. V, p. 29.)

7. Hyphen added.

8. Although Sheridan was out of Dublin for about two years, Dublin seems not to have forgotten him. In describing an evening at the theater, "Geoffrey Jinglestaff, Esq." wrote in *The Dublin Daily Advertiser* of November 27, 1736:

Soon after a Gentleman, dress'd like a Country Squire, came in laughing heartily, and calling Drawer, upon which a young Man with a blue Apron enter'd. *Hark'ee Sirrah,* said the Gentleman, *do you know why a Man in Bed is like a Five-Penny Piece? No, Sir,* said the Drawer. *You Blockhead,* reply'd the other, *are not they both under a Teaster; but run and fetch me a Bottle of Brown Paper and a Bottle of Crooked Stick.* The Drawer went out and soon return'd tell him, that his Master did not understand him. *No, sirrah,* said he, *is not Brown Paper a Sham Pane? and is not a Crooked Stick a Cane a wry? Bring me some Champaign and Canary, but in the mean time you are a thick-skull'd Cur; and if there be any Thing in your Head I'll make a Way for it to come out.* With that he offer'd a Stroke of his Cane, Which the Drawer caught and held in his Hand till he should find an Opportunity of slipping away, and in the Struggle the Gentleman's Waistcoat flew open and discovered something Black under it. Whereupon an old Gentleman, who sat near him in the Gallery, cried out, *Ah, Doctor! Doctor! still at your old Jokes.* The Doctor, who ever he was, seem'd to be uneasy at being discover'd, and affirming that not one of them understood a good *Pun,* withdrew in a great Passion.

The Poems of
THOMAS SHERIDAN

The Poems

In Pity First to Human Kind

Elizabeth MacFadden ?

In pity first to human kind,
   Love taught the art of writing;
But soon deceit stepped in, we find,
   And taught man false inditing.

False vows, false words, nay e'en false tears,   5
   Soon after were invented;
And Love from each account appears
   Almost to have repented

That he disclosed the magic art,
   At first for gods intended,   10
By which he thought the virgin heart
   Would be so much befriended.

What vows, what sighs on paper flow,
   In words as sweet as honey!
They melt away like now-fall'n snow,   15
   In sunshine now of money.

Then Love with indignation saw
   His tender views defeated;
Traitors unpunished broke his law,
   And crime on crime repeated.   20

Then, Love, resume thy wonted power,
   And punish every traitor;
From Jupiter in golden shower,
   Down to the *petit-maître*.

(Written ca. 1710/11)

61

Upon Mr. Sheridan's Turning Author, 1716

Anonymous

My landlord has a little pad
  Can amble for a mile or so;
Just fit for bum of ancient dad,
  What horse one mile can better go?

But add a second to the first,   5
  He straight begins to change his gait;
No horse than Ball can be more cursed;
  Beware, old landlord, of your seat.

Thus like my landlord's little horse,
  You the first mile of life did run,   10
With ease could amble in discourse;
  But when you writ, you were undone.

Now, Ball and Tommy, pause a while
  And mark what I indite:
You Ball shall only ride a mile;   15
  You Tommy cease to write.

                                              (Written 1716)

To Dean Swift

  Dear Dean, since in cruxes and puns you and I deal,
Pray why is a woman a sieve and a riddle?
'Tis a thought that came into my noddle this morning,
In bed as I lay, sir, a-tossing and turning.
You'll find, if you read but a few of your histories,   5
All women, as Eve, all women are mysteries.
To find out this riddle, I know you'll be eager,
And make every one of the sex a Belphegor.
But that will not do, for I mean to commend 'em;
I swear without jest, I an honor intend 'em.   10
In a sieve, sir, their ancient extraction I quite tell;
In a riddle I give you their pow'r and their title.
This I told you before; do you know what I mean, sir?
"Not I, by my troth, sir." Then read it again, sir.

The reason I send you these lines of rhymes double,   15
Is purely in pity, to save you the trouble
Of thinking two hours for a rhyme as you did last,
When your Pegasus cantered in triple, and rid fast.
As for my little nag which I keep at Parnassus,
With Phoebus's leave, to run with his asses,   20
He goes slow and sure, and he never is jaded
While your fiery steed is whipped, spurred, bastinaded.

(Written ca. September 10, 1718)

To the Dean

Don't think these few lines which I send a reproach
From my Muse on a car to your Muse in a coach.
The great god of poem delights in a car,
Which makes him so bright that we see him from far;
For, were he mewed up in a coach, 'tis allowed   5
We'd see him no more than we see through a cloud.

You know to apply this—I do not disparage
Your lines, but I say they're the worse for the carriage.

Now first you deny that a woman's a sieve;
I say that she is.—What reason do you give?   10
Because she lets out more than she takes in?
Is't that you advance for't? You're still to begin.
Your Major and Minor I both can refute;
I'll teach you hereafter with whom to dispute.
A sieve keeps in half, deny't if you can.   15
D. "Adzucks, I mistook it, who thought of the bran?"
I tell you in short, sir, you should have a pair of stocks[1]
For thinking to palm on your friend such a paradox.
Indeed, I confess at the close you grew better,
But you light from your coach when you finished your
      letter.   20
Your thing which you say wants interpretation,
What's name for a maiden, the first man's damnation?
A damsel—Adam's hell—ay, there I have hit it;
Just as you conceived it, just so have I writ it.
Since this I've discovered, I'll make you to know it,   25
That now I'm your Phoebus, and you are my poet.
But if you interpret the two lines that follow,

I'll again be your poet, and you my Apollo.
Why a noble lord's dog, and my school-house this weather,
Make up the best catch when they're coupled together?   30
From my Ringsend car, Sept. the 12, 1718, past 5 in the
morning, on a Repetition Day.

---

1. Begging pardon for the expression to a dignitary of the church.

To the Same

SIR,
   Perhaps you may wonder, I send you so soon
Another epistle; consider 'tis noon.
For all his acquaintance well know that friend Tom is,
Whenever he makes one, as good as his promise.
Now Phoebus exalted sits high on his throne,   5
Dividing the heavens, dividing my crown.
Into poems and business, my skull's split in two,
One side for the lawyers, and t'other for you.
With my left eye I see you sit snug in your stall;
With my right I'm attending the lawyers that scrawl.   10
With my left I behold your bellower a cur chase;
With my right I'm a-reading my deeds for a purchase.
My left ear's attending the hymns of the choir;
My right ear is stunned with the noise of the crier.
My right hand's inditing these lines to your reverence;   15
My left is indenting for me and heirs ever-hence.
Although in myself I'm divided in two,
Dear Dean, I shall ne'er be divided from you.
12 o'clock at Noon, September 12, 1718

To the Dean of St. Patrick's

SIR,
   Your Billingsgate Muse methinks does begin
With much greater noise than a conjugal din.
A pox of her bawling, her *tempora et mores!*
What are times now to me? An't I one of the Tories?
You tell me my verses disturb you at prayers;   5
Oh, ho, Mr. Dean, are you there with your bears?

You pray, I suppose, like a heathen to Phoebus,
To give his assistance to make out my rebus,
Which I don't think so fair; leave it off for the future;
When the combat is equal, this god should be neuter.   10
I'm now at the tavern where I drink all I can;
To write with more spirit, I'll drink no more Helicon;
For Helicon is water, and water is weak;
'Tis wine on the gross lee that makes your Muse speak.
This I know by her spirit and life, but I think   15
She's much in the wrong to scold in her drink.
Her damned pointed tongue pierced almost to my heart:
Tell me of a cart—tell me of a ———.
I'd have you to tell her on both sides her ears,
If she comes to my house that I'll kick her down stairs.   20
Then home she shall limping go, squalling out, "Oh, my knee!"
You shall soon have a crutch to buy for your Melpomene.
You may come as her bully, to bluster and swagger;
But my ink is my poison, my pen is my dagger.
Stand off, I desire, and mark what I say to you: 25
If you come I will make your Apollo shine through you.
Don't think, sir, I fear a Dean, as I would fear a dun;
Which is all at present from yours,

Thomas Sheridan.
(Written ca. September 14, 1718)

To the Dean of St. Patrick's

i

Since your poetic prancer is turned into Cancer,
I tell you at once, sir, I'm now not your man, sir;
For pray, sir, what pleasure in fighting is found
With a coward who studies to traverse his ground?
When I drew forth my pen, with your pen you ran back,   5
But I found out the way to your den by its track.
From thence the black monster I drew, o' my conscience,
And so brought to light what before was stark nonsense.
When I with my right hand did stoutly pursue,
You turned to your left, and you writ like a Jew;   10
Which, good Mister Dean, I cannot think so fair;
Therefore, turn about to the right as you were;
Then if with true courage your ground you maintain,
My fame is immortal when Jonathan's slain,

Who's greater by far than great Alexander,   15
As much as a teal surpasses a gander,
As much as a game-cock's excelled by a sparrow,
As much as a coach is below a wheelbarrow,
As much and much more as the most handsome man
Of all the whole world is exceeded by Dan.   20

> This was written with that hand which in others is
> commonly called the left hand.

                                    ii

Oft have I been by poets told
That, poor Jonathan, thou grows old.
Alas, thy number[s] falling all,
Poor Jonathan, how they do fall!
Thy rhymes, which whilom made thy pride swell,   5
Now jingle like a rusty bridle;
Thy verse, which ran both smooth and sweet,
Now limp upon their gouty feet;
Thy thoughts, which were the true sublime,
Are humbled by the tyrant Time.   10
Alas! What cannot Time subdue?
Time has reduced my wine and you,
Emptied my casks and clipped your wings,
Disabled both in our main springs,
So that of late we two are grown   15
The jest and scorn of all the town.
But yet, if my advice be ta'en,
We two may be as great again:
I'll send you wings, and send me wine;
Then you will fly, and I shall shine.   20

> This was written with my right hand, at the same time with
> the other.

                                   iii

How does Melpy like this? I think I have vexed her;
Little did she know, I was ambidexter.

> (Written ca. September 21, 1718)

Ad Amicum Eruditum Thomam Sheridan

Jonathan Swift

Deliciae Sheridan musarum, dulcis amice,
Sic tibi propitius Permessi ad flumen Apollo
Occurrat, seu te mimum convivia rident;
Aequivocosve sales spargis, seu ludere versu
Malles; dic, Sheridan, quisnam fuit ille deorum,   5
Quae melior natura orto tibi tradidit artem
Rimandi genium puerorum, atque ima cerebri
Scrutandi? Tibi nascenti ad cunabula Pallas
Astitit; et dixit, mentis praesaga futurae,
Heu puer infelix! nostro sub sydere natus;   10
Nam tu pectus eris sine corpore, corporis umbra;
Sed levitate umbram superabis, voce cicadam:
Musca femur, palmas tibi mus dedit, ardea crura.
Corpore sed tenui tibi quod natura negavit;
Hoc animi dotes supplebunt; teque docente,   15
Nec longum tempus, surget tibi docta juventus,
Artibus egregiis animas instructa novellas.
Grex hinc Poeonius venit, ecce, *salutifer* orbi.
Ast, illi causas orant; his infula visa est
Divinam capiti nodo constringere mitram.   20

Natalis te horae non fallunt signa; sed usque
Conscius, expedias puero seu laetus Apollo
Nascenti arrisit; sive illum frigidus horror
Saturni premit, aut septem inflavere triones.

Quin tu altè penitusque latentia semina cernis,   25
Quaeque diu obtundendo olim sub luninis auras
Erumpent, promis; quo ritu saepè puella
Sub cinere hesterno sopitos suscitat ignes.

Te Dominum agnoscit quocunque sub aere natus;
Quos indulgentis nimium custodia matris   30
Pessundat: nam saepè vides in stipite matrem.

Aureus at ramus venerandae dona Sibyllae,
Aeneae sedes tantùm patefecit Avernus:
Saepè puer, tua quem tetigit semel aurea virga,
Coelumque terrasque videt, noctemque profundam.
                    (Possibly written ca. late September-middle October, 1718)

[To My Learned Friend, Thomas Sheridan

[O Sheridan, the muses' pet, sweet friend—
May gracious Phoebus greet you thus upon
Permessus' banks, just as your dinner guests
Laugh at your profuse puns and playful verse.
But, Sheridan, what god gave you at birth   5
The skill to probe into a boy's mind
And delve into the bottom of his brain?
Athena, standing by your cradle, said,
Predicting of your future mind, "Alas,
Unhappy lad who, born beneath our star,   10
Has heart but much less body than a ghost!
Your chirping jokes negate your ghostly frame—
The fly's thighs, mouse paws and the heron's legs.
What nature has not bodily supplied
Your mind will supplement; your teaching soon   15
Will bring about a corps of learned youths,
Their minds instructed in the noble arts.
Behold, Apollo's band will come to heal
The world. But yet they wrangle and ensnarl
The god's great gifts into a tangled knot.   20

["Still, portents of your birth do not deceive
You; and, the confidant always of gods,
You may discover if Apollo's smiled
Upon a newborn child, or if a cold
And horrid future lies in store for him.   25

["As surely as you see the seeds deep down
And you disclose how they may thrust themselves
Aloft and strive at last to reach the gleams
Of light, just so a girl awakes the spark
That sleeps beneath the dormant ash.   30

["That lad will recognize you as his teacher.
No matter what his star, or how his mother
Indulges him; the mother's in the branch.

["And yet the golden branch, the Sibyl's gift,
Has only shown Aeneas' home in Hell: 35
So oft the lad, whom once your golden wand
Has touched, sees heaven, earth and shades profound."]

Vivitur Parvo Malè, Sed Canebat

Vivitur parvo malè, sed canebat
Flaccus ut parvo benè: quod negamus:
Pinguis et lautè saturatus ille
               Ridet inanes.

Pace sic dicam liceat poetae   5
Nobilis laeti salibus faceti
Usque jocundi, lepidè jocantis
               Non sine curâ.

Quis potest versus (meditans merendam,
Prandium, coenam) numerare? quis non   10
Quot panes pistor locat in fenestrâ
               Dicere mallet?

Ecce jejunus tibi venit unus;
Latrat ingenti stomachus furore;
Quaeso digneris renovare fauces,   15
               Docte Patrone.

Vestiant lanae tenues libellos,
Vestiant panni dominum trementem,
Aedibus vestris trepidante pennâ
               Musa propinquat.   20

Nuda ne fiat, renovare vestes
Urget, et nunquam tibi sic molestam
Esse promittit, nisi sit coacta
               Frigore iniquo.

Si modo possem! Vetat heu pudor me   25
Plura, sed praestat rogitare plura,
An dabis binos digitos crumenae im-
              ponere vestrae?
          (Possibly written ca. late September-middle October, 1718)

[Life's bad on just a bit, but
  This Horace quite denies. (Lies!)
  That bard, so fat and bloated, gloated
              At us fools.

[Yet—with respect of course—Horace   5
  Is blessed with wealth and wit; it
  Is jolly, ever joking, stroking
              All his jewels.

[Who could tot up his verses (Curses!)
  When breakfast, lunch and tea flee?   10
  When baker's buns you yearn for? (Earn more
              And ate one?)

[See, ravenous I come; my stom-
  ach barks and hugely rumbles, grumbles;
  Pray, renovate my large gorge,   15
              Wise patron!

[My verses all selected, protected
  With rags, their trembling master, Pastor,
  His Muse with shaking plumes, comes
              To your fold.   20

[Oh, let her not go nude. Would
  You cover her, she'll never ever
  Annoy thee unless depressed
              By the cold.

[I hate to beg. I moan (Ochone!)   25
  Returning to your store for more,
  And plunge my hands again within
                (non dolet?)
                Your wallet.]

Ad Te, Doctissime Delany

Ad te, doctissime Delany,
Pulsus à foribus Decani,
Confugiens edo querelam,
Pauper petens clientelam.
Petebam Swift doctum patronum,   5
Sed ille dedit nullum donum,
Neque cibum neque bonum.
Quaeris quàm malè sit stomacho num?
Iratus valdè valdè latrat,
Crumenicidam fermè patrat: 10
Quin ergo releves aegrotum,
Dato cibum, dato potum.
Ita in utrumvis oculum,
Dormiam bibens vestrum poculum.
          (Possibly written ca. late September–middle October 1718)

[Delany, most learned of men,
  Repulsed from the doors of the Dean,
  I flee now to you and complain—
  A pauper who sought but in vain.

[I sought as my solace Dean Swift   5
  Who offered no food nor no gift,
  Who proffered no shirt nor no shift.
  Wouldst hear how my stomach's bereft?

[It barks oh so fierce, oh so fierce;
  It's almost depleted my purse;
  If only you would ease this curse,
  Give drink or give food, but a mors-

el. 'Neath your beneficent gaze
I'll sleep after drinking your praise.]

To the Dean of St. Patrick's

Dear Dean, I'm in a sad condition,
  I cannot see to read or write;
Pity the darkness of the Priscian,
  Whose days are all transformed to night.
My head, though light's a dungeon grown,   5
  The windows of my skull are closed;
Therefore to sleep I lay me down,
  My verse and I are both composed.
Sleep, did I say? That cannot be,
  For who can sleep that wants his eyes?   10
My bed is useless then to me,
  Therefore I lay me down to rise.
Unnumbered thoughts pass to and fro
  Upon the surface of my brain;
In various maze they come and go,   15
  And come and go again.
So have you seen in sheet burnt black
  The fiery sparks at random run,
Now here, now there, some turning back,
  Some ending where they just begun.   20

(Written ca. October 18, 1718)

To Thomas Sheridan

Jonathan Swift

Dear Tom, I'm surprised that your verse did not jingle;
But your rhyme was not double, 'cause your sight was but
  single.
For, as Helsham observes, there's nothing can chime
Or fit more exact than one eye and one rhyme.
If you had not took physic, I'd pay off your bacon,   5
But now I'll write short, for fear you're short-taken.
Besides, Dick forbid me, and called me a fool;
For he says, short as 'tis, it will give you a stool.

In libris bellis, tu parum parcis ocellis,
Dum nimium scribis, vel talpâ caecior ibis,   10
Aut ad vina redis, nam sic tua lumina laedis:
Sed tibi coenanti sunt collyria tanti?
Numquid eges visu, dum comples omnia risu?

Heu! Sheridan caecus, heu eris nunc cercopithecus.
Nunc bene nasutus mittet tibi carmina tutus: 15
Nunc ope Burgundi, malus Helsham ridet abunde,
Nec Phoebi fili versum quis mittere Ryly.[1]

Quid tibi cum libris? relavet tua lumina Tybris[2]
Mixtus Saturno[3]; penso sed parcè diurno
Observes hoc tu, nec scriptis utere noctu.   20
Nonnulli mingunt et palpebras sibi tingunt.
Quidam purgantes, libros in stercore nantes
Linquunt; sic vinces videndo, mi bone, lynces.
Culum oculum tergis, dum scripta hoc flumine mergis;
Tunc oculi et nates, ni fallor, agent tibi grates.   25
Vim fuge Decani, nec sit tibi cura Delani:
Heu tibi si scribant, aut si tibi fercula libant,
Pone loco mortis, rapis fera pocula fortis.
Haec tibi pauca dedi, sed consule Betty Mi Lady,
Huic te des solae, nec egebis pharmacopolae.
                    Haec somnians cecini,
                    Jⁿ Swift.
                              (Written on October 23, 1718)

1. Pro potis. Horat.
2. Pro quovis fluvio. Virg.
3. Saccharo Saturni.

[At beautiful books, you've too many looks,
And write at a rate 'twould blind any bat,
And drink to the lees, and injure your eyes:
But what of a cure while you're in the mire,
And losing your sight in spreading delight?   5

[Alas, you blind simp, you'll be but a chimp.
Now no satirist will be at a rest;
They'll send you verse letters and unpunished satyrs
While soaked in the sauce bad Helsham guffaws;
To Patrick O'Riley no verses go slyly.   10

[So water and skies be cures for your eyes.
Abandon this writing; cease daily inditing;
Note what I remark—don't write when it's dark.
For eyewash wine piss is thought not amiss;
And books, if you're purging and stools need no urging,   15
Can usefully fit in wiping your shit.
Clean eyes, an' clean bum, an' for books urine summon.
Your eyes and your arse will think you no worse.
Thus foes, if you meet 'em, then you can defeat 'em.
So flee from Delany, flee from the Dean.   20
Alas, if they write, "A feast is tonight,"
Your grave you should choose; escape from their stews.
Sage thoughts I send you, man; but ask Bet, your woman;
And if her you huggest, you'll not need a druggist.
                Daydreaming, this gift   25
                In verse from J. Swift.]

Perlegi Versus Versos, Jonathan Bone, Tersos

Perlegi versus versos, Jonathan bone, tersos;
Perlepidos quidèm; scribendo semper es idem.
Laudibus extollo te, tu mihi magnus Apollo;
Tu frater Phoebus, oculis collyria praebes,
Ne minus insanae reparas quoque damna Dianae,   5
Quae me percussit radiis (nec dixeris ussit)
Frigore collecto; medicus moderamine tecto
Lodicem binum permit, et negat is mihi vinum.
O terra et coelum! quàm redit pectus anhelum.
Os mihi jam siccum, liceat mihi bibere dic cum?   10
Ex vestro grato poculo, tam saepe prolato,
Vina crepant: sales ostendet quis mihi tales?
Lumina, vos sperno, dum cuppae gaudia cerno:
Perdere etenim pellem nostram, quoque crura mavellem.
Amphora, quàm dulces risus queis pectora mulces,   15
Pangitur a Flacco, cum pectus turget Iaccho:
Clarius evohe ingeminans geminatur et ohe;
Nempe jocosa propago, lusit sic vocis imago.
                    (Written ca. October 23, 1718)

[Good Jonathan, I've read your ditty
  Which was, of course, well-turned and pretty;
  It was as always charming, clever,

As you are in your writing ever.
I laud you with the highest praise;   10
To me you shine with Phoebus' rays.
O brother Phoebus, brother poet
Who brings me needed eyewash so it
Repairs the damages of mad
Diana's rays that struck—bedad,   10
Not scorched—and made my eyes a mess
With ever-growing iciness.
My quack prescribes a double blanket,
Then takes my wine and says, "Don't drink it."
O Earth! O Sky! O heaving breast!   15
My mouth is dry, my mind distressed!
Your pleasing cup, so often proferred
With wit and gurgling wine's not offered.
O eyes of mine, I flatly spurn you
When joyous jug, O, I discern you.   20
I'd rather have a jug than eyes;
It more than legs or hide I'd prize.
The jug, which soothes the heart with laughter,
Was praised by Horace, and thereafter,
Whenever breasts were swelled by Bacchus   25
In joyous shouts, then shouts more raucous
Were doubled, doubled and repeated,
And gladness grew and hearts were heated.

[Of course, I propagate your japes,
And thus my voice your image apes.]

I Like Your Collyrium

I like your collyrium,
Take my eyes, sir, and clear ye 'um,
    'Twill gain you a great reputation;
By this you may rise,
Like the doctor so wise,   5
    Who opened the eyes of the nation.
And these, I must tell ye,
Are bigger than its belly;
    You know there's in Livy a story
Of the hands and the feet   10
Denying of meat;

Don't I write in the dark like a Tory?
Your water so far goes,
'Twould serve for an Argus,
   Were all his whole hundred sore;   15
So many we read
He had in his head,
   Or Ovid's a son of a whore.
For your recipe, sir,
May my lids never stir   20
   If ever I think once to fee you;
For I'd have you to know
When abroad I can go,
   That it's honor enough if I see you.

                       (Written ca. October 23, 1718)

To Thomas Sheridan

Patrick Delany

Dear Sherry, I'm sorry for your bloodshedded sore eye,
And the more I consider your case, still the more I
Regret it, for see how the pain on't has wore ye.
Besides, the good Whigs, who strangely adore ye,
In pity cry out, "He's a poor blinded Tory."   5
But listen to me, and I'll soon lay before ye
A sovereign cure well attested in Gory.
First wash it with *ros,* that makes dative *rori;*
Then send for three leeches, and let them all gore ye;
Then take a cordial dram to restore ye;   10
Then take Lady Judith, and walk a fine boree;
Then take a glass of good claret *ex more;*
Then stay as long as you can *ab uxore;*
And then if friend Dick will but ope your back-door, he
Will quickly dispel the black clouds that hang o'er ye,   15
And make you so bright, that you'll sing tory-rory,
And make a new ballad worth ten of John Dory!
(Though I work your cure, yet he'll get the glory.)

I'm now in the back school-house, high up one story,
Quite weary with teaching, and ready to *mori*.   20
My candle's just out too, no longer I'll pore ye,
But away to Clem Barry's—there's an end of my story.

                                    (Written October 1718)

My Pedagogue Dear, I Read with Surprise

My pedagogue dear, I read with surprise
Your long sorry rhymes which you made on my eyes;
As the Dean of St. Patrick's says, "Earth, sea and skies!"
I cannot lie down, but immediately rise
To answer your stuff and the Doctor's likewise.   5
Like a horse with a gall, I am pestered with flies,
But his head and his tail new succor supplies
To beat off the vermin from back, rump and thighs.
The wing of a goose before me now lies,
Which is both shield and sword for such weak enemies.   10
Whoever opposes me, certainly dies
Though he were as valiant as Condé or Guise.
The women disturb me a-crying of pies,
With a voice twice as loud as a horse when he neighs.
By this, sir, you find, should we rhyme for a prize,   15
That I'd gain cloth of gold, when you'd scarce merit frize.

                              (Written ca. October 20, 1718)

You Made Me in Your Last a Goose

You made me in your last a goose;
    I lay my life on't you are wrong,
To raise me by such foul abuse.
    My quill you'll find's a woman's tongue,
And slit, just like a bird will chatter,   5
    And like a bird do something more:
When I let fly, 'twill so bespatter,
    I'll change you to a blackamoor.

                              (Written ca. October 26, 1718)

I'll Write While I Have Half an Eye in My Head

I'll write while I have half an eye in my head;
I'll write while I live, and I'll write when you're dead.

Though you call me a goose, you pitiful slave,
I'll feed on the grass that grows on your grave.

(Written ca. October 26, 1718)

I Can't But Wonder, Mr. Dean

I can't but wonder, Mr. Dean,
To see you live, so often slain.
My arrows fly and fly in vain,
But still I try and try again.
I'm now, sir, in a writing vein;　　　　　　　　5
Don't think, like you, I squeeze and strain.
Perhaps you'll ask me what I mean;
I will not tell, because 'tis plain.
Your Muse, I'm told, is in the wane;
If so, from pen and ink refrain.　　　　　　　　10
Indeed, believe me, I'm in pain
For her and you; your life's a scene
Of verse, and rhymes, and hurricane,
Enough to crack the strongest brain.
Now to conclude, I do remain,　　　　　　　　15
Your honest friend,
TOM: SHERIDAN

(Written ca. October 1718)

To the Dean of St. Patrick's

Dear Sir, since you in humble wise
　　Have made a recantation,
From your low bended knees arise;
　　I hate such poor prostration.

'Tis bravery that moves the brave,　　　　　　　　5
　　As one nail drives another;
If you from me would mercy have,
　　Pray, Sir, be such another.

You that so long maintained the field
　　With true poetic vigor,　　　　　　　　10
Now you lay down your pen and yield;
　　You make a wretched figure.[1]

Submit, but do't with sword in hand,
   And write a panegyric
Upon the man you cannot stand;   15
   I'll have it writ in lyric:

That all the boys I teach may sing
   The achievements of their Chiron,[2]
What conquests my stern looks can bring
   Without the help of iron.   20

A small goose-quill, yclept a pen,
   From magazine of standish,
Drawn forth's more dreadful to the Dean
   Than any sword we brandish.

My ink's my flesh, my pen's my bolt;   25
   When e'er I please to thunder,
I'll make you tremble like a colt,
   And thus I'll keep you under.

                             (Written ca. October 1718)

---

1. A leg awry.
2. A fair open for you.

Another Picture of Dan

Clarissa draws her scissors from their case
To shape the lines of poor Dan Jackson's face.
One sloping cut made forehead, nose and chin; ⎱
A nick produced a mouth and made him grin,   ⎰
Such as in tailor's measure you have seen. ⎰   5
But still were wanting his grimalkin eyes,
For which grey worsted stockings paint supplies.
Th' unravelled thread, through needle's eye conveyed,
Transferred itself into the pasteboard head.
How came the scissors to be thus outdone?   10
The needle had an eye, and they had none.
O wondrous force of art! Now look at Dan:

You'd swear the pasteboard was the better man.
"The dev'l," says he, "the head is not so full!"
Indeed it is—behold the paper skull.   15
                              Tho: Sheridan sculpsit.
                              (Written in 1718, possibly in October)

On the Same

If you say this was made for friend Dan, you belie it:
I'll swear he's so like it that he was made by it.
                              Tho: Sheridan sculpsit.
                              (Written in 1718, possibly in October)

Answer

Probably with George Rochfort

Three merry lads you own we are;
'Tis very true, and free from care,
But envious we cannot bear,
                    Believe, Sir.

For were all forms of beauty thine,   5
Were you like Nereus soft and fine,
We should not in the least repine,
                    Or grieve, Sir.

Then know from us, most beauteous Dan,
That roughness best becomes a man;   10
'Tis woman should be pale and wan,
                    And taper;

And all your trifling beaux and fops,
Who comb their brows and sleek their chops,
Are but offspring of toy-shops,   15
                    Mere vapor.

We know your morning hours you pass
To cull and gather out a face;
Is this the way you take your glass?
                    Forbear it: 20

Those loads of paint upon your toilet
Will never mend your face, but spoil it;
It looks as if you did parboil it;
                Drink claret.

Your cheeks by sleeking are so lean   25
That they're like Cynthia in the wane,
Or breast of goose when 'tis picked clean,
                Or pullet.

See what by drinking you have done;
You've made your phiz a skeleton,   30
From the long distance of your crown,
                T' your gullet.

You say your face is better hung
Than ours—by what? By nose or tongue?
In not explaining, you were wrong   35
                To us, Sir.

Because we thus must state the case,
That you have got a hanging face;
Th' untimely end's a damned disgrace
                Of noose, Sir.   40

But yet be not cast down to see
A weaver will your hangman be;
You'll only hang in tapestry,
                With many.

And then the ladies, I suppose,   45
Will praise your longitude of nose,
For latent charms within your clothes,
                Dear Danny.

Thus will the fair of every age,
From all parts make their pilgrimage,   50
Worship thy nose with pious rage
                Of love, Sir.

All their religion will be spent
About thy woven monument,
And not an orison be sent   55
                To Jove, Sir.

You the famed idol will become,
What gardens graced in ancient Rome,
By matrons worshipped in the gloom
                    Of night, Sir.   60

O happy Dan, thrice happy sure,
Thy fame forever shall endure,
Who after death can love secure
                    At sight, Sir.

So far I thought it was my duty   65
To dwell upon your boasted beauty.
Now I'll proceed a word or two t' ye
                    In answer

To that part where you carry on
This paradox, that rock and stone   70
In your opinion are all one;
                    How can, Sir,

A man of reas'ning so profound,
So stupidly be run aground,
As things so diff'rent to confound   75
                    T' our senses?

Except you judged them by the knock
Of near an equal hardy block,
Such an experimental stroke
                    Convinces.   80

Then might you be by dint of reason
A proper judge on this occasion;
'Gainst feeling there's no disputation
                    Is granted.

Therefore to thy superior wit,   85
Who made the trial, we submit;
Thy head to prove the truth of it
                    We wanted.

In one assertion you're to blame,
Where Dan and Sherry's made the same,   90
Endeavoring to have your name
                    Refined so.

You'll see most grossly you mistook
(The better half you say you took);
If you consult your spelling book,   95
                You'll find so.

S, H, E, *she,* and R, I, *ri,*
Both put together make *Sheri;*
D, A, N, *Dan* make up the three
                Syllables.   100

Dan is but one, and *Sheri* two;
Then, Sir, your choice will never do;
Therefore, I've turned, my friend, on you
                The tables.
                (Written in 1718, possibly in October)

Sheridan to Dan Jackson

Dear Dan, it does amaze me quite,
To see you write, and write, and write,
But how the Devil you can come by't
                's a wonder.

Though 'tis but Grubstreet, yet that same   5
I think so much above thy aim
As the sublime and shining flame
                Of thunder

Does far surpass the sooty blaze
Of slut dispensing kitchen grease;   10
And, if this be the present case,
                Consider

How much your ribaldry provokes,
With fulsome lines and poor, dull jokes.
There's no return but cudgel-strokes,   15
                On hide, Sir,

Can I in honor make to you.
For if you'd finely run me through,
Perhaps I'd take a rapier too,
                And fight you.   20

Thy blood might then my wrath assuage,
When honor called me to engage,
But you're so far below my rage,
                    I slight you.

From barking cur, the mastiff flies,   25
But when behind he bites his thighs,
He turns and pisses out his eyes,
                    Disdaining

So small and pitiful a foe,
From noisy boasting brought so low;   30
The picture's drawn; I'm sure you know
                    My meaning.
                    (Written in 1718, possibly in October)

A Highlander Once Fought a Frenchman at Margate

A Highlander once fought a Frenchman at Margate,
The weapons a rapier, a backsword and target.
Brisk Monsieur advanced as fast as he could,
But all his fine pushes were caught in the wood;
While Sawney with backsword did slash him and nick him,   5
While t' other, enraged that he could not once prick him,
Cried, "Sirrah, you rascal, you son of a whore,
Me'll fight you, begar, if you'll come from your door!"
Our case is the same; if you'll fight like a man,
Don't fly from my weapon, and skulk behind Dan;   10
For he's not to be pierced; his leather's so tough
The devil himself can't get through his buff.
Besides I cannot but say that it is hard
Not only to make him your shield, but your vizard;
And like a tragedian, you rant and you roar   15
Through the horrible grin of your *larva's* wide bore.
Nay, farther, which makes me complain much and frump it,

You make his long nose your loud speaking trumpet,
With the din of which tube my head you so bother
That I scarce can distinguish my right ear from t' other.   20
                    (Written in 1718, possibly in October)

Cur Me Bespateras, Blaterans Furiosè Poeta
T. S. D. I. S. P. D.

Cur me bespateras, blaterans furiosè Poeta
Cum foulo Moutho, putridae cum flaminae Breathae
Me Tootho, et Nailo strivans lacerare Maligno,
Quid faceret grinans aliter spitfiria felis,
Si quis twistaret caudam, si pulleret aures,   5
Dic mihi quid feci, nisi non lisenter aravi
Phizzum, cum dentis suavique honicombio looko,
Et longum nasum wishanti ut longior esset
Protraxi, et bendans makavi touchere Chinnum,
Invidet ut lengtho, strechi Tallboius Heros.   10
Si quis tres Inchos Nosi cutâsset adunci,
Et sic geldâsset Phizzum, non plus tibi furor,
Scintillans oculos firaret, nec tua Quilla
Goosa in perniciem slashantis promptior esset.
Virgilius writat—*Ne saevi magne sacerdos.*   15
Advisum goodum Daniel, si takere posses.
Oh! Jackson, Jackson, quae te dementia seizat
Castos Minaram springes turbare sororum,
Divando ad Muddum, Lampoonos pangere foedos.
                    (Written in 1718, possibly in late October or early
                                                November)

[Why spatter me, you madly babbling bard
 With rancid breath so like a putrid turd,
 Or strive to lacerate me with both nail
 And wicked tooth, just like a cat whose tail
 Is twisted, ears are pulled, and spits? Oh please   5
 Say what I've done. Not 'nough adored your phiz
 With charming smirk and honeyed glance? And then
 My nose pulled long enough to touch my chin?
 He envies my athletic nose, but eke
 Should one have snipped three inches off his beak   10
 And made a gelded gob or phiz castrated,

Then you'd no longer rage or fiercely hate it.
Your eye would be less quick to flash and ravage,
And your goose quill less prone to slash and savage.
The poet Virgil writes, "Great priest, don't rage!"   15
So Daniel, if you'll take advice that's sage—
  Oh! Jackson, Jackson, what mad matter
  Impels you to stir up pure water
  For mud to write your filthy satire?]

The Last Speech and Dying Words of Daniel Jackson

My Dear Countrymen

> ————mediocribus esse poetis
> Non funes, non gryps, non concessere columnae.

To give you a short translation of the two lines from Horace's *Art of Poetry,* which I have chosen for my neck-verse, before I proceed to my speech, you will find they fall naturally into this sense:

> ————For poets who can't tell rocks from stones,
> The rope, the hangman and the gallows groans.

I was born in a fen near the foot of Mount Parnassus commonly called the Logwood Bog. My mother whose name was Stanza conceived me in a dream and was delivered of me in her sleep. Her dream was that Apollo in the shape of a gander with a prodigious long bill had embraced her, upon which she consulted the Oracle of Delphos, and the following answer was made.

You'll have a gosling, call it Dan,
And do not make your goose a swan.
'Tis true because the God of Wit
To get him in that shape thought fit,
He'll have some glow-worm sparks of it.   5
Venture you may to turn him loose,
But let it be to another goose.
The time will come, the fatal time,
When he shall dare a swan to rhyme;

The tow'ring swan comes sousing down   10
And breaks his pinions, cracks his crown;
From that sad time and sad disaster
He'll be a lame, cracked poetaster.
At length for stealing rhymes and triplets,
He'll be condemned to hang in giblets.   15

You see now, Gentlemen, this is fatally and literally come to pass, for it
was my misfortune to engage with that Pindar of the times, Tom Sheridan,
who did so confound me by sousing on my crown, and did so batter my
pinions that I was forced to make use of borrowed wings, though my false
accusers have deposed that I stole my feathers from Hopkins, Sternhold,
Silvester, Ogilby, Durfey, &c., for which I now forgive them and all the
world. I die a poet, and this ladder will be my Gradus ad Parnassum, and
I hope the critics will have mercy on my works.

Then lo! I mount as slowly as I sung,
And then I'll make a line for every rung.
There's nine I see—the Muses too are nine—
Who would refuse to die a death like mine?
1. Thou first rung, Clio, celebrate my name;   5
2. Euterp', in tragic numbers do the same.
3. This rung I see, Terpsicore's thy flute;
4. Erato, sing me to the gods—ah, do't!
5. Thalia, don't make me a comedy;
6. Urania, raise me toward the starry sky.   10
7. Calliope, to ballad strains descend,   ⎫
8. And Polyhymnia, tune them for your friend,   ⎬
9. So shall Melpom'ne mourn my fatal end.   ⎭

                    Poor Dan: Jackson

                                        (Written in late 1718)

From To Mr. Delany

Jonathan Swift

   You wonder now to see me write
So gravely, where the subject's light.
Some part of what I here design
Regards a friend of yours and mine,   90

Who full of humor, fire and wit,
Not always judges what is fit;
But loves to take prodigious rounds,
And sometimes walks beyond his bounds.
You must, although the point be nice,   95
Venture to give him some advice.
Few hints from you will set him right,
And teach him how to be polite.
Let him, like you, observe with care
Whom to be hard on, whom to spare: 100
Nor indiscreetly to suppose
All subjects like Dan Jackson's nose.
To study the obliging jest,
By reading those who teach it best.
For prose, I recommend Voiture's,   105
For verse, (I speak my judgment) yours:
He'll find the secret out from thence
To rhyme all day without offence;
And I no more shall then accuse
The flirts of his ill-mannered Muse.   110

    If he be guilty, you must mend him;
If he be innocent, defend him.

                              (Written November 10, 1718)

Palinodia

Horace, Book I, Ode XVI

Great Sir, than Phoebus more divine,
Whose verses far his rays outshine,
    Look down upon your quondam foe;
O! Let me never write again
If e'er I disoblige you, Dean,   5
    Should you compassion show.

Take those invectives which I wrote
When anger made me piping hot,
    And give them to your cook
To singe your fowl or save your paste   10
The next time when you have a feast;
    They'll save you many a book.

To burn them you are not content;
I give you then my free consent
  To sink them in the harbor;   15
If not, they'll serve to set off blocks,
To roll on pipes, and twist in locks,
  So give them to your barber.

Or when that next you physic take,
I must entreat you then to make   20
  A proper application;
'Tis what I've done myself before
With Dan's fine thoughts and many more
  Who gave me provocation.

What cannot mighty anger do?   25
It makes the weak the strong pursue,
  A goose attack a swan;
It makes a woman tooth and nail
Her husband's hands and face assail
  Or tap him with her fan.   30

Though some, we find, are more discreet,
Before the world are wondrous sweet,
  And let their husbands hector;
But when the world's asleep, they wake;
Then is the time they choose to speak: 35
  Witness the curtain lecture.

Such was the case with you, I find:
All day you could conceal your mind,
  But when St. Patrick's chimes
Awaked your Muse (my midnight curse   40
Which I engaged for better for worse),
  You scolded with your rhymes.

Have done! Have done! I quit the field;
To you, as to my wife, I yield:
  As she does wear the breeches,   45

So shall you wear the laurel crown;
Win it and wear it, 'tis your own,
   And all the poet's riches.
              (Written probably shortly after November 10, 1718)

The Epilogue to *Julius Caesar*

as spoke by Lord Mount Cashell at Mr. Sheridan's School in
Capell Street, 1718, that Tragedy being then Publickly
Perform'd by his Scholars.

   Grandmothers, mothers, aunts and sisters dear,
Before your seats of judgment we appear:
Judges and jury both we'd have you be;
Condemn our Master, not our tragedy.

   With one consent we this indictment draw;   5
Our cause is just as is your law.
When birchin twigs afflict our tender parts,
Where can we fly but to your tender hearts?
There we can refuge find when danger's nigh;
From besoms to your bosoms we must fly.   10

   The first great grievance of our tyrant's reign
Is that he won't permit us to complain:
If so, we're sure to pay for our appeals;
And they're revenged upon our harmless tails.
And, what is worse, he ridicules our woe: 15
"Go tell Mama again! Why don't you go?
I love to whip a fav'rite; that's my joy—
A mother's favorite, not a father's boy."

   Next should we quibble, curse, or lie, or swear,
Oh Heavens above, how he does rant and stare!   20
Passion flies out at both his rolling eyes;
Deaf to our prayers, the stentor loudly cries,
"Up with him, Sir," for that's his term of art.
Then up we go—and oh how we do smart.
Next should we pull a wig, or play in church,   25
Or laugh, next day we're sure to feel his birch.
Should we break windows or with brickbats pelt,
Again this curst machine, his rod, is felt.

Can't we knock out our brains for him I wonder,
But he must cut and slash our flesh asunder?   30
We can't an orchard rob, or plague a neighbor,
But he must come and our poor backs belabor.
Nor can we in a stall a cobbler smoke,
Although it is an inoffensive joke,
But our soft hides with welts are blistered o'er,   35
As if the cobbler mended what he tore.
Should we but tear a book to make a kite,
Which as I think exalts the poet's flight,
He makes it equal to the greatest crime,
Although Longinus teaches the Sublime.   40
Nay, what is worse, if we neglect our books,
With lash severe and terrible rebukes
Our nameless parts he scarifies and rends,
As if we studied with our t' other ends.

　If he taught stumps or logs, why then he might   45
Whip 'em with rods—in this he would be right—
But to teach human flesh by help of wood,
I cannot understand it for my blood.
Is this the way to cultivate our knowledge,
To make us run the gauntlet to the college?   50
Will this exalt us into learnèd men,
To sweep with brooms the cobwebs off our brain?
No, no! 'Twill never do; I think 'tis better
That we should never see nor know one letter.
I've brought a rod to show you. Now see here,   55
How can poor children such a scorpion bear?
'Tis long enough to drive a coach and four;
I vow the very sight on't makes me sore.
Revenge, Revenge, to you we loudly cry;
Condemn the tyrant instantly to die.   60
Here he's within; let him no longer live;
One moment is too long for his reprieve;
With scissors, bodkins, all at once attack him.
Depend upon't, not one of us will back him.

(Written ca. mid-December 1718)

The Pedagogue's Answer

Sir,
 I thank you for your comedies,
 Against the hipps the surest remedies.
 Because Pareus wrote but sorrily
 His notes, I'll read Lambinus thoroughly;
 And then I shall be stoutly set agog   5
 To challenge every Irish pedagogue.
 I like your nice epistle critical,
 Which does in threefold rhymes so witty fall.
 Upon the comic drama and tragedy,
 Your notion's right, but verses maggotty.   10
 'Tis just an hour since I heard a man swear it,
 The Devil himself could hardly answer it.
 As for your friend, the sage Euripides,
 I do believe you give him the slip a-days;[1]
 But mum for that—pray call a-Saturday   15
 And dine with me; you can't a better day.
 I'll give you nothing but a mutton chop,
 Some nappy mellowed ale with rotten hop,
 A pint of wine as good as Falern,
 Which we, masters, God knows, all earn.   20
 We'll have a friend or two at table,
 Right honest men, for few are come at-able.
 Then when our liquor makes us talkative,
 We'll to the fields and take a walk at eve.
   Because I am troubled much with laziness,   25
   These rhymes I've chosen for their easiness.

(Written in 1718)

---
1. N.B. You told me you forgot your Greek.

The Song

My time, O ye Grattans, was happily spent,
When Bacchus went with me wherever I went;
For then I did nothing but sing, laugh and jest—
Was ever a toper so merrily blest?
But now I so cross and so peevish am grown   5
Because I must go to my wife back to town—

To the fondling and toying of "honey" and "dear,"
And the conjugal comforts of horrid small beer.

My daughter I ever was pleased to see
Come fawning and begging to ride on my knee.   10
My wife too was pleased, and to the child said,
"Come, hold in your belly and hold up your head."
But now out of humor I, with a sour look,
Cry, "Hussy!" and give her a souse with my book.
And I'll give her another—for why should she play,   15
Since my Bacchus and glasses and friends are away?

Wine, what of thy delicate hue is become,
That tinged our glasses with blue like a plum?
Those bottles, those bumpers, why do they not smile
While we sit carousing and drinking the while?   20
Ah bumpers! I see that our wine is all done;
Our mirth falls, of course, when our Bacchus is gone.
Then since it is so, bring here a supply;
Begone, froward wife, for I'll drink till I die!

                                        (Written in 1718)

A Letter from Dr. Sheridan to Dr. Swift

I'd have you to know, as sure as you're Dean,
On Thursday my cask of Obrien I'll drain;
If my wife be not willing, I say she's a quean;
And my right to the cellar, egad, I'll maintain
As bravely as any that fought at Dunblain: 5
Go tell her it over and over again.
I hope, as I ride to the town, it won't rain;
For, should it, I fear it will cool my hot brain,
Entirely extinguish my poetic vein,
And then I should be as stupid as Kain,   10
Who preached on three heads though he mentioned but twain.
Now Wardel's in haste and begins to complain;
Your most humble servant, dear Sir, I remain,
                    T—— S——n.

Get Helsham, Walmsley, Delany,   15
And some Grattans if there be any;
Take care you do not bid too many.

                          (Written on December 15, 1719)

From My Much Honored Friend at Heldelville

Patrick Delany

Hail to the sage who, from his native store,
Produced a science never known before,
Science of words, once jargon of the schools,
The plague of wise men and the boast of fools,
Made easy now, and useful, in your rules,   5
Where wit and humor equally combine
Our mirth at once to raise and to refine.
Till now, not half the worth of sounds we knew;
Their virtual value was reserved for you
To trace their various mazes, and set forth   10
Their hidden force, and multiply their worth;
For, if t' express one sense our words we choose,
A double meaning is of double use.

Hail, sacred Art! By what mysterious name
Shall I adore thee, various and the same?   15
The Muses' Proteus, skilled with grateful change,
Through all the pleasing forms of wit to range
In quick succession, yet retain through all
Some faint resemblance of th' original.

Hail, fairest offspring of prodigious birth,   20
At once the parent and the child of mirth!
With Chloe's charms thy airy form can vie,
And with thy smiles as many thousands die;
The pleasing pain through all their vitals thrills,
With subtle force, and tickles as it kills.   25
Thee too, like her, the dying swains pursue,
As gay, as careless, as inconstant too;
To raise yet more thy merit and thy fame,

The Cyprian goddess glories in thy name,
Pleased to be thought the laughter-loving dame.   30
Nor less thy praise, nor less thy pow'r to wound,
Thou lovely, fleeting image of a sound.

(Published in 1719)

The Original of Punning

From *Plato's Symposiacs*

   Once on a time in merry mood,
Jove made a pun of flesh and blood:
A double, two-faced, living creature,
Androgynos, of two-fold nature,
For back to back with single skin,   5
He bound the male and female in;
So much alike, so near the same,
They stuck as closely as their name.
Whatever words the male expressed,
The female turned them to a jest;   10
Whatever words the female spoke,
The male converted to a joke:
So, in this form of man and wife,
They led a merry punning life.

   The gods from heav'n descend to earth,   15
Drawn down by their alluring mirth;
So well they seemed to like the sport,
Jove could not get them back to court.
Th' infernal gods ascend as well,
Drawn up by magic puns from hell.   20
Judges and Furies quit their post,
And not a soul to mind a ghost.

   "Hey Day!" says Jove; says Pluto too,
"I think the devil's here to do;
Here's hell broke loose, and heav'n's quite empty;   25
We scarce have left one god in twenty.
Pray, what has set them all a-running?"

"Dear brother, nothing else but punning.
Behold that double creature yonder
Delights them with a double entendre."   30

"Ods-fish," says Pluto, "Where's your thunder?
Let drive, and split this thing asunder."

"That's right," quoth Jove; with that he threw
A bolt, and split it into two;
And when the thing was split in twain,   35
Why then it punned as much again.
'Tis thus the diamonds we refine;
The more we cut, the more they shine:
And ever since, your men of wit,
Until they're cut, can't pun a bit.   40

So take a starling when 'tis young,
And down the middle slit the tongue;
With groat or sixpence, 'tis no matter;
You'll find the bird will doubly chatter.

"Upon the whole, dear Pluto, you know,   45
'Tis well I did not split my Juno!
For had I done't, when e'er she'd scold me,
She'd make the heav'ns too hot to hold me."

The gods upon this application
Returned each to his habitation,   50
Exremely pleased with this new joke—
The best, they swore, he ever spoke.

(Published in 1719)

Upon the Author

Patrick Delany?

Had I ten thousand mouths and tongues,
Had I ten thousand pair of lungs,
Ten thousand skulls with brains to think,
Ten thousand standishes of ink,
Ten thousand hands and pens to write,   5
Thy praise I'd study day and night.

Oh, may thy work forever live!
(Dear Tom, a friendly zeal forgive.)
May no vile miscreant, saucy cook,
Presume to tear thy learned book   10
To singe his fowl for nicer guest,
Or pin it on the turkey's breast.
Keep it from pastry baked, or flying
From broiling steak or fritters frying,
From lighting pipe, or making snuff,   15
Or casing up a feather muff.
From all the sev'ral ways the grocer
(Who to the learned world's a foe, sir)
Has found in twisting, folding, packing,
His brains and ours at once a-racking.   20
And may it never curl the head
Of either living block or dead.
Thus when all dangers they have passed,
Your leaves, like leaves of brass, shall last.
No blast shall from a critic's breath   25
By vile infection cause their death,
'Till they in flames at last expire,
And help to set the world on fire.

                              (Published in 1719)

Thus Did Great Socrates Improve the Mind

Thus did great Socrates improve the mind
By questions, useful since, to all mankind;
For when the purblind soul no farther saw
Than length of nose into dark Nature's law,
His method cleared up all, enlarged the sight,   5
And so he taught his pupils with day-light.

                              (Published in 1719)

If These Can't Keep Your Ladies Quiet

If these can't keep your ladies quiet,
Pull down their courage with low diet.
Perhaps, dear Sir, you'll think it cruel
To feed 'em on plain water-gruel;

But take my word, the best of breeding,   5
As it is plain, requires plain feeding.
                    Vide Roscom.

(Published in 1719)

Thus Puppies That Adore the Dark

Thus puppies that adore the dark
Against bright Cynthia howl and bark,
Although the regent of the night,
Like us, is gay with borrowed light.

(Published in 1719)

A Punegyric upon Tom Pun-sibi's *Ars Pun-ica*

Anonymous

'Twas sometime in the days of yore,
When th' infancy of Tongue was o'er;
She walked without the hold of nurse,
Of Go-Cart or of Hobby-Horse,
But trod as firm and had the power   5
To run as fast as at this hour.

From top of all Olympus steep,
Great Jove unto the earth does peep
To see how squares go here below,
And whether all are right or no;   10
Which having found in every part,
The god was pleased to th' very heart.

Then to the hole he lays his ear,
That he might mortal language hear,
Know what improvement it had made   15
Since last time he the world surveyed,
Which proves so great he almost fears
Whether or no to trust his ears.
He found the tongue the thoughts could tell,
Could make the bargains, buy and sell,   20
Had got the terms of "rogue" and "whore,"
Of "bitch" and "jade" and twenty more;

And everything said well enough
Excepting such as make one laugh:
It had not learned in all this while   25
One single word would make you smile.

  Jove plainly did perceive this want,
And to himself cries, "Fie upon't,
I now can see into my folly;
These folk are quite too melancholy.   30
But I'll engage that for hereafter
I'll make 'em split their sides with laughter,
Though still I'm in a little doubt
How best to bring this thing about."

  Thus said, he scratched his head awhile,   35
Then thus proceeded with a smile:
"I have it now. The thing is done;
'Tis only teaching them to pun.
And now some of our godships ample
Must make and send one for a sample.   40
Here, Vulcan, let this job be done;
Go make me quickly up a pun."

  The heav'nly smith to Lemnos hies,
And to his work himself applies,
Tries every metal in his shop,   45
From bottom to the very top;
Yet for his heart he could not find
Among so many one to's mind.
Gold was by much too solid stuff,
Not having vacuum half enough;   50
He could not make electrum glister,
Though polished till his fingers blister;
His hopes depended most on lead,
And yet it stood him in no stead.
For when he thought upon its weight,   55
Quoth he, "I must have something light."
He then bethought him where there lay
A grain or two of froth of sea,
Which Venus gave to him a fee as,
When arms he made for great Aeneas.   60
"If this," quoth he, "won't make it up,
There's nothing will in all my shop."

Then on the fire the god did lie
The froth, which 'gan to spit and fry;
But soon as e'er he gave one puft,   65
[Line cropped.]
Quitting both Vulcan and his shop,
It all flew out at chimney top.

   At this poor Vulcan in despair
Does back again to Jove repair;   70
Where falling on his knees, he cried,
"Dread Sir, my utmost art I've tried,
Done all that ever can be done,
Yet can't I make this cursed pun;
I've nothing fit to make it on."   75

   Jove only said, "Who would have thought it?"
And straightway fell himself about it;
So fine a pun he quickly made,
As if he'd served his time to th' trade;
To earth he bids it take its flight,   80
That mortals might make others by't.
To earth the pun no sooner glides,
Than mortals like t' have cracked their sides;
So well it pleased the little elves,
They fell to making puns themselves;   85
And though their clumsy work was rough,
It never failed to make 'em laugh.
From hence began the date of puns,
Being handed down from sires to sons;
Sometimes the art did grow and thrive,   90
And sometimes scarce was kept alive,
Till mortals found it to their cost
That quite and clear the art was lost.
And many a day, I do not doubt it,
The world was forced to be without it,   95
Till taught its value by its want,
Great wits were all resolved upon't,
To use their very utmost cunning
To find again the Art of Punning.
Brave souls. You each deserve a rhyme for't,   100
But I protest I have not time for't.
So I must pass the Scythians o'er,
The Vandals, Goths and many more;

And trudge away with all my speed
To Scotia's hills and banks of Tweed;   105
'Twas here the art first up did peep
After't had lain so long asleep.
They spied her out by second sight,
And catched her e'er she took her flight;
Nay, marry, some o' th' learn'd declare   110
'Twas napping like as Moss caught's mare.
Here many a pretty pun they made,
And bartered 'em by way of trade;
They often tied 'em up in packs
And sent 'em out on pedlar's backs.   115
When James was King of England made,
So much did he promote the trade,
That he for honor of his nation
Was Master of the Corporation.
Encouraged thus, the Scots came o'er   120
In shoals to Anglia's fertile shore,
And brought their puns themselves t' enrich,
As surely as they brought the Itch.
Nor did they on their hands e'er stick;
The best would buy a bishopric;   125
The very worst of all their pack
Would pay for scratching of their back,
From whence our modern custom's hatched,
That for a pun you're always scratched.

  But when alas! Great James was dead,   }   130
And punning would not get one bread,   }
The art again was knocked o' th' head,   }
Though sev'ral sages tried in vain,
If it could be restored again.

  At length Tom Pun-sibi arises   135
(Great Tom who all the world surprises),
And soon as up his head he pops,
He made the puns as thick as hops,
And does the art so well restore,
The like was never known before.   140
For he by either hook or crook
At Jove's own pun did get a look,
And made another by't so well,
You could not one from t' other tell;

Though Jove's was made of flesh and blood,   145
'Twas thought that Tom's was e'en as good.
For Tom, as he was very cunning,
So viewed Jove's archetype of punning,
That he did luckily espy
Where th' knack of all the art did lie,   150
And found that all the mighty trouble
Was how to split and how to double.

   Tom then begins as it was fitting,
And falls a-doubling and a-splitting,
Till every single word he brings   155
To signify at least two things,
So that whatever Tummas spoke
Might be or serious or a joke,
Might signify or cheese or chalk
According as you took his talk: 160
Like mug with ear on either side,
To this or that, as th' hand's applied,
In this or that way hauled with ease
According to the ear you seize;
To right or left, as you shall tug,   165
Obedient goes the willing mug.
So valiant Ralpho's basket-hilt,
By this end taken it would tilt;
By t' other, it was to your wish,
A ladle or a porridge dish.   170

   So here you see lies all the cunning,
The soul, the blood and guts of punning.
Now can he e'er be thought a wit
Whose meaning is not always split?
Or has he to't the least pretence   175
Whose words won't bear a double sense?
Alas now, if you'll but observe't,
How dry, insipid and how starved,
How blunt and dull's our conversation,
How tedious and how out of fashion,   180
For taste and relish how unfitting
Without this wondrous art of splitting?
So oysters have nor taste nor relish,
Until such times as split the shell is.

I think by all men is confessed   185
The worth of what we call dry jest;
Then pray now what can be more fitting
To make it dry than this same splitting?
So Peg to make her haddock dryer
Does split it e'er she hang't by th' fire.   190

The pleasant'st jokes that are a-stirring
Must needs be those of Pickle-herring,
Which makes many ye a man to tickle
To get himself once thought a pickle.
And nought's so good for his invention   195
As this same splitting Tom does mention.
But if you'd have this made more plain,
Think of Peg's haddock once again:
As thus for drying Peg does fit it,
'Tis thus for pickle still she'll split it.   200

Divines by splitting of the text
Make clear what was before perplexed;
And lawyers splitting of their cases
Make 'em as plain as nose on face is.
In short to say no more about it,   205
There's nothing to be done without it.

What thanks to Tom shall be presented,
Who this same splitting first invented?
Come hawkers, with your throats so shrill,
Blackguards and shoe-boys from Cork Hill.   210
What e'er you do, let Tom's great praise
Be still the subject of your lays;
Each shoe you wipe his worth proclaim,
And on the bottom carve his name.
And you with your deep-mouthèd sweep,   215
Do often break poor Echo's sleep,
Make all your pipes and whistles clear,
And split your mouths from ear to ear,
To praise great Tom in numbers fit—
That Tom to whom you owe your wit,   220
That Tom who teaches you to talk,
As subtilly as other folk,
And gives you rules whereby for certain
Your company will be diverting,

As much admired by great and small,   225
As th' learndest doctor of 'em all.

This art requires so little trouble
[Line cropped.]
And then you're sure applause to win,
Though neither meaning's worth a pin.   230

Thus cobbler when he finds his leather
Too thin, he claps his soles together.
You go and cheapen at his stall:
"Pray, Sir, observe this double sole"—
So Cerdon¹ finds by this device   235
The worse his wares, the better price.

But had I lump a dozen pair
By Nature thrown me to my share,
Had I a face of brass, a tongue
As nimble as mill-clapper slung,   240
Or double like to chineown—Pun,
Dear Tom, as certain as a gun
Thy art of punning, doubling, splitting
I ne'er should praise as it is fitting.

But since you'd gladly have me tell ye,   245
How much your puns and you we value,
Your Art of Splitting gives a hint
(Which seems to have a good deal in't),
That if we'd give you praises due
Then we must split as well as you,   250
And show how much we prize and rate ye,
Like Priapus diffissa nate.²

(Published in 1719)

---

1. The Irish M.S. had Sher'dan which must be a Mistake. See *Hudibras*, Part I.
2. Horat. 1. 1. Sat. 8.

A Prologue to a Play Performed at Mr. Sheridan's School Spoke by One of His Scholars

As in a silent night a lonely swain,
Tending his flocks on the Pharsalian plain,
To heav'n around directs his wand'ring eyes,
And every look finds out a new surprise;
So great's our wonder, Ladies, when we view   5
Our lower sphere made more serene by you.
O! Could such light in my dark bosom shine,
What life, what vigor should adorn each line!
Beauty and virtue should be all my theme,
And Venus brighten my poetic flame.   10
Th' advent'rous painter's fate and mine are one,
As he fain would draw the bright meridian sun;
Majestic light his feeble art defies,
And for presuming robs him of his eyes.
Then blame your pow'r, that my inferior lays   15
Sink far below your too exalted praise.
Don't think we flatter, your applause to gain.
No—we're sincere—to flatter you were vain.
You spurn all fine encomiums misapplied,
And all perfections but your beauties hide.   20
Then, as you're fair, we hope you will be kind,
Nor frown on those you see so well inclined
To please you most. Grant us your smiles and then
Those sweet rewards will make us act like men.

(Written possibly in 1719)

The Epilogue

Now all is done, learned spectators, tell
Have we not played our parts extremely well?
We think we did, but if you do complain,
We're all content to act the play again.
'Tis but three hours or thereabout at most,   5
And time well spent in school cannot be lost.
But what makes you frown, you gentlemen above?
We guessed long since you all desired to move,
But that's in vain for we'll not let a man stir
Who does not take up Plautus first and construe.   10

Him we'll dismiss, that understands the play;
He who does not, i' faith, he's like to stay.
Though this new method may provoke your laughter,
To act plays first and understand them after,
We do not care, for we will have our humor,   15
And will try you, and you, and you, Sir, and one or two more.
Why don't you stir? There's not a man will budge;
How much they've read I'll leave you all to judge.

(Written possibly in 1719)

Upon Stealing a Crown When the Dean Was Asleep

Dear Dean, since you in sleepy wise
Have oped your mouth and closed your eyes,
Like ghost I glide along your floor,
And softly shut the parlor door;
For should I break your sweet repose,   5
Who knows what money you might lose,
Since oftentimes it has been found
A dream has giv'n ten thousand pound.
Then sleep, my friend, dear Dean, sleep on,
And all you get shall be your own;   10
Provided you to this agree,
That all you lose belongs to me.

(Written ca. 1719?)

An Elegy on the Much Lamented Death of Mr. Demar, the Famous Rich Man, Who Died on the 6th of This Inst. July, 1720.

with Swift, Stella, and Delany.

Know all men by these presents, Death the tamer
By mortgage hath secured the corpse of Demar;
Nor can four hundred thousand sterling pound
Redeem him from his prison under ground.
His heirs might well, of all his wealth possessed,   5
Bestow to bury him one iron chest.
Pluto, the god of wealth, will joy to know

His faithful steward, in the shades below.
He walked the streets and wore a threadbare cloak;
He dined and supped at charge of other folk;   10
And by his looks, had he held out his palms,
He might be thought an object fit for alms.
So to the poor if he refused his pelf,
He used 'em full as kindly as himself.

    Where'er he went, he never saw his betters;   15
Lords, knights and squires were all his humble debtors;
And under hand and seal the Irish nation
Were forced to own to him their obligation.

    He that could once have half a kingdom bought,
In half a minute is not worth a groat;   20
His coffers from the coffin could not save,
Nor all his int'rest keep him from the grave.
A golden monument would not be right,
Because we wish the earth upon him light.

    Oh London Tavern! Thou hast lost a friend,   25
Though in thy walls he ne'er did farthing spend:
He touched the pence when others touched the pot;
The hand that signed the mortgage paid the shot.

    Old as he was, no vulgar known disease
On him could ever boast a pow'r to seize;   30
But as his gold he weighed, grim Death in spite
Cast in his dart which made three moidores light;
And as he saw his darling money fail,
Blew his last breath to sink the lighter scale.

    He who so long was current, 'twould be strange   35
If he should now be cried down since his change.

    The sexton shall green sods on thee bestow.
Alas, the sexton is thy banker now!
A dismal banker must that banker be,
Who gives no bills but of mortality.   40

EPITAPH

    Beneath this verdant hillock lies
    Demar the wealthy and the wise.

His heirs for winding-sheet bestowed
His money-bags together sewed;
And that he might securely rest,   45
Have put his carcase in a chest:
The very chest in which they say
His other self, his money, lay.
And if his heirs continue kind
To that dear self he left behind,   50
I dare believe that four in five
Will think his better half alive.

(Written on July 6, 1720)

Mr. Sheridan's Prologue to the Greek Play of Phaedra and Hippolytus; Designed to Have Been Spoke by a Boy of Six Years Old

Under the notion of a play, you see,
We're fairly coaxed to act a Tragedy.
Lord! How can any man of reason say
That so much labor should be called a play?
Should any one be so absurd a fool,   5
I'd be the first would kick him out of school;
For I am sure it cost us aching hearts
And aching heads before we got our parts.
Not all the learning of the year behind
Laid half so great a stress upon our mind;   10
As for my part, I wish our school was burned,
And all our books were into ashes turned.
Greek after Greek, book after book, no doubt
Will wear our strongest constitutions out.
My mother told me in these words last night,   15
"Dear Tommy, child, books will destroy you quite;
That you should read at all, I'm very loath;
My life, my dear, I fear they'll spoil your growth."
And she says right; they cost me so much pains,
I wish ten thousand times I had no brains,   20
Nor had a breech to whip; why then I'd play,
But not in Greek—I'd find a better way.
Now, Gentlemen, 'tis worth your while to look:
You see this gig I have—you see this book;
The gig can spin and frisk and hop and tolt,   25

The book's a lazy, sluggish, heavy dolt.
See how much life is in this bouncing ball;
Now smoke the book, it cannot bounce at all.
This top I carry to play Mug and Gloss;
This bone I have it to play Pitch and Toss.   30
But this is neither fit for Gloss or Mug;
A lifeless drone, it is a perfect slug.
I swear the very sight on't makes me sick;
I'm sure it is a cursèd bone to pick.
Next figure I present you is my kite;   35
Had any poet e'er so fine a flight?
See how it skims and soars along the sky;
Come, friend Euripides, let's see you fly.
Down, down he comes—in vain aloft he springs,
A perfect lifeless bat with leathern wings.   40
Behold my bag of marbles—here's a treasure!
A world of joy! A world of real pleasure!
What is this poet good for? Come, let's see—
O yes! 'Tis good—to put beneath my knee.

While thus I play regardless of all care,   45
And wisely act within my proper sphere;
O! Could I thus in happiness and ease
Pass the remainder of my well-spent days,
Secure from birch, regardless of its pain,
I'd never, never see a book again;   50
Rather than ever play a play in Greek,
Grant us, ye Fates, to play at Hide and Seek.

(Written ca. December 1720)

Prologue to *Hippolytus*, Spoken by a Boy of Six Years Old

Richard Helsham

Ye sons of Athens, grant me one request,
And I'll requite you with a pleasing jest.
Protect me from my Master's cruel rod;
Hide me, O hide me, from the tyrant's nod!
He penned a prologue which to me was shown;   5
I liked it not, and told him 'twould not down.

He said it humor had, and wit enough,
But to my thinking it was scurvy stuff;
Howe'er, he made me get it all by heart,
And thus instructed my to play the part: 10

"Dear Tommy, child, repeat the whole with care;
Here you must raise your voice, but sink it there.
Then in due order take your playthings up:
Now whip your gig, now spin your castle-top,
Then take in hand your Virgil and your kite,   }   15
Throw Virgil on the ground, set that to flight,
Then speak these lines, I'm sure they'll give delight."

Thus he desired me to speak and act—
Believe me, Sirs, what I relate is fact;
And now he waits, expecting I should say   20
That trifling prologue to this serious play;
But I must beg in that to be excused;
I would not have the audience so abused.
Such entertainment is not fit for men,
Till they have reached their childish state again—   25
Not like that rev'rend sage in whom appears
New force of reason in advanced years.
O, could I celebrate with equal parts
That patron of religion and of arts,
The stay of right, the church's chief support,   30
His country's champion and her last resort!

But I forbear, and now I must provide
For my own safety, for I fear I've tried
My Master's patience, and his anger moved,
In speaking what he ne'er would have approved.   35
I know my danger, but I can't repent
For being steady to a good intent.

Thus firmly did Hippolytus pursue   }
The slipp'ry paths of virtue, though he knew
His ruin thence would certainly ensue.   40
Since our conditions are so near the same,

They both alike your kind compassion claim:
Grant your protection then, ye sons of wit,
To poor Hippolytus, and poor Tom Tit.

                    (Written ca. December 10, 1720)

The Invitation

In imitation of Horace's *Epistle to Torquatus*
Si potes Archiacis &c. Hor. Lib. I. Epist. 5.

Dear Doctor—Being you're so kind
To take a snack of what you find
With me today, let me just think
How I may make the sequel clink
(For you I know will dine the better   5
When invitation comes in meter);
Hold—let me see—I've found a way.
I borrowed Pegasus today
To ride—to church; and, being Sunday,
I'll make the most of him for one day.   10
Him I ha'n't crossed this year before,
And mayn't again in two years more.
It now is past the eleventh hour,
And faith I dread this heavy shower
(And can you say my fears are vain?   15
Who don't lament this heavy rain?),
For this may change the ladies' minds,
Since they are oft compared to winds;
And lest it should, this note must go
To beg that I mayn't find it so,   20
But that they'll come and take a share
Of such, as here's the Bill of Fare.
With roots, of beef that's boiled, a buttock,
Crammed fowls with oyster sauce, a fat duck.
A side dish made for your own belly—   25
You know what you bespoke—an eel-pie.
These, celery, goose, and nothing worse
This completes; now for second course.
At th' upper end the wild fowl's placed.
The sideboard with a sirloin's graced.   30
Four things more make up the meal,
Our liquors—claret, potent ale,

A quart of rum with juice of lemon,
Which we'll tope off like any seamen;
And then—break up, for too much drinking   35
Dulls the wit and spoils our thinking,
Makes us trip like foundered horses—
Nor tongue nor feet can keep their courses—
Divulges secrets, dims our reason,
Makes (mum for that) the W——gs talk treason.   40
This pocket from your Lady's sight   ⎫
And Mrs. W——, that toast so bright,   ⎬
Whose eyes may light you home at night. ⎭
Be sure you don't forget Miss E——e,
Who I desire may wear her new stays,   45
And come and play and bawl and squeak
Enough to serve her for a week.
I hope, like her, you'll all be merry,
Since nought can more oblige your, Sh——ry.

                                        (Published in 1720)

I Send This at Nine

I send this at nine
To know will you dine
On a beefsteak of mine.
As I'm a divine
I'll give you good wine,   5
Old, gen'rous and fine.
Till death I am thine,
Thomas Sheridine.

                                        (Date uncertain)

Tom Punsibi's Letter to Dean Swift

When to my house you come, dear Dean,
Your humble friend to entertain,
Through dirt and mire along the street,
You find no scraper for you feet:
At this, you storm and stamp and swell,   5
Which serves to clean your feet as well:
By steps ascending to the hall,
All torn to rags, with boys and ball.

Fragments of lime about the floor,
A sad, uneasy parlor door,   10
Besmeared with chalk, and nicked with knives
(A pox upon all careless wives!)
Are the next sights you must expect;
But do not think they're my neglect.
Ah, that these evils were the worst!   15
The parlor still is further curst;
To enter there if you advance,
If in you get, it is by chance.
How oft in turns have you and I
Said thus, "Let me." "No, let me try."   20
"This turn will open it, I engage."
You push me from it in a rage!
Turning, twisting, forcing, fumbling,
Stamping, staring, fuming, grumbling.
At length it opens; in we go;   25
How glad are we to find it so!
Conquests, through pains and dangers, please
Much more than those we gain with ease.

If you're disposed to take a seat,
The moment that it feels your weight   30
Out go its legs and down you come
Upon your reverend deanship's bum.
Hence learn and see old age displayed,
When strength and vigor are decayed,
The joints relaxing with their years;   35
Then what are mortal men, but chairs?

The windows next offend your sight:
Now they are dark, now they are light;
The shuts a-working to and fro
With quick succession come and go.   40
So have I seen in human life
The same in an uneasy wife,
By turns affording joy and sorrow,
Devil today and saint tomorrow.

Now to the fire, if such there be,   45
But now 'tis rather smoke you see;
In vain you seek the poker's aid,
Or tongs, for they are both mislaid.

"Come stir it up." "Ho, Mr. Joker,
How can I stir it without a poker?"   50

"The bellows take; their battered nose
Will serve for poker, I suppose."
Now you begin to rake—alack!
The grate is tumbled from its back;
The coals upon the hearth are laid.   55
"Stay, sir. I'll run and call the maid.
She'll make our fire again complete;
She knows the humor of the grate."

"Deuce take your maid and you together!
This is cold comfort in cold weather!"   60

"Now all, you see, is well again;
Come be in humor, Mr. Dean,
And take the bellows; use them so."

"These bellows were not made to blow.
Their leathern lungs are in decay;   65
They can't e'en puff the smoke away."

"And is your Rev'rence vexed at that?
Get up, a-God's name. Take your hat!
Hang 'em, say I, that have no shift;
Come, blow the fire, good Doctor Swift.   70
Trifles like these, if they must tease you,
Pox take those fools that strive to please you.
Therefore, no longer be a quarr'ler
Either with me, sir, or my parlor.
If you can relish ought of mine—   75
A bit of meat, a glass of wine—
You're welcome to't, and you shall fare
As well as dining with the Mayor."

"You saucy scab, you tell me so!
Why, booby-face, I'd have you know   80
I'd rather see your things in order
Than dine in state with the Recorder.
For water I must keep a clutter,
Then chide your wife for stinking butter,
Or getting such a deal of meat   85

As if you'd half the town to eat.
That wife of yours, the devil's in her—
I've told her of this way of dinner
Five hundred times, but all in vain—
Here comes a leg of beef again!   90
O that that wife of yours would burst!
Get out and serve the lodgers first,
Pox take them all for me! I fret
So much I cannot eat my meat;
You know I'd rather have a slice."   95

"I know, dear sir, you're always nice;
You'll see them bring it in a minute;
Here comes the plate, and slices in it;
Therefore sit down and take your place;
Do you fall to, and I'll say Grace."   100

(Written probably in 1720)

A Prologue Spoke by Mr. Elrington at the Theatre-Royal on Saturday the First of April. In Behalf of the Distressed Weavers

Great cry and little wool—is now become
The plague and proverb of the weaver's loom;
No wool to work on, neither weft nor warp;
Their pockets empty and their stomachs sharp.
Provoked, in loud complaints to you they cry: 5
Ladies, relieve the weavers, or they die.
Forsake your silks for stuffs, nor think it strange
To shift your clothes, since you delight in change.
One thing with freedom I'll presume to tell:
The men will like you every bit as well.   10

See, I am dressed from top to toe in stuff,
And, by my troth, I think I'm fine enough.
My wife admires me more, and swears she never
In any dress beheld me look so clever.
And if a man be better in such ware,   15
What great advantage must it give the Fair!
Our wool from lambs of innocence proceeds;
Silk comes from maggots, calicos are weeds;

Hence 'tis by sad experience that we find
Ladies in silks to vapors much inclined,   20
And what are they but maggots in the mind?
For which I think it reason to conclude,
That clothes may change our tempers like our food.
Chintzes are gaudy and engage our eyes
Too much about the parti-colored dyes.   25
Although the luster is from you begun,
We see the rainbow and neglect the sun.

How sweet and innocent's the country maid,
With small expense in native wool arrayed,
Who copies from the fields her homely green,   30
While by her shepherd with delight she's seen.
Should our fair ladies dress like her in wool,
How much more lovely and how beautiful
Without their Indian drapery they'd prove,
And wool would help to warm us into love.   35
Then like the famous argonauts of Greece,
We'd all contend to gain the Golden Fleece.

                              (First spoken on April 1, 1721)

Prologue to the Farce of *Punch Turned Schoolmaster*

Spoken by Mr. Griffith

Gallants, our business is to let you know,
This night we represent a Puppet-Show,
Where every actor comes to make a figure
Big as the life, and some, indeed, much bigger.
The truth of what I tell you will appear   5
When you behold our Punch and Banimeer.

We found this house was almost empty grown
From the first moment Stretch appeared in town.
What could we do but learn to squeak and hop it,
Each actor change into his fav'rite puppet?   10

Think not in this we banter or abuse you;
We'll turn to anything before we'll lose you.

If you're well pleased with this, you soon shall see
These very puppets act a tragedy;
The Rival Queens we'll play, if you command—   15
Much finer than *The Queen of Ivy Land.*

I now proceed to beg our Punch may meet
As much applause as he in Capel Street.
Our Banimeer speaks Hebrew, Greek and Latin;
Their Punch speaks nonsense, yet is ever prating.   20

0, let not learning want its just reward,
Since Punch, to please you, studied very hard.
Don't let your eager thirst of knowledge cool;
Come and improve your talents—here's your school—
We'll teach the ladies a genteeler squeak,   25
And powdered beaux shall show their parts in Greek.

(Written ca. early April 1721)

From The Puppet-Show

Anonymous

XVI

Tell Tom he draws a farce in vain,
    Before he looks in Nature's glass;
Puns cannot form a witty scene,
    Nor pedantry for humor pass.

XVII

To make men act as senseless wood,   65
    And chatter in a mystic strain,
Is a mere force on flesh and blood,
    And shows some error in the brain.

XVIII

He that would thus refine on thee,
  And turn thy stage into a school,   70
The jest of Punch will ever be,
  And stand confessed the greater fool.

(Written in early April 1721)

A Copy of a Copy of Verses from Thomas Sheridan, Clerk, to George Nim-Dan-Dean, Esq. Written July 15th, 1721, at Night

I'd have you t' know, George, Dan, Dean, 'nd Nim,
That I've learn'd how verse t' compose trim,
Much better b' half th'n you, n'r you, n'r him,
And th't I'd rid'cule their, 'nd your flam-flim.
"Ay' b't then, p'rhaps," says you, "'s a m'rry whim   5
With 'bundance of mark'd notes i' th' rim."
So th't I ought n't for t' be morose 'nd t' look grim,
Think n't your 'p'stle put m' in a megrim;
Though 'n Rep't't'on Day I 'ppear ver' slim,
Th' last bowl 't Helsham's did m' head t' swim,   10
So th't I h'd man' aches 'n 'v'ry scrubb'd limb,
Cause th' top of th' bowl I h'd oft us'd t' skim;
And b'sides D'lan' swears th't I h'd swall'w'd s'v'r'l brim-
mers, 'nd that my vis'ge's cov'r'd o'er with r'd pim-
ples: m'r'o'er though m' skull were ('s 'tis n't) 's strong
  's tim-   15
ber, 't must have ach'd. Th' clans of th' C'llege Sanh'drim
Pres'nt th'r humbl' and 'fect'nate respects; that's t' say,
  D'l'n', 'chlin, P. Ludl', Dic' St'wart, H'lsham, Capt'n
  P'rr' Walmsl', 'nd Longsh'nks Tim.

(Written on July 15, 1721)

To George Nim-Dan-Dean, Esq. upon His Incomparable Verses, &c. of August 2d, M DCC XXI

Hail, human compound quadrifarious!
Invincible as Wight Briareus!

Hail! Doubly doubled mighty merry one,
Stronger than triple-bodied Geryon!
O may your vastness deign t' excuse   5
The praises of a puny Muse,
Unable in her utmost flight
To reach thy huge Colossian height.
T' attempt to write like thee were frantic,
Whose lines are, like thyself, gigantic.   10

Yet let me bless, in humbler strain,
Thy vast, thy bold Cambysian vein,
Poured out t' enrich thy native isle,
As Egypt wont to be with Nile.
O how I joy to see thee wander   15
In many a winding, loose meander,
In circling mazes, smooth and supple,
And ending in a clink quadruple;
Loud, yet agreeable withal,
Like rivers rattling in their fall.   20
Thine, sure, is poetry divine,
Where wit and majesty combine;
Where every line, as huge as seven,
If stretched in length, would reach to Heaven:
Here all comparing would be sland'ring;   25
The least is more than Alexandrine.

Against thy verse Time sees with pain
He whets his envious scythe in vain;
For, though from thee he much may pare,
Yet much thou still wilt have to spare.   30

Thou hast alone the skill to feast
With Roman elegance of taste,
Who hast of rhymes as vast resources
As Pompey's caterer of courses.

O thou, of all the Nine inspired!   35
My languid soul, with teaching tired,
How is it raptured when it thinks
On thy harmonious set of clinks;
Each answ'ring each in various rhymes,
Like Echo to St. Patrick's chimes!   40

Thy Muse, majestic in her rage,
Moves like Statira on the stage,
And scarcely can one page sustain
The length of such a flowing train.
Her train, of variegated dye,   45
Shows like Thaumantia's in the sky;
Alike they glow, alike they please,
Alike impressed by Phoebus' rays.

Thy verse—(Ye Gods! I cannot bear it)
To what, to what shall I compare it?   50
'Tis like, what I have oft heard spoke on,
The famous statue of Laöcoön.
'Tis like—O yes, 'tis very like it,
The long long string with which you fly kite.
'Tis like what you, and one or two more,   55
Roar to your Echo in good humor;
And every couplet thou hast writ
Concludes like Rattah-whittah-whit.

                              (Written ca. August 4, 1721)

With Music and Poetry Equally Blessed

George Rochfort

With music and poetry equally blessed,
A bard thus Apollo most humbly addressed:
"Great author of harmony, verses and light!
Assisted by thee, I both fiddle and write.
Yet unheeded I scrape, or I scribble all day;   5
My verse is neglected, my tunes flung away.
Thy substitute here, Vice-Apollo, disdains
To vouch for my numbers, or list to my strains;
Thy manual signet refuses to put
To the airs I produce from the pen or the gut.   10
Be thou then propitious, great Phoebus, and grant
Relief or reward to my merit or want.
Though the Dean and Delany transcendently shine,
O! brighten one solo or sonnet of mine.
With them, I'm content thou should'st make thy abode,   15
But visit thy servant in jig or in ode.
Make one work immortal; 'tis all I request."

Apollo looked pleased and, resolving to jest,
Replied, "Honest friend, I've considered thy case,
Nor dislike thy well-meaning and humorous face.   20
Thy petition I grant; the boon is not great.
Thy works shall continue, and here's the receipt:
On rondeaus hereafter, thy fiddle-strings spend;
Write verses in circles—they never shall end."

(Written in August 1721)

A Portrait from the Life

Jonathan Swift

Come sit by my side, while this picture I draw:
In chattering a magpie, in pride a jackdaw,
A temper the devil himself could not bridle,
Impertinent mixture of busy and idle,
As rude as a bear, no mule half so crabbed,   5
She swills like a sow, and she breeds like a rabbit,
A housewife in bed, at table a slattern,
For all an example, for no one a pattern.
Now tell me, friend Thomas, Ford, Grattan, and merry Dan,
Has this any likeness to good Madam Sheridan   10

(Written possibly sometime between 1718 and the early
1720s)

A Letter to Tom Punsibi, Occasioned by Reading His Excellent Farce, Called *Alexander's Overthrow, or, The Downfall of Babylon*

Anonymous

Invidiam placare paras. Horat. Sat. 3. Lib. 2.

Dear Tom,
    Nor turkey fat, nor goose from country-hut,
Nor steed when door of stable's left unshut,
Nor silver spoon, nor thimble, bodkin, locket,
Nor watch in fob, nor handkerchief in pocket,   5
Is oft'ner nimmed, when rogue comes fairly by't,

Than are the rhymes we poets do indite.
With watch by night our cattle we secure,
With sturdy mastiff or well-bolted door;
With arms or craft Sir John marks spoons and knives,   10
And honest Ralph with husband's name and wife's;
Dick's geese are known by slit between their toes,
And branded buttock sorrel's master shows.
But plag'ary to baulk none could devise;
He locks and bolts and brands and marks defies.   15
Maugre our utmost care, it does surpass us
To guard th' enclosures we have at Parnassus.
With suchlike fate met Virgil heretofore,
And future ages will the same deplore.
The ravished lock may, ravished once again,   20
Leave Pope with his Belinda to complain.
And plants which Cowley raised from noblest seeds
Be stole and set among some paltry weeds.
Great Gloucester's Royal Grammar may with slyness
Be cribbed, without permission from his Highness.   25

When on some piece we've spared nor care nor pains,
Racked every single thought and squeezed our brains,
Till Envy ne'er a fault sees in the whole;
She then gives out, "The composition's stole."
Or else some pirate of the quill comes on,   30
Seizes our wares and vends them for his own.
In coin like this have poets oft been paid,
Nor Phoebus' self his dearest sons could aid.

But thee, dear Tom, no like disasters wait;
Thy happier genius laughs at such a fate.   35
Should Envy now in human shape appear,
Assume the form and meagre cheeks of G——r,[1]
To tell the world Tom Punsibi's a thief,
Full well she knows, she ne'er could gain belief;
She'll now in every place to great and small   40
Confess that you're a mere original.
Nor need you fear that any can purloin
One page, one thought, one single verse of thine.
Whether you teach us how to Pun by Rule,[2]
Or Punch depute for Master of your school,[3]   45
Whether y' invite the Dean to eat your pullets,[4]
Or arm the Britons stout with Beggar's Bullets,[5]

Such a peculiar manner and design,
Such strokes, such colors glare in every line, ⎫
As prove the hand that touch them to be thine. ⎬   50
Like thine own Caesar[6] thou dost make it known, ⎭
That what is thine, dear Tummas, is thy own.
(Written after December 11, 1721)

---

1. G——r having formerly endeavour'd to prove this Author a Plagiary, upon seeing his *Art of Punning*, declar'd candidly to the World, that he believ'd that Piece to be entirely his own, and none of it stolen.
2. *The Art of Punning*.
3. The Farce call'd *Punch turn'd School-Master*.
4. A famous Poem in imitation of Horace's *Si potes Archaisis*, &c. from Mr. S——n to Dr. S——t, called *The Invitation*.
5. *Alexander's Overthrow*.
6. Vide *S——n's Master-piece, or Tom Punsibi's Folly compleat*.

An Elegy on the Deplorable Death of Mr. Thomas Sheridan, Author of *Alexander's Overthrow or, The Downfall of Babylon*, Who Departed this Mortal Life on Thursday the 8th of March, 1721/22

Anonymous

Assist with mournful strains, assist, my Muse;
Don't at this time your wonted aid refuse.
Bewail his fate; poor Pun-sibi's no more;
In mournful accents now his death deplore.
In vain, alas! for him we hope relief;   5
His fate is certain, certain as our grief;
Nor sighs, nor tears can aught for him procure;
His warrant's sealed, his destiny is sure.
He died with great remorse for former crimes,
Begged Paean's pardon too for murdered rhymes.   10
No more his puns shall please the giddy crowd,
No more sham farces make fools laugh aloud.
But now in common dust his bones must lie;
What pity 'tis that such bright men should die!
He was a stranger to domestic strife.   15
His joys were centered in a handsome wife,
So good, virtuous, of so sweet a mind;

One of such parts, who in this age can find?
He knew the worth of such a mighty prize,
One who the sland'rous tongues of fame defies,   20
And ne'er was known with her to be at strife,
But Betty was the comfort of his life.
His wisdom was so great, so great his name,
My pen is far unfit for such a theme;
The subject is too high for my poor Muse;   25
In commendations I his worth abuse.
His goodness to the poor, all must confess,
In which he ever placed his happiness.
His learning too was equal to his name;
His Grammar shows him not belied by fame.   30
Now join, ye nymphs, and all ye swains combine;
Join all, to let your sorrow equal mine.
What grief's sufficient for so great a man;
Who can express the worth of Sheridan?

                          Epitaph
Stop Travelers; bewail the sad estate   35
Of one, alas! too soon cut down by fate.
Here lies his dust, for wisdom once renowned;
Search Europe, Asia, all the world around:
His fellow surely is not to be found.

                              (Published after March 8, 1721/22)

A Poem on Tom Pun——bi
On Occasion of his late Death, and in Vindication of Some Verses Written, Entitled "Sheridan's Resurrection"

Anonymous

Alas! ye Bards, the Elegies you've made
Are all in vain, for Pun-sibi's not dead.
Happy is he beneath St. Catherine's shades,
Viewing Mountcashel's seat, and flow'ry meads;
With daily raptures he improves his vein,   5
And courts the sporting Muses once again.
We should, dear Tom, have had a loss of thee,
If thou were changèd to a fruitless tree:

No more would comely B——y, thy dear w——e, }
The only joy and comfort of thy life,   }   10
Repeat with thee her own domestic strife;   }
No more thy strains would charm th' unfolding air,
No more thy school would thy just laws revere.
But, sure, a school is far too slight a name
For such a noble and majestic frame.   15
Father of Verse! where all thy state appears,
And with thee all thy sprightly senators;
The lofty fabric where great Julius fell
Could not thy godlike Senate House excel.
But hold! I think some persons say you crib   20
Your verses, Tom; but I believe they fib,
For such true marks in thee, our author, shine   }
In every verse thou writ'st, in every line,   }
That I'll be sworn, dear Tom, they're truly thine. }
For who can think that Spenser's sacred Muse   25
Could write such verse as you, my friend, produce?
Great Addison himself did never yet
Surpass thee, Tom, in eloquence and wit.
Thy farce shall down to future times descend,
While bards thy fancy and thy verse commend,   30
For in that piece there's such poetic flame
'Twould make th' amazèd savages grow tame.
To see great Alexander's sight to fail,
Alas! and drownèd in a pot of ale;
'Tis strange that Virgil never once did think   35
To paint a hero when he raged in drink.
But Pun-sibi to win the sought-for bays
Has led his Muse through new untrodden ways.
If e'er the Muses did a mortal bless
With poetry, 'tis thee, we all confess.   40
Though thou hast grown so very wise of late,
And filled with poetry your learnèd pate,
Yet I do hope you never will despise
To take from me a little kind advice:
Well, to begin, before you do commence,   45
A perfect wit, learn to write common sense.

                                    (Published in 1722)

Tom Pun-Sibi's Resurrection Disproved

Anonymous

Non vana redeat sanguis imagini
Quam virga semel horrida,
Non lenis precibus Fata recludere,
Nigro compulerit Mercurius gregi.
                    Hor. Lib. I. Ode XXIV

Well, Ralph, howe'er you're pleased to strive
To make me think that Tom's alive—
Nay, that he's well as heart can wish,
In goodly plight, and sound as fish,
When there's an Elegy on's death   5
With Epitaph put underneath,
Such as himself has often made
When other men in grave were laid,
Or helped to make ("When Death the Tamer
By Mortgage Seized the Corpse of Damer")—   10
I needs must think it cannot fail,
But Tom is dead as a door nail.
Not only quatenus schoolmaster,
Droll, punster, fiddler, poetaster;
Not dead in sin and foul offense,   15
Or in some other mystic sense;
But cruel Death has made a morsel
Of Thomas' little outward vessel.
If you'd my meaning plainer have,
Why, honest Tom is in his grave,   20
Bum-shot by Obadiah Fizle,
Which makes mine eyes full sorely drizzle,
Or by that Engineer accursed
Hight Fartinando Puffendorst.
But you to prove it all a joke,   25
Tell me he's seen in streets to walk.
What then, have you not often read
Of men that walked when they were dead,
Especially where vital date
Was shortened by untimely Fate?   30
"But he no murderer accuses,
Blames none," you say, "for such abuses,

But cries as loud as tongue can bawl
That he was never dead at all."
Well! Partridge did pretend the same,   35
Swearing his death was all a flam
When the learn'd Squire had proved it plain,
That he was dead and dead again.

Pray go to Bedlam, search it round
For th' maddest man that can be found.   40
Be th' wretch's senses ne'er so bad,
He'll always say he is not mad.
But this you say, "can be no goblin
That walks in Capel Street and Dublin,
'Cause he by night's not only seen,   45
As other goblins oft have been;
But thousands him have set their eyes on
When Phoebus is above horizon.
But goblins, elves," you say, "and sprites
Play all their gambols in the nights;   50
But soon as once the cock does crow,
Away they're all compelled to go.
And every phantom disappear
At Matins sung by chanticleer;
Nor dare they come again in sight   55
Till darkness and succeeding night."

I tell you that's a vulgar error,
Kept up, lest (too much cowed by terror)
Miss ne'er should leave her nurse's sight,
But dread the day as well as night.   60
And so, though Nan and Roger say
That goblins ne'er do walk by day,
We, all our learnèd doctors find
Of other sentiments and mind;
And many of 'em prove downright,   65
They walk by day as well as night.

Admit he thrashed ye two or three,
Who hawked about the Elegy,
And sent his boys, as you have hinted,
To break the press where it was printed: 70
You take this for a reason strong
That Tom's alive; I say you're wrong.

Can't sprites and goblins if they please
Beat, pinch and play such tricks as these?
But Tom, I'm sure, were he alive,   75
Some other method would contrive,
Whereby the world might plainly know
That he is still in *statu quo*,
Than beat poor newsboys into mortar,
Which might be done by any porter.   80
Something peculiar we should see,
Which none could do but only he,
And put us clearly out of doubt
That vital spark's not yet gone out.

So when John Coates, with learnèd lore,   85
Gives out that Whalley is no more,
Pretending by the stars to know
That he's gone down to shades below;
Him Whalley by such art disproves,
As all our scruples quite removes,   90
And shows us plain beyond dispute
That Coates is but a lying brute.
He does not go and thrash his hide,
Nor only tell us he's belied;
This might be credited no better   95
By many than his own *News Letter*;
But to confute his brother quack,
He straight sends out his *Almanack*,
Which, with such learnèd cant he fills,
Such brags and stories of his pills,   100
Stuffed with such astrologic fictions,
Such prophecies and strange predictions,
As not a man alive but he
In all the world can e'er foresee.

Tom was as cunning every whit   105
As Whalley, and had as much wit;
And were he living, I dare say,
Would take the very selfsame way—
Which had he done, I'd then believe
And freely own that he's alive.   110
Had he but only writ a farce,
Or quaint enigma on his a——,
Another Grammar had compiled,

Or vamped up old, anew for child;
Had he but some small paper writ   115
With great assurance, little wit,
And affectation to discerning
A hid'ous, per'lous deal of learning,
Full fraught with many a darling pun,
Some of them pilfered, some his own,   120
Run up on strings like onion heads,
As long as Father Floody's beads,
With style like fabled toad, whose drift's
To swell itself as big as Swift's,
Though there's as much between as is   125
'Tween his birch rod and Tully's fasces.

    Now when I once shall come to find
But some small proof of such a kind,
I'll give my word and protestation
That I'll allow't for demonstration,   130
As plain as two and three make five,
That little Thomas is alive.
Till then, whatever is pretended,
I must believe his life is ended,
And that it is some subtle sprite   135
That does impose upon our sight,
That puts on Thomas' shape and clothes,
So slings its tail, so cocks its nose,
So scrapes sonatas, and so thrums,
So clapper-claws and firks poor bums,   140
And does the nicest judge beguile,
In everything but in his style;
His style, nor goblin, sprite nor elf,
Nor man comes up to but himself.

                          (Written and published ca. June 1722)

From A Description in Answer to *The Journal*

William Percival

As for himself, with draggled gown,
Pure curate-like, he'll trudge the town,
To eat a meal with Punster base,
Or buffoon, call him if you please . . .

                          (Published in 1722)

A Description of Doctor Delany's Villa

Would you that Delville I describe?
Believe me, Sir, I will not gibe;
For who would be satirical
Upon a thing so very small?

You scarce upon the borders enter,   5
Before you're at the very center.
A single crow can make it night,
When o'er your farm she takes her flight;
Yet, in this narrow compass, we
Observe a vast variety;   10
Both walks, walls, meadows and parterres,
Windows and doors, and rooms and stairs,
And hills and dales, and woods and fields,
And hay and grass and corn, it yields;
All to your haggard brought so cheap in,   15
Without the mowing or the reaping—
A razor, though to say't I'm loath,
Would shave you and your meadows both.

Though small's the farm, yet here's a house
Full large to entertain a mouse;   20
But where a rat is dreaded more
Than savage Caledonian boar;
For, if it's entered by a rat,
There is no room to bring a cat.

A little rivulet seems to steal   25
Down through a thing you call a vale,
Like tears adown a wrinkled cheek,
Like rain along a blade of leek;
And this you call your sweat meander,
Which might be sucked up by a gander,   30
Could he but force his nether bill
To scoop the channel of the rill.
For sure you'd make a mighty clutter,
Were it as big as city gutter.

Next come I to your kitchen garden,   35
Where one poor mouse would fare but hard in;

And round this garden is a walk
No longer than a tailor's chalk;
Thus I compare what space is in it,
A snail creeps round it in a minute.   40
One lettuce makes a shift to squeeze
Up through the tuft you call your trees,
And once a year a single rose
Peeps from the bud, but never blows;
In vain then you expect its bloom!   45
It cannot blow for want of room.

   In short, in all your boasted seat,
There's nothing but yourself that's great.

(Written ca. 1722–23)

A Prologue Designed for the Play of *Oedipus*, Written in Greek, And Performed by Mr. Sheridan's Scholars, at the King's Inn's Hall, on Tuesday the 10th of December, 1723

Today before a learn'd audience comes
A play we know too well—witness our bums,
Where deep indenting birch such tragic scenes
Has drawn to life as would amaze your brains:
Believe me, Sirs, I'd many an aching heart,   5
And many a stripe, to make me get my part;
And after all, ah tyrannising r——gue!
Imposes on my memory this damned prologue.
Well faith, if I am fated e'er to squeak
In hollow scenes, it shall not be in Greek;   10
There's such a peal of hard words to be rung,
As spoils the brain and after cracks the lung.
Had he adapted for our waxen age,
A Barring-out to play upon this stage,
Especially considered time of year,   15
He need not its success or our performance fear.
Each boy his part so hero-like had done,
So well employed his powder, pease and gun,
So bravely his assaults repulsed, as you
Could not but be engaged our leave to sue.   20
The Fair, for certain, would have stood our friend,

Charmed that our fortress we'd so well defend,
In hopes one day that the young cavaliers
Would show with better grace in red and bandoliers.
And you, as well as they, will this confess,   25
That this same red has a damned taking grace;
For though black coats as potent be and able,
They're better pleased with gules than they're with sable.
But now I recollect, if more I speak
In English (my performance lies at stake),
The d——l a word I'll have just now in Greek.
                    (Delivered in public on December 10, 1723)

A New Year's Gift for the Dean of St. Patrick's Given Him at Quilca, 1723/24

How few can be of grandeur sure!
The high may fall, the rich be poor.
The only favorite at court
Tomorrow may be Fortune's sport;
For all her pleasure and her aim   5
Is to destroy both pow'r and fame.

Of this the Dean is an example;
No instance is more plain and ample.
The world did never yet produce
For courts a man of greater use.   10
Nor has the world supplied us yet
With more vivacity and wit;
Merry alternately and wise,
To please the statesman and advise.
Through all the last and glorious reign   15
Was nothing done without the Dean,
The courtier's prop, the nation's pride,
But now, alas, he's thrown aside!
He's quite forgot, and so's the queen,
As if they both had never been.   20

To see him now a mountaineer!
Oh! What a mighty fall is here!
From settling governments and thrones,
To splitting rocks and piling stones.

Instead of Bolingbroke and Anna,   25
Shane Tunnelly and Bryan Granna;
Oxford and Ormond he supplies
In every Irish Teague he spies;
So far forgetting his old station,
He seems to like their conversation.   30
Conforming to the tattered rabble,
He learns their Irish tongue to gabble;
And what our anger more provokes,
He's pleased with their insipid jokes.
Then turns and asks them who does lack a   35
Good plug or pipeful of tobacco.
All cry they want; to every man
He gives, extravagant, a span.
Thus are they grown more fond than ever,
And he is highly in their favor.   40

   Bright Stella, Quilca's greatest pride,
For them he scorns and lays aside;
And Sheridan is left alone
All day to gape and stretch and groan,
While grumbling, poor, complaining Dingley   45
Is left to care and trouble singly.

   All o'er the mountains spreads the rumor
Both of his bounty and good humor,
So that each shepherdess and swain
Comes flocking here to see the Dean.   50
All spread around the land; you'd swear
That every day we kept a fair.
My fields are brought to such a pass
—I have not left a blade of grass—
That all my wethers and my beeves   55
Are slighted by the very thieves.

   At night, right loath to quit the park,
His work just ended by the dark,
With all his pioneers he comes
To make more work for whisks and brooms.   60
Then, seated in an elbow-chair,
To take a nap he does prepare,
While two fair damsels from the lawns
Lull him asleep with soft cronawns.

Thus are his days in delving spent,   65
His nights in music and content.
He seems to gain by his distress;
His friends are more, his honors less.

(Written ca. January 1, 1723/24)

The Drapier's Ballad
To the Tune of the London 'Prentice

1

Of a worthy Dublin drapier
  My purpose is to speak,
Who for no private interest,
  But for his country's sake,
By virtuous honor led,   5
  Egregious hazards run,
And so set his country free.
  Could more have undergone?

2

Twice he was persecuted
  By traitors to the state;   10
And twice, by virtue guarded,
  He did their wiles defeat.
Seek all the world about
  And you will hardly find
A man for honor to exceed   15
  This drapier's gallant mind.

3

He was bred in Dublin;
  The chief of wits was he;
From thence went up to London
  A 'prentice for to be.   20
A banker near the court
  Did like his service so,
That a warm farm, in his own land,
  He did on him bestow.

4

When back again to Ireland   25
   This worthy drapier came,
He cast about most nobly
   T' advance its wealth and fame;
And had the simple natives
   Observed his sage advice,   30
Their wealth and fame some years ago
   Had soared above the skies.

5

For oft he them admonished
   To mind the draping trade,
And wear no manufactures   35
   But what themselves had made;
But while by thoughtless mortals
   His scheme neglected lay,
Some foes unto their country's weal
   His person would betray.   40

6

When thus her sons turn enemies,
   What nation free can last!
And now, to quite enslave us,
   A champion over passed,
In copper armor clad,   45
   A wooden tool of might,
Who by his boasts of power did
   All Ireland affright.

7

With just disdain the drapier
   Beheld his brazen pride;   50
He could not hear with patience
   How he our laws defied;
Forgetting his former wrongs,
   Unto our aid he flew,
And with resistless courage soon   55
   This giant overthrew.

8

But oh! The curst ingratitude
   Of some! No matter where,

Let all their names in history
    With infamy appear;   60
For to reward his love
    In saving of the land,
They plotted to deliver him
    Into the traitor's hand.

                                9

The drapier at this treatment   65
    Was not a whit dismayed,
But for his country's safety,
    More than his own, afraid.
He bravely sent them word
    He'd stand the brunt of all,   70
If they would but secure the land
    From Wood's sad brazen thrall.

                                10

Then doth the gallant drapier
    His trade and all expose,
To save the land from foreign   75
    And from domestic foes,
Who, their own turns to serve,
    Most basely would agree
To bring us in dependence
    Who are by nature free.   80

                                11

For he hath shown most clearly
    We can't be free by halves,
And who're to subjects subject
    Can be no less than slaves;
That we no acts have made,   85
    And grant we never may,
To give our brethren title
    To their pretended sway.

                                12

Then with your constant praises
    The drapier's name adorn,   90
While those who would betray him
    Deserve your utmost scorn;
In honoring his worth

Like grateful friends be found,
And with his health next to the King's 95
   Let glasses still be crowned.

(First printed 1724/25)

A Riddle

Because I am by nature blind,
I wisely choose to walk behind;
However, to avoid disgrace,
I let no creature see my face.
My words are few, but spoke with sense, 5
And yet my speaking gives offense;
Or, if to whisper I presume,
The company will fly the room.
By all the world I am oppressed,
And my oppression gives them rest. 10

Through me, though sore against my will,
Instructors every art instill.
By thousands I am sold and bought,
Who neither get nor lose a groat;
For none, alas, by me can gain, 15
But those who give me greatest pain.
Shall man presume to be my master,
Who's but my caterer and taster?
Yet, though I always have my will,
I'm but a mere depender still: 20
An humble hanger-on at best,
Of whom all people make a jest.

In me detractors seek to find
Two vices of a diff'rent kind:
I'm too profuse, some cens'rers cry, 25
And all I get, I let it fly;
While others give me many a curse,
Because too close I hold my purse.
But this I know, in either case
They dare not charge me to my face. 30
'Tis true, indeed, sometimes I save,
Sometimes run out of all I have;
But when the year is at an end,

Computing what I get and spend,
My goings-out and comings-in,   35
I cannot find I lose or win;
And, therefore, all that know me say,
I justly keep the middle way.
I'm always by my betters led;
I last get up, am first a-bed;   40
Though, if I rise before my time,
The learn'd in sciences sublime
Consult the stars and thence foretell
Good luck to those with whom I dwell.

(Written before June 1724)

An Imitation of Anacreon's Grasshopper, Applied to Mr. T. S., Commonly Known by the Name of Skeleton

Anonymous

Hail, happy little animal,
Delight of men and nature, hail!
Seated in thy chair of mirth,
Glad thou view'st the joyous earth,
And inspired by cheerful wine,   5
Mak'st the world around thee shine:
Thine the fruits, and thine the flow'rs,
Thine whate'er the wingèd hours
O'er sea, or earth, or air produce,
All submitted to thy use.   10
All to thee due homage pay,
Monarch thou, and tribute they.

Thee innocence and love commend,
Thee mankind salute their friend;
Pleased they see thee sit and sing,   15
Emblem of the welcome Spring.

Whate'er the bounteous gods bestow,
Thou giv'st with equal bounty too;
And careless of futurity,
Happy thou liv'st extempore.   20

Time before thee flags his wing,
And faster than he flies you sing;
And if duration, as we're taught,
Is measured by successive thought;
Or if, as wisest men confess,   25
'Tis best esteemed by happiness;
You, in the compass of a day,
Live longer than Methuselah.

Hail! bloodless, fleshless animal,
Wise at once, and musical;   30
In thee the Muses all rejoice,
Inspire thy lays, and tune thy voice;
Winter and age before thee fly,
And thou cans't never dread to die;
Death can thee of naught bereave;   35
Thou mock'st the tyrant and the grave:
Thou alcohol[1] of skin and bone,
Angelic airy skeleton,
Body to spirit rectified,
And nearly to the gods allied.

(Published in 1724)

---

1. Alcohol, a term in Chymistry, to signify a Substance so fine it can't be felt.

How Can I Finish What You Have Begun?

How can I finish what you have begun?
Can fire to ripen fruit assist the sun?
Should Raph'el draw a virgin's blooming face,
Exert his skill to give it every gr[ace],
And leave the rest to some Dutch-heavy drone,   5
Would you not rather see that face alone?
Or should Praxiteles the marble take,
A Venus head and neck and shoulders make,
And some rude hand attempt the rest from thence,
Would you not think him void of commonsense?   10

These hints I hope will move you to excuse
The first refusal of my humble Muse.
The task I must decline and think it just
Your piece continue as it is, a bust.

(Written ca. 1724?)

Upon William Tisdall, D. D.

When a Roman was dying, the next man or kin
Stood over him gaping to take his breath in.
Were Tisdall the same way to blow out his brea[th],
Such a whiff to the living were much worse than d[eath].
Any man with a nose would much rather die;   5
So would Jack, so would Dan, so would you, so would I.
Without a reproach to the doctor I think
Whenever he dies, he must die with a stink.

(Written ca. 1724?)

Tom Pun-Sibi Metamorphosed:
Or, The Giber Gibed

William Tisdall

Mirandi Novitate Movebere Monstri.
Ovid. Metam.

Tom was a little merry grig,
Fiddled and danced to his own jig,
Good-natured but a little silly,
Irresolute and shally-shilly:
What he should do, he couldn't guess;   5
They moved him like a man at chess;
S——t told him once that he had wit,
S—— was in jest, poor Tom was bit,
Thought himself second son of Phoebus,
For ballad, pun, lampoon and rebus.   10
He took a draught of Helicon,
But swallowed so much water down,
He got a dropsy; now they say 'tis
Turned to poetic diabetes;

For all the liquor he has passed   15
Is without spirit, salt or taste;
But, since it passed, Tom thought it wit,
And so he writ and writ and writ.
He writ the famous Punning Art,
The benefit of piss and fart;   20
He writ *The Wonder of All Wonders,*
He writ *The Blunder of All Blunders;*
He writ a merry farce for poppet,
Taught actors how to squeak and hop it;
A treatise on the Wooden Man,   25
A ballad on the nose of Dan,
The Art of Making April Fools,
And four-and-thirty quibbling rules.
The learnèd say that Tom went snacks
With philomaths, for almanacs;   30
Though they divided are, for some say
He writ for Whalley, some for Cumpstey.
Hundreds there are who will make oath
That he writ almanacs for both;
And, though they made the calculations,   35
Tom writ the monthly observations.
Such were his writings, but his chatter
Was one continued clitter-clatter.
Swift slit his tongue, and made it talk,
From "cup of sack" and "walk, knave, walk!"   40
And fitted little prating Poll
For wire cage in Common Hall,
Made him expert at quibble jargon,
And quaint at selling of a bargain.
Poll, he could talk in diff'rent lingos,   45
But he could not be taught Distinguos;
Swift tried in vain, and angry thereat,
Into a spaniel turned the parrot;
Made him to walk on his hind legs;
He dances, paws, and fawns, and begs,   50
Then cuts a caper o'er a stick,[1]
Lies close, does whine, and creep, and lick.
Swift put a bit upon his snout;
Poor Tom! he daren't look about;
But when that Swift does give the word,   55
He snaps it up, though 'twere a turd.
Swift strokes his back, and gives him victual,

And then he makes him lick his spittle.
Sometimes he takes him on his lap,
And makes him grin, and snarl, and snap.   60
He set the little cur at me;
Kicked, he leapt upon his knee;
I took him by the neck to shake him,   ⎫
And made him void his *Album Graecum*.   ⎬
"Turn out the stinking cur, pox take him," ⎭   65
Quoth Swift, though Swift could sooner want any
Thing in the world, than a Tantany,
And thus not only makes his grig
His parrot, spaniel, but his pig.

(Published in 1724)

---

1. This is literally true between Swift and Sheridan.

A Letter From A Cobbler In Patrick's Street
to Jet Black

    If any line I write's a hobbler,
Consider, Sir, that I'm a cobbler;
Therefore, I hope you'll give allowance
To an old friend that you did know once.
Nor should I this compar'son offer,   5
Wer't not for Jonathan of Cloffer.

    Now I'm to show the world, d'ee see,
That I'm like you, and you're like me—
Like as two pegs, or as two tacks,
As this to t' other ball of wax.   10

    In all things perfect cousin-germans—
I vamp old boots, you vamp old sermons;
My verses are but so and so,
And yours I think a peg too low.
Like you I oftentimes wax warm,   15
And yet I do no creature harm.
If I've a rupture with a friend,
I patch it up, and there's an end.
I oftentimes am forced to hammer,
Like you, to make my verses grammar.   20

Whole hours prepond'ring in my stall I
Sit for a rhyme to "Shilly shall I";
And after all I think, dear Billy,
I'm forced to make it "shall I, shill I."
You see we both agree in rhymes;   25
Why wits you know will jump sometimes,
In one thing (though in all we're brother-wise)
We differ, which I wish were otherwise:
Our black's applied to diff'rent use;
You blacken men, I blacken shoes;   30
Yet one thing you observe that's mine—
The more you black, the more they shine.
To make us both alike in awl,
Oh, that your rev'rence had a stall!
For you can never hope a mitre,   35
Because you are too fine a writer.

  I must cut short, my verses fail,
'Tis time to take a pot of ale;
Dear Jet, I wish with all my heart
That you were here, and t' other quart.   40
                                    (Published in 1724)

A Scribbler from the Northern Bear

A scribbler from the Northern bear,
This month to Dublin shall repair,
And there shall write, and write, and write,
And vent his gall, and spleen, and spite;
But none alive shall feel the smart;   5
Then home he'll go and break his heart.
                            (Written and published in 1724)

To the Author of "Tom Pun-Sibi Metamorphosed"

Should you want rhymes again for Graecum, ⎫
I'll send you some if you bespeak 'um,   ⎬
But you're conceited and won't take 'um.   ⎭
Take three old wethers and their rumps tie, ⎫
And you will find a rhyme to Cumpsty,   ⎬   5
Or should your fiddle strings your drums tie.[1] ⎭

It shows in rhyming you're not far gone,
Who could not find a rhyme to "jargon,"
That you must call a bargain "bargon";
Had you but drunk a glass of claret—   10
Nay, had you thought upon a carrot—
You might have found a rhyme to "parrot."
You that have bells to ring and chime,
To find you at a loss for rhyme
Makes you a scandal to all piddlers   15
In verse—nay, more I say, to fiddlers!
Were you not very dull and idle,
You might be taught it from your bridle;
The groaning car that goes along
Might furnish you with rhymes for song.   20
When your lampooned our may'r, the tailor,
You called the Chancellor "Chansaylor";
I think you're very much to blame
You did not practise here the same.
Ah, those were happy days of Wit,   25
When you found out the term "Prick-nit"!
But now, alas, thy stubborn brain
Will no such fancies entertain!
Thy wit is palled, thy judgment drowned,
Thy shattered keel is run aground;   30
And you that sailed so well before[2]
Lie stranded on a dirty shore,
There ever destined to be held fast
In a damp miry slough near Belfast.

(Written and published in 1724)

1. These lines are something silly, but they fit you to a hair.

2. I must here inform the Doctor that Virgil in his Georgics makes Poetry to be sailing.

The Rivals
A Poem, Occasioned by *Tom Punsibi, Metamorphosed,* &c.

Anonymous

Men who are out hate those in play,
A case which happens every day;

'Tis worse to lose that very place
Another fills, and that's our case.
The Dean, who realms of wit commands,   5
Like most wise monarchs changes hands;
'Mongst all his subjects picks and chooses
His ministers, as each of use is;
And as he smiles, or frowns, his features
Are joy or grief to all his creatures.   10
T——l would feign at court appear
For what he loves abroad, good cheer.
The Dean in frolic would receive him,
And what he came for freely give him.
He let him sit with Men of Letters,   15
And prate sometimes before his betters;
Would suffer him from three to six,
At proper times, to show his tricks;
Would overhear his *Point of War*
(Of all his tricks the best by far);   20
Bestowed him many a joke and quibble;
At length he licensed him to scribble;
And in his works, to lend him fame,
Here used his wit, and there his phlegm.
Vain of these plumes, he knew were borrowed,   25
The giddy soul grew wondrous forward,
Libelled the Dean, and so repaid
What in his service he had made,
And, prone of old to factious courses,
Now levies independent forces.   30
With arms not his he issues forth,
Declares for Empire in the North;
There utters in imperial strain
Wit which he pilfered from the Dean.
The Dean, his court and hands to clear   35
Of this poor upstart mutineer,
Pronounced in council his disgrace,
And Tom the Punster begged his place,
And hence arose a furious scold
'Twixt the new fav'rite and the old.   40
The war broke out in words and looks,
Then grew the battle of the books;
But those who knew these weapons cried,
"There's no great odds on either side."
And as old heroes in the field   45

Would change their helmet, sword and shield,
And then fall to, to cause disasters,
And make men's arms annoy their masters;
Just so these wits each other gore
With books which hurt them both before.   50
Books have knack 'bove other things
To wound, although they have no stings;
For they their writers, some allege,
Hurt more for want of point or edge.
T——l in wrath and his worst gown   55
Marched slow, with his whole wife, to town;
It happened both were near their times,
She big with child, and he with rhymes;
For he begets a various brood,
Both boys and verse, in heat of blood.   60
So have I seen a bramble bend
And hide in earth its upper end,
Which taking root it could not fail
At once to sprout at head and tail.
Tom, though he little feared the matter,   65
Was rudely used by T——l's satire,
But bearing up at all adventures
Was no more hurt than—the Dissenters.

(Published in 1724)

A Poem,
Or Advice to the Authors of a Satirical Poem, Upon Tom Punsibi and to the (form'd) Dissenting Teacher's Letters to Jett Black

S. Owens

Ye Sons of Levi, Church Divines,
Give ear to these my feeble lines;
Accept the same, as from a friend,
And pardon what I here intend,
Which does set forth you are to blame.   5
It's time to speak when all cry shame
For men of learning and the gown
To expose each other round the town;
In public print with odious words,

More cutting sure than fencers' swords;   10
A bright divine is termed a pig,
Then called silly face for Jig—
But sure they had better called him Whig.
Too harsh a discord, for a fiddle
Dulls all the music, mean or trible.   15
T' other's formed dissenting teacher
That he might better pelt the preacher,
And so falls foul upon Jett Black.
Are these the wits? True wit they lack,
And be't spoken under the rose,   20
The satire's S——t's; it's sure his prose,
As plain appears by his just charge
Against the D——r drawn at large,
But D——n, O D——n, a rhyme for Graecum
Is what you hold an empty vacuum.   25
Let what I've said, I pray, suffice,
And if it won't here's more advice:
Desist such idle way of clashing—
Satire, pun, lampooning, lashing.
Choose virtue's paths therein to walk;   30
Let some great topic be your talk.
New sermons make in your spare hours,
Adorned with rhetoric's sweetest flowers.
Strive who each other shall excel
In seeking Heaven and shunning Hell,   35
In knowing God the chief great cause,
And you that teach, don't break his laws.
But if you say all this you know
(I'm sure you're wrong, you can't say no),
Then view the orbs and earth below.   40
From Arctic to Antarctic pole,
Easting and westing o'er it roll—
Your thoughts I mean. Let it take flight;
Survey those parts that's hid from sight;
Try whether space be infinite.   45
Compose a book of something new;
There's many divines, but very few
Take Gordon's, Fiddes', or Durham's pains,
Or in the least disturb their brains
To show the meaning of those texts   50
Which might convert Socinian sects.
Or study Nature's different parts,

For to improve our curious arts.
O, this is what I'd recommend:
Had I your income, time I'd spend;   55
This way to it, sure I'd incline—
To search things natural, moral and divine.

    N. B. Henceforth keep silence, and be mum;
Touch not the fiddle nor the drum.

(Published in 1724)

To Quilca
A Country House in No Good Repair, Where the Supposed Author, and Some of his Friends, Spent a Summer in the year 1725

Jonathan Swift

Let me thy properties explain:
A rotten cabin, dropping rain,
Chimneys with scorn rejecting smoke,
Stools, tables, chairs, and bedsteads broke.
Here elements have lost their uses;   5
Air ripens not, nor earth produces.
In vain we make poor Sheelah toil;
Fire will not roast, nor waters boil.
Through all the valleys, hills, and plains,
The goddess Want in triumph reigns;   10
And her chief officers of state,
Sloth, Dirt, and Theft, around her wait.

(Written in Summer 1725)

Quilca House to the Dean

Henry Brooke

I plainly see, good Mr. Dean,
That you cannot contain your spleen,
That you must spit it forth at times
In conversation or in rhymes;
Your friends and foes then fare alike,   5
But there are some you dare not strike.

For instance, if you should attack
My lord, he'd lay you on your back
In satire, pun or even poem—
I needn't tell you, for you know him.   10
But you attack his aged house,
Yet I don't matter you a louse.
This language may be low, it's true;
If so, I learned it all from you.
To classic wit I have been used,   15
But when I find myself abused,
I must return the selfsame dirt
Which spatters—but can never hurt.
You've lost all sense of gratitude;
Nay, what is more, you're even rude.   20
Full oft, you know, beneath my garret
You've drunk the best of port and claret;
The best of mutton you have eat;
An apple-pie, too, was a treat.
You might have let my fire alone,   25
For when it's dull, it's like your own;
The doctor, then, laid by his rod;
The servants trembled at your nod;
My dame would list to what you said,
And if she broke poor Priscian's head,   30
She thanked you for your kind correction
Which did not flow from your affection,
But rather to evince your mast'ry
In grammar rules, conserves and pastry.
She always strove to please your palate;   35
As to yourself, why you're a salad.
You praised the meat, you praised the wine,
Called me an inn without a sign;
And if a thought should strike your noddle,
Instead of your own sleepy Poddle   40
You sought the limpid river's side
Where flow'rets bloom in eastern pride.
The sunny mead or tree-topped hill,
The winding stream that turned the mill
Left you in doubt which walk to choose,   45
For Quilca's sacred to the Muse.
My hearth, like my own master's heart,
Congenial glowed, and without art;
And if my chimney chanced to smoke,

It passed away like your own joke.   50
But let me tell you, Polyhymny
Has often sat in that same chimney;
I mean in that same chimney-corner,
But not like you in seat of scorner.
I'm sure my gate was never shut   55
To either full or empty gut;
My master never yet was known   ⎫
On any day to dine alone.   ⎬
"Or pick his chicken to the bone";   ⎭
As you have done, as you've confessed—   60
I'll leave yourself to guess the rest.
But I'm no longer young and trim;
My windows now are rather dim.
For many winters I have stood,
And my old bones (I mean my wood)   65
Are daily yielding to decay,
And like your own will drop away;
But when they're even sunk and rotten,
I'm sure they'll never be forgotten;
My master's fame will lend to me   70
What yours cannot—eternity.

(Written in Summer, 1725?)

A Receipt to Frighten Away the Dean

Peter Murray

Let Kate and Rose and sleepy Ned,
If he can raise his stupid head,
And Shela too, if she has time,
Attend a little to my rhyme,
And I'll give you a choice receipt   5
To save the Doctor's wine and meat—
To save yourself a world of trouble
In boiling praties to a bubble,
In roasting woodcocks to a turn
Before a fire that will not burn.   10
Now my receipt, dear friends, is this—
For which I ought to get a kiss;
If Rosy would but deign to give it,
I'd crown her with a sprig of privet,

The fairest privet in the garden,   15
For which she wouldn't give a farden.
The Doctor, many years ago,
Resolved to plough, resolved to sow.
He ploughed and sowed, but all in vain;
The rooks and crows devoured the grain—   20
I mean the seed when it was sown,
Which cost the Doctor many a groan.
A farmer by experience taught
(Experience isn't got for naught)
Advised him to collect old rags.   25
His lady rummaged all the bags;
Old wigs, old waistcoats and old coats,
The pockets stuffed with classic notes;
Old cassocks too and cast-off bands
Were put into the farmer's hands;   30
A waistcoat soon was stuffed with straw,
And such a paunch you never saw.
He ran a pole up through the middle;
The face was made of an old fiddle
With saucer eyes that would affright   35
Old Nick himself in any night.
This figure formed with so much care
Was hung aloft in open air;
The crows beheld it from afar,
And winged their flight to Mullingar.   40
The Doctor sowed and reaped his grain;
Now listen to another strain—
Oft as the Dean sleeps at your castle,
You know that everyone's his vassal.
The Doctor's self cannot escape;   45
The Dean's as peevish as an ape.
It's "Ned, do this," it's "Ned, do that,"
And "Where's that idle rascal, Pat?"
You know, yourself, what lives you lead;
It is a wretched one, indeed.   50
Now, to get rid of him, attend;
I needn't tell you I'm your friend.
As he's expected every day,
And as he always comes one way,
Hang out for once a tattered shift: 55
You'll see no more of Doctor Swift.

                                    (Written in Summer, 1725?)

To His Excellency Our Lord Carteret, Lord Lieutenant of Ireland: The Humble Petition of Lord Viscount Mont-Cashel, and the Rest of His School-Fellows

Sheweth,
    With greatest respect and most awful submission,
    We send to Your Lordship our humble petition,
    To tell you our Master has basely denied
    To grant us our freedom at Bart'lomy-tide;
    By happy experience, we certainly know   5
    There's naught for your care or your justice too low;
    And therefore we hope you will now condescend
    To be in a case of oppression our friend.

    Our Master most slyly would make it appear
    That we have no such thing as a summer this year;   10
    If we durst speak our minds, we could answer him thus,
    "We are sure that the school is a hot place for us."

    Another expedient he thinks will go down:
    "Dear children, you know I've been long out of town,
    And people will grumble, and say I'm for giving   15
    My school to the dogs, since I've got a living."

    An excellent method of argumentation!
    That for his good luck, we should lose our vacation,
    And that your great goodness to him should destroy
    A custom that gives such a number great joy.   20
    Besides, when he had of his presence bereft us,
    Five Fellows of Trinity College he left us,
    Who did without rods, by the force of their looks,
    Oblige us to sit twice as close to our books:
    Nay more, an Arch-Deacon be joined in commission;   25
    This was in his absence our happy condition.
    So all that we found when our shepherd was gone,
    Through his wonderful caution, six drivers for one.

    Great patron and lover of scholars, redress us;
    Make one Act of Grace—with Liberty bless us.   30

Instead of a fortnight, at present we seek
No longer cessation from books than a week;
Consider our case then, and send your mandamus,
And loudly we'll roar out, "Te Carteret amamus."
We'll make the whole town of your goodness to ring;   35
We'll play for Your Lordship, and pray for the king.
                              (Written in August or early September, 1725)

To the Honorable Mr. D. T.

Great Pattern of Piety, Charity, Learning, Humanity, good Nature, Wis-
dom, good Breeding, Affability, and one most eminently distinguished for
his Conjugal Affection.

Ex Despauterio
O *Tite* Tute *Tati tibi* tanta *Tyranne tulisti.*

What strange disorder often springs
From very light and trivial things!
Which makes philosophers conjecture
They are from Providence a lecture,
To check our vanity and pride,   5
And many other faults beside.
This gave the first creation rise
Of maggots, insects, worms and flies,
Of bugs, wasps, midges, mice and rats,
And barking curs and spit-fire cats;   10
That strive to shun them where you will,
There's one or other at you still;
No man escapes insidious vermin,
From coat of frieze to royal ermine;
From the low joint-stool to the throne,   15
These plagues of Egypt favor none.

And now to paint the sev'ral ways
Such trifles have such power to tease.

The lurking maggot in your meat
Destroys your appetite to eat.   20

Proceed to bed, that place of rest,
Lay down your head and do your best;
One little, skipping, sorry flea
Can chase the God of Sleep away.

The bug, that spawn of rotten wood,   25
Not only sucks, but taints your blood;
At length you seize the worthless prize,
You squeeze, he bursts, and bursting dies;
But still a greater curse you find,
So strong a stink he leaves behind.   30

The crawling louse assails you next;
You grope, and grope, you fret, you're vexed.
This little speck of sweat and dirt,
Although it cannot greatly hurt,
Yet still it makes you scratch and shrug,   35
As much as the adherent bug.

If none of these, a rat or cat,
Or nibbling mouse or buzzing gnat
May come as you're supinely laid,
And break the peace which sleep has made;   40
So slight an accident destroys
The greatest of all human joys!

If to the fields you walk for air,
What num'rous squadrons meet you there.
Flies of all sorts and hues you see,   45
From every ditch and every tree;
Like dust in clouds or powd'ring hail,
Your face on all sides they assail;
Eyes, cheeks, brows, lips, and chin, and nose
Are all attacked by swarming foes;   50
You tap them with your hands in vain—
No sooner off, but on again.
Such are the plagues of human life,
Doomed ever thus to live in strife,
With things so much beneath our care,   55
To wage an everlasting war.

Canst thou, O Man, be vain and proud,
When this must be by all allowed?
One flea, one wasp, one fly, one drone,
The pow'rs of thinking can dethrone;   60
If perched upon your lip or brow,

Can banish what you thought just now,
Can break the lab'ring Fancy's chain,
And set your brains to work again.

What pain the riding trav'ler feels   65
When barking curs are at his heels!
He stops, he turns, he stands at bay,
And frights them for a while away;
But still they tease, and still pursue,
And keep the bounding steed in view,   70
Till one cur bites him to the bone,
And almost brings the rider down.

That case and his is just the same,
Who mounts upon the horse of Fame:
Some envious snarling curs pursue him,   75
With eager malice to undo him,
'Till one more fierce than all, through spite,
Comes up and gives his horse a bite;
The bouncing prancer kicks amain;
The rider holds a strait'ned rein,   80
Clings fast until the horse has done,
The cur flies off, and he rides on.

                    (Written possibly in late September 1725)

The Sick Lion and the Ass

The following Fable is most humbly Inscribed to the Honourable Mr.
D. T. A most Extraordinary Personage, Renowned for his great Quality,
Charity, Hospitality, Liberality, Civility, Piety, Affability, Dignity, Love to
Liberty, and Property, Facility of Speaking, Volubility of Language, Activ-
ity, and Agility, with many other Endowments which I reserve for the
next *Dedication.*
   O Tite Tute Tati tibi tanta Tyranne tulisti. Despaut.

A lion sunk by time's decay,
Too feeble grown to hunt his prey,
Observed his fatal hour draw nigh;
He drooped and laid him down to die.

There came by chance a savage boar,   5
Who trembled oft to hear him roar,

But when he saw him thus distressed,
He tore and gored his royal breast.

A bull came next (ungen'rous foe),
Rejoiced to find him fall'n so low,   10
And with his horny-armèd head,
He aimed at once to strike him dead;
He strikes, he wounds, he shocks in vain;
The lion still conceals his pain.

At length a base inglorious ass,   15
Who saw so many insults pass,
Came up and kicked him in the side;
'Twas this that raised the lion's pride.

He roused and thus he spoke at length
(For indignation gave him strength),   20
"Thou sorry, stupid, sluggish creature,
Disgrace and shame and scorn of Nature!
You saw how well I could dispense
With blows from beasts of consequence;
They dignified the wounds they gave!   25
For none complain who feel the brave.
But you, the lowest of all brutes,
How ill your face with courage suits;
What dullness in thy looks appears!
Thy hanging face! Thy slouching ears!   30
I'd rather far (by Heav'n, 'tis true)
Expire by these than live—by you.
A kick from thee is double death!
I curse thee with my dying breath."

THE MORAL

Rebukes are easy from our betters,   35
From men of quality and letters,
But when low dunces will affront,
What man alive can stand the brunt?

(Written possibly in October 1725)

A Poem Delivered to the Reverend Doctor Swift, Dean of St. Patrick's, Dublin, By a Young Nobleman, November 30, 1725, Being the Dean's Birthday

In Sixteen Hundred Sixty-eight,
A year of most important weight,
A solemn council Jove ordained,
Where all the pow'rs of heav'n convened.
High raised on his imperial throne,   5
In robes of majesty he shone
(Such was the wondrous light displayed,
When first the beauteous world he made).

"Ye Gods and Goddesses," said he,
In sounds becoming his decree,   10
"Be silent all, and all attend,
And hear the work I recommend:
A child's new-born—let's change his fate,
And make him every way complete.

"Whilom we did a woman grace   15
With gifts above a mortal race,
But what marred all—she was designed
To plague and punish all mankind;
But let us now ordain this birth
To polish and refine the earth.   20
Smile all upon the new-born boy;
Send mirth and wit and love and joy;
Eternal funds of these bestow him,
That all may love and learn who know him;
Let every one confer their gift,   25
And all distinguished be in Swift."

Apollo straight assumed his lyre,
His soul with music to inspire,
But struck too eagerly the strings;
With too much violence he sings,   30
For all around he shook the spheres
And stunned the tender infant's ears.

Since that, when harp or fiddles play,
He stops his ears or turns away;
But still the soul of sound remains   35
In easy numbers, easy strains,
That all who read his verse may find
The God of music formed his mind.

The Muses joy'd to see this day,
Flew down from heav'n to sport and play;   40
Around his head in wanton rings,
They fly with wide expanded wings;
Sometimes they skim in level flights
To teach him smoothness when he writes;
Again on lofty wings they rise   45
To raise his poems to the skies,
That though he were confined to rhyme,
He still might keep the true sublime.
Then as a token of their love,
Before they re-ascend to Jove,   50
Each from her wing bestowed a quill:
No less could serve for so much skill,
For so much art—nor wonder then
There's so much magic in his pen.

Jove's daughter next beheld the child;   55
With highest influence on him smiled,
That Reason, firm and clear and strong,
To him as native right belong.
Others with art dispute and plead;
He scorns the help of foreign aid,   60
For all his reas'ning is his own,
And logic falls before his throne.

Venus advanced with her soft train,
Would make him amorous in vain;
No worthy object can he find   65
But the great beauty of the mind.

Jove's gift was this—from him it came
Immortal as the vestal flame—
That his affection knows no end;
No change can be where he's a friend.   70
Others desert when danger's nigh,

The tempest and the thunder fly,
And shrink to see a rocky shore,
But danger makes him love you more.

Hermes, with soft persuasion, strung   75
The well-tuned fibres of his tongue;
Hence he confutes with so much ease,
And conquers with an art to please.

O would the Fates but make it mine,
Like thee to live, like thee to shine;   80
The least perfection men would see
In me would be my quality.
You know the councils of the great;
You know to form the Man of State;
Teach me, though young, to be a man;
Make me a Cart'ret, if you can.

(Written ca. November 30, 1725)

From A Satyr

Jonathan Smedley

Science and Arts are at a stand;
Were't not for Hel——m's *Sleight of Hand,*
For Sherry's quibbles, and thy quill
The dusty press would stand quite still. . . .

(Published in 1725)

From A Letter From D. S——t to D. S——y

Jonathan Swift

Hel——am does truly wit command
And surely writes with sleight of hand.
For Sherry's quibbles, and thy skill
They are as once, and *idem* still.   50

(Published in 1725)

Tom Punsibi's Farewell to the Muses

Anonymous

Ecce iterum Crispinus!

This is to give notice, I Tom the great scribbler,
The punster, the poet, the pedant, the quibbler,
The critic, the antic, the mighty comedian
Of old—but of late the noted tragedian;
Who, like the chameleon, ne'er stuck to one color,   5
Yet still as I changed I ever grew duller;
Who, more than old Ogilby, Hobbes or Sylvester,
The world with voluminous nonsense did pester;
Weak in my attempts, pressed by melancholy,
Bid adieu to my former amusements and folly;   10
In hopes of forgiveness, assure the whole nation
Of this my sincere, though my late, recantation.

Farewell, my false Muse, by whose instigation
I freely submitted to every temptation,
Who for a dull jest have betrayed thy poor master   15
To the envy and malice of each poetaster;
Nay, made me more odious than gruff Punchinello,
And clothed me with fustian instead of prunello;
Yet bad as you are, not one among fifty
Will say (to my sorrow) my wife is so thrifty,   20
That proud crowing hen, that eternal Xantippe—
Parnassus, farewell; farewell, Aganippe.

Apollo, farewell, and ye Muses seraphic;
No longer in meter shall Punsibi traffic:
A wife and a Muse!—no need of the latter;   25
The former may very well serve for a satire,
And since I must dance in a conjugal fetter,
I of the two evils have chosen the better.

O would that I never had tallied with Phoebus,
Or traded in dogg'rel, in puns or in rebus!   30
Ne'er meddled with catches or satires or farces,
And lashed at nothing but at innocent a——!
But Tom was conceited and naught would content him

But forsooth an *exegi* (alas!) *monumentum*.
Moreover, since now you've put me i' the head on't,   35
The dull poetaster undid the good pedant;
For whilst with hard labor and toil I did hammer
Out of my thick noddle an exquisite grammar,
(As Jonathan said) for a word to come pat in,
I maimed all my rules, and I butchered the Latin,   40
But frankly confessed that at length it was silly,
Although I at first had preferred it to Lilly.
In short, to be serious, I now must acknowledge
I'm the jest o' the town and burlesque o' the college.
Thus have I miscarried in all my adventures;   45
Was ever poor mortal so set on the tenters!—
Yet should I not thus my calamity nourish,
But that I see wretcheder criminals flourish,
Who weekly perplex us with journals and libels,
And divert honest folk from reading their Bibles;   50
At least let 'em link me to some barking spaniel,
To C-ffey, Jet Black, or the journalist Daniel,
Who all are (like Balaam's) but talkative asses,
And pound us, if ever we graze on Parnassus.

(Published in 1725)

A New Jingle on Tom Dingle

Anonymous

Though Sh——d-n will
Be Sh——d-n still,
And show his great skill
In writing as ill
As any pupil   5
Or Tom, Jack or Jill
Bred up in a mill,
Built over a rill,
By a country vill,
That han't a door sill,
Nor hardly a spill
Of money in till
To buy them a pill,
Or ale made of Jill,
To take when they're ill;

Yet 'tis the Dean's will,
By good codicil,
He now should be still
Who han't wit at will,
Nor pow'r o'er his drill   20
To save him from nil;
Which if he'd fulfil,
And not his time spill,
Nor let his ink trill
No more from his quill,   25
He'd find by't a bill,
When death Swift did kill,
Would answer all ill,
And crown him with dill;
For thus says Tom Lill,   30
Who lives at the Brill.

(Published 1725–26?)

A True and Faithful Inventory of the Goods Belonging to Dr. Swift, Vicar of Laracor; upon Lending His House to the Bishop of Meath, Until His Own Was Built

An oaken, broken elbow-chair;
A caudle-cup, without an ear;
A battered, shattered ash bedstead;
A box of deal, without a lid;
A pair of tongs, but out of joint;   5
A back-sword poker, without point;
A pot that's cracked across, around,
With an old knotted garter bound;
An iron lock, without a key;
A wig, with hanging quite grown grey;   10
A curtain, worn to half a stripe;
A pair of bellows, without pipe;
A dish, which might good meat afford once;
An Ovid, and an old Concordance;
A bottle bottom, wooden platter,   15
One is for meal, and one for water;
There likewise is a copper skillet,
Which runs as fast out as you fill it;

A candlestick, snuff dish, and save-all,
And thus his household goods you have all.   20

   These, to your Lordship, as a friend,
Till you have built, I freely lend;
They'll serve your Lordship for a shift;
Why not, as well as Doctor Swift?

(Written ca. June 1726?)

To the Dean, When in England, in 1726

   You will excuse me, I suppose,
For sending rhyme instead of prose.
Because hot weather makes me lazy,
To write in meter is more easy.

   While you are trudging London town,   5
I'm strolling Dublin up and down;
While you converse with lords and dukes,
I have their betters here, my books:
Fixed in an elbow-chair at ease,
I choose companions as I please.   10
I'd rather have one single shelf
Than all my friends, except yourself;
For, after all that can be said,
Our best acquaintance are the dead.
While you're in raptures with Faustina,   15
I'm charmed at home with our Sheelina;
While you are starving there in state,
I'm cramming here with butcher's meat.
You say, when with those lords you dine,
They treat you with the best of wine,   20
Burgundy, Cyprus and Tokay;
Why, so can we, as well as they.
No reason, then, my dear good Dean,
But you should travel home again.
What though you mayn't in Ireland hope   25
To find such folk as Gay and Pope?
If you with rhymers here would share
But half the wit that you can spare,
I'd lay twelve eggs, that in twelve days,
You'd make a doz'n of Popes and Gays.   30

Our weather's good, our sky is clear;
We've every joy, if you were here;
So lofty and so bright a sky
Was never seen by Ireland's Eye!
I think it fit to let you know,   35
This week I shall to Quilca go
To see McFadden's horny brothers
First suck, and after bull their mothers;
To see, alas, my withered trees!
To see what all the country sees!   40
My stunted quicks, my famished beeves,
My servants such a pack of thieves,
My shattered firs, my blasted oaks,
My house in common to all folks,
No cabbage for a single snail,   45
My turnips, carrots, parsnips fail,
My no green peas, my few green sprouts,
My mother always in the pouts,
My horses rid or gone astray,
My fish all stol'n or run away,   50
My mutton lean, my pullets old,
My poultry starved, the corn all sold.

A man come now from Quilca says,
"They've[1] stol'n the locks from all your keys";
But what must fret and vex me more,   55
He says,"They stole the keys before.
They've stol'n the knives from all the forks,
And half the cows from half the sturks."
Nay more, the fellow swears and vows,
"They've stol'n the sturks from half the cows."   60
With many more accounts of woe,
Yet, though the de'il be there, I'll go:
'Twixt you and me, the reason's clear,
Because I've more vexation here.

(Written in 1726)

---

1. *They* is the grand thief of the county of Cavan: for whatever is stolen, if you inquire of a servant about it, the answer is, "*They* have stolen it."

From An Epistle in Behalf of Our Irish Poets to the Right Hon. Lady C——t

Anonymous

There's punning Tom Sh-r-d-n, Phoebus's darling,
And eke the tragedian, General St-rl-ng.
But why should I name 'em, for there's to my knowledge
An hundred that set up for wits in the College;
And that for no reason that I ever knew,
But because they're persuaded 'emselves that 'tis true.
Take any of these, then, as well as we love 'em;
The soul of Great Britain perhaps may improve them.
But if Sw——t or D-1——y should go off to London,
Poor Dublin, alas! would be perfectly undone.
Then take whom you will of the musical herd,
But Patrick and Jonathan cannot be spared.
So now I have done, and, without being rude,
Permit me, dear Madam, at once to conclude.

(Published in 1726)

The Humble Petition of Stella's Friends

Possibly with Delany and others

Poor Stella hourly is perplexed
Betwixt this world here and the next,
Her friends imploring her to stay
And angels beck'ning her away.
Behold the balance in suspense!   5
She's unresolved for here or hence.
Ah, let our friendship turn the scale.
Let friendship over heav'n prevail,
Till you have lived what time is due,
And then we'll all expire with you.   10

(Written on June 11, 1727)

An Invitation to Dinner, from Doctor Sheridan to Doctor Swift. Written in the Year M DCC XXVII

I've sent to the ladies this morning to warn 'em
To order their chaise, and repair to Rathfarnham,
Where you shall be welcome to dine, if your Deanship
Can take up with me, and my friend Stella's leanship.
I've got you some soles and a fresh bleeding bret   5
That's just disengaged from the toils of a net;
An excellent loin of fat veal to be roasted,
With lemons, and butter, and sippets well toasted;
Some larks that descended, mistaking the skies,
Which Stella brought down by the light of her eyes;   10
And there, like Narcissus, they gazed till they died,
And now they're to lie in some crumbs that are fried.
My wine will inspire you with joy and delight;
'Tis mellow, and old, and sparkling, and bright—
An emblem of one that you love, I suppose,   15
Who gathers more lovers the older she grows.
Let me be your Gay, and let Stella be Pope;
We'll wean you from sighing for England I hope:
When we are together there's nothing that is dull;
There's nothing like Durfey, or Smedley, or Tisdall.   20
We've sworn to make out an agreeable feast,
Our dinner, our wine, and our wit to your taste.

   Your answer in half an hour, though you are at prayers;
you have a pencil in your pocket.

(Written in 1727)

To The Right Honorable the Lord Viscount Mont-Cassel:

This Fable is most humbly dedicated by a person who had some share
in his education.

   A peacock nobly born and bred
Once took a fancy in his head,
Whether for pleasure, health or food,
To ramble in a neighb'ring wood.
The birds around from every tree   5

Crowded in flocks the sight to see.
His train, adorned with glitt'ring rays
Provokes their malice not their praise.
But soon his envied splendor drew
Censure from all the vulgar crew.   10
Each bird, as if by mankind taught,
Turned all his wit to find a fault;
And whereso'er he took his flight,
They always kept him full in sight.
Of him alone the forest rung;   15
He grew the talk of every tongue.
Wise Goodman Owl was heard to say,
"The peacock scratched his head today."
The Raven swore in hollow tone,
He saw him pick a dirty bone.   20
"For all his pride," says Gossip Quail,
"He wants a feather of his tail."
A Linnet came and whispered low,
He saw him bill a carrion Crow.
Others observed he spoiled the wood   25
By nipping every tender bud,
Did all the mischief in his pow'r
To every plant and every flow'r;
The blossoms enviously he gathers,
For fear they should outvie his feathers;   30
For new-laid eggs he searched about,
Broke every one that he found out;
Nor was he satisfied to plunder—
He tore the very nests asunder.
In short whate'er he said or did   35
Could not by any means be hid.

But now for what was first in view,
My Lord, I turn myself to you;
To you, I make the application,
The rising honor of our nation,   40
From school translated to a college,
There to acquire superior knowledge;
To have your noble blood refined
By what can best adorn your mind.
You enter on a public stage   45
In the first wildness of your age,
And all around you every eye,

On everything you do, a spy;
Where not a trivial act can be
From the severest censure free.   50

  If smallest faults can give a handle
For calumny, reproach and scandal,
If true or false, the world will talk,
How circumspectly must you walk!

  You know, my Lord, 'tis wisely said   55
(And you the passage often read),
"The higher any persons rise,
The more exposed to cens'ring eyes."
And if a vicious course they steer,
How monstrous will their crimes appear!   60

  Your fellow-students will each day
Find something right or wrong to say:
"Our Lord Mont-Cassel missed a prayer,
In spite of all his tutor's care;
Instead of lecture in the hall,   65
His Lordship was engaged at ball;
The little sorry theme he writ
Was scribbled without fear or wit;
He fell in company with rooks
Who choused him out of half his books."   70

  But should you copy vulgar Lords,
Whose actions only vice records,
Whose very footmen show more sense,
Appear of greater consequence,
How foes will smile! how friends will grieve!   75
To find you ruined past retrieve.
Nay, all the world about will stare
To see you slip through all our care.

  Then listen, while I now describe
The grand achievements of your tribe.   80
They drink, they quarrel, swear and game,
And Dick the footman does the same.
Behold a knot of peers approach;
They just have bilked a hackney-coach.
Behold them in their tavern airs,   85

Kicking the drawers down the stairs.
Behold their conduct at a play;
What comedy so good as they!
The valor of a noble rake
At midnight makes a city quake; 90
The hero breaks the watchman's head,
And fights the tradesman from his bed.
His lordly soul undaunted hears
The windows clatt'ring round his ears;
With busy hands he keeps a-doing, 95
Nor dreads at all the jingling ruin.
And though his comrades all are flown,
He stays to throw the t'other stone.
(Now change, my Muse, no longer jest;
A graver style becomes the rest.) 100
He blasts his fortune, health and fame
Without the least regard to shame.
At length when all his credit's gone,
No tradesman left to be undone,
A peer reduced he makes pretension 105
To royal bounty for a pension;
Becomes to get a mean support
A truckling vassal to the court.

O let it never once be said,
My Lord, that you are thus misled! 110
Let not your early parts be lost,
Which so much pains and labor cost.
Ill-natured folks will say with joy,
"That Lord was once a hopeful boy."
And every friend will grieve to see 115
So fine a plant a stunted tree.

I know, my Lord, you can with ease
Command your passions as you please;
If they break loose, you are undone,
And down a precipice you run. 120

Let prudence every action guide
And only virtue be your pride.
Be just the same you were at school
(I cannot give a better rule),
Where your example has done more 125

Than rods could ever do before.
Preserve your honor and your truth,
Those lovely ornaments of youth,
By which you have distinguished been
To the first dang'rous year, sixteen, 130
When too like Icarus we rise,
And spurn at what our friends advise,
Till sad experience brings to view
How rash and giddily we flew.
Apply this hint, and take it thus; 135
Your tutor is your Daedalus;
His care will show the safest way;
Your duty must be to obey,
Till rip'ning judgment makes you see
The safest course as well as he; 140
As he directs, if you can fly,
With honor live, with honor die.

(Published in 1727)

Prologue Spoken at Mr. Sheridan's School

Enter Scholar, riding on an Ass

The scenes are new, and everything compact,
And all our younkers ready just to act.
But why this racket? Why this hurly-burly?
Some laugh, some sneer, and some look very surly.
You're mighty judges in your own conceit: 5
Am I the only ass that rides in state?
Our play's th' *Adelphi*—I'm to be a brother,
And my supporter ass to be another—
But, gentlemen, forbear; for, as it passes,
The greater part among us are but asses. 10

If you came hither to imbibe instruction,
And to receive some wonderful production,
Expect half-wit from th' officers of schools;
Asses produce no prodigies but mules.
Don't think that I intend to be uncivil; 15
I shall not ride, like beggars, to the devil.
Too oft, alas, am I accoutered thus,
And forced to mount the standing Pegasus.

Our Master still, which you will think a wonder,
Exalts the dull and keeps the witty under.   20
But ah! the tyrant then without remorse
The rider lashes, who should lash the horse;
And in promotion takes away command,
For still the under has the upper hand.

But hold—how's this!—who's that that yonder scuffles   25
With beaver, powdered wig and cambric ruffles?
I value not his pageantry a louse!
Sir Fopling, know this is no coffee-house;
Since you're so prudent as to come to school,
You must observe the true scholastic rule;   30
Our Master hates a self-conceited elf,
And bears no noise but what he makes himself.

He writes—but I shall not reveal the myst'ry;
We must beware of *scandalum magistri.*
He that tells tales is worse than he that mitches;   35
That man may come to school without his breeches.
Who'd purchase vain applause with real sorrow?
Your bays tonight would turn to birch tomorrow.

                                        (Published in 1727)

From Tim and the Fables

Dear Tim, no more such angry speeches,
Unbutton and let down your breeches,
Tear out the tail, and wipe your a—— ———
I know you love to act a farce.
                    (Probably first published ca. 13–16 July, 1728)

Ballyspellin

All you that would refine your blood,
    As pure as famed Llewellyn,
By waters clear, come every year
    To drink at Ballyspellin.

Though pox or itch your skin enrich   5
    With rubies past the telling,

'Twill clear your skins before you've been
   A month at Ballyspellin.

If lady's cheek be green as leek
   When she comes from her dwelling,   10
The kindling rose within it glows
   When she's at Ballyspellin.

The sooty brown who comes from town
   Grows here as fair as Helen;
Then back she goes to kill the beaux,   15
   By dint of Ballyspellin.

Our ladies are as fresh and fair
   As Ross or bright Dunkelling;
And Mars might make a fair mistake,
   Were he at Ballyspellin.   20

We men submit as they think fit,
   And here is no rebelling;
The reason's plain: the ladies reign;
   They're queens at Ballyspellin.

By matchless charms, unconquered arms,   25
   They have the way of quelling
Such desperate foes as dare oppose
   Their pow'r at Ballyspellin.

Cold water turns to fire, and burns;
   I know because I fell in   30
A stream which came from one bright dame
   Who drank at Ballyspellin.

Fine beaux advance, equipped for dance,
   To bring their Anne or Nell in;
With so much grace, I'm sure no place   35
   Can vie with Ballyspellin.

No politics, no subtle tricks,
   No man his country selling;
We eat, we drink, we never think
   Of these at Ballyspellin.   40

The troubled mind, the puffed with wind,
    Do all come here pell-mell in;
And they are sure to work their cure
    By drinking Ballyspellin.

Though dropsy fills you to the gills,   45
    From chin to toe though swelling,
Pour in, pour out, you cannot doubt
    A cure at Ballyspellin.

Death throws no darts through all these parts;
    No sextons here are knelling;   50
Come, judge and try, you'll never die,
    But live at Ballyspellin.

Except you feel darts tipped with steel,
    Which here are every belle in;
When from their eyes sweet ruin flies,   55
    We die at Ballyspellin.

Good cheer, sweet air, much joy, no care,
    Your sight, your taste, your smelling,
Your ears, your touch, transported much
    Each day at Ballyspellin.   60

Within this ground we all sleep sound,
    No noisy dogs a-yelling,
Except you wake for Celia's sake
    All night at Ballyspellin.

There all you see, both he and she,   65
    No lady keeps her cell in,
But all partake the mirth we make,
    Who drink at Ballyspellin.

My rhymes are gone; I think I've none,
    Unless I should bring hell in;   70
But, since I'm here to heav'n so near,
    I can't at Ballyspellin.

(Written ca. middle September 1728)

You That Would Read the Bible . . .

You that would read the Bible, turn all
To April 6, *The London Journal,*
And by a letter there you'll see
How much the text will owe to me.
Five thousand years and more—'tis odd   5
None could explain the word of God!
Of all the learnèd in all ages,
Through all their long, laborious pages,
Till I, the top of Irish Deans,
Have made it out with wondrous pains.   10
I've read the dev'l and all of books;
The world may read 'em in my looks:
Above ten wagonload at least,
Within my skull in order placed,
From thence to sally forth anew,   15
One Universal Single View.
I've likewise ransacked books profane
Which I shall muster to explain
Whate'er is hid, obscure, perplexed:
As plain as pikestaff, every text.   20
Most articles, whereof I treat,
Have been the subject of debate
Full often o'er a pot of ale,
When I was rabbi at Kinsale.
But then, for want of ancient learning,   25
The Scripture sense not well discerning,
Our nights were passed in great confusion,
No mortal making one conclusion.
To find a remedy for this,
I hope it will not be amiss   30
To furnish my associate *quondam*
(That they no more dispute at random)
With choice Collected Dissertations,
Answers, Rejoinders, Replications,
That each may have enough to say,   35
And hold the Scripture his own way.
Profecto legi plus quam satis,
More languages than Mithridates,
All which I learned (as will appear
Since I left Ireland) in one year;   40

Where such, as knew my stock, can tell
I scarcely could read English well.
In this one book I've done much more
Than all the world has done before;
No bibliotheque that is now extant   45
Has half so well explained a text on't;
With so much ease I can command it,
The greatest dunce may understand it.
If any thinks the work too long
For one man's head, I'll show he's wrong,   50
Because the way which I intend
Will bring it quickly to an end.
In chapters here and there I'll dip,
Whole books not worth the reading skip;
Whate'er's poetical or moral,   55
To them I have a mortal quarrel;
What merely is historical,
I shall not touch upon at all;
You'll see me such a Bible-trimmer,
That I'll reduce it to a primer.   60
As for the Fathers, they are all met
In Pool, Petavius and Calmet;
I've read 'em page by page, and find
No gleaning work for me behind.
And when I cut one folio short,   65
Will not the reader thank me for't?
For I have so much ancient lore
I could have swelled 'em into four.
We wait subscriptions coming in;
We're just beginning to begin;   70
'Tis this the printer's sole pretence is:
We've paper, types, amanuensis,
And all but what few pence are owing
To set the press and me a-going.
One thing I beg leave to remark—   75
For young divines who're in the dark,
And English readers who are straining
In every chapter for a meaning,
For men of letters and good sense,
Here's learning at a small expense;   80
They'll find my books, when well examined,
Will do by help of Pool and Hammond;
And if the parsons can afford once

A Bible with a large Concordance,
I know not anything they lack   85
Except it be an Almanac.
In my Compilement they shall see
Opinions, great variety,
That every schismatic with ease
May find a gloss himself to please.   90
Now Monsieur Calmet (like an olio)
Dished up nine tracts of his in folio;
To all his countrymen revealed
What Latin, Hebrew, Greek concealed,
So plain in French that every peasant   95
Breaks out with rapture in the praise on't.
O what a glorious learnèd heap is't!
A wondrous author for a papist!
I wish in English 'twere translated,
And mine to wipe his Rev'rence fated.   100
To what perfection had he brought
His books, with liberty of thought!
But all along he's cramped I find,
And therefore durst not speak his mind;
For had he said a word 'gainst Popery,   105
The laws would turn his neck with rope awry.
Thus foreign Pop'ry is a curse,
But English Popery is worse.

    Remember all, before you're told,
That what I write for new is old;   110
If any man of reading looks,
He'll find it all in other books;
As I'm an orthodox divine,
I've stol'n my comments, every line.
There's all the wrangling tracts I know   115
Collected here, both con and pro,
So well disposed of, every man
May find the truth out, if he can.
From the Creation to the Flood
(To show you that my work is good),   120
I've drawn a sketch, as I thought best,
To form a judgment of the rest.
A word or two before I close all:
One Doctor Innis makes proposal—
A poor insipid moral tool,   125

He'd have the world to walk by rule.
He thinks I've naught to do but nose him;
I'd see him hanged ere I oppose him.
He strives to make men good, but I, Sir,
Resolve to make them worse, and wiser.   130
It ever was my way to love
The serpent, rather than the dove.
The doctor, by a vain pretension,
Depends upon his own invention;
But I, who always lived on loan,   135
Shan't write a sentence of my own.

(Probably first published ca. October 8–12, 1728)

The Tale of the T——d

A pastry-cook once moulded up a t——
(You may believe me when I give my word)
With nice ingredients of the fragrant kind
And sugar of the best, right doubl' refined.
He blends them all, for he was fully bent   5
Quite to annihilate its taste and scent.
With outstretched arms, he twirls the rolling-pin,
And spreads the yielding ordure smooth and thin,
'Twas not to save his flour, but show his art,
Of such foul dough to make a sav'ry tart.   10
He heats his ov'n with care, and baked it well,
But still the crust's offensive to the smell;
The cook was vexed to see himself so soiled,
So works it to a dumpling, which he boiled;
Now out it comes, and if it stunk before,   15
It stinks full twenty times as much, and more.
He breaks fresh eggs, converts it into batter,
Works them with spoon about a wooden platter,
To true consistence, such as cook-maids make
At Shrovetide, when they toss the pliant cake.   20
In vain he twirls the pan; the more it fries,
The more the nauseous, fetid vapors rise.
Resolved to make it still a sav'ry bit,
He takes the pancake, rolls it round a spit,
Winds up the jack, and sets it to the fire;   25
But roasting raised its pois'nous fumes the high'r.
Offended much (although it was his own),

At length he throws it where it should be thrown;
And in a passion, storming loud, he cried,
"If neither baked, nor boiled, nor roast, nor fried,   30
Can thy offensive, hellish taint reclaim,
Go to the filthy jake from whence you came."

The Moral

This tale requires but one short application:
It fits all upstart scoundrels in each nation,
Minions of fortune, wise men's jest in pow'r,   35
Like weeds on dunghills, stinking, rank and sour.
                    (Probably first published ca. 29 October–2 November, 1728)

Prologue Spoken Before a Greek Play, At the Reverend Dr. Sheridan's School, At the Breaking-Up of His Scholars for Christmas, 1728

Come out my lads, make haste, come out and play,
For here's a lovely night, a night like day.
No star did ever in our sky appear
So pleasing, blushing, bright, serene, so clear.
The glancing rays are for my eyes too strong;   5
See what it is to be in prison long.
But hold—my sight's regained! O sweet surprise,
They are not stars which blind my sight, but eyes!
Fool that I was, when stars can only move
Our silent admiration, not our love;   10
But you move both, you wound at once and please,
And though you kill, yet still you love to gaze.
What lightning's this? Heav'ns, with what force it passes!
Dear ladies, hold away your burning glasses.
Pity our youth; be tender as you're fair;   15
So many painted arrows who can bear!
A truce, dear foes, we beg; we make proposal—
Just for three hours, those twinklers you would close all.
Or how can we pretend to act our parts
When you have pre-engaged our eyes, our hearts?   20
Conceal, sweet foes, your charming pretty looks;
Keep them as close as we would keep our books;
Or if you don't withdraw those killing graces,
I vow we'll swear the peace against your faces.

Hide them at least until the play be over,   25
And then let every lady kill her lover.

(Written ca. mid–December 1728)

The Five Ladies' Answer to the Beau, With the Wig and Wings at His Head

You little scribbling beau,
    What demon made you write?
Because to write you know
    As much as you can fight.

For compliment so scurvy,   5
    I wish we had you here;
We'd turn you topsy-turvy
    Into a mug of beer.

You thought to make a farce on
    The man and place we chose;   10
We're sure a single parson
    Is worth a hundred beaux.

And you would make us vassals,
    Good Mr. Wig and Wings,
To silver clocks and tassels—   15
    You would, you thing of things!

Because around your cane
    A ring of diamonds is set,
And you in some by-lane
    Have gained a paltry grisette,   20

Shall we of sense refined
    Your trifling nonsense bear,
As noisy as the wind,
    As empty as the air?

We hate your empty prattle,   25
    And vow and swear 'tis true,
There's more in one child's rattle
    Than twenty fops like you.

(Written in 1728)

To My Worthy Friend T S——, D. D. On His Incomparable Translation of and Notes on Persius

Anonymous

Quis expedivit Psittaco suum Xaīpe?
Quis leget haec?

Pers.

Hail Bard triumphant! Whose poetic fire
Apollo and the Sacred Nine inspire.
Thou Light! Who for Hibernia's glory rose
To make cramp Persius speak in Irish prose.
The sense of whose dark numbers to restore   5
Was often tried, but never gained before.
Here Stapleton exerts his art in vain;
Here Dryden sunk, nor could the load sustain.
This was the work reserved for THEE, to bring
A Latian bard the Irish cry to sing.   10

Your first attempt turned Lilly's rules to rhyme.
Now Persius speaks through thee in prose sublime.
O wondrous genius! who can thus transpose,
Turn Lilly's prose to verse, and Persius' verse to prose.

Thou Dunster[1] of the age, the puzzling text   15
Can now no more by critics be perplexed.
Beneath, the swelling notes in order stand,
And with the comment chime, at thy command.
The upper planets thus their powers dispense,
And govern mortals by their influence.   20
Thy early notes in music now appear[2]
In strains exalted in a nobler sphere.
The prattling parrot now his Greek[3] forsakes,
And in a more familiar language speaks.
Now the "Grim Horns"[4] in rattling numbers roar,   25
And sound a sense they never knew before.
The proud calf's head a horrid aspect lies,[5]
And when it's ravished from his body dies.

Thou truly did'st on Mount Parnassus dream[6]
And glut the purest Heliconian stream.   30

May ivy leaves[7] around thy temples spread
In shape like tongues, and lick thy sacred head.
The crooked Horns shall serve to sound thy fame,
And Echo[8] shall reiterate thy name.

(Published in 1728)

---

1. He translated Horace into prose.
2. He learned to play on the fiddle.
3. *Xaĩpe* in the Prologue to Persius.
4. See his translation of *Torvo Mamillones,* &c. Sat. I. line 99.
5. *Et raptum Vitulo Caput ab atura Superbo Passaris.* Sat. I. line 100.
6. In allusion to the first two lines of the Prologue.
7. See the Note, p. 3 on

        ——Quorum imagines lambunt
        Hoedere sequaces.

8. Reparabilis adionat Echo.

An Ode

To be Performed at the Castle of Dublin, March the 1st, 1728/29. Being the Birth-day of Her Most Serene Majesty Queen Caroline. By the Special Command of their Excellencies, the Lords Justices of Ireland.

Recitativo: Early Queen of Light arise,
        Blend thy colors, paint the skies;
        Every grace like her display,
        Who gives luster to this day.

Aria: Let the lovely smiles of morning   5
  Give the cheerful warblers warning,
  All in sprightly notes to sing,
  "The Queen of Britain is the Queen of Spring."
  Phoebus loudly strike thy lyre;
  Now let heav'n and earth conspire;   10
  In sound sublime make both at once combine
  To sing the glorious birth of Caroline.

DA CAPO.

Rec: Of Caroline to sing the birth,
      Gift of heav'n, and pride of earth!

Aria: Joyful Nature   15
                 In each feature,
                 Grace and beauty
                 All transcending,
          Mixed with every powerful charm;
                 Love and duty   20
                 Thence intending,
          Every British heart should warm.

                      DA CAPO.

Rec: Who was ever known before
         In the lines of royal race,
         Should we all their virtues trace,   25
         Happy with such an unexhausted store?

Aria: All that can adorn a Queen,
         Soft address and easy mien,
         Every motion is endearing,
         Every word commands a hearing,   30
         Every sentence from her tongue
         Sounds as if an angel sung.
         All her actions thus refined
         Show the early seasoned mind,
         Show the parents' prudent care,   35
         Who adorned the rising fair
         With whate'er is great and good,
         Equal to her princely blood.

                      DA CAPO.

Rec: Happy monarch, who can see
            All that you can wish to have   40
         In thy blest consort and illustrious progeny
            Daughters no less divine
            Than thy great Caroline,
            Sons as their father brave!
              Her forming hand,   45
              To bless the nation,
         By thy example and her education,
         Will fit them for council and command.

Aria: Their godlike father's martial fire,

Unrivalled by the sons of Fame,   50
Shall make them gloriously aspire
To add new trophies to the Brunswick name.
Thus with unbounded reputation,
Their courage and their wisdom shall increase,
   Alike for war or peace,   55
   And all their care shall be
Still to preserve our golden liberty
To be the bulwark of the reformation.

Aria: Our secret and our open foes
   In vain shall plot, in vain oppose;   60
   Britain, secure, all other power defies
   Under a king so valiant and so wise.
   All Europe's balance George shall hold,
   In spite of foreign arms and Spanish gold.
   His matchless fleet shall teach 'em to obey;   65
   For they must rule the land, who rule the sea.

DA CAPO.

Chorus: Rouse then, ye British hearts;
   Ireland against your foes will join,
   And draw that sword to take your parts,
   Which flew like lightning o'er the banks of Boyne. 70
   The same high courage flows within our veins
   That streamed through Flanders' twenty long campaigns.
   Lead on, and we shall make the world surrender;
     We long in arms to shine,
   To serve our country, and our faith's defender,   75
     His royal issue, and our Caroline.
           (First performed March 1, 1728/29)

From The Critical Minute

Michael Tracey

O Thou! What e'er may thy attention draw—
Priest, pedant, Punsibi, et cetera—
Whether you choose t' adopt a solemn air,
Or sit and doze in Busby's easy chair,
Or praise yourself, or vilify mankind,   5

Or what the head may want, lash in behind:
Though mean my verse, yet be thy spleen witheld;
Grieve not, my Tom, to see thy own excelled.

(Published in 1731)

A New Simile for the Ladies

With Useful Annotations

To make a writer miss his end,
You've nothing else to do but mend.

I often tried in vain to find
A simile[1] for womankind—
A simile, I mean, to fit 'em,
In every circumstance to hit 'em.[2]
Through every beast and bird I went;　　　　　　5
I ransacked every element;
And, after peeping through all nature
To find so whimsical a creature,
A cloud[3] presented to my view,
And straight this parallel I drew:　　　　　　10

Clouds turn with every wind about;
They keep us in suspense and doubt;
Yet, oft perverse, like womankind,
Are seen to scud against the wind.
And are not women just the same,　　　　　　15
For who can tell at what they aim?[4]

Clouds keep the stoutest mortals under,
When bell'wing,[5] they discharge their thunder;
So, when the alarm-bell is rung
Of Xanti's[6] everlasting tongue,　　　　　　20
The husband dreads its loudness more
Than lightning's flash or thunder's roar.

Clouds weep, as they do, without pain;
And what are tears but women's rain?

The clouds about the welkin roam,[7]　　　　　　25
And ladies never stay at home.

The clouds build castles in the air,
A thing peculiar to the fair;
For all the schemes of their forecasting
Are not more solid, nor more lasting.   30

A cloud is light by turns, and dark;
Such is a lady with her spark:
Now with a sudden pouting⁹ gloom,
She seems to darken all the room;
Again she's pleased, his fear's beguiled,¹⁰   35
And all is clear when she has smiled.
In this they're wondrously alike¹¹
(I hope the simile will strike);
Though in the distant dumps¹² you view 'em,
Stay but a moment, you'll see through 'em.   40

The clouds are apt to make reflection,¹³
And frequently produce infection;
So Celia, with small provocation,
Blasts every neighbor's reputation.

The clouds delight in gaudy show,   45
For they, like ladies, have their bow;
The gravest matron¹⁴ will confess
That she herself is fond of dress.

Observe the clouds in pomp arrayed;
What various colors are displayed: 50
The pink, the rose, the vi'let's dye,
In that great drawing-room, the sky.
How do these differ from our Graces¹⁵
In garden-silks, brocades and laces?
Are they not such another sight,   55
When met upon a birthday night?

The clouds delight to change their fashion;
Dear ladies, be not in a passion,
Nor let this whim to you seem strange,
Who every hour delight in change.   60

In them and you alike are seen
The sullen symptoms of the spleen;

The moment that your vapors rise,
We see them dropping from your eyes.

In evening fair you may behold   65
The clouds are fringed with borrowed gold;
And this is many a lady's case,
Who flaunts about in borrowed lace.[16]

Grave matrons are like clouds of snow;
Their words fall thick and soft and slow,   70
While brisk coquettes,[17] like rattling hail,
Our ears on every side assail.

Clouds, when they intercept our sight,
Deprive us of celestial light;
So when my Chloe I pursue,   75
No heav'n besides I have in view.

Thus, on comparison,[18] you see,
In every instance they agree,
So like, so very much the same,
That one may go by t' other's name.   80
Let me proclaim[19] it then aloud,
That every woman is a cloud.

(Published ca. August 1732)

---

1. Most ladies, in reading, call this word a *smile;* but they are to note, it consists of three syllables, si-mi-le. In English, a likeness.

2. Not to hurt them.

3. Not like a gun or pistol.

4. This is not meant as to shooting, but resolving.

5. The word "bellowing" is not here to be understood of a bull, but a cloud, which makes a noise like a bull when it thunders.

6. Xanti, a nickname for Xantippe, that scold of glorious memory, who never let poor Socrates have one moment's peace of mind; yet, with unexampled patience, he bore her pestilential tongue. I shall beg the ladies' pardon, if I insert a few passages concerning her; and at the same time I assure them, it is not to lessen those of the present age, who are possessed of the like laudable talents; for I will confess that I know three in the city of Dublin, no way inferior to Xantippe, but that they have not as great men to work upon.

When a friend asked Socrates, how he could bear the scolding of his wife Xantippe, he retorted and asked him how he could bear the gaggling of his geese. "Ay, but my geese lay eggs for me," replied his friend. "So does my wife bear children," said Socrates.—*Diog. Laert.*

Being asked at another time by a friend how he could bear her tongue, he said she was of this use to him, that she taught him to bear the impertinences of others with more ease when he went abroad. *Plut. de Capiend. ex host. utilit.*

Socrates invited his friend Enthydemus, to supper. Xantippe in great rage went in to them and overset the table. Enthydemus, rising in a passion to go off: "My dear friend, stay," said Socrates, "Did not a hen do the same thing at your house the other day, and did I show any resentment?" *Plut. de irâ cohibendâ.*

I could give many more instances of her termagancy and his philosophy, if such a proceeding might not look as if I were glad of an opportunity to expose the fair sex; but to show that I have no such design, I declare solemnly that I had much worse stories to tell of her behaviour to her husband, which I rather passed over, on account of the great esteem which I bear the ladies, especially those in the honorable station of matrimony.

7. Ramble.

8. Not vomiting.

9. Thrusting out the lip.

10. This is to be understood not in the sense of wort, when brewers put yeast or barm in it; but its true meaning is "deceived" or "cheated."

11. Hit your fancy.

12. Sullen fits. We have a merry jig called "Dumpty Deary," invented to rouse ladies from the dumps.

13. Reflection of the sun.

14. Motherly women.

15. Not Grace before and after meat, nor their Graces the Duchesses, but the Graces which attended on Venus.

16. Not Flanders lace, but gold and silver lace. By borrowed, I mean such as run in honest tradesmen's debts, for what they were not able to pay, as many of them did for French silver lace, against the last Birthday. *vid.* the Shopkeepers' books.

17. Girls who love to hear themselves prate, and put on a number of monkey-airs to catch men.

18. I hope none will be so uncomplaisant to the ladies as to think these comparisons odious.

19. Tell it to the whole world, not to proclaim them as robbers and rapparees.

A Prologue to *Julius Caesar,* As It Was Acted at Madam Violante's Booth, Dec. the 15th, 1732, By Some of the Young Gentlemen in Dr. Sheridan's School.

Ladies, our Master chose a dreadful play,
With base intent to drive you all away,
But bravely stand your ground and fear him not;

I'll tell the secret, and betray the plot.

Thunder and lightning first begin the night;   5
Let not this trick your tender hearts affright;
One drum unbraced the thunder's roar supplies,
And pounded rosin in blue flashes flies:
A harmless noise, where no dire bolt is thrown,
And lightning much less dang'rous than your own.   10
Witness those eyes, which through my bosom dart;
How shall I bear them? O my bleeding heart!

Next you shall see a murdered king. What then?
In two hours more you'll see him live again.
Though sev'ral daggers seem to pierce his breast,   15
Upon my honor they're but wounds in jest.
And all the blood that streams along the floor
Is but a bladder of sheep's blood—no more.

When you shall see the rabble on our stage
Tear the dunce laureate, Cinna, in a rage,   20
Kind-hearted ladies, do not weep for him;
The poet's safe and sound in every limb.

The thing I fear will work your fancies most
Is the phantasma—Julius Caesar's ghost—
Which to the life he acts in every view,   25
Yet he's no more a ghost than one of you;
Though he stalks jointless, though he looks so pale,
'Tis all a sham; we drudged his face with meal.

When trumpets sound, and drums begin to rattle,
And gen'rals march in sullen pomp to battle,   30
Be not dismayed at the tremendous sight,
Nor think in earnest they intend to fight.
They only fight to jest behind the scene;
Though hundreds fall, there's not one mortal slain,
And each mama shall have her child again.   35
Thus far through tenderness I undeceive you;
Ladies, adieu—how loath am I to leave you!
                    (Written somewhat before December 15, 1732)

Now to Lampoon Myself for My Presumption

Your verses, Doctor, crawl on gouty feet;
You've made those waters bitter which were sweet;

Your chaos we must grant is truly good;
Like the first chaos 'tis completely mud.

(Written on January 5, 1734)

I Ritu a Verse o Na Molli o Mi Ne

I ritu a verse o na molli o mi ne,
Asta lassa me pole, a laedis o fine,
I ne ver neu a niso ne at in mi ni is;
A manat a glans ora sito fer diis;
De armo lis abuti hos face an hos nos is   5
As fer a sal illi, as reddas aro sis.
Ac is o mi molli is almi de lite;
Illo verbi de, an illo verbi nite.

(Written on June 28, 1734)

His Modest Apology for Knocking Out a News-Boy's Teeth, Who Told Him His Works Would Not Sell

I must confess that I was somewhat warm;
I broke his teeth, but where's the mighty harm?
My works, he said, could ne'er afford him meat,
And teeth are useless where there's naught to eat.

(Published in 1734)

Tanti Vi Sed I Tanti Vi

Tanti vi sed I tanti vi
Hi fora Dic in apri vi.

(Written on July 15, 1735)

A Letter of Advice to the Right Hon. John Earl of Orrery

My Lord, I know not what you mean,
By such encomiums on the Dean,
By choosing all your time to waste,
With one of his exploded taste!

From whence, my Lord, I plainly see   5
You've just as bad a taste as he;
Therefore to gain a reputation,
As you're a stranger in the nation,
Take my advice, avoid him quite,
And choose companions more polite.   10
'Twill cost you but a little pains
To single out a score of Deans,
Whose equals are not to be found
In Irish or in English ground;
For, here you can't be at a loss,   15
There is Dean D——l and Dean C——,
And Dean I——r and Dean S——ne;
These are the men will make you shine,
And make mankind's united voice
Applaud you for so wise a choice.   20

    Another fault—forgive a friend—
You show, which I would have you mend;
I mean your pouring over books
(And one may see it in your looks)
While folks as noble born as you   25
More rational delights pursue,
As horses, drabs, and dogs, and dice,
And drinking hard, and dressing nice.
If thus, my Lord, you'd show your parts,
How soon you'd gain the ladies' hearts!   30
Not all the witty things you say,
Within the compass of day,
Could half that strong impression make,
As solitair, toupee and snake;
And this, experiment shall show: 35
Observe Clarinda with a beau,
While you yourself are sitting by;
She'll scarce vouchsafe you half an eye,
But rather hear him hum one tune,
Than hear you speak from June to June.   40

    Another scand'lous thing, my Lord—
You walk the streets without a sword,
Alone without your footman Dick,
Without the ornamental stick;
I can assure you that some folks   45

On this occasion have their jokes.
I heard a beau, who shall be nameless,
Declare he thought your lordship shameless;
And thus went on: "I cannot bear
To see that lord without a chair;   50
The weather's fair I own; what then?
Peers should not walk like other men.
It is beneath their noble feet
To tread upon a filthy street."
This is the current cant that goes   55
Among the wisest of our beaux.
Pray don't give them such dire offence,
But shun the puppies of low sense,
Who make you basely turn aside
From nonsense, vanity and pride,
Those princely qualities which grace
The inward man of outward lace;
And then, my Lord, and not till then,
You may be justly ranked with men.

(Published in July 1735)

While Footman-like He Waits in Every Hall

While footman-like he waits in every hall,
His ill-matched wife is well received by all;
Graceful and comely she, he scarce a man,
A dire contrast of scald-crow with a swan.

(Written on April 3, 1736)

From Upon a Certain Bookseller, or Printer, in Utopia

Thou lowest scoundrel of the scoundrel kind,
Extract of all the dregs of all mankind. . . .
I'll make thy dunghill reputation s——k,
Write thee to death with thy own pens and ink.

(Completed ca. May 12, 1736)

My Hens Are Hatching

My hens are hatching,
My house is thatching,

My geese a-gaggling,
My wife a-draggling,
My corn a-threshing,   5
My sheep a-washing,
My turf a-drawing,
My timber sawing,
My gravel walk raking,
My rolling-stone making,   10
My ale a-brewing,
Myself a-stewing,
My boys a-teaching,
My webs a-bleaching,
My daughters reading,   15
My garden weeding,
My lime a-burning
My milk a-churning.
   In short, all nature seems to be at work,
   Busy as Kouly Kan against the Turk.   20

(Written ca. May 24, 1736)

My Walk It Is Finished

My walk it is finished,
My money diminished;
But when you come down,
I'll hold you a crown
You'll soon make me rich,   5
Or I'll die in a ditch.

(Written on June 3, 1736)

You Shall Want Nothing Fit for Mortal Man

You shall want nothing fit for mortal man
To eat or drink; 'tis all that I do can.
   And all that's expedient,
   From your most obedient.

(Written on June 3, 1736)

Grouse Pouts Are Come In

Grouse pouts are come in;
I've some in my bin,
To butter your chin;
When done with our din–
ner, through thick and thin   5
We'll walk out and in,
And care not a pin
Who thinks it a sin.
We make some folks grin,
By lashing their kin, &c.

(Written on June 23, 1736)

I Wish Your Reverence Were Here to *Hear* the Trumpets

I wish your reverence were here to *hear* the trumpets;
Mistake me not, for I mean not the strumpets.

(Written on June 23, 1736)

Our River is Dry

Our river is dry,
And fiery the sky;
I fret and I fry,
Just ready to die;
Oh, where shall I fly
From Phoebus's eye?
In bed when I lie,
I soak like a pie;
And I sweat, oh, I sweat, like a hog in a sty.

(Written on July 6, 1736)

Grouse Pouts

Grouse pouts,
Fine trouts,

Right venison
For my benison.
Leave your stinking town in haste,   5
For you have no time to waste.

(Written on July 20, 1736)

To the Rev. Doctor Swift, Dean of St. Patrick's.
A Birthday Poem. Nov. 30, 1736

To you, my true and faithful friend,
These tributary lines I send,
Which every year, thou best of Deans,
I'll pay as long as life remains;
But did you know one half the pain,   5
What work, what racking of the brain,
It costs me for a single clause,
How long I'm forced to think, and pause,
How long I dwell upon a proem,
To introduce your birthday poem,   10
How many blotted lines; I know it,
You'd have compassion for the poet.

Now to describe the way I think:
I take in hand my pen and ink;
I rub my forehead, scratch my head,   15
Revolving all the rhymes I read—
Each complimental thought sublime,
Reduced by fav'rite Pope to rhyme,
And those by you to Oxford writ,
With true simplicity and wit.   20
Yet after all I cannot find
One panegyric to my mind.
Now I begin to fret, and blot
Something I schemed but quite forgot;
My fancy turns a thousand ways   25
Through all the sev'ral forms of praise,
What elegy may best become
The greatest Dean in Christendom.
At last I've hit upon a thought—
Sure this will do—'tis good for naught—   30
This line I peevishly erase,

And choose another in its place;
Again I try, again commence,
But cannot well express the sense;
The line's too short to hold my meaning;   35
I'm cramped and cannot bring the Dean in.
O for a rhyme to "glorious birth"—
I've hit upon't—The rhyme is "earth"!
But how to bring it in, or fit it,
I know not, so I'm forced to quit it.   40

   Again I try—I'll sing the man—
"Ay do," says Phoebus, "if you can;
I wish with all my heart you would not;
Were Horace now alive he could not;
And will you venture to pursue   45
What none alive or dead could do?
Pray see, did ever Pope or Gay
Presume to write on his birthday?
Though both were fav'rite bards of mine,
The task they wisely both decline."   50

   With grief I felt his admonition,
And much lamented my condition,
Because I could not be content
Without some graceful compliment.
If not the poet, sure the friend   55
Must something on your birthday send.

   I scratched and rubbed my head once more:
Let every patriot him adore.
Alack a day, there's nothing in't—
Such stuff will never do in print.   60

   Pray, Reader, ponder well the sequel;
I hope this epigram will take well:

   In others, life is deemed a vapor;
In Swift, it is a lasting taper,
Whose blaze continually refines;   65
The more it burns, the more it shines.

   I read this epigram again;
'Tis much too flat to fit the Dean.

Then down I lay some scheme to dream on,
Assisted by some friendly demon.
I slept, and dreamed that I should meet
A birthday poem in the street;
So after all my care and rout,
You see, dear Dean, my dream is out.

(Published ca. November 27, 1736)

A Birthday Poem on the Anniversary of the Birth of the Rev. Dr. Swift, D.S.P.D. Nov. 30, 1737.

Illum aget penna metuente solvi.
Fama superstes.

This day, the fav'rite of the year,
To each Hibernian heart most dear,
The gods and goddesses convene
In honor of St. Patrick's Dean,
To celebrate his genial day,   5
And now their brightest pomp display.
The grand procession led by Jove,
To Sol's bright palace on they move,
Where ent'ring at his golden gate,
The god received them all in state.   10
Behold them in their proper places,
The gods, the goddesses and Graces,
In their celestial best attire;
And now the birthday song require.
The Muses, placed on either hand,   15
Wait for the signal of command;
For none durst touch the trembling strings,
Before the god of music sings.

The god begins; they straight obey;
By turns they sing; by turns they play;   20
Again at once they all agree
In blest concerted harmony;
No voice exempt, no finger mute,
The well-tuned notes and numbers suit
So well that every various tone   25
By symphony appears as one.

The vaulted roof exalts the sound,
And guides the floating charms around.
Each heav'nly bosom pants with pleasure,
Approves the song, applauds the measure, 30
For Phoebus both composed, to raise
His fav'rite Swift to deathless praise.
They sang how gloriously he stood
Against the dark invader, Wood,
Though armed with tenfold plates of brass; 35
How bravely Swift maintained the pass;
How wary, vigorous and stout,
He kept the lurking ruin out;
That famed Hibernia now can say,
She owes her safety to that day. 40
Now softly sweet to Lydian airs
They shift their hands and soothe the spheres,
The spheres that harmony employ
In sympathetic, tuneful joy;
Well-pleased to join in such a choir 45
Where Swift is sung and gods inspire
With numbers high, and sweet like those
Which he for matchless Stella chose—
Stella, the glory of her age,
Who lives in his immortal page; 50
And now repeats those lines above,
Where Wisdom best expresses Love.
While thus advanced the smiling Hours,
And transport filled the heav'nly pow'rs.
Far-flying Fame came flutt'ring in, 55
As if her wings had wounded been,
And thus with falt'ring accents faint
The weary goddess makes complaint.

"Ye gods and goddesses," said she,
"See, what a wretch ye made of me: 60
To send me from among the blest
To one who never gave me rest,
Who every hour new bus'ness finds,
Compels me to outstrip the winds,
Though every region, every nation 65
To sound his endless reputation;
Though I through all the world have flown,
Beyond the stars have made him known,

Yet must I never cease to fly
Till heav'n shall order him to die."   70

   Jove smiling heard, and thus replies,
"You'll have more labor when he dies;
Whenever I immortal make him,
You never can, nor shall forsake him."

(Completed ca. November 30, 1737)

O Would That Enemy I Dread, My Fate

O would that enemy I dread, my fate,
Place me with you in some obscure retreat,
My wishes then would have their utmost bound,
And all I want in your dear arms be found.
By Love's soft passion willingly betrayed,   5
I'd court the idol which great Love has made,
Thy lovely face, my fancy's only joy,
Whose smiles revive me, and whose frowns destroy.
Yet you, too cruel to the truest heart
That ever loved you, hence resolve to part,   10
And leave me in return of all my love
A pain which no physician can remove,
No pow'r of reason ever can subdue,
Nor time nor place, nor all the world, [but you].

(Written possibly ca. 1730–36)

When G——le Has Her Mind at Ease

When G——le has her mind at ease,
Her only study is to please;
You cannot find in all the nation
Her parallel for conversation.
And be the subject which it will,   5
With pleasure you can hear her still.
Nay, though she should employ her wit
Against you, you are fond of it,
And like it more, the more that she
Eclipses yours by repartee.   10
But if one grievance comes athwart her,
No nettles sting or touch you smarter.

Her passion void of all restriction
To plainest truths gives contradiction.
She nods her head, begins to pout   15
And throws her arms three yards about;
Prepared each word you say to scan,
Spreads out her fingers like a fan;
Taunting, teasing, fretting, quarr'ling,
Like monkey sick or lily snarling.   20
But when her storm of anger's over,
Again you're reconciled and love her;
Thus as she's better, as she's worse,
She is a blessing or a curse.

                                        (Written possibly ca. 1730–36)

Joshua Battus's Spepeech to the Paparliament

My Lalalards I cucomplain,
Ofof a mamalicious Dean.
He scribibibled (for I know him)
A Jacococobite popoem,
Where he empopoployed his wit on   5
The gogovernment of Bebritain,
And said such ugugugly things
Of miministers and kikings,
'Twill set the Irish peepeepeers
And them together by the ears,   10
If we don't use poproper means
To pupupunish witty strains
And let 'em see paparty zeal
Shall over wiwiwit prevail.
We'll pull down all who dare peprate   15
In lililibels 'gainst the State.
O GoGoGod, I'm in a fright,
That they and we should fafafight;
I'd rather swallow down a turd
Than see a nennannaked sword.   20
Damn LibLibLibLibLiberty,
What googoogood is it me,
Who from a race of slaves am sprung?

Give me LibLiberty of Tongue.
When other fofolks draw their swords,   25
I nononothing draw but words.

(Written probably in 1730)

So on the Stream the Silver Swan

So on the stream the silver swan
Gracefully slow is wafted on
  Adown the gentle tide.
Unseen her [flying] feet she plies;
Erect her chest, abashed her eyes   5
  With decent modest pride.

Behold her move along the green;
Behold her shape, her air, her mien!
  What dignity! What ease!
But if she dance, the Graces seem   10
Employed to harmonise each limb,
  And guide her through the maze.

(Written possibly ca. 1730–36)

Be Still, Thou Busy Foolish Thing

Be still, thou busy foolish thing,
Nor urge me more of her to sing
  Who [causèd] all thy pain.
Why wilt thou dwell upon a theme
Which serves but to increase your [flame],   5
  That still must burn in vain?

Thus to my heart I oft have said,
But as the dear enchanting maid
  Has seized my soul entire,
My reason with my love combined   10
Is grown to every danger blind,
  And joins to fan the fire.

Why pay we to the pow'rs above
Our adoration and our love,
   But that they perfect are?   15
Though mortals cannot perfect be,
The nearest to perfection she,
   The next our love should share.

                (Written possibly ca. 1730–36)

Some Nymphs May Boast External Grace

Some nymphs may boast external grace,
An easy mien, a beauteous face,
   Whilst others more refined
Possess superior excellence,
Though not the object of our sense,   5
   The beauties of the mind.

Her gifts thus Nature various pours:
Without she spreads the gayest flow'rs
   Where dung's concealed within;
And underneath the barren shore   10
The sparkling gem and shining ore
   More precious lie unseen.

Here she has tried her utmost pow'r,
Here has exhausted all her store
   To make the work complete;   15
Beauty than fairest flow'rs more fair,
Virtues than brightest gems more rare
   Are in Lucinda met.

Yet more, for in the mortal clay
She blended a celestial ray   20
   To animate the whole;
That beaming forth effulgence bright
Makes visible to mortal sight
   The beauties of her soul.

Around her lips in dimpled cells   25
Good nature sweetly smiling dwells,
   Whilst bashful modesty

Fain in her cheek would lie concealed,
But by her blushing is revealed
   Conspicuous to each eye.   30

Truth, candor, innocence serene
On her unclouded front are seen
   Majestically bright;
Reason, first offspring of the skies,
Darts from his citadel, her eyes,   35
   A mild though piercing light.

So the pure stream that gently flows
At once its crystal clearness shows;
   At once our wond'ring eye
Surveys within its bosom fair   40
The radiant glories of the sphere,
   And all the spangled sky.

(Written possibly ca. 1730–36)

From Some Critical Annotations, on Various Subjects Which Have Been Handled by Several Authors

Laurence Whyte

  T-m Punsibi gave us his Art,
With wit and humour played his part;
With serious air he recommends
The Art of Punning to his friends,
Such as no irony could see,   65
Were sure that puns like f—ts are free.
They strain their wits, all hazards run,
To be delivered of a pun,
That commonly is too farfetched
And in the tenters too long stretched.   70

(Published in 1740)

Appendix I: Verse Translations

After Lucretius

All men of mirth and sense admire and love
Those words which like twin brothers doubtful prove;
When the same sounds a diff'rent sense disguise,
In being deceived the greatest pleasure lies.

(Published in 1719)

After Claudian

From word to word th' ambiguous sense is played;
Laughing succeeds, and joyful tears are shed.

(Published in 1719)

After Martial?

Cinna, give me the man, when all is done,
That wisely knows to crack a jest and pun.

(Published in 1719)

After Petronius

Jokes, repartees, and laugh, and pun polite
Are the true test to prove a man is right.

(Published in 1719)

After Lucan?

He's King of Mirth that slyly cheats our sense
With pun ambiguous, pleasing in suspense;
The shoulders lax become; the bending back
Upheaved with laughter makes our ribs to crack;
Ev'n to the liver he can joys impart,   5

205

And play upon the fibres of the heart,
Open the chambers of the lungs, and there
Give longer life in laughing, than in air.

(Published in 1719)

After Horace

If any man can better rules impart,
I'll give him leave to do't with all my heart.

(Published in 1719)

After Martial?

He that would move another man to laughter
Must first begin, and t' other soon comes after.

(Published in 1719)

Chorus From Sophocles' *Philoctetes*

Strophe I

I heard of those eternal pains
    Which racked Ixion feels,
Fast bound by adamantine chains
    To ever-turning wheels.

Doomed to this fate by angry Jove   5
    For tempting to embrace
The Queen of heav'n with impious love,
    His torments never cease.

For never did I hear or see
    A man so racked before,   10
As Philoctetes seems to me;
    What suff'rings can be more?

He never did an act was wrong,
    But justice still maintained;
I wonder much that he so long   15
    Such torments has sustained.

Tell me the cause, ye angry Pow'rs;
  In Fortune's stormy seas,
He's tossed so many tedious hours,
  Without one moment's ease.   20

Antistrophe I

Exposed to all the storms that blow
  From whence he cannot fly;
And not a friend to feel his woe,
  Returning sigh for sigh.

Not one the healing herb applies   25
  To soothe his angry wound,
But torn with anguish there he lies
  Extended on the ground.

The instant that his pains abate
  He like an infant creeps   30
To find a plant to quell that heat,
  And thus the venom sleeps.

Strophe II

Not from the sacred earth his food,
  Nor from the tiller's care
Does he recruit his streaming blood,   35
  But from the bird-flown air.

When soaring fowls advance this way,
  He lets his arrows fly;
To certain death the feathered prey
  Falls flutt'ring from the sky.   40

Ah! wretched soul, thy fate was hard,
  To live ten years in pain,
To be from joyful wine debarred,
  To drink the tasteless rain.

                      (Published in 1725)

Choral Song from *Philoctetes*

Soft sleep, thou stranger to all pain,
  Breathe on him with thy softest gale;

Thou prince of a most happy reign,
  Upon his eyelids gently steal.
Keep off the bright extended rays of light,   5
And gather all the gloomy shades of night.
  Come hither, thou physician sure,
  Thou the universal cure.

(Published in 1725)

After Horace

Thus after plain repast each cheerful guest
With useful conversation crowns the feast—
Not trifling chat on this or t' other place,
Or Lepos dancing with a better grace—
But what is more concern to humankind,   5
To mend our manners and improve the mind.
On philosophic questions wisely bent:
As whether wealth or virtue gives content;
What cause directs us in the choice of friends,
Our private int'rest or more noble ends;   10
What road to choose, what end we should pursue,
And how to keep the good supreme in view.

(Published probably on June 1, 1728)

Tasso's *Amore Fuggitivo*

  Down from the realms of light above,
I, Queen of Heav'n and Queen of Love,
Am come in search to find my son;
The cruel brat away has run.
Last night as in my lap he lay,   5
With artful toying, wanton play,
He slyly took a golden dart,
And pierced my side and touched my heart;
Whether by chance or by design,
I cannot easily divine.   10
But when he saw the wound was giv'n,
In haste he took his flight from heav'n
(So conscious of the crime committed!),
Nor know I whither he has flitted.
And as it is the mother's fashion   15
To change her anger to compassion,
I've used my utmost skill to find

The dear disturber of my mind;
I've traversed o'er, with utmost care,
My own and every other sphere,   20
Where stars are fixed, or move around;
In heav'n he's nowhere to be found.

  O, tell me then, ye mortal swains,
If this low world my son contains.
I know that he's a frequent guest   25
To every soft and tender breast.

  Ye beauteous nymphs, I must despair
To find him out among the fair;
Though strong delight incites the boy
Among your golden curls to toy,   30
Yet he in vain for pity waits,
And finds no entrance at your gates;
For none can Cupid entertain
Whose breasts have fierceness and disdain.

  To you, ye courteous men, I come;   35
Your tender bosoms are his home.
To you, who always on him smiled,
O, tell me where's my lovely child!
Whatever swain discovers this,
I'll give him a celestial kiss—   40
A kiss of love with much more sweets
Than mortal e'er in mortal meets.
Who e'er shall send him home again,
In heav'n shall in my kingdom reign.
I'll make him King of Love, and then   45
Of course he must be King of men.
All pow'r with me he shall partake;
I swear it by the Stygian lake.
O, tell me where's my lovely child!
Undone! Distraction turns me wild.   50
You're silent all, and none will tell
In which retreat he chose to dwell.
Perhaps incognito he roves
Through flow'ry fields and shady groves,
By purling streams and glassy springs;   55
Has plucked the feathers from his wings,
Thrown off his quiver to disguise

Himself from our pursuing eyes.
But I shall give you every mark
To know the little vagrant spark,   60
Although he uses every art
To hide himself and wound your heart,
Unseen, by cunning to prevail—
In vain he shall himself conceal.
Though like an infant he is seen,   65
In size, in shape, in limbs, in mien,
If I should tell, you'll think it odd,
In heav'n there's not an older god.
Yet he, just like a child, will play
A thousand tricks the livelong day.   70
But every jest and trick he shows,
Create in you ten thousand woes.
Here joy and anger shift their place,
Alternate in his various face;
The cheek where dimpled smile appears,   75
Next moment see it bathed in tears.
His locks are spangled o'er with gold
As full of curls as they can hold;
And as Dame Fortune is defined
With hair before and none behind,   80
So he the very selfsame way,
His bushy forehead does display,
But look behind—you cannot spy
One single lock to catch him by.
If on his lively face you gaze,   85
'Tis brisker than a dancing blaze;
And, though his front be smooth and fair,
A wanton boldness revels there.
His sparkling eyes with fire abound
Where smiles alluring bask around,   90
Through which he slyly looks askew,
To wound the heart he has in view.
His little words he lisps so well,
No music can his tongue excel.
That sweetness, which he gives his voice,   95
Makes every ear that hears rejoice.
His cheeks adorned with dimpled smiles,
The heart, which thinks them true, beguiles.
So flow'rs that hide the serpent bring
Th' unwary swain to feel the sting.   100

At first with looks demure and meek,
To lodge within your house he'll seek;
But once he's in, he lays aside
His humble mien and swells with pride.
Nor will he from your house depart   105
Without the key that locks your heart.
And when he thus has gained his ends,
He drives away your former friends,
Makes you foresake the old and true,
To love and entertain the new.   110
Where he usurps tyrannic sway,
The vassal Reason must obey.
He rules with such resistless force,
No pow'r on earth can stop his course;
For they who dare oppose his might   115
Are either slain or vanquished quite.

   Now I have told you every sign
By which to know this child of mine.
If he concealed among you be,
I beg you'll bring him straight to me.   120
What? Silent all! Will none discover,
No swain betray the patent rover?
You hide, like fools, what ne'er was yet
Concealed by pow'r of mortal wit.
For through your eyes and tongue he'll fly,   125
And seen by every stander-by;
Though fast in pris'n, away he'll break,
And out or in your heart must ache.
Now, after this my declaration,
If any soul in all this nation   130
Shall dare to hide my fav'rite boy,
He shall not know one moment's joy.
But shall be like that senseless swain,
Who strove to hide a snake in vain;
For when it stung, he roared aloud   135
And showed his folly to the crowd.

   But hold, I shall not yet return—
On earth I will a while sojourn,
To make a stricter search advance;
Perhaps I'll find him out by chance.   140
                       (Written early 1730s?)

Pere Bouhours' Fountain Made Muddy
by the Translator

Here in surpirising chaos, doubly sweet,
Both heav'n and earth within this fountain meet;
The pleasing cheat with rapture strikes us all
In gay confusion as the figures fall.
Here on the branches fishes perched repose,   5
And on the angler's hook you see the rose;
Thus the deluding idol charms the eye,
While birds appear to swim and fishes fly.

(Written ca. January 5, 1734)

From Lucan

Why? thou great ruler of Olympus, why
Hast thou to timorous mortality
Added this care, that men should be so wise,
To know by omens, future miseries?
Free us from this unnecessary care;   5
Unlooked for send the ills thou dost prepare;
Let human minds to future things be blind,
That hope, amidst our fears, some place may find.

(Written ca. 1736)

Appendix II: Educational Verses upon Latin Grammar, Prosody, and Rhetoric

Thus Cacus-like, His Calves He Backwards Pulls

Thus Cacus-like, his calves he backwards pulls,
And shades his den by dark'ning Lily's rules;
But to regain what's lost in this dire place
Requires more wit than strength of Hercules;
With so much pains, boys prejudice receive   5
With much more labor what they can't retrieve.

(Published in 1714)

Of the Genders of Nouns

General Rule 1
Gods, angels, men, months, rivers, wind
Must ever be with "hic" declined;
Thus every common name for "He"
Must of the better gender be.

General Rule 2
Goddesses, women, cities, isles   5
All "haec" a true grammarian styles;
So Sirens, Furies, Harpies, Graces,
Because they are all female faces;
Nymphs, Muses, Fates, this gender crave;
And every common name they have,   10
As "haec virago." To these nouns
Add counties, villages and towns.

General Rule 3
Decline with "haec" most names of trees,
Because they've female properties;
By bearing fruit, and summer's pride,   15
They're nearly to the sex allied.

General Rule 4
All names of metals, pulse and fruit
Do with neuter gender suit;
But if both fruit and tree they sound,
The female "haec" still keeps its ground.   20

215

Rule the 5th
Nouns that express both kinds are common,
As "senex" an old man and woman;
But yet by epithets we find
Some are to one side more inclined.

Remarks upon Rule 5
We must observe nouns that are common   25
Sometimes for man, sometimes for woman;
But by the sense we soon may see
With what sex they can best agree.
Some words we know, by Nature bent,
To either sex indifferent.   30
Others are found again t' incline
Chiefly to be o' th' masculine.
And some by Nature too there are
That to the female must adhere.
Verbals in *a* must follow these,   35
And nouns denoting offices,
In which the male and female are
Obliged to have an equal share.

(Published in 1714)

From Of Knowing the Gender of Nouns by Termination

Declension 1
All nouns in *a* make Feminine,
If you like "Musa" them decline,
Except they're from a Graecian line,
Or by their sense are Masculine.

From Of Prosody

Of Derivatives and Compounds
Words from their root their quantity
Do borrow, so the like we see
In compound words: they still retain
Their primitive and native strain.
But let us not on this depend;   5

Some cross the strain whence they descend:
From fathers short long sons arise,
And parents tall a pigmy size.
Look in this Index; there you'll find
How diff 'rent some are from their kind.   10

(Published in 1714)

Of Quantity Which Depends upon the Authority of the Poets

Another kind of Quantity
There is, we call Authority;
In first and middle syllables,
This liberty of poets dwells;
Where we may find *A, E, I, O*   5
Short commonly, but *U's* not so:
For *U* much oft'ner long we find,
Because by nature so inclined.
All that do not with this agree,
Comprised in burlesque you shall see.   10

(Published in 1714)

Of Figures Peculiar to Prosody

Synaeresis
Concurring vowels that agree
To make two syllables, we see
By poets melted into one,
To make a verse more smoothly run.

Diaeresis or Dialysis
One syllable the poets split   5
The better to compose their feet.

Synaloepha
One word beginning, ending one
With vowel, make a simple tone.
So melting dipthongs the same way
Become as friendly quite as they.   10

Eclipsis
When "m" concludes, and vowel follows,
The vowel straight this letter swallows.

Systole
Words that were made by nature long,
The poet shortens for his song;
To let us know his pow'r the better,   15
He robs position of a letter.

Ectasis
Another time with wanton sport,
He does extend such as are short;
And what from words he robbed before
He does bestow, though not restore.   20

Prothesis and Aphaeresis
One a beginning newly makes;
T' other from words beginnings takes.

Epenthesis and Syncope
Such are these two, that black and white
In nature aren't more opposite:
The former to the middle gives;   25
The latter from the midst receives.

Paragoge and Apocope
One to a word does something add;
T' other takes off from what it had.

Tmesis
This figure makes a mighty pother;
It puts one word within another.   30

Antithesis and Metathesis
This changes letters, that transposes,
Though seldom this observed in prose is.

(Published in 1714)

Figures of Speech

Simile
A simile's the likeness of a thing
The poet does for illumination bring,
A bright reflection of a brighter mind
In which right judgment and true fancy's joined.
Thus Phoebus in a cloud, his skill to show,   5
With silver pencil paints his golden bow.

Metaphor
When words we from their genuine sense transfer
To stand for others, let us first take care
That they true likeness and proportion bear.
Hence golden phrases come, and metaphor   10
By a new stamp makes words to pass for more.

It pleases much when poets do translate
Their terms from living things t' inanimate;
Thus they give life and motion to their strains
By frowning mountains and by smiling plains.   15

From dead to living all those terms are good
In which there's found a just similitude.
Such metaphors we see give life to life;
Thunder and lightning best illustrate strife.
So from the dead we to the dead translate,   20
And add more life to things inanimate.

Allegory
Thus we refine the gold 'till by degrees
We run in metaphors whole sentences;
Hence liquid streams of allegory flow,
All of a piece and regularly slow.   25

Antonomasia
Another name to metaphor we give
When that a proper's made appellative;
Antonomasia's the word; no doubt
He was a Molo that first found it out.

Catachresis

A catachresis next is known to be   30
A metaphor of mere necessity;
Forced headlong in where other language fails,
So much our passion o'er our sense prevails.
Thus Master Witty on poor scholar dull
Calls him a leaden or a wooden skull.   35

Metonymia

A metonymia is another kind
Of metaphor by which we often find
That authors make some proper names to stand
For their invention and for their command.
Read Homer, Virgil, Horace, Lucan through;   40
In them you'll find that what I say is true:
When lovely Ceres makes her autumn smile,
With golden grain rewards the ploughman's toil,
He sits contented and his work surveys,
Forgets his labors for his present ease.   45

Synecdoche

To this synecdoche is near allied
When by a part the whole is signified;
But care must be, lest we obscure the sense,
Always to choose some part of eminence;
I've lived some autumns, yet I wonder why   50
Men make a part the whole to signify:
"Some love with rapid wheels to raise
Olympian dust, and gather praise."

Hyperbole

Hyperbole is an exceeding lie
Made to diminish things or magnify,   55
Which, by a monstrous falseness, is designed
To bring the truth the nearer to our mind.
It makes a giant wade the deepest sea,
Contracts a pigmy to a litle flea.

Ironia

An irony for raillery's designed;   60
In this the tongue runs counter to the mind;
The keenest satire can't so sharply bite,
As when we thus compare things opposite:

So when I would the vicious wretch reclaim,
I praise what he has not, his virtue, to his shame.   65
Thou pretty boy that never mind'st thy book,
'Tis hence thy Master gives the kind rebuke.

Antithesis
Antithesis agrees with this, so far
As we do qual'ties opposite compare;
In the same line a contradiction springs,   70
But 'tis in epithets and not in things.
Much I conceive, but little can express
How sweet's the turn of this poetic dress.
"Not fierce but awful in his manly page,
Bold is his strength, but sober is his rage."   75

Correction
Correction does a wondrous pleasure give,
Whether of thoughts affirmed or negative;
When poets, on condition pleasing more,
Unsay whatever they have said before.
Sweet are their melting strains when soft they sing,   80
Sweet are their numbers joined with warbling string,
But neither melting strains, nor numbers joined
To string, so much as this engage the mind.

Suspension
Suspension follows next, a grateful stay
That holds the eager mind a while at bay,   85
Reserves a pleasure which we long to know,
And does at last its latent beauty show.
As evening clouds, pleased at the sun's farewell,
With blushing joy the coming dawn foretell;
As the grey dawn smiles through the dusky gloom   90
Of summer's night, and shows that Sol's to come
To beautify the skies and bless the day—
Suspension courts us with the like delay.

Change
Judgment pursues when Fancy's on the wing,
Feign would his mistress to sedateness bring,   95
While she does all his arguments despise,
And from his magisterial precepts flies;
Not faster runs the hare before the hound;

Not faster he pursues her mazing round:
But such enchanting music's in her tongue,   100
Judgment's convinced she does good sense no wrong,
For though she backward sings her froward lays,
The diff'rent turns she gives deserve new praise.

Action
When in few lines much action is expressed
With lively thoughts, the active soul is pleased;   105
We love the bounding of a deer much more
Than crawling worm flat-moving on a floor.
Who will not startle when he hears this sound:
"Air blackens, rowls the thunder, groans the ground."

Of Figures Occasioned by Passion
Passions have language proper to declare   110
Whether the soul's inclined to peace or war,
Whether soft love sheds poison through the veins,
Aversion cools, or hope low thoughts disdains.
Or joy transports, or loads of grief depress,
Or envy wastes, or fear destroys no less—   115
All these require a diff'rent air and dress.
Nature alone instructs us best to find
The secret springs and movements of the mind.

Exclamation
First then she teaches to describe our woes,
And pressing grief by exclamation shows.   120
The tortured slaves, as well as injured chief,
In deep-fetched groans do place their best relief:
"Oh, 'tis vain to beg relief from thee,
Thou black contriver of my misery!"

Prosopopoeia
Prosopopoeia, when the breast is filled   125
With swelling grief, makes our expressions wild;
Hence we each rock, each grove and stream address
As if they could commis'rate our distress;
Love's pleasing raptures make us do no less.

Aposiopesis
But if great floods of passion higher swell,   130
We then want words our sentiments to tell.

Asyndeton
When wild surprise or anger makes us speak,
Asyndeton conjunctions does forsake.

Doubting
When we do with ourselves expostulate
For being treated at the basest rate, 135
By doubts and questions we resolve to try
How to return or bear the injury.

Interrogations
The reader best to questions does attend
When we some thing of moment recommend.
Interrogations first his mind assail; 140
Such arguments can very seldom fail.

Repetitions
If our expressions from true passions fall,
Most repetitions are emphatical.

(Published in 1714)

Of Epigram

An epigram does many things require,
A poignant wit and quick poetic fire,
Of style a natural simplicity
In which there's beauty, point and brevity.
No puns or quibbles here a place should find; 5
They're but the squibs of thoughts that please a vulgar mind.

(Published in 1714)

Appendix III: Poems of Doubtful Attribution

A Hunting Song

Hark! hark! I think I hear the horn,
  That chides my long repose;
The dew-drop twinkles on the thorn,
  The stream in music flows.

Hark! hear! I hear black Betsy snort,   5
  Impatient of the rein;
When Nature thus proclaims the sport,
  Shall man cry out, "It's vain"?

For this she lent the gentle hart
  The vivid lightning's speed;   10
She taught the hare her mazy art,
  And winged the generous steed.

Let sages then of human race,
  The slaves of musty saws,
Decry the pleasures of the chase,   15
  The fruit of Nature's laws.

The chase supplied our ancient sires
  With food and raiment too—
Till cursed Ambition fanned her fires,
  And bent the sounding yew.   20

Then Law stretched forth her artful toils,
  And Cunning laid her snares,
And Plunder gloried in her spoils
  And filled the world with cares.

But Care dare not as yet pursue   25
  The hunter's bounding hoof;
And if she even takes a view,
  The view must be aloof.

(Written ca. 1699?)

Verses on a Wooden Leg

Divines, especially your old ones,
Will gravely tell you, if they're cold ones,

227

That you may father on the devil
Each act and deed of moral evil;
His back is broad enough, we know,   5
To bear them all, like Richard Roe.
In every suit Old Nick's engaged,
Yet strange to tell, he's never caged;
For he's at large and runs about—
The devil's in, the devil's out.   10
Thus grave divines have made up pills
To cure us of all human ills:
If you have lost a horse or mare,
Then you're cut off from so much care;
If death deprives you of your wife,   15
Why, there's an end to all your strife;
Or should she crown your brow with horns,
Bear them with patience like your corns—
They've remedies for each disaster,
For every broken head a plaster.   20
For instance, now there's Ellis Clegg,
You know the man has broke his leg—
No matter how, no matter where;
It's known that Ellis loves the fair.
At first he wept and called on death,   25
But now he's glad he kept his breath;
What has he gained then by the loss?
To use the words of Jerry Cross:
"In point of saving, let us see,
The first great thing's economy: 30
He saves a stocking and a shoe,
And half a pair of boots will do.
And then, if he should chance to ride,
One spur's sufficient for a side;
And if that side should move, you'll find   35
The other will not lag behind:
It's easy proved from *Hudibras;*
Nay, you may prove it by your ass.
What next? He'll save a yard of garter,
And then the gout will catch a Tartar;   40
If it should think to seize his oak,
How Clegg will laugh and tell the joke!
We haven't done with savings yet,
In wear and tare, and even tret:
The buckle's saved that binds the knee,   45

Or tape in bow-knots three times three.
The buckle's saved that binds the shoe,
And any buckle now will do;
Provided it will hold the latchet,
There's no occasion, Sir, to match it;   50
Odd buckles sell for one-third price,
So there's a saving in a trice.
Then soap and washing's saved, you see,
Upon the wooden deputy;
Though if you judge by shoe and shirt,   55
Clegg seems to like a little dirt;
And it will serve him all his life,
To bear him up, or beat his wife.
Another thing, if he should beg,
There's nothing like a wooden leg;   60
And when he moves upon his pins,
He's not afraid of broken shins;
Besides he stands a fourth relation
To every blockhead in the nation,
And every place of public trust   65
Is filled with all these blockheads first."
Now, reader if you please we'll stop,
And moralize upon the prop.
What is a leg of flesh and bone?
If well proportioned, I must own   70
It adds new beauties to the fair,
And always marketable ware.
Like every other charm, they last
Until the honeymoon is past;
With age they shrivel and they shrink,   75
And then, alas! what must we think?
Sure it should mortify our pride,
To think the best are thrown aside.

                              (Written ca. 1699?)

The Enigma in the Last *Mercury* Explained

Your house of hair and lady's hand
At first did put me to a stand;
I have it now—'tis plain enough—
Your hairy business is a muff.
Your engine fraught with cooling gales,   5

At once so like to masts or sails;
Your thing of various shape and hue
Must be some painted toy I knew;
And for the rhyme to "you're the man,"
What fits it better than a fan?   10

(Published in May, 1707)

Paddy's Choice

Young Pat was heir to fourscore cows,
Five hundred sheep and sixty sows,
Two lordly bulls, four breeding mares,
A house with half a flight of stairs,
Well thatched and plastered round with clay,   5
Of diff 'rent colors, blue and gray,
As snug as any thrush's nest:
Proceed, dear Muse, and tell the rest.
Before you bring him on the stage,
Pray tell the reader Paddy's age: 10
"Just twenty-four"—I think you're right,
For I was told the same last night.
The gods to honest Pat were kind
In gifts of body and of mind;
For he could read, and write, and sing,   15
And touch with art the trembling string;
The foremost in the fight or chase,
And never known to lose a race;
In wrestling skilled; oh Muse divine,
Around his rival how he'd twine!   20
His legs well made, a better pair
Was never seen at any fair,
Proportioned well in every part,
And add to this a gen'rous heart.
As yet our swain ne'er thought of love;   25
Youth, like the bee, delights to rove
From flower to flower, from tree to tree:
Oh Cupid! mind thy just decree,
Prepare thy bow, evince thy power,
And wound the breast that wounds a flower.   30
Let not the wretch 'scape like the bee,
And lay the fault on destiny.
This was not Paddy's case I own;

Sometimes he thought to lie alone
Was not so pleasant as it might,   35
Provided everything went right,
That half a bed, an honest soul,
Was often better than the whole,
Provided Sally filled the other;
Why not as well as her fair mother?   40
With thoughts like these amused one night,
He sunk to rest, his sleep was light:
He dreamt, and in the pleasing trance
He thought he saw a nymph advance
With swimming mien and measured pace;   45
Her locks were bound with silver lace,
And decked with buds of every hue,
The pansy pale, the violet blue;
The lightest summer cloud her veil,
While vestments floating on the gale,   50
With trembling dew-drops sprinkled o'er;
The like was never seen before.
Pat thought at first she was the queen
Of love, or goddess of the green;
At all events resolved to wait,   55
With courage like a man, his fate.
He wasn't held in long suspense;
There's nothing like the present tense;
In love, at least, it is the best,
For time, you know, destroys the zest.   60
With honeyed words and accents mild,
Conducted by fair Venus' child:
"I'm come to offer you my hand,
Not for the sake of house or land,
For I despise your dirty pelf;   65
I love you only for yourself;
Your gen'rous worth has fired my breast;
Forgive—my eyes will tell the rest.
That fleecy coat I'll quickly change;
With cows and sheep no more you'll range;   70
Your hair with riband shall be bound,
Your hat with roses decked thrice round;
Your homespun hose shall yield to silk,
Your gloves as white as snow or milk;
Potatoes vile shall yield to truffles,   75
And wristbands plain to flowing ruffles;

Wax tapers shall flame round in brass,
And wooden cups give way to glass."
Pat heard with wonder; we'll suppose
At every gaze new charms arose;   80
He pressed her hand, but was afraid
To kiss so bright, so fair a maid.
His breast was filled with soft alarms:
She knew the magic of her charms;
And left him to reflect awhile,   85
Then softly vanished in a smile.
That he might have his choice of two,
Another just appeared in view,
That was not fit to be her maid,
In point of dress, so coarse arrayed;   90
Her coat was poplin, home-made stuff,
Her stockings blue, and somewhat rough;
But there was something in her eyes
That might command the richest prize;
But modesty forbade the trial,   95
And every look spoke self-denial.
Her modest eye, 'stead of her tongue,
Spoke thus, as by the fairies sung:
"Young Pat, I see your heart is won;
If so, poor Shela is undone: 100
Your house, that braves the rudest storm,
Must change, alas! its pleasing form;
Your locks, that wanton in the wind,
The gaudy riband now must bind;
Your kine and swine must all be sold,   105
And wooden cups exchanged for gold;
Your father's homely cheer you'll quit,
The plain roast joint and wooden spit;
Potatoes must not show their face,
And whiskey sink into disgrace.   110
But say, dear Pat, when all is past,
How long you think this game will last;
When all is spent, and friendship fled,
Will beauty serve you in its stead?
Or will the fair, whose pride is dress,   115
Remain with you in deep distress?
In such a case, what would you do?
I'd live, and love, and die with you;
At night I'd trim the little fire,

And knit your stockings on fine wire;   120
I'd stuff your pumps with softest hay,
And hang your hat out of the way;
From every bush I'd pluck the wool,
And when I'd have my apron full,
I'd spin it on my fav'rite wheel,   125
And wind it on a hand-cross reel;
In heath well dyed a purple black,
How it would shine upon your back!
And when you went at night to bed,
I'd wash your shirt, and bind your head;   130
With verdant moss I'd fill your pillow,
And wreath the window with a willow;
Green rushes on the floor I'd strew,
And thus I'd live and die with you.
If fate should bless us with a race,   135
I'd trace the father in each face."
Pat paused a while, and Shela stood
Like the pale primrose in the wood.
The youth advanced, and seized her hand,
And kissed it thrice at love's command.
He waked, and knew where Shela dwelt;
Her eyes confessed the pangs she felt:
Hymen was ready with his torch,
And led them to the sacred porch.

(Written ca. 1709?)

An Impromptu on Parting from Elizabeth MacFadden

You ask how long I'll stay from thee;
    Suppress those rising fears;
If you should reckon time like me,
    Perhaps ten thousand years.

(Written ca. 1710–11?)

Amplissimo Doctissimoque Viro Ricardo Bulstrode, Equiti Aurato &C., Propter Poemata Sacra Super ab Ipso Scripta

En etiam nostro sua sunt miracula saeclo
    posteritas quibus est vix habitura fidem.

Votivo faciles venerantur thure Camenas
  non jam nummorum numina sola sonis.
En cui lustra novem citius geminaverit aetas
  torrida quam surgat quinta per arva seges.
Virgilio dignos pangit vel Apolline versus,
  Pieriumque fluit Nectar ab ora senis.
Quam Phoebo charus primano in flore juventae!   5
  cuius adhuc tali sanguine vena calet.
Fallor: non Phoebus, pietas haec carmina fundit;
  talia non umquam ludere Apollo solet.

(Probably written ca. 1712)

[To That Most Splendid and Learned Gentleman, Sir Richard Bulstrode, on Account of the Sacred Poems Recently Written by Him

See, even our age has its miracles—miracles which future generations
  will scarcely believe.
The ready Muses we worshipped with votive incense; it is not just the
  spirit of money that you celebrate.
Here is one for whom time will have doubled nine five-year periods
  before a fifth crop grow in the sun-baked fields.
He composes verses worthy of Virgil or Apollo; and the Muses' nectar
  flows from the old man's lips.
How dear to Phoebus he was in the flower of his early youth! a man
  whose veins are still warm with such blood.
I am wrong: it was not Phoebus but devotion which poured forth these
  songs; Apollo is never accustomed to play such compositions.]

Lines Written on a Window in the Episcopal Palace at Kilmore

Thus spake great Bedel from his tomb:
"Mortal, I would not change my doom
To live in such a restless state,
To be unfortunately great,
To flatter fools and spurn at knaves,   5
To shine amidst a race of slaves,
To learn from wise men to complain,
And only rise to fall again.

No! let my dusty relics rest
Until I rise among the blest."   10
                                          (Written ca. 1717–18?)

Assist Me, My Muse, Whilst I Labor to Limn Him

Assist me, my Muse, whilst I labor to limn him.
Credite, Pisones, isti tabulae persimilem.

You look and you write with so diff'rent a grace,
That I envy your verse, though, Lord, not your face;
And to him that thinks rightly, there's reason enough,   5
'Cause one is as smooth as the other is rough.
But much I'm amazed you should think my design ⎫
Was to rhyme down your nose or your Harlequin grin, ⎬
Which you yourself wonder the de'il should malign. ⎭
And if 'tis so strange that your Monstership's crany   10
Should be envied by him, much less by Delany.
Though I own to you, when I consider it stricter,
I envy the painter although not the picture;
And greatly she's envied, since a fiend of hell
Was never drawn well, but by her and by Raphael.   15

Next as to the charge, which you tell us is true,
That we were inspired by the subject we drew:
Inspired we were, and well, Sir, you knew it,
Yet not by your nose, but the fair one that drew it.
Had your nose been the Muse, we had ne'er been inspired,   20
Though perhaps it might justly be said, we were fired.

As to the division of words in your staves,
Like my countryman's horn-comb into three halves,
I meddle not with it, but presume to make merry;
You called Dan one half, and t' other half Sherry: 25
Now if Dan's a half, as you call't o'er and o'er,
Then it can't be denied that Sherry's two more.
For pray give me leave to say, Sir, for all you,
That Sherry's at least of double the value.
But perhaps, Sir, you do it to fill up the verse, ⎫   30
So crowds in a consort (like actors in farce) ⎬
Play five parts in one, when scrapers are scarce. ⎭

But be that as it will, you'll know more anon, Sir,
When Sheridan sends to merry Dan an answer.

(Written in 1718)

Enigma

I never did eat, yet I'm still at a feast;
I'm rude, yet distinguish a man from a beast.
Close pent up in prison, by closure I'm barred
With a numerous white and sometimes black guard;
Yet freedom I love; and, like fiery gunpowder,   5
The more I'm confined, I shall break out the louder.
I never was thought very witty at best,
Yet always make one at the end of a jest.
You'd swear by my size that I've naught of ill nature,
Yet my greatest delight's for the most part in satire;   10
But no more of the matter, lest when you all know it
Too much of the Enig be bestowed on the poet.
    The Solution—Laughter

(Written possibly ca. 1720)

Directions for Laughing

Your riddle does feed though it never could eat;
Else how could poor mortals with laughing grow fat?
A horselaugh's so crude it defiles your learn'd jest,
For it changes a beau to the form of a beast.
You may laugh in the day if your teeth remain white;   5
If black, you discreetly must laugh in the night;
If loose, I advise you to get them some binders,
For a gunpowder laughter may blow out your grinders.
With the drolls, that your wit may obtain a good grace,
Be sure you tee-hee it still in the right place;   10
Most satires in frowning do chiefly delight,

But Horace's laughter has still the most spite;
But, Sir, be of comfort, though your riddle moves laughter,
'Tis a laughing of liking, not the ha-ha of satire.

(Written possibly ca. 1720)

Sheridan's Masterpiece; or, Tom Pun-Sibi's Folly Complete, *Alexander's Overthrow, or The Downfall of Babylon,* As It Was Acted At Mr. Lyddal's in Dame Street, December 11th, 1721.

Scriptis Patet Scriptor

Enter Julius Caesar and Casephalamus.

Cas.	What man are you that dares to come this way, Sir?	
Jul.	What man? An't please you, I am Julius Caesar.	
Cas.	What made you to these British isles to come?	
	Had you no victuals of your own at home?	
	Get off, I say, or else I'll take a cudge:	5
	Gaffer, I'll thrash you, that you shall not budge.	
Jul.	Stand off I say, and quit the field;	
	I fear no cudgel while I bear a shield;	
	A Roman soldier knows not how to fear.	
	Look at my sword; behold my massy spear.	10
	Should you approach this little boat, or think to trouble it,	
	By stick or stone, i' faith, I'd pink your doublet.	
Cas.	O, fight, ye Britons, fight to save your pullets;	
	Drive off these Romans with your beggar's bullets;	
	Hear what he says, the swagg'ring fool is cracked;	15
	Believe me, Sirs, what I relate is fact.	
	I'd have you know, Sir, that this land is mine,	
	And I possess it by a right divine.	
Jul.	What's that to me, if I can get your throne?	
	I'd make you know, Sir, that what's mine's my own.	20
Cas.	We're all destroyed, or I am much mistaken;	
	Oh! Fight, ye Britons, fight to save your bacon.	
	But see! The winds to our assistance blow;	
	Safe is the word, and so away ye go.	

Exeunt.

Enter Xerxes and a Messenger.

Mes.	Most high and mighty monarch of the East,	25

The cook dispatched me in the greatest haste
To tell you that your buttered ale is made,
But none will trust you for a loaf of bread.

Xerx. I, whose dominions reach from pole to pole,
Can't now be trusted for one single roll,   30
Learn hence, ye monarchs, what the Fates may do:
I've lost my battles and my breakfast too.

Exeunt.

Enter Alexander and Lysimachus.

Alex. Since Babylon must fall, what is't to me?
Lys. It is to you, for so the Fates decree.
Alex. Down then with all your tow'rs since fall they must;   35
These glittering spires must tumble into dust.
Fall on, my boy, begin the brisk attack;
Here lies the cakes, you see, and there the sack.
Lys. Be witness for me, all ye Powers Divine,
If they're not eaten, 'tis no fault of mind.   40

They scramble out.

Enter Cassander before he poisons Alexander.

Cas. The morning rises black; therefore, 'tis night;
'Tis either dark, or I am blinded quite.
Go fetch a candle, boy, go quickly go,
That I may see whether I am blind or no;
But I am apt to think this sudden gloom ⎫   45
Foretells the mighty Alexander's doom; ⎬
Or else they've shut the windows of my room. ⎭

Exit.

Enter Alexander.

Alex. Hey Day, what's this I feel, a sudden thirst?
I've drank and drank until I'm like to burst.
Call fill to me; I fear that jackadandy,   50
That made my hot-pot, poured in too much brandy.
My head turns round, my sight begins to fail,
And I am drownèd in a pot of ale.
Oh! Dismal death, I'm just upon thy brink;
I die in honor since I die in drink.   55

FINIS

(Written ca. December 11, 1721)

Verses Written on One of the Windows at Delville

A bard, grown desirous of saving his pelf,
Built a house he was sure would hold none but himself;
This enraged good Apollo, who Mercury sent,
And bid him go ask what his votary meant:
"Some foe to my empire has been his adviser;   5
'Tis of dreadful portent when a poet turns miser!
Tell him, Hermes, from me, tell that subject of mine,
I have sworn by the Styx to defeat his design;
For wherever he lives, the Muses shall reign;
And the Muses, he knows, have a numerous train."   10

(Written ca. 1722–23?)

Punch's Petition to the Ladies

—Quid non mortalia pectora cogis,
Auri sacra fames?

Fair ones! To you who hearts command
And gently sway, with fan in hand,
Your fav'rite, Punch, a suppliant falls,
And humbly for assistance calls.
He humbly calls and begs you'd stop   5
The gothic rage of Vander Hop,
Wh' invades without pretence or right,
Or any law but that of might,
Our Pigmy land—and treats our kings
Like paltry, idle, wooden things;   10
Has beat our dancers out of doors,
And called our chastest virgins whores.
He has not left our Queen a rag on,
Has forced away our George and Dragon,
Has broke our wires, nor was he civil   15
To Doctor Faustus or the Devil;
E'en me he hurried with fell rage
Most hoarsely squalling off the stage.
And faith, our fright was very great
To see a minister of state   20
Armed with power and fury come
To force us from our little home.

We feared, as I am sure we'd reason,
An accusation of high treason.

Till starting up, says Bannameer,   25
"Treason, my friends, we need not fear;
For 'gainst the Brass we used no power,
Nor strove to save the Chancellor.
Nor did we show the least affection
To Rochfort on Westmeath election,   30
Nor did we sing." —"'MacHugh,' he means;
The villain, I'll dash out his brains.
'Tis no affair of state that brings
Me here, nor business of the king's;
I'm come to seize you all as debtors,   35
And bind you fast in iron fetters,
From sight of every friend in town,
Till fifty pound to me's laid down."

"Fifty!" quoth I, "a dev'lish sum,
But stay till the new half-pence come;   40
Then we shall all be rich as Jews,
From Castle down to lowest stews;
That sum shall to you then be told,
'Though now we cannot furnish gold."

Quoth he, "Thou lovest, Punch, to prate   45
And could'st forever hold debate,
But think'st thou I have nought to do
But thus *fuer le temps* with you;
Or dost thou think that I am come
To carry naught but farthings home?   50
Thou fool, I ne'er do things by halves;
Farthings were made for Irish slaves.
No brass for me; it must be gold,
Or fifty pound in silver told,
That can by any means obtain   55
Freedom for thee and for thy train."

"Votre tres humble serviteur,
I'm not in jest," said I, "I'm sure;
But from the bottom of my belly
In sober sadness I must tell ye,   60
I think it is good reasoning

That we fictitious men should bring
Brass counters made by William Wood,
Which may as well be understood
Right sterling—as we, flesh and blood.   65
And since we are but mimic men,
Pray let us pay in mimic coin.
Add too, 'tis said that you and I
Are of the selfsame family;
And, faith, I'm apt to think so too,   70
For who is liker me than you?
Just the same grave and awkward grace
Shows forth itself in either face,
And each of us with labor struts
Behind a flasket huge with guts.   75
We tally well in these respects,
But best of all in intellects;
For, when you took the diff'rence learned
'Twixt the words 'sorry' and 'concerned,'
And when upon a grave affair   80
Amazed you gazed behind a chair,
Then cried, 'Lord, how like Punchinello
Is that same soft, beef-witted fellow!'
Then, pretty cousin, let us buss,
And cease to treat your kindred thus."   85

Quoth he, "Thou vile misshapen beast,
Thou knave, am I become thy jest?
Now not a puppet of you all
Shall stir a step without this wall,
Nor Merry Andrew beat thy drum,   90
Until you pay th' aforesaid sum."

Then marching off with solemn pace
To write dispatches for his Grace,
The Revel-Master left the room,
And us condemned to fatal doom.   95
Now, fair ones, if I e'er found grace,
Or if my jokes did ever please,
Use all your int'rest with the Sec
(They say he's at the ladies' beck);
And, though he thirsts as much for gold   100
As ever Midas did of old,
Your charms I'm sure can never fail;

Your eyes must influence, must prevail.
At your command he'll set us free;
Let us to you owe liberty.   105
Get us a licence now to play,
And as in duty bound we'll pray, &c.

(Possibly written in January 1723)

A Faithful Inventory of the Furniture Belonging to _____ Room in T.C.D. In Imitation of Dr. Swift's Manner. Written in the Year 1725

—*Quaeque ipse miserrima vidi*—VIRG.

Imprimis, there's a table blotted,
A tattered hanging all bespotted.
A bed of flocks as I may rank it,
Reduced to rug and half a blanket.
A tinder-box without a flint,   5
An oaken desk with nothing in't,
A pair of tongs bought from a broker,
A fender and a rusty poker,
A penny pot and basin—this
Designed for water, that for piss—   10
A broken-winded pair of bellows,
Two knives and forks, but neither fellows;
Item, a surplice, not unmeeting
Either for table cloth or sheeting;
There is likewise a pair of breeches,   15
But patched and fallen in the stitches,
Hung up in study very little,
Plastered with cobweb and spittle.
An airy prospect all so pleasing,
From my light window without glazing.   20
A trencher and a college bottle,
Piled up on Locke and Aristotle.
A prayer-book which he seldom handles,
A save-all and two-farthing candles.
A smutty ballad, musty libel,   25
A Burgursdicius and a Bible.
The C—— Seasons and the Senses
By Overton, to save expenses.

Item (if I'm not much mistaken),
A mouse-trap with a bit of bacon.   30
A candlestick without a snuffer,
Whereby his fingers often suffer.
Two odd old shoes I should not skip here;
Each strapless serves instead of slipper.
And chairs a couple, I forgot 'em,   35
But each of them without a bottom.
Thus I in rhyme have comprehended
His goods, and so my schedule's ended.

(Written in 1725)

The Linnet and the Jay

By a friend of Stella's

Mona, by nature formed a jay,
  Observed a little linnet
Warbling melodious on a spray,
  Like Handel on his spinnet.

Attentive, she resolved each note;   5
  And, ere the season ended,
As much improved her tuneless throat
  As nature could be mended.

Lin silent heard, but Poll, rejoiced,
  Exerts his clumsy tongue   10
To praise a jay so heav'nly voiced,
  And pity Lin outsung!

Lin smiled and sighed, "My little lays
  Are native, artless, few;
Content, I quit all higher praise   15
  To Mona and to you."

(Written mid–1720s?)

On Fabricius

That when the good man lowly bent
Cooked his own cabbage in his homely tent,

And when the Sammites sent a golden sum
To tempt him to betray his country, Rome,
The dross he scoffingly returned untold   }   5
And answered with a look serenely bold,
That Roman sprouts would boil without the Grecian gold;
Then eat his coleworts for his meal designed,
And beat the Grecian army when he dined.

(Written ca. 1725)

On Potatoes

Vos Hiberni, collocatis,
Summum bonum in potatoes.

[Strive to sate us, Irish tillers,
 With potatoes, best of fillers.]

(Written ca. 1725?)

Wonderful Man, Part the Third

Inscribed to the Right Honourable M. C.
Difficile est proprie communia dicere.   HOR.

  I sing a subject sung by no man,
A common man and yet uncommon;
For I may venture to declare,
Such common men are very rare;
A man, who rightly understood   5
Is wonderful, though not of WOOD.[1]
This point I think is very plain,
For though he's common, he is clean:
No lawyer, advocate or proctor,
And yet he's all, and is a doctor,   10
Common to landmen and to seamen,
Common to churchmen and to laymen,
The common and the sure resort
Both of the country and the court,
Common to rich and poor—nay more, he   15
Is common both to Whig and Tory;
And some will swear it to their knowledge,
To every creature in the college.

In short, as far as I can find,
He's common to all humankind: 20
Common at morning, noon and night;
Common as water, air or light.

His favors never yet were bought,
And often come, though never sought;
And, though they reach both dead and living,   25
He gives 'em, for the sake of giving:
What more a paradox may seem,
Thus cheap, he is in high esteem!

Now Reader, I perceive you'd fain
Know what this commonness can mean;   30
I'll tell you then and save your guessing—
Why, C——g——ll is a common blessing.

(Written ca. 1725–27)

---

1. In allusion to some Papers upon the Wooden Man in Essex-Street, under the title of the Wonderful Man.

The Blunder of All Blunders, on the Wonder of All Wonders

Or Gulliver Devoured by Butterflies, or the Fop's Observation on Lilliput, &c.

—Stars beyond a certain Height,
Are said to give the World no Light.
Cad. & Van.

As mercenary canting quacks
Who deal in penny almanacs,
Gazing through telescopic glasses,
Pretend to read whatever passes
Above our sphere, pray God defend us,   5
As well as Newton or Gassendus,
Although they know no more the while
Than John O'Noke or John O'Style.
So beaus and fops of small discerning,
With powdered wigs and little learning,   10

At coffee houses hold their lectures,
Making a thousand strange conjectures.
Poor Lemuel's laid upon the table,
And everyone, as he is able,
In blust'ring words and smart orations,   15
Begins to vent his observations;
While I and other poetasters,
Gaping to find out new disasters,
According to our form diurnal,
Like Don Arbuckle in his journal,   20
Stand by in heedless manner, list'ning,
As mild as strumpet at a christ'ning;
Prepared tomorrow to rehearse
Their wretched prose in wretched verse,
And make up whatsoever's wanting   25
By similes and formal canting;
For stories still, like folks in selling,
Do lose or gain something in telling.
But lest I should, by long digression,
Be guilty of an indiscretion,   30
And prove to critics troublesome,
Let me unto the purpose come;
That is, that I should give a sample
Of their opinions for example:
Some said, "It must be so and so,"   35
And others stiffly answered,"No!"
Quoth one, "These lines in such a print
At such and such a person hint;
My intimate acquaintance said it,
And I may take it on his credit;   40
For he assured me that he saw
The man that knew—," et cetera.
Another vowed to Gad 'tis antic,
Abominable and romantic,
An incoherent piece of myst'ry;   45
He never read the like in hist'ry.
Another vapored, "Without pumping,
I know his meaning by his mumping."
"Yes," quoth another, "you have hit it;
Much good may do the man that writ it;   50
But, as for me, I'd be unwilling
To be the author for a shilling;
It's founded on a crooked model."

He said, and shook his empty noddle.
Another adds, "Think what you will on't,   55
But I think neither good nor ill on't.
I would not give this dish of coffee
For all his wit and philo-sophy."
To this, but little purpose, each
As far as lungs and stuff could reach,   60
Without remorse (a hopeful gang!)
Vented his critical harangue.
Have you not seen in rainy weather
A flock of geese on flight together,
With whistling pinions clap and flutter,   65
Gaggle and make a hideous splutter?
Such, but much louder, as I take it,
Was this intolerable racket,
When these immortal politicians
Summoned their weighty suppositions;   70
And all the burden of their chat
Ended in either THIS or THAT.
Thus fops, to show their skill in letters,
Are ever railing at their betters,
Till their impertinence and noise   75
Become the jest of girls and boys;
For though you spend much time in wrapping
The sluggard-ass in gaudy trapping,
Yet in the end, and take my saying,
'Twill be discovered by its braying.   80

   Per pauca Desunt, * + * + * + * +
+ * + + + + + + + * + + + + * + * + + + + +
Yet after all we must agree
Some are so blind they will not see.

                                        (First published in 1726)

Epilogue Designed to Be Spoken by Alonzo, at the Acting of *The Revenge* by Some Schoolboys

Since none in virtue to perfection rise
But those who oft its precepts exercise,
We who dare greatly in the dawn of age
Heroic actions copy on the stage;

Think glory cheap though purchased oft with pain,   5
And pleasure when 'tis bought with guilt disdain;
Learn all the graces of a godlike mind,
In friendship gen'rous, and in love refined;
By great examples growing early wise,
When men must sure to noblest heights arise;   10
Like Romans in our country's cause appear,
And be the heroes we have acted here.
Yet to what end should we those heights attain?
The patriot acts, the scholar thinks in vain;
Here no Southamptons[1] on the Muses smile;   15
No bounteous Dorsets bless our drooping isle.
But what, alas, is harder to be born;
Her native honors are by strangers worn!
Then, sure Hibernia's sons may justly fear,
Science will soon be out of fashion here;   20
Who for life's stage would study liberal arts,
When British actors play the nobler parts?

(First published ca. 1726)

1, The Earl of Southampton gave Shakespeare a thousand Pound for the Dedication of *Venus and Adonis* to him.

A Riddle by T-m Pun——I, Addressed to D——h

There's a thing in the East, that inhabits the South,
Which swallows the ocean, without throat or a mouth.
It's made up of opium, with lungs from the moon,
And never can speak, without aid of a spoon.
The doctors are drunk when they think to define   5
The properties various twixt me and the vine.
Howsoever this ease to their stomachs I give;
I die to relieve them; they die whilst I live.
You know all the secrets that are hid in the town,
And legerdemain will show for a crown;   10
Why then two shillings more, I'll give you my leech
If this you unriddle in writing or speech.

(Published ca. 1726)

On Paddy's Character of "The Intelligencer"

As a thorn-bush or oaken bough
Stuck in an Irish cabin's brow,

Above the door, at country fair,
Betokens entertainment there,
So bays on poets' brows have been   5
Set for a sign of wit within.
And as ill neighbors in the night
Pull down an ale house bush for spite,
The laurel so, by poets worn,
Is by the teeth of Envy torn—   10
Envy, a canker-worm which tears
Those sacred leaves that lightning spares.
And now t' exemplify this moral,
Tom having earned a twig of laurel
(Which measured on his head was found   15
Not long enough to reach half round,
But like a girl's cockade was tied
A trophy on his temple side),
Paddy repined to see him wear
This badge of honor in his hair,   20
And thinking this cockade of wit
Would his own temples better fit,
Forming his Muse by S——'s model,
Let's drive at Tom's devoted noddle,
Pelts him by turns with verse and prose,   25
Hums like a hornet at his nose;
At length presumes to vent his satire on
The Dean, Tom's honored friend and patron.
The eagle in the tale, ye know,
Teased by the buzzing wasp below,   30
Took wing to Jove and hoped to rest
Securely in the Thunderer's breast;
In vain; even there to spoil his nod
The spiteful insect stung the god.

(Written in 1728–29)

Dean Smedley Gone to Seek His Fortune

Per varios casus, per tot discrimina rerum. Virgil, *Aeneid*, I, 204.

The very reverend Dean Smedley,
Of dullness, pride, conceit, a medley,
Was equally allowed to shine
As poet, scholar and divine.
With godliness could well dispense,   5

Would be a rake, but wanted sense.
Would strictly after truth inquire
Because he dreaded to come nigher.
For liberty no champion bolder,
He hated bailiffs at his shoulder.   10
To half the world a standing jest,
A perfect nuisance to the rest.
From many (and we may believe him)
Had the best wishes they could give him.
To all mankind a constant friend,   15
Provided they had cash to lend.
One thing he did before he went hence,
He left us a laconic sentence,
By cutting of his phrase and trimming,
To prove that bishops were old women.   20
Poor Envy durst not show her phiz,
She was so terrified at his.
He waded without any shame,
Through thick and thin, to get a name.
Tried every sharping trick for bread,   25
And after all he seldom sped.
When fortune favored, he was nice;
He never once would cog the dice;
But if she turned against his play,
He knew to stop *à quatre trois*.   30
Now sound in mind and sound in corpus
(Says he), though swelled like any porpoise,
He hies from hence at forty-four
(But by his leave he sinks a score),
To the East Indies, there to cheat,   35
Till he can purchase an estate;
Where after he has filled his chest,
He'll mount his tub and preach his best,
And plainly prove by dint of text
This world is his, and theirs the next.   40

    Lest that the reader should not know
The bank where last he set his toe,
'Twas Greenwich. There he took a ship,
And gave his creditors the slip.
But lest chronology should vary,   45
Upon the ides of February,
In seventeen hundred eight and twenty,

To Fort St. George a pedlar went he.
Ye Fates, when all he gets is spent,
Return him beggar as he went.   50

(First published on May 7, 1729)

An Answer to the Christmas-Box

In Defence of Doctor D———n-y, by R———t B———r

Si, Perguma dextra
Defendi possent, etiam hoc defensa fuissent.   En: 2

Ye damnable dunces, ye criblers, what mean ye,
To fall with your dogg'rel on Doctor D———n-y?
Such poor silly critics as you may go whistle;
You ne'er can run down his familiar Epistle,
That brilliant Epistle which glitters and shines   5
In music, in numbers, in diction, in lines,
In substance, in spirit, in force and in wit,
In compliments such as Augustus might fit;
Though what he has said of his patron is faint—
Nor wonder, since no man his virtues can paint,   10
For no poet ever attempts to express
A man truly great but he must make him less.
Besides he divided; he gave the one half
Of all the encomiums to himself and Sir Ralph.
O! Wonderful prowess of genius, when he   15
With so little trouble could compliment three!
His Lord and the Speaker shall live in his poem;
Six thousand years after all readers shall know 'em,
While Pindar and Horace and Virgil forgotten
Shall be, like their heroes, sunk, buried and rotten;   20
For all other authors his writings shall banish;
Like ghosts at the sight of the daylight they'll vanish.
His glorious Epistle so shining and high
Shall be like his Phoebus, that lord of the sky,
Who, when on his chrysolite throne he appears,   25
A star dare not peep in the sky for its ears.
Now a word, by the by, for I think it my duty,
Since you're so mistaken, to point out each beauty.
Observe with what judgment he shows this, our isle;
A patron so artful our cares can beguile.   30

How that very peevish, cross grumbler, the Dean,
Does nothing at Court but of courtiers complain;
Such impudence 'tis, in a man of his station,
To put in one word for the good of the nation,
That he with submission sits silently list'ning,   35
Like a clerk when the parson holds forth at a christ'ning.
But ventures at last, like a man of true spirit,
To cry out, "My Lord, you must know I have merit
Much more than a thousand, and is it not hard
That virtue so wondrous should have no reward   40
But a pitiful pittance, five hundred a year,
At a time that our very potatoes are dear?
My Lord, what I tell you is true to a tittle,
Or may I be banished from licking your spittle."
"Why then," quoth my Lord, "since you give me this trouble,   45
I tell you, in short, you are every way double—
As poet, as doctor, as rector, as vicar,
As dealer, as builder, as planter, as quicker,
But if you've a mind to be triple, rely on
My word, and I'll make you a second Geryon."   50
Ye critic malicious, now read what he says
In those matchless verses on Fermanagh ways,
Where all the rough pebbles are polished so fine,
Like em'ralds they sparkle, like diamonds they shine.
Whoever hereafter that fell on these stones   55
Shall think it an honor to break half his bones.
Now see the finesse of a true politician:
He'd change for the worse, and he'd thrash like a Priscian;
From thumping the cushion to make those that nod,
Instead of a sermon he'd brandish a rod.   60
But Charley (though Charley) is not such a tool,
To change for more trouble a sinecure school.
Four hundred per annum, not one shilling under,
To preach in two churches twelve long miles asunder,
And wade it a-horseback in dirt to the knee,   65
When Paddy can better wade through it than he.
Observe his address; with what artful submssion,
He tells his rich patron his grievous condition:
Quite ruined and bankrupt, reduced to a farthing,
By making too much of a very small garden.   70
By squand'ring his money in dribs to the poor,
He's ready to leave the key under the door;
And grieves that his patron has so much to give,

While he (more's the pity) is shifting to live.
Again he solicits in manner most nice,   75
By another more subtle and cunning device:
Because he has heard that his patron's well read,
He lays by his belly and begs for his head;
For writing three riddles had cost him such pains,
That he scarce had remaining three scruples of brains.   80
For want of some money, he's quite off the hooks
To pay off old scores and to buy him new books,
To rebuild a house that he pulled down already,
And to buy a fine ribband to give a fine lady.
These are but a few that I chose from the rest,   85
Though not one thought in it but can stand the test.
Nay more, I will venture to swear it surpasses
All poems that ever were hatched at Parnassus.
Ev'n Horace to Caesar, to this is but barely
A thing called a poem; and Swift to his Harley,
That poem so valued, so often read over,
While Pat's is a reading may sleep in its cover.

(Published in 1729)

A Letter of Advice to the Reverend Dr. D-la-y, Humbly Proposed to the Consideration of a Certain Great Lord

What, doctor, if great Carteret condescends
To chat with Swift and you as private friends,
Must you so silly be to tell the town,
And boast of freedoms he may blush to own?
Is this the modest dutiful behavior   5
You show your patron for so great a favor?
Think you these honors to your merit due?
What equal honors can reflect from you?
You may perhaps propose immortal fame,
Under the shelter of your patron's name;   10
If you presume too far, you miss that end,
For the like course lost Swift his Gaulstown friend,
And may in time disturb your patron too,
To see the simple choice he's made of you.
But is my lord still short of his intent?   15
Or is your merit of that vast extent,

That nothing less than thousands can content?
There was a time when Paddy, out of hope,
Thought a West Indian jaunt his utmost scope.
The world's well mended since with Patrick; now   20
Nothing but vistas and canals will do.
But pray, great sir, what friend of common sense
Would labor to promote such vain expense?
And must your brethren all in hamlets dwell
T' adorn your busts, and young St. Patrick's cell?   25
Why may not some of 'em, for aught you know,
Have a desire to build and to bestow?
Retrench then, and be modest if you can, sir,
Or raise objections stronger than your answer.
Think, doctor, after double vicar, double rector,   30
A dignity in Christ Church lecture—
And something else, which you have still forgot,
A college place. Won't all this boil the pot?
Then judge how very awkwardly it looks—
"You have not yet enough to buy your books."   35
Good Patrick, take advice, and first read o'er
The books you have before you call for more;
Resign some of those cures you labor hard in;
If you must spend whole summers in your garden,
Attend some one at least, and quit Glasnevin,   40
Which will destroy your credit, if you live in;
Let Barber, though polite, at counter wait;
No longer be caressed in pomp and state:
Quickly do this, or you may some provoke
To say you mean to fleece, not feed, the flock.   45

(First printed early 1729/30)

From An Ode

To be Performed at the Castle of Dublin, On the 1st. of March, 1729/
30. Being the Birthday of Her most Serene Majesty Queen Caroline:
By the Special Command of His Excellency, John Lord Carteret.

DA CAPO.

Rec: See! the sacred scion springs,
           See the glad promise of a line of kings.

Aria: Royal youth, what bard divine   25
            Equal to a praise like thine,
            Shall in some exalted measure
            Sing thee Britain's dearest treasure;
            Who her joy in thee shall tell;
            Who a sprightly note shall swell?   30

DA CAPO.

Aria: Ye golden lights who shine on high,
            Ye potent planets who ascend the sky,
            On this happy day dispense
            All your kindest influence;
            Heav'nly Pow'rs be all prepared   35
            For George and Caroline's guard.
            Britannia's Angel, be thou near;   }
            The growing race is now thy care:
            Oh! spread thy wings above the fair.

DA CAPO.

Rec: Hence then with every anxious care;   40
            Begone, pale Envy, and thou cold Despair;
            But thou, Hope with smiling cheer,
            Do thou bring the ready year.

Aria: Flora sweet, her bounty spreads,
            Smelling gardens, painted meads;   45
            Ceres crowns the yellow plain;
            Pan rewards the shepherd's pain.
            All is plenty, all is wealth,
            And on the balmy air sits rosy-coloured health.

DA CAPO.

Chorus: Father of thy country, hail!   50
            Always everywhere prevail;
            Pious, valiant, just and wise,   }
            Better suns for thee arise;
            Purer breezes fan the skies.

Earth in fruits and flow'rs is dressed;   }   55
Joy abounds in every breast;
For thee thy people all, for thee the year is blessed. }

(First performed on March 1, 1729/30)

A Fable of the Lion and Other Beasts

One time a mighty plague did pester
All beasts domestic and sylvester.
The doctors all in consort joined
To see if they the cause could find,
And tried a world of remedies,   5
But none could conquer the disease.
The lion in this consternation
Sends out his royal proclamation,
To all his loving subjects greeting,
Appointing them a solemn meeting;   10
And when they're gathered round his den,
He spake: "My lords and gentlemen,
I hope you're met full of the sense
Of this devouring pestilence;
For sure such heavy punishment   15
On common crimes is rarely sent.
It must be some important cause,
Some great infraction of the laws.
Then let us search our consciences,
And every one his faults confess: 20
Let's judge from biggest to the least,
That he that is the foulest beast
May for a sacrifice be given
To stop the wrath of angry heaven.
And since no one is free from sin,   25
I with myself will first begin.

"I have done many a thing that's ill
From a propensity to kill,
Slain many an ox, and, what is worse,
Have murdered many a gallant horse,   30
Robbed woods and fens and, like a glutton,
Devoured whole flocks of lamb and mutton;
Nay, sometimes, for I dare not lie,
The shepherd went for company."

He had gone on, but Chancellor Fox   35
Stands up: "What signifies an ox?
What signifies a horse? Such things
Are honored when made sport for kings.
Then for the sheep, those foolish cattle,
Not fit for courage or for battle,   40
And being tolerable meat,
They're good for nothing but to eat.
The shepherd too, your enemy,
Deserves no better destiny.
Sir, Sir, your conscience is too nice;   45
Hunting's a princely exercise;
And those, being all your subjects born,
Just when you please are to be torn.
And, Sir, if this will not content ye,
We'll vote it *Nemine contradicente.*"   50

Thus after him they all confess
They had been rogues, some more, some less;
And yet by little slight excuses
They all get clear of great abuses:
The bear, the tiger, beasts of fight,   55
And all that could but scratch and bite;
Nay, ev'n the cat of wicked nature,
That kills in sport her fellow creature,
Went scot-free; but his gravity,
An ass of stupid memory,   60
Confessed, as he went to a fair,
His back half broke with wooden ware,
Chancing unluckily to pass
By a churchyard full of good grass,
Finding they'd open left the gate,   65
He ventured in, stooped down and eat.

"Hold," says Judge Wolf, "these are the crimes
Have brought upon us these sad times;
'Twas sacrilege, and this vile ass
Shall die for eating holy grass."

(First printed November 7, 1730)

A Trip to Temple-Oge, Stephen's Green and the Bason: Or, An Election of Dublin Beauties

Since bailiffs and mayors, to evade all objection,
By bribing old women obtain an election;
Since poets and cobblers their talents exert
And strive by translating for the term of expert;
Nay, even the Clergy (forgive the expression)   5
By merit or int'rest obtain a fair session.

Though frolicsome beaus who ensnare the whole city,
By Nature made fools, would conceit they're damned witty,
Yet the pride of the fair in abundance surpasses
Mayors, bailiffs and cobblers, wits, prelates and asses;   10
And scarce a spruce cook-maid puts on a silk gown,
But thinks she outshines all the nymphs of the town.

Some amorous prigs, who considered the cause,
Resolved to prevent such cabals by fixed laws;
So pitched on a judge, who well learned in grimace,   15
Could explain a defect in mind, body or face,
And published advice to the fair lovely creatures
To repair to the Green for a judgment of features.

When soft blooming May, in her luster displayed,
Had woven the trees to a cool verdant shade,   20
Judge Apollo advanced to the court of his duty,
To elect for the town a top mistress of beauty,
Where nymphs who were zealous for fame and renown
Sought to captivate fools or to purchase the crown.

A gay buxom widow, long stripped of her shame,   25
First sailed to Apollo and whispered her name,
When the young powdered god, with a formal protest,
Declared on his soul she deserved it the best;
But a fop standing by let the auditors know
Though bright Sol's in face, she's damned fusty below.   30

The widow thus passed, two sisters appeared
Whom the beaus like divinities worshipped and feared;
Apollo himself stood aghast in surprise
To behold the fierce glances that shot from their eyes;

Yet declared them both fools to expect such a station   35
Since C——t had gave them the applause of the nation.

    The nymphs, who imagined so great a man's word
Could have raised a poor peasant as great as a lord,
Wheeled round in a huff and declared 'twas odd,
That so much ill manners should dwell in a god;   40
But Apollo to tickle the audience with sport
Swore a statesman's good word should pass only at court.

    A young miss being next, at the front of the press,
In blushes and sighs, seemed to make her address;
Whilst a beau standing by proclaimed with a sneer,   45
"God's curse, it's hers, for her sire was a peer."
But the damned toupee judge swore by God she had no right,
For the assembly complained of her shortness of sight.

    Miss B——ly advanced, with the pretty Miss C——s,
The pride of each play and delight of the boxes;   50
Young T——h and M——C——l beseeched the divine
That the former beneath his bright garland might shine.
Apollo made answer, 'twixt smiling and passion,
"Her bubbies are white, but too small for the fashion."

    The others observing their friend so abused   55
Sheered off in a huff and were highly excused;
Whilst Monikee Gaul, midst a laughter rushed in
And cheered up the god with a smack o' the chin;
Who bid her stand off and go practise her tricks
Of attending the playhouse and groping for——.   60

    A Capel Street beauty exalting her charms,
To encompass the crown extended her arms,
When a gaudy young beau strove to tarnish her fame
And swore her fine clothes had procured an ill name;
But Mon. much more apt at a scurvy lampoon,   65
Cried, "G-d D——n, her face looks as broad as the moon."

    After fifty young belles were despised by the god,
And sighing shrunk back at the frown of a nod,
The Quality pressed with the multitude's weight
Thought fit to draw off from a trampling fate,   70
Whilst a torrent of girls, of each calling and size
Thronged in on the fop, demanding the prize.

There chamber and kitchen-maids flocked in a cluster,
Who jostling for room, made a damnable bluster;
Whilst the citizen boys fought to bring in their doxies,   75
The beaus made a bustle at sight of their proxies;
And Apollo, to quiet the clamorous squabble,
Cursed, damned, drew and swore he'd destroy the whole rabble.

The storm being appeased, Miss H——s walking forth
Began to recount a long tale of her worth;   80
And Apollo declared by the wonderful Nelly
She should reign, were it not for her damned cockit-belly.
The dame sigh and answered, "Sir, what you think fit."
"Pshaw! curse her," says Mon. "She sets up for a wit."

Jenny Griffith spoke next, with pipe like a lark,   85
Who swore she surpassed all the nymphs of the park,
Protesting no knave who maintained her by trade,
When in bed should her slumbering moments invade;
Which heroic lecture would doubtless prevail,
But Mon. cried, "G-d Damn her, her father sells ale."   90

The objection on all sides was granted for just,
"For though," says Apollo, "the best are but dust,
Yet were honors like these to encompass her lot,
Love-trials may change at the word of a sot."
Then the crowd, who applauded a speech so polite,   95
Hissed poor Madam Fill-Pot quite out of his sight.

A painter and seamstress next fronted the crowd,
But the audience conjectured each minx was too proud;
She also declared by their languishing parts,
None less than esquires should vanquish their hearts;   100
But the prig told 'em both, were the charms the defence,
Each ought to have pleaded a dozen years since.

Miss W——l, Miss D——l, and Miss P——er,
In hopes of the wreath, flocked in all together;
Apollo confessed, that of all he had seen,   105
The first was best formed for a goddess or queen;
And fixing the garland, was raptured to find
A queen for the city shaped just to his mind.

Then echoing shouts swelled through the whole gang,
Whilst Apollo proclaimed, with a solemn harangue: 110
The Belle of Hibernia, to regulate all
That under the judgment of beauty can fall;
Demanding henceforward no swain shall dare pray ⎫
To Venus for aid, from those presents of May, ⎬
Whilst their queen keeps the charms of Et Cetera. ⎭   115

(First published 1730)

On the Revd. Dr. Swift, D.S.P.D. Leaving His Fortune to Build an Hospital for Idiots and Lunatics

The Dean must die?—Our idiots to maintain!
Perish ye idiots!—and long live the Dean!

(First published January 1734)

On the Same

Lo! Swift to idiots bequeaths his store:
Be wise, ye rich—consider thus the poor.

(First published January 1734)

To the Editor of *The Dublin Journal*

Poor, honest George, Swift's works to print:
Thy fortune's made, or nothing's in't.
Subscribers, a vast number, show
There is no want of money now.
The Dean's so great a man of taste,   5
I'll covet to read him in haste,
More from thy press, than any other:
Let what will happen to Fairbrother.

(First published ca. February 1, 1734)

Peg Ratcliff the Hostess's Invitation to Dean Swift

Written with a design to be spoken by her on his arrival at Glasnevin,
  Doctor Delany having Complimented him with a House there.

Though the name of this place may make you to frown,
Your Deanship is welcome to Glass ne vin town;
A glass and no wine, to a man of your taste,
Alas! is enough to break it in haste.
Be that as it will, your presence can't fail   5
To yield great delight in drinking our ale;
Would you but vouchsafe a mug to partake,
And, as we can brew, believe we can bake.
The life and the pleasure we now from you hope,
The famed Violante can't show on the rope;   10
[Your genius and talen]ts outdo even Pope.
[Then while, Sir, you live] at Glasnevin and find
The benefit wished you by friends who are kind,
One night in the week your favor bestow
To drink with Delany and others you know: 15
They constantly meet at Peg Ratcliff 's together,
Talk over the news of the town and the weather,
Reflect on mishaps in church and in state,
Digest many things as well as good meat,
And club each alike, that no one may treat.   20
This, if you will grant, without coach or a chair,
You may in a trice cross the way and be there;
For Peg is your neighbor, as well as Delany,
[An] housewifely woman, full pleasing to many.

(Published June, 1735)

While Fame Is Young, Too Weak to Fly Away

While fame is young, too weak to fly away,
Envy pursues her, like some bird of prey.
But once on wing then all the dangers cease;
Envy herself is glad to be at peace,
Gives over, wearied with so high a flight,   5
Above her reach and scarce within her sight.
But such the frailty is of human kind,

Men toil for fame, which no man lives to find.
Long rip'ning underground, this china lies;
Fame bears no fruit, till the vain planter dies.

(Written ca. 1736?)

Now in This Thankless World the Givers

Now in this thankless world the givers
Are envied ev'n by the receivers;
'Tis now the cheap and frugal fashion,
Rather to hide than pay the obligation.
Nay, 'tis much worse than so;   5
It now an artifice does grow,
Wrongs and outrages to do,
Lest men should think we owe.

(Written ca. 1736?)

How Are They Bandied Up and Down by Fate

How are they bandied up and down by fate,
By so much more unhappy as they're great:
Greatness, thou gaudy torment of our souls,
The wise man's fetters, and the range of fools.

(Written ca. 1736?)

Love, the Most Gen'rous Passion of the Mind

Love, the most gen'rous passion of the mind,
The softest refuge innocence can find,
The safe director of unguided youth,
Fraught with kind wishes, and secured by truth,
That cordial drop heav'n in our cup hath thrown   5
To make the nauseous draught of life go down;

On which one only blessing God might raise
In lands of atheists subsidies of praise;
For none did e'er so dull and stupid prove,
But felt a God, and blessed his pow'r in love.

(Written ca. 1736?)

He That Imposes an Oath

He that imposes an oath, makes it—
Not he that for convenience takes it;
Then how can any man be said
To break an oath he never made?

(Written ca. 1736?)

Notes

Abbreviations

Ball	*Swift's Verse* (London, 1929).
BL	British Library, London.
Brewer	E. Cobham Brewer, *The Dictionary of Phrase and Fable* (Leicester, 1990).
Cambridge	Trinity College Library, Cambridge.
Concanen	*Miscellaneous Poems, Original and Translated, By Several Hands . . .* (London, 1724).
DNB	*Dictionary of National Biography.*
Fairbrother	*Miscellanies in Prose and Verse.* Vol. IV. (Dublin, 1735).
Folger	The Folger Shakespeare Library, Washington, D.C.
Forster	Forster Collection, Victoria and Albert Museum, London.
Foxon	D. F. Foxon, *English Verse, 1701–50* (Cambridge, 1975).
Gilbert	Gilbert Collection, Dublin Central Library.
Huntington	Henry E. Huntington Library, San Marino, California.
JIL	*The Journal of Irish Literature.*
Newberry	The Newberry Library, Chicago, Illinois.
Nichols	*A Supplement to Dr. Swift's Work . . . Vol. XXIV of the Works* (London, 1776).
NLI	National Library of Ireland.
OED	*Oxford English Dictionary.*
Penn	University of Pennsylvania Library, Philadelphia.
Rogers	Pat Rogers, ed., *Jonathan Swift, the Complete Poems* (Harmondsworth, Middlesex, 1983).
Rothschild	Collection of Lord Rothschild, Library of Trinity College, Cambridge.
TCD	Library of Trinity College, Dublin.
Whartoniana	*Whartoniana: Or Miscellanies, In Verse and Prose. . . .* Two volumes (1727).
Williams	Harold Williams, ed., *Collected Poems of Jonathan Swift*, 3 vols., 2d ed. (London, 1958).

265

WM   *The Whimsical Medley,* Vol. III. Library of Trinity Col-
                        lege, Dublin.

In Pity First to Human Kind (MacFadden?)

The previous appearance of this poem was in Wilson's *The Polyanthea,*
Vol. I (pp. 27–28). One might gather from the remarks of Con. Sheridan
quoted therein that Elizabeth MacFadden wrote these lines sometime
during her courtship:

> I believe I was the first he [Sheridan] consulted on the subject of his marriage
> with that lady; for he was afraid to mention it to his father; who, no doubt, like
> all fathers, thought himself a better judge of an affair of so important a nature
> than his son himself. Be that as it may, it was not the business of a day; many
> letters passed between the youth and the maid; they were written in a strain
> of unaffected simplicity; many of them were shewn to me after their marriage,
> but I did not think it would have been delicate to have asked a copy of any of
> them; I only recollect some lines that Miss Mac Faden wrote, which I can
> repeat, for I was in those days as fond of reading poetry as others were of
> writing it; particularly if it flowed from a female pen. Stay, let me recollect;
> now I remember them: I forget the occasion on which they were written.

During her courtship, Elizabeth may possibly have written such a poem
about love in order to impress her literary swain. After marriage, it seems
certain that she took very little interest either in books or in her husband's
literary friends. A strong reason for distrusting the reported remarks of
Con. Sheridan is that his description of both Elizabeth and of her relations
with Sheridan tallies with few others; see the Note to "An Impromptu
on Parting from Elizabeth MacFadden."

15 *now-fall'n.* One wonders if this is not a misprint for "new-fall'n."
24 *petit-maître.* Dandy, coxcomb.

Upon Mr. Sheridan's Turning Author, 1716 (Anon.)

The manuscript of this previously unpublished piece is in the library
of Trinity College, Dublin. Whatever it was that Sheridan published in
1716 has not come to light.

To Dean Swift

This printing is based on the first appearance of the poem which is in
WM (p. 345), where it is attributed to Sheridan. Its first appearance in

print is probably a broadside of possibly 1727 (TCD), in which it is titled "Answer'd by Mr. S——g," and in which it is coupled with a poem by Swift there called "A Riddle by Doctor R——se." It has often been printed in Swift collections, such as Fairbrother, *Miscellanies,* Vol. IV (1735, pp. 193–194); Faulkner, *Works,* Vol. VI (1738, pp. 192–94); Sheridan, *Works,* Vol. VII (1784, pp. 159–60); *Miscellaneous Pieces, in Prose and Verse* (1789, pp. 206–07); in Scott, Browning, Horrell, Williams (pp. 971–72), *JIL,* Vol. XVI, No. 1 (p. 33), and elsewhere. The title given in *WM* is "Tho: Sheridan to Dean Swift," and in Faulkner is "The Reverend Dr. SH——N to J. S. D. D. S. P. D."

Swift's answer, which is called by Faulkner "D——n S——'s answer to the Reverend Doctor SH——n," denies that a woman is either a sieve or a riddle, and proposes another problem:

> Now tell me a thing that wants interpretation,
> What name for a maid, was the first man's damnation?

Sheridan answers Swift's riddle in his next poem, "To the Dean."

Fairbrother dates Swift's reply as 1712, which is several years before Swift and Sheridan became acquainted, and *Miscellaneous Pieces* dates it as 1719. However, the dating in *WM* reads "From my hackney-coach, Sept. 11, 1718, past 12 at noon." This date is convincingly accepted by Williams, and so Sheridan's poem must have been written either on the day before or earlier on the same day.

A solution to Sheridan's riddle in line 2 occurs probably in line 6: "All women, as Eve [or "a sieve"] are mysteries."

1   *cruxes.* Tormenting and perplexing puzzles.

2   The broadside has "Pray tell me, Why is a Woman a *Sieve* and a *Riddle?*"

8   *Belphegor.* Machiavelli has a *Novella di Belfagar arcidiavolo* about the devil who takes refuge in Hell to avoid a scold. The tale was later reworked by Jean de la Fontaine in one of his Contes where an archdemon undertakes an earthly marriage but flees back to Hell to escape it. Arthur Wilson also has an English tragicomedy of 1691 called *Belphegor, or the Marriage of the Devil.* Sheridan apparently simply means "make every woman a devil."

9   *Commend.* The broadside and Fairbrother have "come-mend," which points up the pun of to praise and to come and fix. 1784 and 1789 have "commend."

14   *"Not I, by my troth, sir."* Faulkner prints these words in italics to indicate a direct quotation, and adds the footnote "The Dean's Answer."

15 Not indented by Faulkner.
16 *in.* Faulkner has "through."
19 Indented by Faulkner.

To the Dean

This printing is based on Sheridan's holograph (NLI, Ms. 1494). There it is titled "No. 5—To the Dean." "No. 5" would suggest that this was the fifth poem Sheridan sent to Swift as a result of their pact to write each other a poem a day for a year.

The poem was copied into *WM* (pp. 346–47), and attributed to Sheridan. The first printing that I have seen is an undated Dublin broadside. The poem was reprinted in *Miscellaneous Pieces* (1789, p. 208); in Scott, Williams (pp. 973–74), *JIL,* Vol. XVI, No. 1 (pp. 33–34), and elsewhere.

1 *WM* adds as the first word, "Sir."
2 *on. WM* has "on." The NLI holograph looks like "on," but the "o" is dotted, as is "in" later in the line.
4 *from.* "So" is crossed out in Sheridan's manuscript and replaced by "from." *WM* has "so." 1789 has "from."
6 *We'd see. WM* has "We should see," which does not fit the basic metrical pattern of an iamb followed by three anapests. 1789 has "We'd see."
7 *WM* and 1789 do not indent this line.
10 *do you.* 1789 unmetrically has "d' you."
12 *Is't that you. WM* has "Is that your."
14 *to. WM* and 1789 have "you."
16 *I mistook it. WM* has "I gramercy." 1789 has "you."
17 *of.* 1789 has "'o."
23 *A damsel—Adam's Hell. WM* has "Adam's Hell, a Damsel."
24 *have I. WM* has "I have."
Postscript: Ringsend car. Peter Somerville-Large notes in *Dublin* (London: Hamish Hamilton, 1979) that the passage from Dublin Bay into the Liffey was difficult because of a sandbank lying across the mouth of the river. This problem was solved by dredging a channel and by building the North and South Walls to contain the river. By 1728, both the North and South Wall had been extended to the village of Ringsend. But until then "The majority of passengers disembarked at Ringsend. From there they were taken in a rickety vehicle known as a Ringsend Car across the sands towards Townsend Street [in Dublin]" (pp. 135–36, 177). Why Sheridan should have been traveling in a Ringsend Car is unknown.

Repetition Day. A term not in *OED*. However, Andrew Carpenter, noting that Dr. Johnson's Dictionary defines "repetition" as "Recital from memory, as distinct from reading," suggested to the present editor that the term might possibly refer to a day given over to testing the students in Sheridan's school. This seems a plausible surmise, as one of the definitions of "repetition" in *OED* is "The action of reciting in a formal manner, *esp.* recitation of something learned by heart; a piece set to be learned and recited." A seventeenth-century example is given of the word used in this sense: "There must daily repetitions and examinations." And also a nineteenth-century example: "Seeing that his boys learn their repetitions and get up in time for morning school."

The Postscript is not in *WM*.

To the Same

This piece, unlike its companion, immediately preceding, does not appear in *WM*. Probably its first appearance, upon which this printing is based, was in *Miscellaneous Pieces* (1789, p. 209). It is reprinted by Scott, Williams (p. 975), *JIL,* Vol. XVI, no. 1 (p. 34), and others. The dating, obviously by Sheridan, was printed in 1789 at the beginning of the verse letter.

To the Dean of St. Patrick's

This poem is a response to one by Swift, called in *WM* "The Dean of St. Patrick's to Tho: Sheridan" (Williams, pp. 975–77), which was written at the same time on the same day, noon on September 12, 1718, as Sheridan's amiable piece "To the Same." However, Swift's poem is a reply to Sheridan's more irascible one written earlier on that same day ("Don't think these few lines which I send a reproach"). Swift's poem refutes Sheridan's first poem on the matter of the sieve and the riddle, and remarks:

> But keep a good tongue, or you'll find to your smart,
> From rhyming in cars, you may swing in a cart.

And concludes:

And thus I am fully revenged for your late tricks,
Which is all at present from the

                             Dean of St. Patrick's

Sheridan's poem picks up certain of Swift's arguments such as Sheridan's poems being delivered to the cathedral and interrupting the Dean at his prayers, and it also picks up Swift's occasional phrase, such as "O tempora, O mores!"

However, Sheridan's poem is also a response to Swift's poem of September 15, which begins "Sir, When I saw you today, as I went with Lord Anglesey," which Williams (pp. 978–80) mistakenly prints after Sheridan's. From this Swift poem also, Sheridan repeats certain words, such as "Melpomene" and "Billingsgate," and he refutes certain arguments and even rephrases some of Swift's lines. Compare particularly Sheridan's lines 24 and 25 to Swift's lines 21 and 22:

Your ink is your poison, your pen is what not:
Your ink is your drink, your pen is your pot.

This printing of Sheridan's poem is based on the transcription in *WM* (p. 349). It was first printed in Barrett (1808, pp. 150–151), and then in Scott, Roscoe, Browning, Horrell, Williams (pp. 977–978), and in *JIL*, Vol. XVI, No. 1 (p. 35). *WM* differs slightly from the printed versions: in line 12 it includes "more" before "Helicon," and the inclusion helps the meter; in line 23 it uses the word "bluster" where some later editors, although not Williams, have used "blunder."

3   *tempora et mores.* Times and customs.
8   *rebus.* A pictorial representation of a word or phrase, in which each picture usually suggests one of the syllables, as in two gates and a head for Gateshead.
12 *Helicon.* "Name of a mountain in Boeotia, sacred to the Muses, in which rose the fountains of Aganippe and Hippocrene . . . used allusively in reference to poetic inspiration." *OED.*
22 *Melpomene.* The Muse of Tragedy.

To the Dean of St. Patrick's

This printing is based on the first appearance of these verses, in *WM* (pp. 352–53), where they were attributed to Sheridan. They were first printed in Barrett (1808, pp. 153–54) and have since been reprinted in Scott, Browning, Horrell, Williams (pp. 969–70), *JIL,* Vol. XVI, No. 1 (pp. 35–36), and elsewhere.

These verses were a response to Swift's "A Left-Handed Letter," dated
September 20, 1718. In part, Swift wrote:

> I must now, at one sitting, pay off my old score.
> How many to answer? Here's one, two, three, four.
> But, because the three former are long ago past,
> I shall, for method's sake, begin with the last. . . .
> My offers of peace you ill understood.
> Friend Sheridan, when will you know your own good?
> 'Twas to teach you in modester language your duty;
> For, were you a dog, I would not be rude to you.
> As a good quiet soul, who no mischief intends
> To a quarrelsome fellow, cries, "Let us be friends."
>   But we like Antaeus and Hercules fight,
> The ofter you fall, the ofter you write;
> And I'll use you as he did that overgrown clown,
> I'll first take you up and then take you down:
> And, 'tis your own case for you never can wound
> The worst dunce in your school, till he's heaved from the ground.

> I beg your pardon for using my left hand, but I was in great haste, and the
> other hand was employed at the same time in writing some letters of business.
> September 20, 1718.—I will send you the rest when I have leisure: but pray
> come to dinner with the company you met here last.

Swift's poem first appears in *WM,* and that wording is followed in the
above quotation. The poem was first printed by Faulkner in 1762, and
subsequently in most editions of Swift's poems, the most recent being
Williams (pp. 967–68) and Rogers (pp. 173–74). Rogers, whose printing
does not take note of the variants in *WM,* also prints the poem out of
sequence. In his edition, it should follow Swift's next poem, "The Dean
to Thomas Sheridan," which is dated five days earlier, on September 15.
The sentiments about politeness in raillery look forward to Swift's verse
letter "To Mr. Delany" of November 10, 1718. According to Faulkner's
note in his 1762 printing, Swift did write the poem with his left hand, and
in his note above Swift claims that he was writing business letters with
his right hand. In line with their usual One-Upmanship, Sheridan in his
poem claims also to write poetry with both hands simultaneously.

i 2   *I.* Barrett and Scott print "I'll."
i 10   Sheridan seems to say here that Swift not only used his left hand,
       but that he also wrote from right to left, as Hebrew is written.
i 11   The word "cannot" occurs in *WM.* Barrett, Scott, Williams and
       others print "can't," which hurts the meter.

i 20   *Dan.* Probably the Rev. Daniel Jackson, whose prominent nose is the subject of a number of poems by Sheridan, Swift and their friends.

ii 2   *grows.* Barrett, Scott and others print "grow'st."

ii 3   *number[s] falling.* WM incorrectly has "number." Barrett and Scott have the plural, and I follow Williams by including the "s" in brackets. Browning has "failing," which appears to be a mistranscription.

ii 4   *they do.* Williams has "do they."

ii 9   *and.* Browning has "you."

iii 2   *Melpy.* Melpomene, the Muse of Tragedy.

Ad Amicum Eruditum Thomam Sheridan (Swift)

This admiring but somewhat bantering Latin poem, which Swift apparently valued, was copied into *WM*, where it was preceded by the following covering letter from the fictitious "Pat. Reyly," its nominal author:

> REVEREND AND LEARNED SIR,
>   I am teacher of English, for want of a better, to a poor charity-school, in the lower end of St. Thomas's-street; but in my time I have been a Virgilian, though I am now forced to teach English, which I understand less than my own native language, or even than Latin itself; therefore I made bold to send you the enclosed, the fruit of my Muse, in hopes it may qualify me for the honour of being one of your most inferior ushers; if you will vouchsafe to send me an answer, direct to me next door but one to the Harrow, on the left hand in Crocker's-lane.
>   I am yours, reverend sir to command.
>   PAT. REYLY.
> Scribimus indocti doctique poemata passim.—Horat.

The concluding Latin line from Horace (Ep. 2, 1, 117) is translated by H. Rushton Fairclough as "but, skilled or unskilled, we scribble poetry, all alike."

The poem's first publication was in Faulkner's 1735 edition of the *Works;* and the present printing, with the contractions expanded and the capitalization normalized, is based on that. In Faulkner, the poem is dated October 1717, and that date is accepted by Williams, Davis, and Rogers. It is uncertain precisely when Sheridan and Swift first met, but there are no other extant poems between Swift and Sheridan in 1717, and I am inclined to date "Ad Amicum Eruditum" about a year later. By October 1718, Swift and Sheridan knew each other well enough to engage in extensive and initially playful verse insults, and it is not until October 23, 1718, in his "To Thomas Sheridan" poem, that Swift refers to the Reyly pieces.

The poem has been included in the significant collections of Swift's verse. It was first published in Faulkner's 1735 edition of the *Works* (pp. 475–76), and more recently in Williams (pp. 211–14), Davis (pp. 157–58), and Rogers (p. 569). Its last previous appearance was in *JIL*, Vol. XVI, No. 2 (pp. 49–51), which also included the English translation included here. The English versification by the present editor is a loose rendering of a literal prose translation by Dwight Peterson. It has been cast into uncharacteristic blank verse because Swift's original was unrhymed and also because Swift frequently seemed to be striving for a quite sober effect. One problem in the translating was that a direct quotation appears to begin in line 10 from Athena, with "Heu puer infelix!" Whether the quotation ends with that verse paragraph or continues until the end of the poem, I am not sure.

2 (l. 3 in English)   *Permessi.* A river in Boeotia sacred to Apollo and the Muses.

13   *Musca . . . mus.* Musca (fly) and mus (mouse) are puns on Musae (Muses), which I have been unable to render in English.

18   *Poeonius.* Referring to Apollo, the god of medicine as well as of the arts.

23–24 (ll. 24–25 in English)   *frigidus horror / Saturni . . . septem . . . triones.* The phrase "frigidus horror Saturni" is literally "the cold horror of Saturn," and is definitely pejorative. Saturn, however, was the god of sowing and of harvest. He is sometimes identified with Cronus who was defeated by Zeus and then came to Latium and set up a kingdom that instituted a Golden Age. The phrase "septem . . . triones" possibly refers to the seven bright stars of Ursa Major that constitute the Dipper and part of the Plough. I have truncated these vaguely into "a cold and horrid future."

32–33   Rogers notes that these lines reflect "Swift's habitual interest in the *Aeneid,* Book VI"; Peterson notes also that Swift's lines are "perfect dactylic hexameters, worthy of Virgil."

Peterson further notes that "deliciae" in line 1 "has definite sexual connotations: a sexual toy"; that "rimandi" in line 7 from the verb "rimor" means to tear open, but the noun from which it comes, "rima", means crack and concludes "We might have a vague peder-astic pun here since the poem has to do with Sheridan's new teach-ing position"; and finally that "penitus" and "semina" in line 25 may contain some farfetched homosexual content. In the translation, I have included none of these overtones, and doubt they are meant to be there.

Vivitur Parvo Malè, Sed Canebat and Ad Te, Doctissime Delany

These two Latin verses first appeared in *WM* (pp. 355–57). They are almost certainly by Sheridan, and appear to be a response to Swift's Latin poem "Ad Amicum Eruditum Thomam Sheridan." In *WM*, Swift's poem is introduced by a prose letter in English presumably written by "Patrick Reyly," an impecunious teacher who is begging for a position in Sheridan's school, and who includes "Ad Amicum Eruditum Thomam Sheridan" as an indication of his abilities.

Although Swift's Latin poem is highly complimentary about Sheridan's abilities as a teacher, it also contains a few critical barbs. It was usually Sheridan's habit in such matters to continue the joke (see, for instance, his Dan Jackson and his George-Nim-Dan-Dean poems below), and to give back as good as he got, or, indeed, rather more. In this instance, the continuation of Swift's joke was considerably elaborated. It opened with "Reyly's" Latin poem to Delany, petitioning him for aid now that "Reyly" has been repulsed by the Dean. The Latin poem is then followed by a short prose note to Delany that introduces a long begging letter "Reyly" had written to Swift:

Quaeso, reverende vir, digneris hanc epistolam inclusam cum versiculis perlegere, quam cum fastidio abjecit et respuebat Decanus ille (inquam) lepidissimus et Musarum at Apollinis comes.

Reverende Vir,
De vestrâ benignitate et clementiâ in frigore et fame exanimatos, nisi persuasum esset nobis, hanc epistolam reverentiae vestrae non scripsissem; quam profectò, quoniam eo es ingenio, in optimam accipere partem nullus dubito. Saevit Boreas, mugiunt procellae, dentibus invitis maxillae bellum gerunt. Nec minus, intestino depraeliantibus tumultu visceribus, classicum sonat venter. Ea nostra est conditio, haec nostra querela. Proh Deûm atque hominum fidem! quare illi, cui ne libella nummi est, dentes, stomachum, viscera concessit natura? mehercule, nostro ludibrium debens corpori, frustra laboravit a patre voluntario exilio, qui macrum ligone macriorem reddit agellum. Huc usque evasi, ad te, quasi ad asylum, confugiens, quem nisi bene nôssem succurrere potuisse, mehercule, neque fores vestras pultûssem, neque limina tetigissem. Quàm longum iter famelicus peregi! nudus, egenus, esuriens, perhorrescens, despectus, mendicans; sunt lacrymae rerum et mentem carnaria tangunt. In viâ nullum fuit solatium praeterquam quod Horatium, ubi macros in igne turdos versat, perlegi. Catii dapes, Maecenatis convivium, ita me picturâ pascens in-

ani, saepius volvebam. Quid non mortalium pectora cogit Musarum sacra fames? Haec omnia, quae nostra fuit necessitas, curavi ut scires; nunc re experiar quid dabis, quid negabis. Vale.

[I beg, reverend sir, that you deign to peruse this letter enclosed with these little verses, which, with contempt, that Dean rejected and spat upon—that most charming Dean, comrade of the Muses and Apollo.

[Reverend Sir,
[If I hadn't been persuaded, breathless about your kindness and mercy in cold and hunger, I would not have written this letter to your excellency; I have no doubt whatsoever that you will receive this with the best of intentions, since you are of such good character. The North Wind rages; storms low; my jaws with teeth unwilling wage war. No less does the stomach sound its trumpet, its innards battling with intestinal strife. This is our condition; this is our complaint. Oh, the faith of gods and men! Why does nature give to that man who has not even one penny, teeth, stomach and guts? My God, he is a plaything in debt to his body; in vain has he labored in voluntary exile from his father, and has rendered an already thin little plot of land even thinner by farming. From this place now I have escaped, fleeing to you, as if to sanctuary; and if I hadn't been completely certain that I could come to you for help, by God, I would neither have knocked on your door nor touched your threshold! How long did I pursue my way, absolutely famished! Naked, in great need, despised, begging! "There are tears for the human condition and things of the flesh touch the mind." On the way there was no companionship but Horace whom I read over and over, especially where he roasts little thrushes over a fire. The feasts of Cato, the banquets of Maecenas—very often did I ponder these things, feeding myself on an empty picture. Why does hunger not touch the holy hearts of the immortal Muses! All of these things, what my great need was, I have taken pains for you to know. Now I will see what you will allow or deny. Farewell.]

Then follows "Reyly's" Latin poem to Swift, which begins "Vivitur parvo malè."

The two later "Reyly" poems and letters were printed by several of Swift's early editors without being attributed to any particular writer. Sheridan, however, is by far the most likely composer; for Sheridan and Delany come off well, but Swift, who refuses Reyly, does not. Swift's line about Reyly in his poem to Sheridan of October 23, 1718, is "Nec Phoebi fili versum quis mittere Ryly," and it is a little ambiguous, but it certainly could mean to send verses *from* Reyly. If that is the meaning, it is a definite attribution of the sequence to Sheridan.

On its first publication in Faulkner's 1735 edition of the *Works,* Swift's Latin poem was dated October 1717. This date was probably given by Swift himself, and it has been accepted by Williams, Davis, and Rogers.

It is not precisely certain when Swift and Sheridan first met, but it could not have been greatly before October 1717. Nevertheless, there are no other Swift/Sheridan poems before 1718, and such an early date for the jokingly critical "Reyly" poems and letters seems a bit implausible. Consequently, I lean to assigning the "Reyly" pieces to the following October, when Swift and Sheridan knew each other better, when they were engaging in a series of initially playful verse insults, and when Swift himself referred to the "Reyly" pieces.

In *WM*, the Delany poem precedes the Swift one. The order is here reversed, however, to agree with the fictional time of composition.

The versification of the Latin poems into English is the present editor's and is based upon a prose translation by Dwight Peterson who also translated the prose.

To the Dean of St. Patrick's

The first appearance of the poem, upon which this printing is based, is in *WM*, (pp. 361–62), where it was attributed to Sheridan. It was printed in Barrett (p. 159), and in Scott, Roscoe, Browning, Horrell, *JIL*, Vol. XVI, No. 1 (pp. 38–39), and elsewhere. Unlike *WM*, Barrett prints the poem in four-line stanzas. Also, in line 6, Barrett seems to have miscopied "soul" for "scull," and to have been followed by Scott and others.

The approximate date of the poem may be inferred by working backward in this particular exchange from Swift's poem ("Dear Tom, I'm surprised that your verse did not jingle"), dated October 23, 1718.

> 3 *Priscian.* Grammarian. Priscian was a Roman grammarian of the early sixth century A.D.

To Thomas Sheridan (Swift)

Swift's poem was transcribed in *WM*, (pp. 364–65), which is the copy-text used here. It was first printed by Barrett (pp. 162–63), and has been reprinted by Scott, Williams (pp. 980–81), Rogers (pp. 175–76), and other editors, although not by Davis who regards the trifles as "often no better than rhymes strung together as fast as possible in a sort of competitive game." The verse translation of the Latin portion is by the present editor following a prose rendering by Dwight Peterson. It seems not to have been previously translated, and first appeared in *JIL*, Vol. XVI, No. 2 (pp. 49–52).

3   *Helsham.* Dr. Richard Helsham, physician, Fellow of Trinity College, and jovial friend of both Swift and Sheridan. See Biographical Index.

7   *Dick.* Helsham.

17 *Ryly.* This certainly refers to "Pat. Reyly," the nominal author of a letter by Swift to Sheridan in English and Latin prose and in Latin verse (see "Ad Amicum Eruditum Thomam Sheridan"). The Reyly character was then used by Sheridan for two further Latin poems (See "Vivitur Parvo Malè, Sed Canebat" and "Ad Te, Doctissime Delany"). Rogers (p. 679) appears to regard Reyly as a real person.

29 *Betty Mi lady.* I have mistranslated this bit of Anglo-Latin as "Bet, your woman" to indicate Sheridan's wife, Elizabeth MacFadden. If Swift addressed her as "Mi lady," he was being heavily ironic, for the two heartily disliked each other. The other possibility would be Lady Betty Rochfort—in which case, Sheridan would have been ill at Gaulstown. However, his own poems on his illness would indicate that he was at home in Capel Street.

footnotes. Not included by Williams and Rogers.

Perlegi Versus Versos, Jonathan Bone, Tersos

This printing is based on the transcription in *WM* (p. 365). The poem was first published by Barrett (p. 164), and then reprinted by Scott, Horrell, Williams (pp. 981–82), *JIL,* vol. XVI, No. 1, (pp. 40–41), and others. Another of the pieces written during Sheridan's eye trouble, it is probably a reply to the Latin portion of Swift's poem above which begins "Dear Tom, I'm surprised that your verse did not jingle." As Sheridan notes in his concluding couplet, his form of internal rhyming imitates Swift's in his Latin verses, and we may probably then conclude that Sheridan's piece was composed on October 23 or 24. Browning, as Williams notes, incorrectly asserts that the piece replies to Swift's "Tom, for a goose you keep but base quills."

The English versifying of the Latin is by the present editor and is based on a prose rendering by Dwight Peterson.

18 *lusit* Barrett and Scott have "hesit."

I Like Your Collyrium

This printing is based on *WM* (p. 363). It was printed in Barrett (p. 161), Scott, Browning, *JIL,* Vol. XVI, No. 1 (p. 39), and elsewhere. It is usually considered a reply to the poem, generally attributed to Delany, which begins "Dear Sherry, I'm sorry for your bloodshedded sore eye." However, the amiability of this poem and the irascibility of "My pedagogue dear, I read with surprise" might suggest that this poem was written as an answer to Swift and the other as an answer to Delany. Further, Swift's English and Latin poem, "Dear Tom, I'm surprised that your verse did not jingle," suggests some remedies to which Sheridan's lines 1–2 and 13 appear to reply.

1   *collyrium.* Eye-salve.
5   *the doctor so wise.* "Probably Dr. Davenant." Barrett's note. If, as the context suggests, Dr. Davenant was a physician, I have been unable to identify him. There are no plausible candidates cited among the graduates of Oxford, Cambridge, or Trinity; there is no reference in Gilbert's *History of the City of Dublin* or in J. B. Lyons's *Brief Lives of Irish Doctors*, and indeed that latter authority, when queried, was unable to identify a Dr. Davenant.
9-12   *Livy.* A check of the Latin words for hand, feet, and meat in the *Concordance to Livy* has suggested no plausible source in the historian.
14-18   *Argus . . . Ovid.* Argus was the hundred-eyed keeper of Io after she was changed into a heifer by Jupiter. After Argus was slain by Mercury at Jupiter's bidding, his eyes were placed by Juno in the tail of the peacock. Ovid tells his story in Book I of *The Metamorphoses.*

To Thomas Sheridan (Delany)

This poem first appeared in *WM* (p. 362), and was first printed by Barrett (p. 160). It has been reprinted in various Swift editions, although not in the most recent by Williams, Davis and Rogers.

7   *Gory.* Possibly Gorey in County Wexford.
8   *ros.* Oil of roses possibly.
11   *Lady Judith.* Unidentified.
      boree. From boreen, the Irish for path or little road.
12   *ex more.* As usual.
13   *ab uxore.* From your wife.
14   *friend Dick.* Dr. Richard Helsham.
16   *tory-rory.* An obsolete word meaning uproarious or boisterous.
17   *John Dory.* This would seem to be the name of a ballad that I have been unable to locate. It is also the name of a fish, the best known

of the six species of Dory found in the Mediterranean and off the Atlantic coast of Europe.

20   *mori.* Die.

22   *Clem Barry.* According to Burtchaell and Sadleir, Clement Barry was born in Dublin, the son of Joseph Barry, a solicitor. He studied under Mr. Jones of Dublin, and was admitted as a pensioner to Trinity, aged sixteen, on September 27, 1697. In his edition of Swift's letters, Williams mentions that Barry "lived at Saggart near Dublin. He was a distant cousin of the then Lord Santry. In *Gulliveriana* he is described as 'Mr. Barry, chief Favourite and Governour of *Gallstown*.' "

My Pedagogue Dear, I Read with Surprise

The first extant appearance of this poem, upon which this printing is based, is in *WM* (pp. 363–64). It was first printed by Barrett (p. 162), and then by Scott, Browning, Horrell, *JIL,* Vol. XVI, No. 1 (pp. 30–40), and elsewhere. It would seem because of its crambo form to be a response to Delany's "Dear Sherry, I'm sorry for your bloodshedded sore eye," which goes to rather farfetched lengths to make twenty-two lines on one double rhyme.

12   *Condé.* Condé, Louis II, de Bourbon. Eminent French noble, general and patron of literature during the seventeenth century.
     Guise. Probably Francis of Lorraine, second Duke of Guise (1591–1563). Like Condé, an eminent French noble and general.

16   *frize.* Frieze, a course woolen cloth, usually with the nap only on one side.

You Made Me in Your Last a Goose and I'll Write While I Have Half an Eye in My Head

This printing is based on the poems' first appearance in *WM* (p. 368), where they were untitled. They were first printed by Barrett (p. 166), and then by Scott, Williams (p. 984), *JIL,* Vol. XVI, No. 1 (p. 41), and others. They appeared in *WM* immediately following the poem that begins "A Highlander once fought a Frenchman at Margate," and the form in which they were transcribed has suggested to various editors, such as Scott and Williams, that they were meant to constitute one poem. There is, however, no justification for such a conclusion. In many pages of *WM* two red lines are drawn across the page to separate poems, but that is not the case on pages 352–85 which contain these poems. In those pages, the poems are separated only by a blank space. On p. 367, for instance, only such a space separates Swift's "Lean Tom, when I saw him last week" from "A Highlander," and no one has ever concluded that these were parts of the same poem. Similarly, on p. 368, only a space separates "I'll write while I have half an Eye" from Swift's following "Tom, for a Goose you keep but base quills"; again no one has ever concluded that the two were parts of the same poem.

In their form and content also, the pieces are demonstrably not one, but three separate poems. Scott, nevertheless, considers them as one poem written in response to "To the Rev. Daniel Jackson," which Swift wrote in the character of Sheridan. This conclusion seems improbable, however: the twenty lines of "The Highlander" do in content appear to belong to the verse warfare over Dan Jackson's nose, which was waged possibly in October, 1718, but, "You Made Me in Your Last a Goose" and "I'll Write While I Have Half an Eye in my Head" belong to a quite different verse warfare waged at about the same time, from September to November 1718, in which Sheridan attacked Swift's allegedly declining poetic powers. Williams, who also treats the three verses as parts of one poem, does not discuss "A Highlander," but thinks that the other parts were written in response to the poem he titles "Sheridan, a Goose," that begins, "Tom, for a goose you keep but base quills." However, that line would seem a direct answer to Sheridan's "My quill you'll find's a woman's tongue, / And slit, just like a bird will chatter. . . ." (lines 4–5 of "You Made Me in Your Last a Goose"). And Swift's concluding couplet ("As for you're writing I am dead, / I leave it for the second head") seems a direct response to Sheridan's line 2 ("I'll write when you're dead") and to his line 4 ("I'll feed on the grass that grows on your grave") in "I'll Write While I Have Half an Eye in My Head." As Swift's poem is dated October 27, 1718, we may, then, with fair certainty place the writing of Sheridan's two little pieces on about October 26. Lines 12 and 17 of Swift's "Mary the Cook-Maid's Letter to Dr. Sheridan," one of his best pieces about Sheridan, also seem to refer to "You made me in your last a goose" and "I'll write while I have half an eye in my head."

I Can't but Wonder, Mr. Dean

This printing is based on *WM* (p. 369), where the poem was untitled. It was first printed by Barrett (p. 167), and then by Scott, Williams (pp. 1018–19), *JIL,* Vol. XVI, No. 1 (pp. 41–42), and others. Its dating is a problem. Williams includes it in the 1719 poems, and remarks that it evoked Swift's poem which begins, "Poor Tom, wilt thou never accept a

Defiance." However, there seems little reason for assigning either poem to 1719, as they are in content much closer to the verse warfare between Swift and Sheridan of September and October, 1718.

8   *'tis.* Barrett, Scott, Roscoe and Browning have "it's."
9   *I'm told.* Barrett, Scott, Roscoe, and Browning have "I am told," which harms the meter.

To the Dean of St. Patrick's

This printing is based on *WM* (p. 359). The poem was first printed by Barrett (p. 158), and reprinted by Scott, Roscoe, Browning, and *JIL,* Vol. XVI (No. 1, p. 42). It may be given a possible approximate date of October 26, 1718, because of another allusion, in line 21, to "a small goosequill." However, what Swift's humble recantation (referred to in lines 1 and 2) is remains a problem.

18   *Chiron.* Mentor or teacher, a function performed by Chiron the centaur.
fn. 1   *A leg awry.* Transcribed in *WM* and apparently Sheridan's note.
fn. 2   *A fair open for you.* Transcribed in *WM* and apparently Sheridan's note.

Another Picture of Dan

In 1718, possibly in October, Swift, Delany, Sheridan, and the young clergyman, Dan Jackson, were staying at Gaulstown House, and Betty Rochfort cut out Dan Jackson's profile in silk. Apparently it was quite recognizable as he had a large nose, and Delany, George Rochfort, and Sheridan all wrote gibing poems about his profile. Jackson seems to have replied with the poem that begins, "Three merry lads with envy stung" (Williams, pp. 994–95). Probably at the same time, Swift replied with the poem that begins "Whilst you three merry Poets traffick: (Williams, pp. 993–94), and a verse battle, in which Swift and Sheridan were the principal combatants, began. Ehrenpreis describes the whole enterprise as "laborious fun," and goes on to say that "Too many of these squibs are preserved, for they can amuse few readers today." This opinion strikes the present editor as somewhat phlegmatic, and the sequence of poems seems so ingenious and droll that one can but marvel at the wit of the company.

This printing is based on *WM* (p. 332), which contained the signature

"Tho: Sheridan sculpsit." The poem was first printed in Fairbrother's 1735 volume and then in the London *Miscellanies. The Tenth Volume . . .* of 1745. Fairbrother entitled it "Another. By Sh——n," but omitted the signature, and the 1745 volume entitled it "Another" and included the signature. The most recent printings were by Williams (p. 992) and *JIL,* Vol. XVI, No. 1 (p. 44.)

1   *Clarissa draws her scissors from their case.* A more famous Clarissa connected with scissors was the heroine of Pope's *The Rape of the Lock.* Note especially lines 127–28 from Canto IV:

> Just then, Clarissa drew with tempting grace
> A two-edged weapon from her shining case. . . .

2   *shape.* 1745 has "draw."
5   *measure.* 1735 has "Measures."
7   *stockings.* 1745 has "Stocking."
9   *the.* 1745 has "his."
14   *dev'l.* 1735 has "Devil."

On the Same

This printing is based on *WM* (p. 331), which includes the signature "Tho: Sheridan sculpsit." Fairbrother reprinted the couplet in Vol. IV of his *Miscellanies* of 1735 (p. 196), but used the title "Another. By D—— S——," and omitted Sheridan's signature. The couplet was not included in the *Miscellanies* of 1745, but appeared in Barrett (p. 145), Scott, Browning, Horrell, Williams (p. 991), and *JIL,* Vol. XVI, No. 1 (p. 44).

2   *I'll.* Fairbrother has "I."

Answer (probably with George Rochfort)

This poem is a retort to the clever and logic-chopping "D-n J——n's Answer" (Williams, pp. 333–34).

There is a question of how much of this poem Sheridan wrote. In *WM* (pp. 336–38), it is called "Answer," and all twenty-six verses are printed as one poem and attributed to Sheridan. Fairbrother omits stanza three, but also prints the verses as one poem. However, other editions, including the 1745 *Miscellanies,* attribute most of the poem, beginning with stanza nine ("You say your face is better hung"), to George Rochfort and print that part separately. Thus Faulkner, 1763, Vol. X (pp. 379–81), calls that segment "Answer to Dan. Jackson, by Mr. George Rochfort"; Roscoe and Browning call it "Mr. Rochfort's Reply"; and Horrell and Williams (pp. 994–95) call it "Answer to D-n J——n, by Mr. G——rge R——rt."

As his gibing poem against Sheridan, which begins "With music and poetry equally blessed," amply demonstrates, Rochfort was perfectly capable of turning out adroit and clever verses. Also, as the attack on Dan Jackson was originally launched by Delany, Sheridan, and Rochfort in separate poems, it is plausible that each would separately defend his own attack. And finally, Sheridan's son had supplied the printer of the 1745 *Miscellanies* with his father's papers, and this is persuasive evidence for Rochfort having written the latter stanzas.

A case, nevertheless, can be made for Sheridan's sole authorship of the verses as the one continuous poem that appears in *WM*. There, the poem is immediately followed by the two Swift pieces written in Dan Jackson's name, which begin "Wearied with saving Grace and Prayer" and "Three days for Answer I have waited." (Williams, pp. 1002–4, prints them in reverse order; Rogers, pp. 183–85, does not, and the content of the poems would seem to bear him out.) "Wearied," which is the more direct response, seems to refer to "Answer" as one poem. Its sixth stanza is a direct reply to the eighth stanza of "Answer," which is in the "Sheridan" section, but its eighth stanza is a direct reply to the fourth stanza of the "Rochfort" section, and its four concluding stanzas are a direct reply to the last five stanzas of the "Rochfort" section. Further, both Swift replies refer to only one author who is indisputably Sheridan. Line 23 of "Wearied," for instance, alludes to Sheridan's slight build by referring to him again as "a skeleton" (see also lines 11–12 of Swift's "Ad Amicum Eruditum Thomam Sheridan"). Line 44 refers to Sheridan as "dull Pedant," and, of course, he and not Rochfort was a teacher. In addition, line 17 of "Three days" addresses him directly as "Tom." Finally, in favor of all of the verses being Sheridan's, stanza nine does seem to continue the argument of stanza eight. In any event, in lieu of certainty, and although I lean to Rochfort having written the later stanzas, I have printed them together as one poem, as they were in *WM* upon which this printing is primarily based. The piece was most recently printed in *JIL*, Vol. XVI, No. 1 (pp. 44–47).

6 *Nereus*. Spelled "Nireus in *WM*. "A greek hero, King of Naxos, famed for his beauty." Williams' note. See *Iliad*, II, lines 673–74.
7 *We*. 1745 has "She," which makes no sense.
9–12 Not included by Fairbrother.
11 *woman*. 1745 has "women."

15   Fairbrother and 1745 include "the" before "offspring," which hurts the meter.

29   *drinking you have done.* In lieu of these words, Fairbrother has asterisks.

38   *you have.* Fairbrother has "you've" which hurts the meter.

39   *damned.* Fairbrother has "sad."

41   *to see.* Fairbrother and 1745 have "I see."

55   *an.* 1745 has "one."

57–60   *You the famed idol.* . . . "Statues of Priapus, stained vermilion, with club, sickle, and phallic symbol, were commonly placed in Roman gardens. *Cf.* Virg. *Ecl.* vii. 33; Hor. *Sat.* I, viii. 1–7." Williams's note.

58   *What. WM* and Fairbrother have "What"; 1745 has "As," which might seem to make more sense.

60   *of night, Sir. WM* and 1745 have only "of night," but, as the fourth line of each stanza otherwise always has three syllables, I have followed Fairbrother and added "Sir."

63   *love.* Fairbrother has "live."

64   *at sight, Sir.* Again, *WM* and 1745 have only "at sight."

66   *thy.* Fairbrother has "your."

67   *to t'ye.* This is the reading of Fairbrother and 1745. *WM* has, more awkwardly, "two to you."

70–71   *This paradox . . . all one.* These lines refer to some word play on the name of Rochfort in "D-n J——n's Answer." See lines 19–20:

> The 'Squire in *French* as hard as Stone,
> Or strong as Rock, that's all as one. . . .

73   *reas'ning.* This is the printing of 1745. *WM* and Fairbrother have "reasoning," which hurts the meter.

75   *diff'rent.* Fairbrother and 1745 have "different," which is unmetrical.

76   *T' our senses.* Fairbrother has a line of four syllables, "to our Senses"; 1745 has plausibly "T' our Senses." It is impossible to make out which version *WM* has.

77   *them.* 1745 has "'em."

89–104   These lines refer to some wordplay in "D-n J——n's Answer" on "Sherry" and "Dan." See lines 29–38.

92   *so.* Fairbrother and 1745 have "Sir."

94–95   1745 reverses these lines.

96   *so.* Fairbrother and 1745 have "Sir."

98   *Sheri. Wm* and Fairbrother have *"Sherri"*; 1745 has *"Sherry."*

99   make. 1745 has "makes."
101   Sheri. WM, Fairbrother and 1745 have *"Sherri."*

Sheridan to Dan Jackson

These stanzas in form and content may be a direct reply to Swift's "Wearied with saying Grace and Prayer" and "Three days for Answer I have waited" and particularly to the poem that immediately follows them in *WM*, and begins "To you victorious and brave." Nevertheless, the exact order and even the authorship of several of the Dan Jackson poems seem impossible to resolve.

The printing of this piece is based on its first published appearance, in Fairbrother, Vol. IV (1735, p. 211). It was reprinted by Williams (pp. 1007–8), who remarks that it appears also in *WM*, but I have not found it there. Its most recent appearance was in *JIL*, Vol. XVI, No. 1 (pp. 47–48).

A Highlander Once Fought a Frenchman at Margate

This printing is based on the poem's first appearance, in *WM* (pp. 367–68). There it immediately precedes the two verses that begin "You Made Me in Your Last a Goose" and I'll Write While I Have Half an Eye in My Head," and the arrangement of the poems on the page could suggest that they were intended as three parts of one poem, as some editors, indeed, have taken them. This opinion seems improbable, however, not only because the verse form of the three pieces is different, but also because in content "A Highlander" clearly belongs to the Dan Jackson's nose sequence, and the content of the other two belongs to the verse warfare between Swift and Sheridan that was going on at about the same time over Swift's alleged declining poetic powers. Lines 10–20 of this piece, however, clearly refer to Swift's having written several of the nose poems in the character of Dan Jackson.

5   Sawney. A mildly disparaging name for a Scot, as Teague is for an Irishman.
16   larva's. Mask's.

Cur Me Bespateras, Blaterans Furiosè Poeta

Williams, in his reprinting of this poem (p. 996), dismisses it as "doggerel." He is doubtless referring to such Englishified Latin as "foulo Moutho," "spitfiria," "Phizzum," "honicombio," and "Muddum." Such typical Sheridan playfulness, however, is vigorously counterpointed by a vehemence of expression that makes this piece the most violent of the Dan Jackson poems and to Swift, doubtless, one of the most abrasive.

This poem does not appear in *WM*, and its first publication, upon which this printing is based, was apparently by Fairbrother (pp. 200–1); its most recent appearance was in *JIL,* Vol. XVI, No. 1 (pp. 48–49). The poem was not heretofore been attributed to any author, and Fairbrother initiated some confusion about its authorship by heading it with these lines:

> Merry Dan, as 'Tis Fitting,
> To Sh——n Sendeth Greeting
> T.S.D.I.S.P.D.

Williams in his reprinting followed Fairbrother's lead. However, the initial couplet of the heading does appear in *WM* and belongs to a Dan Jackson poem probably written by Swift and entitled "In Vindication of poor Dan's Picture." Further, the content of this Latin poem makes it quite clear that the piece is not from but to Dan Jackson.

My reason for attributing the piece to Sheridan is partly that the "Englishified" Latin is more in his manner than in that of any of the other combatants. Also, Sheridan was aware that some of the Dan Jackson poems which particularly attacked him were written by Swift, and that fact might account for some of the ferocity of the diction, as well as the goose quill reference in lines 13–14, and also Virgil's "magne sacerdos" which is more appropriate for Swift than for Jackson. Finally, T.S.D.I.S.P.D. is a standard Roman greeting, in which T. S. would stand for Thomas Sheridan, and D. I. for Dan Jackson, and S.P.D. for "salutem plurimam dicere" or "to send warmest greetings."

As the couplet used by Fairbrother for the title is palpably wrong, I have used the first line as the title. The English versifying is by the present editor and is based on a prose rendering by Dwight Peterson.

1 *Cur me bespateras.* Possibly an allusion to Swift's line "Pray do they praise me or bespatter?" in the poem that begins "Wearied with saying grace and prayer."

14 *slashantis.* Miscopied as "shlashantis" by Williams.

The Last Speech and Dying Words of Daniel Jackson

This printing is based on *WM* (pp. 342–44). The piece was then printed by Fairbrother and by Barrett, and has often been reprinted in collections of Swift's poems, most recently by Williams (pp. 1008–10) and in *JIL*, Vol. XVI, No. 1 (pp. 48–49). No earlier commentator has attributed it to any writer (save Ehrenpreis who vaguely thought it might by "Jackson or somebody"), but it is probably, on the basis of its ironic content, by Sheridan. Also, line 2 of the first verse ("And do not make your goose a swan") is a clear reply to Swift's poem of October 27, 1718, which begins "Tom, for a goose you keep but base quills." In that poem, Swift wrote:

> You're my goose, and no other man's;
> And you know all my geese are swans. . . .

And, of course, the true swan in this poem is identified as "that Pindar of the Times, Tom Sheridan."

The epigraph, as Browning and Williams note, is an alteration of these lines from Horace:

> ———mediocribus esse poetis
> Non homines, non di, non concessere columnae.
> *Ep. ad Pisones,* lines 372–73

H. Rushton Fairclough translates them as "But that poets be of middling rank, neither men nor gods nor booksellers ever brooked." Sheridan's English version, with its allusions to rocks and stones, would appear to be a retort to the wordplay on George Rochfort's name in lines 19–20 of the poem usually called "D-n J——n's Answer." In his printing, Barrett added, before "rocks" in the first line of the epigraph's translation, the word "high" to fill out the meter.

Neck-verse. "A verse, usually . . . set before a claimant to benefit of clergy, by reading which he might save his neck." Williams's note.
of Delphos. This is the transcription in *WM*. Fairbrother has "at Delphos."
I, 7 to. Williams omits this word.
I, 10 comes sousing. Fairbrother has "come." Williams notes that "sousing" is "A hawking phrase. A 'souse' is the act of the hawk in swooping."
I was forced to make use of borrowed wings. An allusion to the poems written by Swift in the name of Dan Jackson.
Hopkins, Sternhold, Silvester, Ogilby, Durfey. "Examples of versifiers. Hopkins and Sternhold were joint versifiers of the psalms; Josuah Sylvester, 1563–1618, translated Du Bartas; John Ogilby, 1600–76, published verse translations of Aesop, Virgil, Homer; Thomas

D'Urfey, dramatist and songwriter, was still alive when this was written." Williams's note.

Gradus ad Parnassum. Stair to Parnassus.

Signature   Poor Dan: Jackson. Not included by Fairbrother.

From To Mr. Delany (Swift)

This poem was originally published by Deane Swift in the *Works* of 1765. The original and its covering letter to Delany are among the Forster Mss. in the Victoria and Albert Museum. The poem has been reprinted in all important collections of Swift's poems, and this reprinting follows that of Rogers (pp. 179–82). That portion not printed here and not directly concerned with Sheridan contains a brief discussion of wit and humor that may owe something to Congreve. It might be noted that Swift's practice did not always follow his own strictures in the poem, and that his objective theorizing was really a strategy for winning a verse contest with Sheridan in which he was apparently coming off second best.

105 *Voiture.* "Vincent Voiture (1598–1648), courtier and writer, best known in England for his letters, which were much read, translated (as by Dryden), and imitated as models of courtly style in amatory correspondence. Swift owned two editions of his works." Rogers' note.

Palinodia

In September and particularly in October 1718, Swift's and Sheridan's private verse exchanges took on an increasingly ferocious tone. Despite some testimonials from both poets about the other's excellence, and despite some initial playfulness in the concurrent Dan Jackson sequence, what had begun as good-natured raillery on both sides became increasingly abrasive. For instance, in his poem of September 21, Sheridan referred irritatingly to Swift's "Billingsgate Muse." In that poem and others, he noted that Swift's Muse was on the wane, and these remarks culminated in an elaborate lost poem in which Sheridan proclaimed Swift's Muse to be dead. As Swift remarked in "The History of the Second Solomon" (*PW*, V, p. 222), Sheridan "without the least provocation made a funeral solemnity with asses, owls, &c. and gave the copy among all his acquaintance." Accustomed as he was to deference, the older man was apparently considerably irritated. His strategy, however, was not to reply in kind, but to take a higher ground, as he did in his dignified poem to Delany of November 10, 1718. There, Swift made distinctions between humor, raillery, and wit, discussed their use in polite conversation, and drew a line between "raillery and gross abuse." He then applied these standards to

> a friend of yours and mine
> Who full of humour, fire and wit,
> Not always judges what is fit. . . .

Swift obviously meant his poem, as well as its covering letter, to be shown to Sheridan. His strategy was successful, for Sheridan seems never to have published the piece, and may even have called all of the copies of his poem back, for none has ever come to light. The "Palinodia" was very possibly written at this time, around the middle of November, and Swift and Sheridan were reconciled. The poem is a graceful and nominally abject apology; nevertheless, among other lightly satiric touches, one might note the extravagance of the first two lines.

The poem has not previously been attributed to Sheridan, but it closely fits the situation outlined above, and there is good internal evidence that the piece is his. For instance, there is the reference to the goose and the swan in line 27, which refers to several previous pieces including "The Last Speech and Dying Words of Daniel Jackson" and to Swift's "Mary the Cook-Maid's Letter." Also, there are the references to a hectoring wife, as Elizabeth Sheridan notoriously was, in stanzas 5, 6, and 8.

Horace's Ode has quite the same general subject as Sheridan's poem, but "Palinodia" is a parallel piece rather than a translation. Francis Sylvester Mahony translated Horace's poem as "The Satirist's Recantation," and his version reads in part:

> Blest with a charming mother, yet
>   Thou still more fascinating daughter!
> Prythee my vile lampoons forget—
> Give to the flames the libel—let
>   The satire sink in Adria's water! . . .
>
> Oh, be appeased! 'twas rage, in sooth,
>   First woke my song's satiric tenor;
> In wild and unreflecting youth,
> Anger inspired the deed uncouth;
>   But, pardon that foul misdemeanour.
>
> Lady! I swear—my recreant lays
>   Henceforth to rectify and alter—
> To change my tones from blame to praise

Should your rekindling friendship raise
The spirits of a sad defaulter!

The "Palinodia" was transcribed in *WM* (pp. 360–61) and was reprinted in various collections of Swift's poems, the earliest being Vol. XVI of Faulkner's *Works* of 1767. Its most recent appearance was in *JIL,* Vol. XVI, No. 1 (pp. 43–44). This printing is based on *WM*, but the division into six-line stanzas is the present editor's and has been made to emphasize the form of the poem. A few significant differences of wording from Faulkner are noted below.

Title   *Palinodia*. The Recantation.
  7   *invectives*. Faulkner has "Iambicks."
 19   Faulkner has "Or when you next your physick take."
 30   Faulkner has "While he's no longer man."
 35   *Then*. Faulkner has "That."
 39   *chimes*. Scott has "schemes," which is pretty obviously wrong.
 41   *Which*. Faulkner has "When."
 45   *does*. Faulkner has "must."
 48   *And all the poet's riches*. Faulkner has "The poet's only riches."

The Epilogue to *Julius Caesar*

This printing is based on *WM* (pp. 273–74). There the poem is not ascribed to Sheridan, but he usually wrote the prologues and epilogues to the plays performed at his school; the jokey nature of the poem, as well as the assumption of another persona, make it seem highly likely that the piece is his. Indeed, the basic joke of the later poem, "Mr. Sheridan's Prologue to the Greek Play of Phaedra and Hippolytus," of a small boy criticizing his master, is precisely the same as that of this poem. Also, several details in the two poems are similar (compare, for instance, lines 37–40 of "The Epilogue" to lines 35–40 of "The Prologue.")

William Clark Smith, working from the papers of W. J. Lawrence, in *The Early Irish Stage, The Beginnings to 1720* (Oxford: Clarendon Press, 1955) assigns the production of *Julius Caesar* to 1718. Sheridan did not, however, publish the piece until 1728 or early 1728/29. Then it appeared in a broadside (TCD) together with a "Prologue Spoken Before a Greek Play, at the Reverend Dr. Sheridan's School, at the Breaking-Up of his Scholars for Christmas, 1728." This fact might suggest that Sheridan used the epilogue in 1718 (*WM* having been completed no later than 1721), and then dusted it off again for a new generation of students in 1728. Edward Davys, Third Viscount Mountcashel, the speaker of the epilogue, would have been about seven years old in 1718, but Sheridan occasionally assigned a prologue or an epilogue to one of his youngest students as he did in the prologue he wrote for the *Hippolytus* two years later.

Except for a few matters of punctuation and spelling, the two versions do not significantly differ, but the present printing is based on the broadside that Sheridan seems likely to have sent to the printer himself. The most recent appearance of the piece was in *JIL*, Vol. XVI, No. 2 (pp. 19–20).

13–14 *WM* has "If that we do, we pay for our appeals; / Our tongue's revenged upon our harmless tails."
17 *WM* has less metrically "I love to whip a favourite; that is my joy. . . ."
20 *rant. WM* has "stamp."
21 *rolling. WM* has "rowling."
27 *brickbats. WM* has "brickbat."
28 *this. WM* has "that."
29 *for him.* These words from the broadside are omitted in *WM*, but needed for the meter.
33 *cobbler. WM* has "gaoler."
36 *WM* has "He cried in jest, but we in earnest roar."
38 *as I think. WM* has "very much."
43 *scarifies. WM* appears to have "sacrifies."
45 *logs. WM* appears to have "Leggs."
47 *nets. WM* has "help."
52 *off. WM* has "of."
    brain. WM has "brains."
54 *one. WM* has "a."

The Pedagogue's Answer

Sheridan's poem replies to Swift's "A Letter to the Reverend Dr. SH——N" (Williams, pp. 987–89). Swift's piece is a short discourse on comedy and tragedy, with allusions to Terence, Plautus, Aeschylus, Sophocles, and Euripides. The rhyming is trisyllabic and includes "profane is" with "Aristophanes"; "Euripides" with "dip a-days"; "Stagirite" with "fadge aright"; "best piece is" with "Thespis's"; and "Eschylus" with "please, kill us." Swift concludes with the challenge, to which Sheridan refers in his lines 25–26:

> And now I find my Muse but ill able,
> To hold out longer in Trysyllable.

I chose these Rhymes out, for their Difficulty.
Will you return as hard ones, if I call t'ye?

This printing is based upon the poem's first appearance which was in
Fairbrother, Vol. IV (1735, pp. 192–93). Fairbrother assigns the poem to
the year 1718. A slightly different version was printed by Scott in his
second edition, Vol. XV (1724, p. 59), and there the title was given as
"The Answer, by Dr. Sheridan." The most recent appearance of Scott's
version was in Williams (pp. 989–90), and the most recent appearance of
Fairbrother's was in *JIL*, Vol. XVI, No. 1 (pp. 20–21).

  2 *hipps.* "Morbid depression of the spirits, the 'blues.'" *OED.* Scott
        has for this line "I'll stay and read 'em now at home a-days."
3–4 *Pareus . . . Lambinus.* "Johann Philipp Wangler, or Pareus, 1576–
        1648, the German philogist, editor of Plautus, Terence, and Sallust,
        and compiler of a *Lexicon criticum, seu thesaurus linguae latine,*
        and Denis Lambin, French classical scholar, 1520–72." Williams's
        note.
  4 *His.* Scott has, less sensibly, "Thy."
  9 *drama.* Scott has, more metrically, "dram."
11 *just.* Scott has "but."
13 *footnote.* Scott, who attaches the footnote to the beginning of line
        14, has "I believe you give him now the slip o'days," which is metri-
        cally better.
15 *call.* Scott has "come."
20 *masters.* Scott has "poor masters," which helps the meter.
21 *two at table.* Scott has "two, sir, at table," which harms the meter.
22 *few are* Scott has "few're."
        come at-able. Scott has "comeatable."
25 *I am.* Scott has "I'm," which helps the meter.

The Song

This song appeared in *WM* (p. 333), and was first printed by Fairbrother,
Vol. IV (1735, pp. 198–99). No author is listed in *WM*, but Fairbrother
plausibly attributes the piece to Sheridan, for the Grattans were Sheri-
dan's friends, and there is a grousing allusion to the speaker's wife. This
printing is based on *WM*, and the poem appears there among some other
Sheridan pieces written in 1718. It was reprinted by Barrett, Scott,
Browning, and others, and most recently in *JIL,* Vol. XVI, No. 2
(p. 21).
Sheridan's three stanzas parody portions of the ten-stanza poem "A

Pastoral," which is a lament for a lost nymph, was written by John Byrom (1692–1763), and first appeared in *The Spectator* of October 6, 1714. Sheridan's first four lines parallel the first four lines of Byrom's first stanza:

> My Time, O ye Muses, was happily spent,
> When *Phebe* went with me wherever I went;
> Ten thousand sweet Pleasures I felt in my Breast:
> Sure never fond Shepherd like *Colin* was blest!

Sheridan's fifth line repeats line 5 of Byrom's second stanza, but thereafter strongly deviates from Byrom's

> But now I so cross and so peevish am grown,
> So strangely uneasy as never was known.
> My Fair one is gone, and my Joys are all drown'd,
> And my Heart—I am sure it weighs more than a Pound.

Sheridan's second stanza, however, closely parodies Byrom's fifth:

> My dog I was ever well pleased to see
> Come wagging his Tail to my fair one and me;
> And *Phebe* was pleas'd too, and to my Dog said,
> Come hither, poor Fellow; and patted his Head.
> But now, when he's fawning, I with a sour Look
> Cry, Sirrah; and give him a Blow with my Crook:
> And I'll give him another; for why should not *Tray*
> Be as dull as his Master, when *Phebe's* away?

Sheridan's last stanza parallels, although not quite so closely, Byrom's eighth:

> Rose, what is become of thy delicate Hue?
> And where is the Violet's beautiful Blue?
> Does aught of its Sweetness the Blossom beguile,
> That Meadow, those Daisies, why do they not smile?
> Ah! Rivals, I see what it was that you drest,
> And made your selves fine for; a Place in her Breast:
> You put on your Colours to pleasure her Eye,
> To be pluckt by her Hand, on her Bosom to die.

5   *so peevish.* Fairbrother unmetrically omits "so."
8   *small beer.* Beer of weak or inferior quality.
10 *ride.* Fairbrother has "sit."

19   *smile.* Fairbrother has "smite," which does not make too much sense.

20   *while.* Fairbrother has "White."

21   *Bacchus.* Fairbrother has "liquor."

A Letter from Dr. Sheridan to Dr. Swift

This verse is a response to Swift's long and clever verse letter, dated December 14, 1719, Nine at night (Williams, pp. 1012–15). Sheridan's verse also called forth a response from Swift, dated December 15 (Williams, pp. 1017–18).

This printing is based on the manuscript in Sheridan's hand among the Theophilus Swift papers in the Huntington Library. The poem was first printed by Deane Swift (1765, 4to, Vol. VIII, p. 200; 8vo, Vol. XVI, p. 322) and by Faulkner (1765, Vol. XIII, pp. 329–30). It was also printed by Scott, Roscoe, Browning, Horrell, Williams, and *JIL,* Vol. XVI, No. 2 (pp. 21–22).

2   *Obrien.* "I.e. Haut-Brion." Williams's note. Haut-Brion is a variety of fine quality claret.

3   *be.* Deane Swift has "is."
        quean. Whore.

5   *Dunblain.* "At Sherrifmuir, two and a half miles from Dunblane, a sanguinary but indecisive battle was fought on 13 November, 1715, between the Jacobites led by the Earl of Mar and a government force under the command of the Duke of Argyle." Williams's note.

10   *Kain.* Unidentified, but obviously a clergyman.

12   *Wardel.* Unidentified, but obviously a servant.

15   *Helsham, Walmsley, Delany* For Dr. Richard Helsham and Dr. Patrick Delany, see Biographical Notes. Williams's note about Walmsley (p. 857) reads: "John Walmsley, who became a fellow of T.C.D. in 1703, Senior Fellow in 1713, B.D. and D.D. in 1716. In 1723 he was presented to the living of Clonfeacle, co. Tyrone, where he often officiated though he did not reside. He died at Armagh, 12 Dec. 1737. Leslie, *Armagh Clergy.*"

16   *some Grattans if there be any.* "In Dublin, for they were country-clergy, living near to the city." Faulkner's note.

From My Much Honored Friend at Heldelville (Delany)

This piece was one of the prefatory poems in Sheridan's *Ars Pun-ica* . . . (Dublin: James Carson, 1719), and this printing is based on that edition. A second edition appeared in Dublin in 1719, and a London edition was published by J. Roberts, in which the title page wrongly identifies Tom Pun-sibi as Swift. The essay was also attributed to Swift in *Miscellanies* (London, 1722). It was reprinted in Nichols's *A Supplement,* Vol. XXIV (1776), in Scott, Roscoe, and elsewhere.

The title of the poem is obviously Sheridan's and Heldelville was the name of the house and grounds in Glasnevin bought by Helsham and Delany. Its name was taken from the first syllables of both their names. Later, when Delany alone owned it, it was called Delville.

16 *Proteus.* "Neptune's herdsman, an old man and a prophet. . . . There was no way of catching him but by stealing upon him during sleep and binding him; if not captured, he would elude anyone who came to consult him by changing his shape, for he had the power of changing it in an instant into any form he chose." Brewer.

22 *Chloe.* "The shepherdess beloved by Daphnis in the pastoral romance of Longus, entitled *Daphnis and Chloe.*" Brewer. A figure of exquisite loveliness.

29 *Cyprian goddess.* Venus.

The Original of Punning

This was one of several prefatory poems published in Sheridan's *Ars Pun-ica . . .* (Dublin: James Carson, 1719; London: J. Roberts, 1719). The pamphlet has been several times reprinted and occasionally attributed to Swift, as in the fourth edition of the *Miscellanies* of 1722. In Dublin, if not in London, it was, however, well known that Tom Pun-sibi was Sheridan. The pamphlet has been reprinted in various editions of Swift, such as Fairbrother's, Nichols's, and Scott's. This poem was reprinted separately in *Gulliveriana* (pp. 79–82), and its most recent printing was in *JIL*, Vol. XVI, No. 2 (pp. 22–23). This printing is based on the first Dublin edition.

In Plato's *Symposium,* Aristophanes tells the story of how Zeus split the body of fractious primeval man who originally had four hands and feet, one head with two faces and so on. In Jowett's translation: "I have a plan which will humble their pride and mend their manners and then they will be diminished in strength and increased in numbers; this will have the advantage of making them more profitable to us. They shall walk upright on two legs, and if they continue insolent and will not be quiet, I will split them again and they shall hop about on a single leg." In his Art of Splitting Words, Sheridan is paralleling this fable.

The indentations in lines 23, 28, 31, and 33 have been included by the present editor for the purpose of clarity.

Upon the Author (Delany ?)

This piece was one of the prefatory poems in *Ars Pun-ica*, and this printing is based on James Carson's first edition of 1719. Nichols, Vol. XXIV (1776, p. 548), attributes it to Swift, as does Ball (p. 154). But in *Ars Pun-ica,* the piece follows "From My Much Honored Friend at Heldelville," and is described as "Upon the Author. By the same hand." The difficulty is that between the two poems is printed "The Original of Punning" by Sheridan himself. Although it is possible that Sheridan wrote "Upon the Author" about himself, the piece has a jovial friendliness to "Dear Tom" that inclines me to think it Delany's but placed out of proper order perhaps by the printer. However, see the similar lines in "Palinodia," in which Sheridan notes other uses for the paper on which verses are written. There, "To singe your fowl" is very close to line 11 of "Upon the Author," and lines 16–18 are similar in content to lines 21–22 of "Upon the Author." Scott titles the poem "Recommendatory Verses to Dr. Sheridan, on his Art of Punning."

24 *leaves of brass.* Possibly a pun is intended here combining the meanings of brass as metal alloy and of brass as impudence.

Thus Did Great Socrates Improve the Mind

From *Ars Pun-ica.*

6 *day-light.* A pun involving the Dublin pronunciation of "delight."

If These Can't Keep Your Ladies Quiet

From *Ars Pun-ica.*

1 *these.* Various punishments, such as whipping and locking them up.
Vide Roscom. Apparently a reference to Wentworth Dillon, 4th Earl of Roscommon (1633?–85), poet, translator of Horace, and friend of Dryden. There are a couple of lines in his "The Ghost of the Old House of Commons, to the New One, appointed to meet at Oxford," which seem applicable in this context:

> I feel (but, oh! too late) that no Disease
> Is like a Surfeit of Luxurious Ease. . . .

But the poem is generally not relevant to Sheridan's.

Thus Puppies That Adore the Dark

From *Ars Pun-ica*.

2   *Cynthia*. The moon.

A Punegyric upon Tom Pun-sibi's *Ars Pun-ica* (Anon.)

The previous printing of this long poem was a small quarto pamphlet of seven pages. In the National Library of Ireland copy, which is the only one I have discovered, the title page is missing, and the bottom of the pages is cropped causing a couple of lines to be lost. The National Library catalog seems to attribute the poem to Swift, and that is a possibility, although not to my mind a strong one.

43   *Lemnos*. An island in the Aegean, sacred in ancient times to Vulcan.
51   *electrum*. A natural pale yellow alloy of gold and silver.
105 *Scotia*. Scotland.
111 *Moss caught's mare*. A variant of a proverbial phrase meaning unlooked for, as in "napping, as Mosse took his Mare." Cited in *OED* from Randle Cotgrave's *A dictionarie of the French and English tongues* (1611).
147 *Tummas*. Thomas.
167 *valiant Ralpho's basket-hilt*. Ralpho is the squire of Samuel Butler's *Hudibras*. A basket-hilt is the hilt of a sword provided with narrow plates of curved iron in the shape of a basket to protect the hand.
192 *Pickle-herring*. Ball in his edition of the *Correspondence* remarks that "The sobriquet . . . perhaps finds to-day its best equivalent in the term merry-andrew. It was first applied early in the seventeenth century as the name of a humorous character in a German play, and was afterward adopted by the Dutch, whose use of it has been made famous by Addison in the 'Spectator'" (Vol. V, App. IV, p. 446).
210 *Cork Hill*. Cork Hill is the site of the City Hall in modern Dublin. Maurice Craig, describing the area in Sheridan's time, wrote:

The widely celebrated "Hell-Fire Club" was founded by the first Earl of Rosse, Colonel Jack St. Leger, and a humorous painter named Worsdale in about 1735, meeting in the Eagle Tavern in Cork Hill. Cork Hill was of course very much the centre of things, on the doorstep of the Castle and only a step or two from Essex Bridge. Just across the road from the Eagle Tavern was the Stationers' Hall, where one might see such innocent spectacles as "a painting by Raphael, and several fleas tied by gold chains." (*Dublin, 1600–1860.* Dublin: Allen Figgis, 1969, p. 154.)

216   Echo's. Echo was the nymph who loved Narcissus. As he did not return her love, she pined away till only her voice remained.

235 and fn. 1   Cerdon. In Butler's *Hudibras,* Cerdon is introduced in the First Part, Canto II, lines 409–440. A part of his description seems particularly applicable to Sheridan:

> Learned he was, and could take note,
> Transcribe, collect, translate and quote.
> But *Preaching* was his chiefest Talent,
> Or Argument, in which b'ing valiant,
> He us'd to lay about and stickle,
> Like Ram or Bull, at *Conventicle. . . .*

252   Priapus diffissa nate. Priapus's rump was cleft asunder. In his *Satires* (Book I, Satire 8), Horace writes in the character of a piece of wood, which has been fashioned into the figure of Priapus, the garden god, and is being used as a scarecrow in a cemetery. The cemetery is mainly used for paupers and criminals, and is 'frequented at night by "witches who with spells and drugs vex human souls." The Priapus statue observes two such witches tearing "a black lamb to pieces with their teeth" and burying "a wolf's beard and the tooth of a snake." In H. Rushton Fairclough's translation, the statue "shuddered at the words and deeds of the two Furies" and "as loud as the noise of a bursting bladder was the crack when my fig-wood buttock split" ["nam displosa sonat quantum vesica pepedi / diffissa nate ficus . . ." Lines 45–46].

A Prologue to a Play Performed at Mr. Sheridan's School. . . .

This prologue and its accompanying epilogue were apparently to a play by Plautus (see "The Epilogue, line 10), and first appeared in *WM* (pp. 370–71). These were not attributed to Sheridan, but they are pretty certainly his as it was his custom to write the prologues and epilogues to the school plays. Indeed, it was a kind of school tradition. Their first printing was by Barrett in a section titled "Poems by Swift and Sheridan" (pp. 168–70). They were reprinted by Scott, Roscoe, and Browning, and their most recent appearance was in *JIL,* Vol. XVI, No. 2 (p. 24). The dating of 1719 for both pieces is conjecture. However, *WM* was completed no later than the very early 1720s, and we have a prologue for 1718 and 1720. This printing is based on *WM.*

2 *Pharsalian plain.* Site of a great battle in Thessaly, Greece, in which Julius Caesar overcame Pompey in 48 B.C.

The Epilogue

For details of composition and printing, see "A Prologue" above.

10 *construe.* Barrett notes that Sheridan intended the word to be pronounced as "conster."

Upon Stealing a Crown When the Dean Was Asleep

This piece was first printed in the London *Miscellanies,* Vol. X (1745, pp. 231–32), and then by Faulkner, Vol. VIII (1746, pp. 336–37). It has since been reprinted by Scott, Roscoe, Browning, Horrell, and Williams (pp. 1032–33). For Swift's amusing reply, see "The Dean's Answer" (Williams, p. 1033; Rogers, pp. 199–200). In his poem Swift refers to "the lady at St Catherine's," by whom he meant Lady Mountcashel. Her son was enrolled in Sheridan's school, and Sheridan occasionally visited them at their home in Leixlip. Indeed, Swift has two poems of December 1719, which refer to Sheridan's visiting St. Catherine's. Rogers, consequently, deduces that "Upon Stealing a Crown" may have been written around the same time, and the surmise seems plausible. Williams assigns Sheridan's and Swift's poems to 1731.

An Elegy on the Much Lamented Death of Mr. Demar. . . .

On the death of some notable figure, it was not unusual for a broadside elegy, adorned with a mourning border and concluded with an Epitaph, to be issued in commemoration. The anti-elegy on Demar, which appeared originally in two poorly printed broadsides of 1720 (TCD), effectively utilizes this form. Delany in his *Observations* (p. 53) remarks, "The writing an elegy upon DEMAR, was a subject started, and partly executed

in company, SWIFT, and STELLA, and a few friends present. Every one
threw in their hint." And then he quotes lines 31–34, which he says were
Stella's contribution. The exactness of Delany's remarks here, and gener-
ally in the *Observations,* suggests that he was one of the party; in which
case, he himself almost surely contributed. Another contemporary, the
knowledgeable anonymous author of "Tom Pun-sibi's Resurrection Dis-
proved" (see lines 9–10), remarks that Sheridan "helped to make" the
poem. The third and fourth printings of the piece, in London, noted that
they were "By the AUTHOR of the Art of Punning," although it is possi-
ble that Swift may have been meant. Nevertheless, as Williams notes,
"The correspondent who forwarded the 'Elegy' to *The Weekly Journal:
or, British Gazetteer* professed to have known 'Deamur' for 'upward of
fifty Years.' He gives him a high character for kindliness and generosity.
'I look upon his Death to be one of the greatest Losses Ireland cou'd
labour under, . . . The Death of Mr. Demur *[sic]* produc'd the following
Elegy, written by the Celebrated Author of the Art of Punning.'" As the
first four printings of the poem appeared quickly after Demar's death—
that is, between July 6 and the appearance in *The Weekly Journal* on July
23—it might appear that one of the joint authors was responsible for
sending it around. Further, the tongue-in-cheek tone of the covering letter,
as well as the attribution to the author of *The Art of Punning,* could make
it possible that Sheridan had a hand in the matter.

There is also a contemporary attribution to Sheridan and Swift in the
anonymous poem "An elegy on the much lamented death of Jack Clifford,
the News-Cryer, formerly Packet-carrier to Billy Whichet" (TCD). This
piece, apparently from the early 1720s, is a mock elegy like the Demar
poem, and contains the following lines:

> He, that so often has made others cry,
> in justice should not want an elegy;
> he, that so often has made others laugh,
> in justice should not want an Epitaph.
> Tom Sheridan, I'm sure, will give a lift,
> To pen his praises, so will Doctor Swift,
> as they lamented Damer's fate before;
> Damer was very rich, and Clifford poor.
> But yet, should Swift and Sheridan refuse
> to pay the grateful tribute of their Muse,
> though thou, Great Clifford, art forever hurled
> from the dull region of this Upper World,
> yet you may still remain in statu quo,
> and cry thy packets in the Shades below.

This piece has been recently reprinted in Patrick Fagan's *A Georgian*

Celebration, Irish Poets of the Eighteenth Century (Dublin: Branar, 1989, pp. 174–75).

Sir Walter Scott notes, "My late regretted friend, Mr. Cooper Walker, favoured me with the following notices concerning this elegy: 'The subject was John Demar, a great merchant in Dublin, who died 6th July 1720. Swift, with some of his usual party, happened to be in Mr. Sheridan's, in Capel Street, when the news of Demar's death was brought in to them; and the elegy was the joint composition of the company.'" Williams notes, however, that John Cooper Walker was not born until 1761, and so his report is hearsay.

Scott appends a further note that his friend Walker found in the diary of a deceased friend: "As I passed through Smithfield (Dublin), I saw the house, No. 34, in which the remarkable John Demar, the usurer, lived and died. He was buried in the S. W. corner of St. Paul's churchyard.— No tombstone for many years."

Williams lists the following early printings of the poem:

An Elegy on the much Lamented Death of Mr. Demar, the Famous rich Man, who died the 6th of this Inst. July, 1720. Broadside.
An Elegy . . . Mr. Joseph Demar, . . . who died in Dublin. . . . Broadside.
St. James's Post, July 20, 1720.
Weekly Journal: or, British Gazetteer, July 23, 1720. Described as "By the AUTHOR of *The Art of Punning.*"
A Defence of English Commodities. . . . To which is Annexed, An Elegy upon the much lamented Death of Mr. Demar, . . . Printed at Dublin: And Reprinted at London, by J. Roberts in Warwick-Lane. MDCCXX, p. 25. Described as "By the AUTHOR of *the Art of Punning.*
Pinkethman's Jests: Or, Wit Refined. . . . London: . . . 1721, 2nd part, p. 121.
Miscellanies, written by Jonathan Swift, D.D. . . . The Fourth Edition. London: Printed in the Year M.DCC.XXII, pp. 194–96.
Miscellanies. The Last Volume, 1727, p. 286 (1731, p. 318; 1733, p. 318). Only the Epitaph printed, which might suggest that it was by Swift.
Gulliveriana, 1728, p. 82.
The Drapier's Miscellany. . . . Dublin: Printed by and for James Hoey, 1733, p. 26.
Faulkner, 1735, Vol. II, p. 137 (1737, Vol. II, p. 109).
A Collection of Poems, &c. Omitted in the Fifth Volume of Miscellanies in Prose and Verse. London: . . . Charles Davis, . . . MDCCXXXV, p. 433.

Among the more recent printings are Faulkner, *Works,* Vol. II, (1763, pp. 137–39); Scott, Roscoe, Browning, Horrell, Williams (pp. 232–35), Davis, and Rogers (pp. 214–15). This printing is based on the 1720 broadside in TCD.

Title *Demar. Weekly Journal* has "Demur"; *Gulliveriana* has the more usual spelling and pronunciation of "Damer."

  1 *Know all men by these presents.* The conventional opening of a legal document, which is satirically appropriate as Demar had undoubtedly in his money-lending activities, drawn up many such documents.

  8 *steward.* As Rogers notes, "servant; but alluding to the function of land-agent and broker, which generally involved putting money out at interest."

 17 *And under hand and seal.* As Rogers notes, "the closing formula of a document, next to the signature."

 18 *obligation.* As Rogers notes, a "state of indebtedness, with overtones of a legal usage."

 20 *a groat.* One of the 1720 broadsides and *The Drapier's Miscellany* have "one Groat." A groat was an obsolete coin of small value.

 22 *int'rest.* Rogers notes several appropriate meanings: "(1) money paid for a loan; (2) self-interest; (3) legal concern or title."

 24 *Because we wish the earth upon him light. Miscellanies* of 1722 appends to this line the footnote "Sit tibi Terra levis," or "May the earth lie lightly upon you," an inscription found frequently on tombstones and sometimes abbreviated to S.T.T.L.

 25 *London Tavern.* "A tavern in Dublin where Mr. Demar kept his office." Faulkner's note. Rogers adds, "According to *Gilbert,* I, 65–7, the establishment was located in Fishamble Street, conveniently close to St. Patrick's for Swift's acquaintance with Demar. The tavern was destroyed by fire in 1729." Fishamble Street is no more than a good ten minutes' walk away from St. Patrick's.

 27 *touched the pence.* In the first use of the word "touched" in the line, it means, as Rogers notes, "received money by underhand means."

 28 *shot.* Bill or reckoning.

 32 *moidores.* "A Portuguese gold coin current in England during the first half of the eighteenth century, and accepted at a value between 27s. and 28s." Williams's note.

 36 *change.* Rogers sees here a play on words involving Demar's "change of mortal state" and exchange or "broking centre."

43–44 These lines are omitted by Faulkner, 1735.

 44 *sewed.* The broadside has "sow'd," which makes no sense.

 45 *And that he might securely rest.* Faulkner, 1735, has "His heirs that he might safely rest."

47   *The. Gulliveriana* has "That."
52   *half.* Faulkner, 1735, has "self."

Mr. Sheridan's Prologue to the Greek Play of Phaedra and Hippolytus . . .

Of this poem, Deane Swift remarked:

It was customary with Dr. Sheridan to have a Greek play acted by his head class just before they entered the University; and accordingly, in the year 1720, the Doctor having fixed on Hippolytus, wrote a prologue in English, to be spoken by Master Tom Putland, one of the youngest children he had in his school. The prologue was very neat and elegant, but extremely puerile, and quite adapted to the childhood of the speaker, who, as regularly was taught, and rehearsed his part, as any of the upper lads did theirs. However, it unfortunately happened, that Doctor King, the Archbishop of Dublin, had promised Sheridan that he would go and see his lads perform the tragedy. Upon which Doctor Helsham writ another prologue, wherein he laughed egregiously at Sheridan's, and privately instructed Master Putland how to act his part; and, at the same time, exacted a promise from the child, that no consideration should make him repeat that prologue which he had been taught by Sheridan. When the play was to be acted, the Archbishop attended according to his promise, and Master Putland began Helsham's prologue, and went through it to the amazement of Sheridan; which fired him to such a degree, (although he was one of the best natured men in the world) that he would have entirely put off the play, had it not been in respect to the Archbishop, who was indeed highly complimented in Helsham's performance. When the play was over, the Archbishop was very desirous to hear Sheridan's prologue; but all the entreaties of the Archbishop, the child's father, and Sheridan could not prevail with Master Putland to repeat it, having, he said, promised faithfully that he would not, upon any account whatever; and therefore, that he would keep his word. (*A Supplement* . . . , Vol. XXIV, 1776, pp. 363–64)

Sheridan's prologue was first published as a Dublin broadside dated 1721 (Rothschild, Texas), and was reprinted in *Whartoniana,* Vol. I (1727, pp. 13–15), in *A Supplement,* Vol. XXIV (1776, pp. 541–42), and most recently in *JIL,* Vol. I, No. 1 (pp. 25–26). The broadside contains four more lines than the reprintings, and there are a few differences of wording. This printing is based upon the broadside.

Title   Hippolytus. Spelled "Hyppolitus" in the broadside. The title in *Whartoniana* is "Prologue to a Greek Play, Intended to be Spoken by a Boy of six Years old."
   4   *should. Whartoniana* and *A Supplement* have "can."

 6 *would. Whartoniana* and *A Supplement* have "should."
10 *stress. Whartoniana* and *A Supplement* have "load."
11–14 These lines are omitted by *Whartoniana* and *A Supplement*.
15 *Whartoniana* and *A Supplement* indent this line.
21 *Nor had a. Whartoniana* and *A Supplement* have "Or had no."
23 *Whartoniana* and *A Supplement* indent this line.
24 *gig.* A top, a whirligig.
25 *tolt.* To take up, raise or lift. *Whartoniana* and *A Supplement* slightly vary the word order: "The Gig can spin, and hop, and frisk, and tolt."
27–28 The lines make clear that young Putland was to have accompanied his recital with props and gestures. On line 27, he would have bounced and caught the ball; on line 28, he would have dropped the book. *Whartoniana* and *A Supplement* indent line 27. In line 28, "smoke" means to have an understanding of something.
29 *Whartoniana* and *A Supplement* indent this line.
    Mug and Gloss. Mug is a game of marbles and also the hole into which a ball is rolled or thrown in certain games. Gloss is the game of pegging tops.
30 *I have it to play Pitch and Toss. Whartoniana* and *A Supplement* have "I have to play at Pitch and Toss."
31 *this.* The book; as line 38 makes clear, a copy of Euripides's *Hippolytus.*
35 *Whartoniana* and *A Supplement* indent this line.
36–40 During these lines, the kite is tugged about, and the book is tossed and dropped.
36 *Had any poet e'er. Whartoniana* and *A Supplement* have "What poet ever had."
37 *it. Whartoniana* and *A Supplement* have "he."
41 *Whartoniana* and *A Supplement* indent this line.
42 *Whartoniana* and *A Supplement* print "Here is a World of Joy, a World of Pleasure!"
43 *What is this poet good for? Whartoniana* and *A Supplement* print "Now, what is this Book good for?"
44 *Whartoniana* omits the dash.
45–52 *Whartoniana* does not indent line 45, but in the broadside a pointing hand indicates all of these lines as, perhaps, a peroration.

Prologue to *Hippolytus,* Spoken by a Boy of Six Years Old (Helsham)

See the note to "Mr. Sheridan's Prologue to the Greek Play of Phaedra and Hippolytus." Helsham's poem was first printed in a Dublin broadside

of 1721 (TCD), and given the title of "D——n S——t's Prologue to Hip-
polytus, Spoken by a Boy of Six Years Old," which might indicate that
Swift had a hand in the composition. The piece was reprinted in *Wharton-
iana* (pp. 16–18) with the title of "Prologue to the Same, spoken by the
Boy of six Years old," and attributed to Swift. Nichols reprinted it in *A
Supplement* (pp. 542–43), and gave it the title of "Another Prologue, spo-
ken by Master Putland, instead of Dr. Sheridan's." Helsham was con-
nected to the Putland family. This printing is based mainly on the
broadside.

2   *jest. Whartoniana* has "Test," which seems in error.
10 *the. Whartoniana* has "my."
14 *gig.* Something that whirls, a top.
22 *beg.* Although omitted in the broadside, this word appears in *Whar-
    toniana,* and is necessary both for the sense and the iambic pen-
    tameter.
23 *the. Whartoniana* has "this."
26 *rev'rend sage.* "The Bishop of Dublin, who was there." This note
    in *Whartoniana* refers to Archbishop King, who was then in his
    seventieth year.

The Invitation

This poem was originally printed as a broadside in Dublin in 1720
(Rothschild, Texas). It was then described as "Written by Mr. T. S——
to D——r *[sic]* S——." Its most recent printing was in *JIL,* Vol. XVI,
No. 2 (pp. 27–28).

Epigraph   Horace's "Epistle to Torquatus" was, as is Sheridan's poem,
    an invitation to dine. Sheridan or his printer incorrectly spelled
    "Archiacis" as "Archaicis," as also did the anonymous "A Letter
    to Tom Punsibi . . ." in referring to this poem. John Conington
    translates the first lines of Horace as:

    > If you can lie, Torquatus, when you take
    > Your meal, upon a couch of Archias' make,
    > And sup off potherbs, gathered as they come,
    > You'll join me, please, by sunset, at my home.

    A couch by Archias would have been a simple, unassuming piece
    of furniture.

11–12   These lines would seem to indicate that Sheridan had not recently
    been writing poetry.

40 *W——Gs.* Whigs.
42 *Mrs. W——.* Possibly Dorothy Walls, the wife of Archdeacon Thomas Walls, Master of St. Patrick's School.
44 *Miss E——e.* "Eustace" would be a typical Sheridan rhyme for "new stays." Possibly Clotilda Eustace who married Thomas Tickell in 1726. Ball in his edition of the *Correspondence* describes a Miss Eustace as "a lady who had been known to the Deanery circle as 'the brat,' and who is said by the public prints of that day to have been the possessor of 'a great fortune and singular accomplishments.' She was the daughter of Sir Maurice Eustace, one of the nephews and heirs of a Lord Chancellor of Ireland in Restoration times, and with her mother, who was Sir Maurice's second wife, and who had been for many years a widow, was a frequent guest at the Deanery, where they enjoyed the distinction of being allowed to choose their own dinner at a cost not exceeding one shilling and sixpence." (Vol. III, p. 304 n.)

On the same page of the conclusion of the manuscript copy of "Punch's Petition to the Ladies" (Huntington) appears this short poem:

> On Miss Eustace
> Such Graces ye Hibernian Fair adorn
> 'Tis well that Cecil was in England born
> Else Beauty, noted Isle! must yield ye Prize
> And English Hearts submit to Irish eyes.

I Send This at Nine

This previously unpublished piece is contained in a manuscript volume titled *Poems by Swift,* housed in the Royal Irish Academy, Dublin (24.C.31). There is no way of dating the poem other than to place it sometime before 1735 when Sheridan moved to Cavan. I have arbitrarily placed it here, following the similar poem "The Invitation"; on such a basis, of course, it could have appeared after "An Invitation to Dinner" of 1727, or elsewhere.

Tom Punsibi's Letter to Dean Swift

Sheridan's son remarked about this poem:

> When he was disengaged, the Dean used to call in at the Doctor's about the hour of dining, and their custom was to sit in a small back parlour *tête-a-tête,*

and have slices sent them from the common room, of whatever was for the family dinner. The furniture was not in the best repair, being often frequented by boarders, of which the house was seldom without twenty; but was preferred by the Dean as being more snug than the state parlour, which was used only when there was company. The state of the poem is an account of one of these casual visits.

The poem first appeared in a transcript by Swift's friend, Anthony Raymond, the Vicar of Trim, in the endpapers of a manuscript contained in the library of TCD (Ms. H.3.6. [1325]). It was first printed as a Dublin broadside in 1727 (TCD, BL, Cambridge). A slightly shorter version was printed by Sheridan's son in his life of Swift (1784, pp. 444–47), and this version was followed by Scott. Williams (pp. 1045–48) reprinted from the broadside, which the version printed here also basically follows, as does the most recent printing in *JIL*, Vol. XVI, No. 2 (pp. 27–28). The chief differences in the versions are that 1784 contains two lines of dialogue not in the others, and that the others have twenty lines which were shortened to these twelve in 1784:

> Are you disposed to take a seat;
> The instant that it feels your weight,
> Out go its legs and down you come
> Upon your reverend deanship's bum.
> Betwixt two stools, 'tis often said,
> The sitter on the ground is laid;
> What praise then to my chairs is due,
> Where one performs the feat of two!
> Now to the fire, if such there be,
> At present naught but smoke we see.
> "Come stir it up."—"Ho, Mr. Joker,
> How can I stir it without a poker?"

The last two lines above are the new ones that do not appear in the early versions.

In their article "Swift's 'O'Rourke's Feast' and Sheridan's 'Letter': Early Transcripts by Anthony Raymond" (*Proceedings of the First Munster Symposium on Jonathan Swift*, Hermann J. Real and Heinz J. Vienken, eds. (München: Wilhelm Fink, [1986], pp. 27–46), Andrew Carpenter and Alan Harrison argue that the 1784 version is greatly superior to the Raymond transcript and the similar broadside. In one or two specific instances, they are quite persuasive, and I have adopted the 1784 readings; however, other than the differences noted above, I find the variations both few and slight, and consequently have based this printing on the longer broadside version.

The Raymond transcript differs from the 1727 broadside mainly by printing the broadside couplets as one continuous line. All of the versions are confusing and illogical in their indentation and punctuation, and this printing has attempted by indentation and quotation marks to indicate more clearly the two different speakers.

Scott dates the poem 1724; Williams, following the broadside, gives 1727. Raymond, however, died in 1726, and the title of the poem in his transcript is "A Letter to the Revd. Doctor Swift Dean of St Patrick's in the year 1720." The year 1720 was also the year in which Sheridan's similar poem "The Invitation" was written.

16   further. Raymond's transcript has "farther."
21   I. Raymond's transcript has "I'll."
23–24   Raymond's transcript and the 1727 broadside have:

> Twisting, turning, trifling, rumbling,
> Scolding, stairing, fretting, grumbling. . . .

In Raymond, "fretting" is spelled with one "t."

I have adopted the 1784 version because it seems better and because Carpenter and Harrison reasonably suggest that the change may have been authorial rather than editorial.

29   If you're. Raymond's transcript and 1784 have "Are you."
31–32   Raymond's transcript and the 1727 broadside have:

> Nay take the best in all the Room,
> Out go it's Legs, and down you come.

I have adopted the 1784 version, for, as Carpenter and Harrison justly remark, "it is obviously the best of the three."
49–50   These lines occur only in the 1784 printing.
64   The broadside confusingly does not indent this line, although the sense indicates a new speaker, the Dean.
69   have. Raymond has "has."
71   The broadside indents this line.
75   The broadside indents this line.
79   The broadside does not indent this line and thereby confuses the meaning as the Dean is now speaking.
80   Why. Raymond and 1784 have "Why"; the broadside has "You," which is not quite as effective because of the "You" in the previous line.

82 *the Recorder.* Dublin legal official who kept the rolls of the city and the records of the courts of Quarter sessions.
83 The broadside confusingly indents this line although the Dean is still speaking.
87 *devil's.* Raymond has more awkwardly "Dev'l is."
90 *leg.* Raymond has "Rump."
91 The broadside indents this line although the Dean is still speaking.
93 *them.* 1784 has "'em."
94 *cannot.* Raymond has "shall not."
96 The broadside does not indent this line although the speaker has changed to Sheridan.
    you're always. The year 1784 has "you are not," and Carpenter and Harrison argue that that is a much better reading and that the broadside version is nonsensical. It seems to me, however, that either version makes sense and that it is difficult to call either inferior.

A Prologue Spoke by Mr. Elrington . . .

Williams notes that "Archbishop King estimated that the number of families in the weaving trade in dire want was nearly seventeen hundred, and the number of persons six thousand. . . . The government ordered £100 for relief purposes; collections were made in churches; and a play, realising £73, was given for the benefit of distressed weavers. The play chosen for performance was *Hamlet* (*Gentleman's Journal,* 15 April, 1721)." For this performance, Sheridan wrote the prologue, and Swift wrote the epilogue. An answer to both poems (see *A Supplement,* Vol. XXIV, 1776, pp. 528–29) is sometimes attributed to Delany, but Foxon says that there is no support for this attribution. Foxon, however, is incorrect in assigning the prologue and epilogue to 1720.

This printing is based on the earliest publication I have seen of Sheridan's prologue, a broadside printed in Dublin by John Harding in 1721 (BL). Swift's epilogue is printed on the verso. Williams notes an earlier separate printing of both poems as broadsides, and also cites printings in *St. James's Post* of April 10–12, and in *Gentleman's Journal* of April 15. Later reprintings occurred in Concanen's *Miscellaneous Poems* (pp. 205–7); in *The Drapier's Miscellany* (pp. 3–5) where the prologue is attributed to Swift; in *A Supplement,* Vol. XXIV (1776, pp. 527–28); in Scott, Roscoe, and Browning. Recent separate printings of Swift's epilogue are in Williams (pp. 273–76), Davis (pp. 214–16), and Rogers (pp. 228–29). Recent separate printings of Sheridan's prologue are in *JIL,* Vol. XVI, No. 2 (p. 29), and in Fagan's *A Georgian Celebration* (pp. 165–66). The catalog of the Gilbert Collection does list a Sheridan prologue, probably not this one, printed by J. Carson in 1720, but I have not been able to compare it as it has been cut out from the volume in which it was bound.

Title Concanen and Fagan, following him, print the title as "A Prologue spoken by Mr. Elrington at the Theatre Royal in Dublin on behalf of the distressed weavers." Thomas Elrington (fl. 1688–1732) was the actor-manager of the Theatre Royal, Smock Alley.

1 *Great cry and little wool.* According to Fagan, "a proverb denoting a disappointing result." *The Concise Oxford Dictionary of Proverbs* cites uses in 1475, 1659, and by Addison in *The Spectator* of December 18, 1711.

7 *stuffs.* Woolen fabrics.

18 *Silk comes . . . are.* Concanen and Fagan have "silks come" and "from."

34 *Indian drapery.* Silk dresses.

37 *We'd.* Concanen and Fagan have "we'll."

Prologue to the Farce of *Punch Turned Schoolmaster*

In a letter of April 15, 1721, to Charles Ford, Swift wrote, "Sheridan put the Players upon acting a Puppet shew, but his Subject was ill chosen, and his performance worse, and it succeeded accordingly" (Williams, *Correspondence,* Vol. II, p. 381). Sheridan's play has been lost, but this printing of his prologue is based upon its apparently first publication in Mathew Concanen's *Miscellaneous Poems* (pp. 398–400). It appeared also in *A Supplement,* Vol. XXIV (1776, p. 539), and most recently in *JIL,* Vol. XVI, No. 2 (pp. 29–30). This printing follows Concanen.

Sub-title *Griffith.* Thomas Griffith, popular Dublin actor of the day.

6 *Banimeer.* A character in a puppet show.

8 *Stretch.* An English puppet-master.

15 *The Rival Queens.* Nathaniel Lee's play of 1667.

16 *The Queen of Ivy Land.* Unidentified.

18 *Capel Street.* Where Stretch performed.

From The Puppet-Show (Anon.)

Probably in early April 1721, Sheridan's play *Punch Turned Schoolmaster* was produced in Dublin. The central comic device of the play was that real actors should take the roles of puppets (see previous note). In his letter to Ford of April 15 Swift also noted that Sheridan's play:

. . . gave Occasion to a very pretty Copy of Verses on Puppet shews printed here but not published, yet I shall soon get one, and would send it to you if I could Frank it; We cannot find the Author, and it is not Delany. (*Letters of Swift to Ford.* Oxford: Clarendon Press, 1935, pp. 89–90)

Nichol Smith and Williams both regard these remarks as strong evidence that Swift was not the author of "The Puppet Show," as "Swift is not given to mystifying Ford." Williams, however, does add that "The familiar reference to Sheridan as 'Tom,' and to his besetting sin of punning, is quite in Swift's style." Ball in *Swift's Verse* (p. 162) definitely attributes the poem to Swift.

The earliest copy of the poem, and apparently the one referred to by Swift, is a Dublin broadside of 1721 printed by John Harding (Huntington). It was reprinted in the London *St. James's Post* on April 21, and then printed as Swift's in Faulkner's *Works,* Vol. VIII (1762, p. 175), and also by Scott and other editors. The printings are nearly identical.

69 thee. Refers to Stretch the puppet-master.

A Copy of a Copy of Verses . . .

Sheridan's poem evoked Swift's jocular appreciation entitled "George Nim-Dan-Dean, Esq. to Mr Sheridan on his Verses, Written July 15, 1721, at Ten in the Morning" (Williams, pp. 1020–22; Rogers, pp. 231–33), which said in part:

> Thy Verse like Bricks, defy the Weather,
> When smooth'd by rubbing them together:
> Thy Words so closely wedg'd, and short are,
> Like Walls, more lasting without Mortar:
> By leaving out the needless Vowels,
> You save the Charge of Lime and Trowels.
> One Letter still another Locks;
> Each groov'd, and Dove-tail'd, like a Box.

Sheridan's *jeu d'esprit* was first printed by Faulkner (1762, Vol. X, and 1763, Vol. XI, p. 318), and this printing is based upon 1763 but attempts to correct several problems of Faulkner's spacing, which might confuse. The poem's most recent printings are by Williams (pp. 1019–20) and *JIL,* Vol. XVI, No. 2 (p. 30).

Title George Nim-Dan-Dean. George Rochfort, John Rochfort, Daniel Jackson, and Swift who were all staying at the Rochfort family seat, Gaulstown House, near Duleek, Co. Meath. Faulkner notes that John Rochfort was "called Nim, because he was a great hunter, from Nimrod."

 1 *t' know.* Faulkner has "t'know."
 3 *b' half.* Faulkner has "b'half."
 9 *I 'ppear.* Faulkner has "I'appear."
10 *bowl 't.* Faulkner has "Bowl't."
12 *I h'd.* Faulkner has "I'h'd"; Williams has "I' h'd."
    t' skim. Faulkner has "t'skim."
13 *I h'd.* Again Faulkner has "I'h'd."
14 *pim-.* Faulkner, although not Williams, mistakenly prints the entire
    word, "Pimples," in the line.
15–18 These lines appear incorrectly aligned by Williams.
15 *('s 'tis n't).* Faulkner has "(s'tis n't)."
16 *must have ach'd. Th' Clans of th' C'llege Sanh'drim.* Williams in-
    correctly has "must have ask'd Th' Clans." Sanhedrim, council.
17 *t' say.* Faulkner has "t'say." He also indents this line.
18 *D'l'n', 'chlin, P. Ludl', Dic' St'wart, H'lsham, Capt'n P'rr' Walmsl',
    'nd Longhsh'nks Tim.* Delany. Probably the Rev. John Echlin whom
    Swift mentions in a letter to Lord Carteret of July 3, 1725, as being,
    with Delany and others, among the contemporary clergymen "most
    distinguished for their Learning and Piety." According to Delany in
    his *Observations,* Swift consulted Echlin on all matters relating to
    the cathedral choir. Delany also adds that Echlin was "as complete
    a man, and as fine a gentleman, as any of his age." Echlin became
    Vicar-General of Tuam in 1734. Peter Ludlow, Irish M.P. Dick Stew-
    art; Burtchaell and Sadleir note that Richard Stewart, described as
    Generosus or Gentleman, sent his son Richard to Trinity in 1722
    when the son was seventeen. Helsham, Captain Perry Walmsley,
    and, according to Faulkner's note, "Mr. Stopford of Finglas. Minis-
    ter of that Parish, afterwards Bishop of Cloyne." "Tim" was origi-
    nally written "Timm," but I suspect that this was a misprint for
    "Jim." The phrase "Long Shanks Jim" is used in "George Nim-Dan-
    Dean's Invitation," and Stopford's first name was James.
        Faulkner prints "D'l'n'" as "D'ln'."
The dating. Faulkner assigns the composition of Sheridan's poem to
    July 15 "at night" and of George Nim-Dan-Dean's answer to July
    15 "at Ten in the Morning." As Rogers notes, "if taken literally, this
    would mean that the answer preceded the original poem."

To George Nim-Dan-Dean, Esq., upon His Incomparable
Verses . . .

Sheridan's playful shortening of lines by eliminating vowels in "A Copy
of a Copy of Verses" evoked two replies by Swift, George and John

Rochfort, and Dan Jackson. One, "George Nim-Dan-Dean, Esq. to Mr. Sheridan" (Williams, pp. 1020–22; Rogers pp. 231–33) is an ironic admiration of Sheridan's form, and the other, "George Nim-Dan-Dean's Invitation to Mr. Sheridan" (Williams, pp. 1022–23; Rogers, pp. 233–34) is an Ogden Nashery, which is the antithesis of Sheridan's form. It was written in long, rambling, seemingly meterless lines that unexpectedly end in the overwhelming form of quadruple rhyme. For instance:

> Dear Tom, this verse, which however the beginning may appear, yet in the *end's good metre*,
> Is sent to desire that, when your August vacation comes, your *friends you'd meet here.*

Sheridan's poem "To George Nim-Dan-Dean, Esq. Upon His Incomparable Verses" in content satirizes this form and in its own form attempts to one-up it. Sheridan's manuscript has not survived, but Deane Swift has described its ingenious form: "These verses were all written in circles, one within another, as appears from the observations in the . . . poems by Dr. Swift."

There has been some question about the authorship of "To George Nim-Dan-Dean, Esq. Upon his Incomparable Verses." Deane Swift, who first published them (*Works*, 1765, 4to, Vol. VIII ((2)), pp. 233–39), said that they were "Written by Dr. Delany in the name of Thomas Sheridan." However, Swift's reply is addressed "To Mr. Thomas Sheridan, Upon his Verses Written in Circles" (Williams, pp. 1026–27; Rogers, pp. 234–37); and George Rochfort's reply, "On Dr. Sheridan's Circular Verses," goes further and directly satirizes Sheridan's constant versifying and fiddle-playing, and in one line even remarks that Swift's and Delany's poems are much better. Finally, Delany in his *Observations* (p. 107) directly refers to Sheridan's having written the poem. All of these matters point conclusively to Sheridan's authorship.

Sheridan's poem was reprinted by Faulkner, Vol. XIII (1765, pp. 366–68) and later by Scott, Roscoe, Browning, Horrell, Williams (pp. 1024–26), and *JIL*, Vol. XVI, No. 2 (pp. 30–31). This printing is based on Deane Swift.

2   *Wight Briareus.* In Greek mythology, Briareus and his brothers, Cottus and Gyges, were each possessed of a hundred arms and fifty heads. In one legend, they assisted Zeus in repelling the Titans who were consigned to Tartarus, the gates of which were guarded by Briareus and his brothers. See Virgil, *Aeneid,* VI, line 287.

4   *triple-bodied Geryon.* In Greek mythology, Geryon was the king of the island of Erytheia and usually represented as a monster with

three heads or bodies. One of the labors of Hercules was to carry off his cattle. See Lucretius, V, line 28, and Virgil, *Aeneid,* VII, line 662, and VIII, line 202.

12 *Cambysian.* Cambyses was the son of Cyrus the Great, and, according to Herodotus and Darius, a drunken, murdering despot. Browning also notes that he was "the emblem of bravado." In Act II, Scene iv of *Henry IV, Part 1,* Falstaff says, "I must speak in passion, and I will do it in King Cambyses' vein." Shakespeare probably had in mind Thomas Preston's ranting play on Cambyses of 1569.

34 *Pompey's caterer of courses.* The meaning would seem to be long, long meals, but the only reference in Plutarch with even a dim relevance is "Pompey," XL, 4–5. In Volume I of his *Apothegms* (Gilbert, Ms. 123, pp. 95–96), Sheridan relates, however, a story with some relevance:

> When *Pompey's* Stomach did nauseate common meats, his Physician prescribed him a Thrush to eat; but upon search, there was none to be bought, (for they were not then in season) and one telling him, they were to be had at the house of *Lucullus,* who had them all the year round, Why then, said he, if it were not for *Lucullus's* Luxury, must not *Pompey* live? Not minding the Physician's Prescription, he took up with plain food.

42 *Statira.* One of the heroines of Nat Lee's *The Rival Queens, or the Death of Alexander the Great* of 1677. Browning also notes that she is "Represented as the perfection of female beauty in *Cassandra,* a romance by La Calprenède, romancier et auteur dramatique. 1610–1663." I suspect that Sheridan, however, had the Lee play in mind, for he refers to it in his "Prologue to the Farce of *Punch Turned Schoolmaster,*" and he seems to lampoon it in his *Alexander's Overthrow.*

46 *Thaumantia.* "Iris, daughter of Thaumas, and the messenger of Juno, descending and returning on the rainbow." Browning's note.

52 *The famous statue of Laöcoön.* The statue by three Rhodian sculptors—Agesander, Polydorus, and Athenodorus—dates probably from the second century B.C., and is now in the Vatican Museum. It depicts Laöcoön and his two sons enmeshed in the coils of two great sea serpents, and Sheridan means that George Nim-Dan-Dean's verses twist and twine interminably, if not fatally. For Laöcoön's story, see Virgil, *Aeneid,* II, lines 56–316.

56 *Echo.* "At Gallstown there is so famous an Echo, that, if you repeat two lines of Virgil out of a speaking-trumpet, you may hear the

nymph return them to your ear with great propriety and clearness."
Deane Swift's note.

56 *Rattah-whittah-whit.* "These words allude to their amusements
with the Echo, having no other signification but to express the sound
of stones returned by the Echo, when beaten one against the other."
Deane Swift's note.

With Music and Poetry Equally Blessed (Rochfort)

George Rochfort's clever poem was written in reply to Sheridan's "To
George Nim-Dan-Dean, Esq., Upon his Incomparable Verses, &c. of Au-
gust 2d, M DCC XXI." The first printing that I have discovered was by
Orrery in his *Remarks* (p. 55). Orrery did not identify the author, but
printed the lines, as a presumably just summation of Sheridan, at the
end of his own character sketch. Delany, in his *Observations upon Lord
Orrery's Remarks* (pp. 73–75) identified the author as George Rochfort
and apparently worked from a different and probably more authentic
manuscript. He added two lines missing in Orrery, and has occasional
variations in wording, spelling, and punctuation. The poem, as printed
here, is based on Delany's version which Nichols reprinted (p. 682) under
the title of "Mr. George Rochfort's Epigram on Dr. Sheridan." The piece
was reprinted in Scott under the title of "On Dr. Sheridan's Circular
Verses," as well as in Roscoe, Browning, and Williams (pp. 1027–28).

3   *harmony, verses.* Printed as "poetry, music" by Orrery.
4   *Assisted.* Printed as "Instructed" by Orrery.
6   *My verse is neglected, my tunes flung away.* Printed as "My tunes
are neglected, my verse flung away" by Orrery.
7   *Vice-Apollo.* "Dr. Swift." Orrery's note. In Delany's "News from
Parnassus," also written in 1721, Apollo had selected Swift as his
"Vicegerent."
9   *signet.* Printed as "sign he" by Orrery.
15–16 Not printed by Orrery.
19 *thy.* Printed as "your" by Orrery.
20 *thy well-meaning and humorous.* Printed as "your unmeaning and
innocent" by Orrery.
21 *Thy.* Printed as "Your" by Orrery.
22 *Thy.* Printed as "Your" by Orrery.
23 *rondeaus.* "A song, or peculiar kind of poetry, which returns to the
beginning of the first verse, and so continues in a perpetual rota-

tion." Orrery's note. Orrery also spells the word as "Roundos," and prints "your" for "thy."

A Portrait from the Life (Swift)

This poem was first published by Deane Swift in 1765, and then included in all of the significant collections of Swift's poems, and most recently by Williams (pp. 954–55) and Rogers (p. 266). Rogers correctly notes that there is no way of dating the piece exactly. However, Swift did allude to Dan Jackson as "Merry Dan" in 1718 in the exchange of poems about Jackson's nose, so one is tempted to think of the piece as occurring early rather than late in Swift's friendship with Sheridan.

The antipathy between Swift and Sheridan's wife has been attested both by Swift and Sheridan.

9 *friend Thomas, Ford, Grattan, and merry Dan.* The first cited is Sheridan, the second Charles Ford, and the fourth the Rev. Daniel Jackson. Re Grattan, the original footnote by Deane Swift cites the Rev. John Grattan, but Rogers cites "Robert Grattan, probably," who was one of Swift's executors.

A Letter to Tom Punsibi, Occasioned by Reading His Excellent Farce . . . (Anon.)

This printing is taken from a four-page Dublin pamphlet of late 1721 or early 1722 (Newberry). The piece was reprinted in *Whartoniana* (pp. 57–60), and is one of several poems that the production of Sheridan's *Alexander's Overthrow* on December 11, 1721, gave rise to. The anonymous author obviously knew Sheridan well over a period of years, and the prime suspects would be Delany, Helsham, or George Rochfort. The piece is particularly interesting because it seems definitely to identify the broadside "S——s Master Piece Or, Tom Pun-sibi's Folly Compleat" as Sheridan's production.

Epigraph   Horace's entire line reads "Invidiam placare paras virtute relicta?" Philip Francis translates it as "Think you the Wrath of Envy to appease?"
2 *from. Whartoniana* has "in."
6 *oft'ner nimmed. Whartoniana* has "often." Nimmed means stolen.
24–25   This couplet is a gibe at Sheridan's Grammar that took over, practically intact, much from the Royal Grammar.

25 *from. Whartoniana* has "of."
26 *nor care nor. Whartoniana* has "no care nor."
47 See line 14 of "S——s Master Piece," which reads "Drive off these Romans with your beggar's bullets."
51 *thine own Caesar.* A character in Sheridan's *Alexander's Overthrow.*
52 *Dear Tummas.* The author of "A Punegyric upon Tom Pun-sibi's Ars Punica" also calls Sheridan Tummas.
fn 1 In the Newberry Library copy of the poem, part of the last line of the footnote is missing, but the missing words may be supplied from the reprinting in *Whartoniana,* and appear to be "entirely his own and none of it stolen." G——r is John Greer who wrote the pamphlets accusing Sheridan of plagiarism.
fn 4 *Horace's Si potes Archaisis.* The author should have written "Si potes Archiacis," the first words from Horace, Epistle V, Book I. This epistle is a verse invitation to dinner, and its entire first sentence reads:

> Si potes Archiacis conviva recumbere lectis
> nec modica cenare times holus omne patella,
> supremo te sole domi, Torquate, manebo.

H. Rushton Fairclough translates the lines as, "If you can recline at my table on couches made by Archias, and are not afraid of 'a dinner of herbs' only, from a modest dish, I shall expect you, Torquatus, at my house at sunset." A couch made by Archias would have been a small, unpretentious one.
    In *Whartoniana,* "S——n" and "S——t" are spelled out.
fn 6 *S——n's.* In *Whartoniana,* the word is spelled out, "Sheridan's."

An Elegy on the Deplorable Death of Mr. Thomas Sheridan . . .
(Anon.)

The only previous printing of these lame verses with their heavy-handed irony was in a Dublin broadside of 1721/22 (TCD). Celebrating the fictional death of an opponent was, of course, no new or original joke. In 1708, Swift concocted just such a trick on Partridge, the London almanac-maker. Swift certainly, however, had no hand in this elegy on Sheridan, even though its title and to some extent its form follow Swift's "An Elegy on Mr. Partridge, the Almanack-maker, who Died on the 29th of this Instant March, 1708." Both the poetic craft and the quality of the humor in this piece on Sheridan are distinctly third-rate. Perhaps the only telling point, other than the usual allusions to Sheridan's marital unhappiness and to his half-plagiarized grammar, is the use of Swift's original joke against his friend.

What happened on March 8 might have been a revival of *Alexander's Overthrow,* which was originally produced on the previous December 11; however, I have discovered no record of such a revival.

10   *Paean's.* In Greek religion, Paean was the physician of gods; it is
       unknown whether he was a separate entity or an aspect of Apollo.
       Here, Paean probably stands for Apollo.

A Poem on Tom Pun-bi . . . (Anon.)

Apparently the only previous printing of this anonymous poem was a Dublin broadside of 1722 (Yale). The acute accents in lines 8, 32, 34, and 42 have been added here to make the lines conform to the basic iambic pentameter.

Title   Poem. Curiously spelled "Poam" in the original.
           "Sheridan's Resurrection". This poem has not survived.
3–4   *St. Catherine's shades . . . Mountcashel's seat.* St. Catherine's was
         the home of the Mountcashels.
   9   *B——y, thy dear w——e.* "Betty" and "wife."
 12   *th'.* Originally printed as "the," which muddles the meter.
 29   *thy farce. Alexander's Overthrow.*
 32   *th' amazed.* Originally "the amazed." I have altered it to fit the
         metrical pattern.

Tom Pun-sibi's Resurrection Disproved (Anon.)

The first publication of this poem, upon which this printing is based, was apparently a Dublin broadside of 1722. The Huntington Library copy has written on it "June 1722: Tho: Sheridan is alive." The piece was reprinted in *Whartoniana* (pp. 64–69).

If we are to credit this poem (lines 69–70 and 79), Sheridan was irritated by "An Elegy on the Deplorable Death," thrashed some newsboys who were selling it, and sent some of his own students "To break the press where it was printed."

Epigraph   Joseph P. Clancy translates the lines as:

Would the blood come back to his thin ghost
Whom Mercury once and for all
(he does not take kindly to prayers to open the gates)
With his grim staff has gathered to the flock of shades?

4   *sound as fish.* Possibly from the phrase "sound as a roach." According to Brewer: "Quite sound. A pun upon *roach* or *roche* the fish, and the French *roche,* a rock."

9–10   These lines contain a near quotation from "An Elegy on . . . Demar . . ." which Sheridan probably wrote with Swift, Stella, and Delany.

13   *quatenus.* As.

21   *Obadiah Fizle.* Fizzle is the nominal translator of the anonymous pamphlet of 1722 titled *The Benefit of Farting Explain'd: or, the Fundament-all Cause of the Distempers incident to the FAIR-SEX Enquired into. Providing* a Posteriori *most of the Dis-ordures Intail'd upon them, are owing to Flatulencies not seasonably vented* (TCD). In passing, this farrago of miserable half-puns and adolescent vulgarities attributes to Sheridan the authorship of the considerably abler pamphlet *The Wonderful Wonder of Wonders. Being an Accurate Description of the Birth, Education, Manner of Living, Religion, Politicks, Learning, &c. of Mine A-se,* which was also published in 1722 (TCD). Of *The Benefit of Farting Explain'd,* Swift wrote to Knightley Chetwode on March 13, 1721/22, "Surely you in the country have got the London fancy, that I am the author of all the scurvy things that come out of here. The slovenly pages called the Benefit of _____ was writ by one Dobbs a surgeon."

24   *Fartinando Puffendorst.* Don Fartinado Puff-indorst, described as the Professor of Bumbast in the University of Crackow, nominally wrote, in Spanish, *The Benefit of Farting Explain'd.*

25   *a joke. Whartoniana* has "meer Talk."

29   *where. Whartoniana* has *when.*

35   *Partridge.* An allusion to Swift's 1708 joke which claimed that Partridge, the London almanac-maker, was dead.

37   *the learn'd Squire.* Swift, writing under the pseudonym of Isaac Bickerstaff.

85–104   John Whalley (1653–1724) was a Dublin almanac-maker and publisher. See Biographical Index. John Coates, or Coats, was an almanac-maker from Cork, who published *Vox Stellarum,* a rival almanac to Whalley's. If we are to credit this poem, Coates played such a trick on Whalley as Swift had on Partridge and as the anonymous author of "An Elegy on the Deplorable Death of Mr. Thomas Sheridan" had on Sheridan.

112   *Or quaint enigma on his a———.* This seems a definite attribution to Sheridan of the poem which is here printed with the title of "A Riddle." The attribution would put the composition of "A Riddle" some time before June, 1722.

118   *per'lous. Whartoniana* has "Par'lous."

140   *clapper-claws and firks.* Clapper-claws is to thrash soundly. Firks is also to thrash or whip, whips poor bums being an allusion to Sheridan's schoolmastering.

From A Description in Answer to "The Journal" (Percival)

Swift's poem "The Journal" of 1721 was a generally genial satire of how life was lived at Gaulstown House where he had stayed with the Rochforts from June to October. However, toward the end of the poem, William Percival, the Dean of Emly, came in for some rather more biting remarks, as also did his wife. The poem led to some criticism of Swift for abusing the hospitality of friends, and Percival's contribution was this poem from which I have taken a few lines that refer to Sheridan as well as Swift.

This printing is based on the Dublin broadside of 1722 (TCD). The piece was reprinted by Scott, Vol. I (1814, p. 272).

A Description of Doctor Delany's Villa

F. Elrington Ball in his *History of County Dublin* notes that on May Day, 1719, Helsham and Delany leased from Dorothy Berkeley a tract of land called the Glen, containing a large stone house, in the village of Glasnevin.

Helsham, who had an advantage over Delany in being born to an assured position, acted probably the part of the rich friend in joining in the lease of the Glen, and appears to have soon relinquished whatever connexion he may have had with it. But the joint-tenancy lasted sufficiently long to allow Swift an opportunity of excercising his power of verbal manipulation in using the first syllables of his tenants' names to confer on the Glen the designation of Heldelville, which was soon changed to its diminutive Delville, either, as has been suggested to avoid inconvenient associations, or to suit the changed conditions when Helsham's interest terminated. Throughout his life Delany displayed an ambition of making a figure in the world, and in order to do so he lived in a style that his means did not justify. At Delville he sought to gain the reputation of an improver, and for many years he indulged there in reckless outlay. The house, which had been occupied by Mrs. Berkeley, was levelled with the ground, and another was designed without any regard to the dimensions of his purse, while the few acres of land were made the subject of an attempt to show how "the obdurate and straight line of the Dutch might be softened into a curve, the terrace melted into a swelling bank, and the walks opened to catch the vicinal country." (Part VI, 1920, pp. 130–31)

Delany had as much as twelve acres of land, and the description, as well as two photographs of the house in Ball, indicate that it was quite imposing. Weston St. John Joyce in his 1912 volume, *The Neighbourhood of Dublin,* was still able to describe the estate thusly:

The gardens are laid out to the best advantage, and retain, in their main features, the design of their originator. They contain a number of magnificent trees and shrubs, among which are arbutus, ilex and yew, many of them of venerable appearance. A pretty stream, spanned by rustic bridges, flows through the grounds which are well enclosed, forming a delightful retreat.

Maurice Craig, the architectural historian, visited the house as a young man, and remarked in conversation with the present editor that it was a comfortable rather than a distinguished building. The house existed in good repair until the 1940s when it was torn down by an order of nuns who then owned the property. The modern Irish clergy have been possibly more destructive to Ireland's great houses than Cromwell. When staying in the hospital, Bons Secours, which now is built on the grounds, in 1987, I was told by one of the nuns that a grotto of the Virgin outside my bedroom window was supposed to be on the spot of Stella's bower. Otherwise, the only memento of Delville that remains is an ornate fireplace in one of the receiving rooms downstairs.

The point of Sheridan's poem would seem to be not that Delany's estate was tiny, but an ironic gibe that it was too large for a churchman and scholar and too small for so many improvements. The clever details of the poem are Sheridan's own inventions, but his idea was undoubtedly derived from Martial. See Epigram 18 of Book Eleven:

Lupus, a farm near town you gave to me;
A larger plot I in my window see;
Such scrap of earth a *farm* 'twere hard to prove,
When one small rue-plant makes Diana's grove.
This, which a locust's wing might overlay!
Whose crops would feed an ant one single day!
This, which a folded rose-leaf might have crown'd,
Where not a herb can any more be found
Than eastern scents or fragrant spices rare,
To please a palate or perfume the hair;
Where e'en a cucumber must crooked lie;

A snake to coil its tail would vainly try.
Such garden scarce one caterpillar feeds;
The willow-bed no second insect breeds;
The mole alone my farm does plough and dig;
No mushroom here can gape; no early fig,
Nor smiling violet, here has room to grow;
The devastated land a mouse lays low,
More dreaded by the owner than of yore
Was that huge beast the Caledonian boar.
Aloft my crops are carried in the straw,
Caught by the flying swallow's slender claw.
Priapus here can scarce find room to stand,
Though half his size, and reft of wooden brand.
One snail-shell holds our yearly grain, and more;
In one pitch'd nut-shell all the wine we store.
Lupus, your kindness by one letter err'd;
To call such gift a *favour* was absurd:
Take back your farm; more grateful far to me
The *savour* that your kitchen yields, would be.

This translation appeared in the *English Journal of Education* for January 1856 and was reprinted in *The Epigrams of Martial* (London: Henry G. Bohn, 1860), pp. 507–8. See also Swift's critical remarks in "An Epistle upon an Epistle" (Williams, pp. 475–79).

Sheridan's poem was first printed by Concanen in *Miscellaneous Poems* (pp. 239–42). It was first attributed to Sheridan by Nichols in *A Supplement,* Vol. XXIV (1776 and 1779, pp. 212–14). It was also attributed to Sheridan in *Additions to the Works of Alexander Pope,* Vol. I (1776, p. 119); however, the most convincing attribution is by Sheridan's son in his edition of Swift, Vol. VII (1784, p. 250), where he remarks of the poem, "This was not Swift's, but written by Dr. Sheridan." A transcript (Harley 7316, p. 420) in the British Library also attributes the poem to Sheridan, and Ball in *Swift's Verse* remarks, "There is no good reason to disbelieve that the piece . . . was also written by Sheridan" (p. 230). I stress the attributions so much because Sir Frederick Falkiner and Browning disagree. In Temple Scott's edition of Swift's prose, Vol. XII (pp. 79–82), Falkiner weakly argues that the poem may be by Swift because of some similarity to Swift's poem on Vanbrugh's House, and Browning in his 1910 edition of Swift's poems asserts, without argument, that the piece is "unquestionably by Swift." In addition, two late printings—in the *Pennsylvania Magazine* (Vol. I, May 1775, p. 231), and in the *Hibernia Magazine* (1782, p. 216)—attribute the poem to Swift.

Other printings are in *Miscellaneous Pieces in Prose and Verse* (1789, pp. 212–14); Sheridan-Nichols, Vol. XVI (1808, pp. 300–1); Scott, Roscoe, and *JIL,* Vol. I, No. 2 (p. 32). This printing is based on Concanen.

15   haggard. A stock-yard, an enclosed place near a farmhouse.

A Prologue Designed for the Play of *Oedipus* . . .

The poem first appeared in a broadside, probably printed in Dublin in December 1723 (Huntington). It was reprinted by Wilde in *The Closing Years of Dean Swift's Life* (Dublin: Hodges and Smith, 1849), pp. 159–60. Wilde thinks that, because the schoolboy speaker was critical of his master, the poem could not have been Sheridan's. This, however, was a joke that Sheridan had used in several other prologues.

11   peal. Spelled "Pale" in the broadside.
14   Barring-out. "A practice of barring the master out of the school-room in order to dictate terms to him. It was once common, but is now numbered with past customs. Miss Edgeworth has a tale so called." Brewer.

A New Year's Gift for the Dean of St. Patrick's

This printing is based on Sheridan's manuscript in the Huntington Library. It was printed from that manuscript by Scott, Vol. XV (1814, pp. 115–17), by Williams (pp. 1039–41), and by *JIL,* Vol. XVI, No. 2 (pp. 36–37). The title in Williams's printing is "To the Dean of St. Patrick's"; the title printed here is Sheridan's endorsement on the back of the manuscript.

3   Favorite. I have substituted "Favorite" for Sheridan's "Fav'rite," in order to retain his iambic pentameter.
11   us. Scott prints "as."
25   Bolingbroke and Anna. Henry St. John, First Viscount Bolingbroke (1678–1751), leading Tory politician and Swift's good friend; Anne, Queen of England (1665–1714).
26   Shane Tunelly and Bryan Granna. Probably Cavan neighbors. MacLysaght in *The Surnames of Ireland* lists Townley as a name occurring in Louth, Cavan, and Dublin, and Ó Grianain as a rare name found in Cavan and Sligo.
27   Oxford and Ormond. Robert Harley, first Earl of Oxford (1661–1724), leading Tory politician with Bolingbroke in the reign of Queen

Anne, and a friend of Swift and Pope; James Butler, second Duke of Ormonde (1665–1745), Tory politician, Lord Lieutenant of Ireland, prominent Jacobite, and a friend of Swift.

60   *whisks.* Scott prints "whisk."

64   *cronawns.* Humming.

The Drapier's Ballad

This song first appeared as an anonymous broadside, printed by John Harding in Dublin in 1724/25 (TCD). It was reprinted anonymously with the title "Song III" in *Fraud Detected* (pp. 220–22). When reprinted under the same title in *The Hibernian Patriot* (pp. 257–61), it was attributed to Sheridan. The version printed here is based mainly upon the broadside, but the principal variants are listed.

9   *he was. Fraud Detected* has "was he."

10   *traitors.* The broadside has "t——s"; *Fraud Detected* and *The Hibernian Patriot* print the word out.

15   *exceed. Fraud Detected* and *The Hibernian Patriot* have "excel."

16   *This drapier's gallant mind. Fraud Detected* and *The Hibernian Patriot* have "Our gallant *Drapier's* Mind."

19   *went up. Fraud Detected* and *The Hibernian Patriot* have "sent o'er."

28   *T'. Fraud Detected* has "To."

32   *soared. Fraud Detected* and *The Hibernian Patriot* have "reach'd."

44ff   *A champion. . . .* The allusion is to William Wood and his proposed coinage against which Swift wrote *The Drapier's Letters.*

47   *boasts. Fraud Detected* and *The Hibernian Patriot* have "Boast."

58   The broadside prints "Of some —— No Matter where," which would seem to be wrong, for it suggests the inclusion of one or two more syllables into what should be an iambic trimeter line. *Fraud Detected* and *The Hibernian Patriot* have "Of some! (no matter where)."

64   *traitors.* Again the broadside has "t——s," while *Fraud Detected* and *The Hibernian Patriot* print the word out.

72   *sad.* Not included in the broadside, it does appear in *Fraud Detected* and *The Hibernian Patriot,* and is necessary to fill out the meter.

83   *who're. Fraud Detected* and *The Hibernian Patriot* print "those," which is perhaps less awkward.

85   *That we no acts have made. Fraud Detected* and *The Hibernian Patriot* print "As yet, no Acts we've made."

96   still be crowned. Fraud Detected and *The Hibernian Patriot* print
"go all round."

A Riddle

The copy-text of this riddle is its first publication in Vol. III of Swift's
Works of 1735 (pp. 384–86). Of this and seven other riddles, George Faulk-
ner there remarked:

> About Nine of Ten Years ago, some ingenious Gentlemen, Friends to the
> Author, used to entertain themselves with writing Riddles, and send them to
> him and their other Acquaintance, Copies of which ran about, and some of
> them were printed both here and in England. The Author, at his leisure Hours,
> fell into the same Amusement; although it be said that he thought them of no
> great Merit, Entertainment, or Use. However, by the Advice of some Persons,
> for whom the Author hath a great Esteem, and who were pleased to send us
> the Copies, we have ventured to print the few following, as we have done two
> or three before, and which are allowed to be genuine; because, we are informed
> that several good Judges have a Taste for such Kind of Compositions.

One of the riddles had already been printed as a broadside "By the Revd.
Doctor D——y," but the authorship of the others has remained uncertain.
However, we may confidently ascribe this one about "The Posteriors" to
Sheridan because it is on the same subject as his essay, "The Wonderful
Wonder of Wonders," and also because it uses some of the same examples
and even occasionally a similar wording. For instance:

> He is a perpetual hanger on. . . . "Wonderful Wonder."
> An humble hanger-on at best. . . . "A Riddle."
>
> . . . as fast as he gets he lets it fly. "Wonderful Wonder."
> And all I get, I let it fly. "A Riddle."
>
> He is generally the first abed in the family, and the
>   last up. . . . "Wonderful Wonder."
> I last get up, and first a-bed. "A Riddle."

In a letter to Pope, dated December 5, 1726, Swift remarked that he
was tempted to have the riddles printed as a batch. However, the anony-
mous "Tom Pun-Sibi's Resurrection Disproved" in line 112 definitely at-
tributes "A Riddle" to Sheridan, and this would put the composition of
the piece sometime before June 1724. Also, the 1731 pamphlet *A Full
Vindication of the Revd. Tho. Sheridan, D. D. and his Sermon on St.*

Cecilia's Day . . .'' seems to attribute "The Wonderful Wonder" to Sheridan and may also refer to this riddle. See, too, Swift's *"Bons Mots de Stella."*

The riddles were reprinted in the fifth volume of the *Miscellanies* in 1735, 1736, and 1745. They also appear in Sheridan, Scott, Browning, Horrell, Williams (this riddle appearing on pp. 917–18), and Rogers (this riddle appearing on pp. 303–4). This riddle most recently appeared in *JIL,* Vol. XVI, No. 3 (p. 27).

16   But. Williams incorrectly prints "By."

An Imitation of Anacreon's Grasshopper . . . (Anon.)

This printing is based upon the first publication which I have traced, in Concanen (pp. 235–37). In his 1724 pamphlet, *Letter from a Dissenting Teacher to Jet Black,* Sheridan remarked that he was "all day . . . as laborious as a Bee, and at Night as cheerful as a Grasshoper, which made one of my Friends write a Poem, call'd The Grasshoper" (pp. 10–11). Some of the details in this poem resemble some in Swift's "Ad Amicum Eruditum Thomam Sheridan." Thomas Moore translates Anacreon's grasshopper Ode thusly:

> Oh thou, of all creation blest,
> Sweet insect! that delight'st to rest
> Upon the wild-wood's leafy tops,
> To drink the dew that morning drops,
> And chirp thy song with such a glee,
> That happiest kings may envy thee!
> Whatever decks the velvet field,
> Whate'er the passing seasons yield;
> Whatever buds—whatever blows—
> For thee it buds—for thee it grows,
> Nor yet art thou the peasant's fear,
> To him thy friendly notes are dear;
> For thou art mild as matin dews,
> And ever, when the summer hues
> Begin to paint the bloomy plain,
> We hear thy sweet, prophetic strain;
> Thy sweet, prophetic strain we hear,
> And bless the notes and thee revere!
> The Muses love thy shrilly tone;
> Apollo calls thee all his own;
> 'Twas he who gave that voice to thee,

'Tis he who tunes thy minstrelsy.
Unworn by age's dim decline,
The fadeless blooms of youth are thine.
Melodious insect! child of earth!
In wisdom mirthful, wise in mirth;
Exempt from every weak decay,
That withers vulgar frames away;
With not a drop of blood to stain
The current of thy purer vein;
So blest an age is pass'd by thee,
Thou seem'st—a little deity!

How Can I Finish What You Have Begun?

This graceful piece appears untitled in an undated fragment of a letter (NLI, MS. 8718). Although neither the heading nor the conclusion of the letter survives, the handwriting appears to be that of Sheridan, and the content strongly suggests that the recipient was Swift. For instance, this poem is introduced by the remark, "You desired me to finish some lines you writ at Dunshaghlin." Dunshaghlin (or, as it was sometimes spelled, Dunshaughlin or Dunshallan) was a village that Swift would have passed through on his way to or from Quilca. In a letter to Swift dated October 5, 1735, Sheridan sketches out the Dean's route to Quilca thusly:

> Leave *Dublin* on *Wednesday;* ride to *Dunshaughlin* that day, 12 miles; from thence to *Navan* on *Thursday,* 11 miles. A *Friday* to *Virginia,* 15 miles, where I will meet you that evening with a couple of the best bottles of wine in *Ireland,* and a piece of my own mutton, &c.

The dating of the poem is conjecture, but, as the letter also contains the critical squib entitled "Upon William Tisdall, D. D.," I have placed it with the two anti-Tisdall poems of 1724. Williams also regards 1724 as the probable date of writing.

The piece was printed by Scott in his *Memoirs of Swift* (1814, pp. 74-75), by Ball in his edition of the *Correspondence* (Vol. IV, p. 479), and by Williams (pp. 1122–23). This printing is from the manuscript.

4   gr[ace]. The manuscript is somewhat tattered, and the last three letters of the word are missing.

14   There follow four marked over and indecipherable lines.

Upon William Tisdall, D. D.

This poem appears in the fragment of a letter (NLI, MS. 8718) discussed in the previous note. The poem was introduced by these remarks:

> Being in a vein of writing Epigrams I send you the following Piece upon Tisdall wch I intend to send to all his acquaintance for he goes from house to house to shew his wit on me for w^ch [I] think it reasonable he shou'd have something to stare[?] him [in?] the face.

For Sheridan's enemy Tisdall, see the Biographical Index.

Of this piece, Williams remarks, "On a presumption that this lampoon is of Swift's (or Sheridan's) composition it should probably be assigned to 1724." His reason is that in that year Tisdall published his attack upon Sheridan, "Tom Pun-Sibi Metamorphosed: Or The Giber Gibed." In that poem Sheridan was treated harshly while Swift was not, and so in 1724 Sheridan had a stronger reason than Swift for replying.

   3   *brea[th].* The manuscript is somewhat tattered, and the last two letters of the word are missing.
   4   *d[eath].* Only the initial letter of the word survives in the manuscript.

Tom Pun-Sibi Metamorphosed . . . (Tisdall)

This vicious attack first appeared in a Dublin broadside of 1724 (TCD). It was reprinted with a few slight variations in *Whartoniana,* Vol. I (pp. 52–54), and in *Gulliveriana* (pp. 260–64), and then by Scott, Vol. XIII (1814, pp. 359–60). With the omission of thirteen lines, it also appeared as a Dublin broadside of 1728 under the title of "The True Character of the Intelligencer. Written by Pady Drogheda." This printing is primarily based on the 1724 broadside.

The piece is particularly interesting for its list of Sheridan's writings and for its charge that Sheridan wrote for the Dublin almanacs. The treatise on the Wooden Man and "The Art of Making April Fools" I have not discovered, but the latter may refer to *Ars Pun-ica.* The poem was unsigned, but "The Rivals" (see below), which is an answer to it, clearly identifies Tisdall as the author.

When Smedley reprinted the poem in his *Gulliveriana,* he added this prefatory note:

> The following Poem was writ by a very Ingenious *Clergyman* of *Ireland,* in contempt of *Gulliver's* Insolence to his Friends and Acquaintances, and to expose the servile Behaviour of the *Captain's Underlings;* amongst whom this *Clergyman* places *Tom Punsibi;* so nam'd by himself, on account of his *Art of Punning,* altho', bad as the performance is, *Gulliver* has a chief Share in it, as you may see, by the Agreement which there is, between the Method and *Analysis* of that Book and the *Bathos.* I can't but think this Poem worthy this Collection, from the Spirit of it, and because it exposes, not only the *Captain,* but his chief *Underling,* SHERIDAN, an *Irish* Schoolmaster.

Smedley's charge that Swift had a hand in *The Art of Punning* may well have some truth in it, and also it is probable that Tisdall's poem occasioned the anonymous Dublin pamphlet of 1725 entitled "AN ESSAY ON GIBING, with a *Project for its Improvement.* This is a work somewhat similar to Sheridan's *Art of Punning.* It gives an historical background of gibing as well as an account of its effect upon the individual disposition and upon society, a criticism of poor gibing, and suggestions for the advancement and improvement of gibing. The pamphlet also contains a brief discussion of punning, but is less facetious than *The Art of Punning* and more general. Nevertheless, the following passage seems to refer to Sheridan's pamphlet and also to Swift:

> I should have followed the Conduct of the Author, who not long since, obliged the World with an elaborate Treatise on a Sister Art; and insinuated at my Weekly Club, that this Work of immense Erudition was digested, lick'd, par'd, and polish'd by my Friend *Jonathan,* a great Dab at Joakes and Gibing.

There may be also in the pamphlet a covert reference to Tisdall who in the last line of "Tom Pun-Sibi Metamorphosed" refers to Sheridan as Swift's parrot, spaniel, and pig. The author of *AN ESSAY ON GIBING* writes:

> The meanest Giber of lowest Humour can apply the terms *Punch,* and *Pig,* and *Parrot,* and *Spaniel,* to Persons possessed of these Qualities in an eminent Degree; but to draw the Pictures of *Buffoons, Pets,* and *Trencher Guests,* in so clear a Light, that they may be known at once, without such gross Appellations, and the World be able to decypher them by Intuition, from their Features, Colouring, and Resemblance of the Originals, is the Essence and Perfection of refin'd Gibing.

In sum, although the Gibing pamphlet was not claimed by Sheridan, and although it is not quite an overt reply to Tisdall, there are enough hints in it to suggest that "Tom Pun-Sibi Metamorphosed" caused Sheridan to write "AN ESSAY ON GIBING."

Epigraph   Slightly misquoted. In Book 7 of Ovid's *Metamorphoses,* line 758 reads "Accipe mirandum! novitate movebere facti." Or, in Frank Justus Miller's translation, "Hear the wonderful story: you will be moved by the strangeness of the deed." Tisdall's version means "You will be impressed by the novelty of such a strange creature."

1   *grig.* Most of the usual definitions of this word will fit: dwarf, cricket, or grasshopper; a gay, lively, lighthearted small person.

5   *couldn't. Whartoniana* has "could not."

6   *They moved. Gulliveriana* has "Sw——t us'd."

7   *S——. Whartoniana* has "Swift." *Gulliveriana* has "He."

8   *Whartoniana* spells out "Swift." *Gulliveriana* has, a little more smoothly, "But 'twas in jest, and Tom was bit."

14   *to. Whartoniana* has "t' a."

18   *therefore. Gulliveriana* has "so he."

19   *The benefit of piss and fart.* Italicized in *Whartoniana.* This line probably refers to the 1722 pamphlet entitled *The Benefit of Farting Explain'd* (TCD). Its authorship was denied by Sheridan in his *A Letter from a Dissenting Teacher to Jet Black,* and also by Swift in a letter to Knightley Chetwode dated March 13, 1721/22. Swift added that it was written by a surgeon named Dobbs.

25   *the Wooden Man.* A famed door-post in Dublin. Of it, Sir John Gilbert writes in *A History of the City of Dublin,* "From the latter part of the seventeenth century an oaken figure, notorious in Dublin as the 'Wooden Man,' stood on the southern side of Essex-street, not far from Eustace-street; and frequent jocose references to it, under the name of the 'Upright Man,' are to be found in the local jeux d'esprit of the city wits."

29   *went snacks.* Went equal shares with.

30   *philomaths.* Lovers of learning, a term formerly popularly applied to astrologers or prognosticators.

32   *Whalley . . . Cumpsty.* John Whalley (1653–1724) and Andrew Cumpsty (d. 1714). Dublin almanac-makers. For both, see Biographical Index.

46   *Distinguos.* Distinctions in thought or reasoning.

50   *paws, and fawns.* This is the reading of the broadside and *Whartoniana. Gulliveriana* and Scott have "fawns, and paws."

56   *turd. Whartoniana* has "T——d."

64   *And. Whartoniana* has "I."

Album Graecum. List of Greek words, dictionary.
67   *Tantany.* An obsolete form of Tantony, from St. Anthony who was the patron of swineherds. A tantony pig was the runt of the litter. Also, figuratively, an obsequious follower.
fn   Not in *Whartoniana.*

A Letter from a Cobbler in Patrick's Street to Jet Black

In a letter of June 16, 1724, to Charles Ford, Swift remarked, "Sheridan pursues Tisdall with Ballads and Verses, and there is one very good, called the Cobler to Jet Black" (Williams, *Correspondence,* Vol. III, p. 15). The Cobbler poem first appeared as an anonymous broadside in 1724 (Cambridge), and Foxon calls it a satire on Jonathan Smedley. It is, but only partially. The "Jonathan of Cloffer" referrred to in line 6 is Smedley who was installed as Dean of Clogher on June 24, 1724. Further, the cobbler's comparison of himself to Jet Black (that is, William Tisdall) is reminiscent of Smedley's irritating comparison of himself to "t'other *Jonathan,* viz. *Swift*" in his begging "Epistle to his Grace the Duke of Grafton, Lord Lieutenant of Ireland" that initially appeared as two nearly identical broadsides of 1724. In the cobbler's letter, the use of "t'others" in line 10 and 40 seems a jeering reference to Smedley's poem, and lines 34–37 of the cobbler's letter are definitely based on the following lines from Smedley's "Epistle":

> It was my Lord, the dextrous Shift,
> Of t'other *Jonathan,* viz. *Swift,*
> But now, St. *Patrick's* sawcy Dean,
> With Silver Verge, and Surplice clean,
> Of *Oxford,* or of *Ormond's* Grace,
> In looser Rhyme, to beg a Place:
> A Place he got, yclypp'd a *Stall,*
> And eke a Thousand Pounds withal;
> And, were he a less *witty Writer,*
> He might, as well, have got a *Mitre.*

Nevertheless, the main satiric thrust of the cobbler's "Letter" is at Tisdall's anti-Sheridan poem, "Tom Pun-Sibi Metamorphosed: or, the Giber Gibed" of 1724. For instance, in line 4 of his poem, Tisdall had coined the word "shally-shilly" because he needed a rhyme for "silly," and the cobbler's lines 21–24 criticize this makeshift. The identical criticism is made by Sheridan in his *A Letter from a Dissenting Teacher to Jet Black,* which also criticizes Tisdall's grammar, as does the cobbler in lines 19–20.

Possibly Sheridan first attacked Tisdall in the cobbler's "Letter," and then amplified his points in the "Dissenting Teacher" pamphlet.

33   awl. A half-pun on the shoemaker's tool and "all."

A Scribbler from the Northern Bear

The only previous printing of this piece is in the 1724 pamphlet "A Letter from a Dissenting Teacher to Jet Black" (NLI). The pamphlet is an answer to William Tisdall's broadside poem of 1724, "Tom Pun-Sibi Metamorphosed: Or the Giber Gibed." The pamphlet is signed "Phila-lethes," and a note in the bound volume containing it in the National Library of Ireland ascribes the work to Delany. The only apparent reason for the attribution is that Delany once used that pseudonym; however, so did a number of other writers. James Woolley attributes the authorship to Sheridan, and this judgment seems unquestionably correct. The "author" of the pamphlet, Philalethes, is at pains to establish that he is not Tom Pun-sibi, but this adoption of another persona is a technique that Sheridan had employed elsewhere, as in his pamphlet against John Greer. In its very informed content, and certainly in the style and tone of its verses, the pamphlet seems definitely Sheridan's production. (For speculation about Sheridan's possible authorship of another pamphlet seemingly occasioned by Tisdall's poem, see the Notes to "Tom Pun-Sibi Metamorphosed.")

One particularly interesting point in the pamphlet is the acknowledg-ment of the correctness of Tisdall's charge in "Tom Pun-Sibi Metamor-phosed," that Sheridan had written for almanacs. In fact, "A Scribbler from the Northern Bear" is prefaced by these lines:

> *The Monthly Observations* [in Whalley's Almanac] He cannot disallow, but wonders, that you were not warned from scribbling, by a very remarkable *Prediction,* which is as follows, in an almanack for the present Year.
> *February hath 29 Days.*
> *The Lunation peculiar to this month will be at the 13th Day at 49 Minutes past Twelve at Night. Mighty things are now on the Stage.*

Title   Northern Bear. A term applied to Russia. As Tisdall resided in Belfast, Sheridan is indulging in hyperbole.

To the Author of "Tom Pun-Sibi Metamorphosed

This printing is based on the first untitled appearance of the poem in the 1724 pamphlet "A Letter from a Dissenting Teacher to Jet Black." It was reprinted with the above title in *Whartoniana,* Vol. I (pp. 55–56). The poem is a criticism of the technique of Tisdall's "Tom Pun-Sibi Metamorphosed," and chiefly of Tisdall's forced rhymes. Sheridan, of course, was frequently guilty of the same fault, although it might be said that his rhyming is sometimes so purposely bad that he makes rather a comic virtue out of it.

    1   *Graecum.* In "Tom Pun-Sibi Metamorphosed," Tisdall had written:

> I took him by the neck to shake him,
> And made him void his *Album Graecum.*

An Album Graecum would have been a list of Greek words or a dictionary.

2–3 *'um. Whartoniana* has "'em."
   5 *Cumpsty.* Andrew Cumpsty, Dublin teacher and almanac maker. See Biographical Index.
   7 This line is indented in *Whartoniana.*
8–9 In lines 43–44 of "Tom Pun-Sibi Metamorphosed," Tisdall had written:

> Made him expert at quibble jargon,
> And quaint at selling of a bargain.

10–12 In lines 47–48 of "Tom Pun-Sibi Metamorphosed," Tisdall had written:

> Swift tried in vain, and angry thereat,
> Into a spaniel turned the parrot. . . .

 15 *piddlers. Whartoniana* has "Pedlars."
 18 *your. Whartoniana* has "the."
21–26 These lines would seem to refer to some unidentified previous satirical poem by Tisdall.
 32 *dirty. Whartoniana* has "barren."
 34 *damp. Whartoniana* has "deep."
      Belfast. Tisdall was Vicar of Belfast.
Footnotes Omitted in *Whartoniana.*

The Rivals (Anon.)

This answer to Tisdall's "Tom Pun-Sibi Metamorphosed" first appeared in a Dublin broadside of 1724 (TCD, Gilbert). Its author would appear well acquainted with Swift's set, and a prime suspect would be Delany.

19 *Point of War.* Undiscovered.
32 *Empire in the North.* Tisdall was Vicar of Belfast.
68 *the Dissenters.* A gibe at Tisdall's 1712 work, *Conduct of the Dissenters in Ireland.*

A Poem . . . (Owens)

The only previous appearance of Samuel Owens's piece is a Dublin broadside of 1724 (Gilbert). The broadside is as ill-printed as the poem is ill-written, but, as a plea to Tisdall and to Sheridan not to disgrace their priestly calling, it is of some interest. Owens was a Dublin locksmith, given to versifying and sympathetic to Swift and Irish nationalism.

A poem of 1734, "Advice to the Clergy" (BL), has a few superficial resemblances to Owens's piece. The title page indicates a Dublin origin; if so, Foxon concludes, the dedicatee was presumably Sheridan. There is little in the poem, however, to connect it either with Dublin or Sheridan.

1 *sons of Levi.* Loosely, priests or ministers.
20–25 Owens here attributes to Swift the 1724 pamphlet "A Letter from a Dissenting Teacher to Jet Black." It is more probably by Sheridan.
23 *D——r.* Possibly "drummer" from "Drum Ecclesiastic," which Brewer defines as "The pulpit cushion, often, vigorously thumped by what are termed 'rousing preachers.'" See also l. 59.
48 *Gordon's, Fiddes', or Durham's pains.* Three fairly recent writers on theology. Richard Fiddes (1671–1725) wrote *Theologia Speculativa* (1718), *Theologia Practica* (1720), and other works. James Durham (1622–58) wrote *A Commentarie upon the Book of Revelation* (1658) and other works. Gordon is more difficult to identify, but the chief candidates would appear to be Robert Gordon (1687–1764), a biblical scholar long engaged in translating the New Testament into English; James Gordon (1615?–86), who wrote *Some Charitable Observations on a Late Treatise of Church Lands and Tithes* (1706); and the prolific miscellaneous writer Thomas Gordon (d. 1750) who sometimes wrote on religious subjects.
51 *Socinian.* Having to do with the sect founded by two sixteenth-century Italian theologians, Laelius and Faustus Socinus, who denied the divinity of Christ.

To Quilca (Swift)

Until the seventeenth century, the Sheridan family had owned large tracts of land in Cavan. These, however, were forfeited because of their

Jacobite sympathies, but a portion of them had been awarded to the man who was to become Sheridan's father-in-law, and upon his death they came into Sheridan's possession. This small estate near Virginia in Co. Cavan was called Quilca, and both Sheridan and his son Thomas were inordinately proud of it and carried out, as much as their purses would allow, extensive improvements. Swift stayed in Quilca on several occasions and even worked on *Gulliver's Travels* there. Sheridan's pride in Quilca is rather undercut by Swift's various descriptions of it as uncomfortable, primitive, and slovenly. See, for instance, Swift's amusing prose piece, "The Blunders, Deficiencies, Distresses, and Misfortunes of Quilca" (*Prose Works,* Vol. V, pp. 219–21). See also the three short pieces of doggerel in Swift's letter to Sheridan of June 25, 1725 (Williams, *Correspondence,* Vol. III, pp. 63–65).

This printing is based on the poem's first publication by Faulkner in 1735. The piece has appeared in all of the important editions of Swift's poems, and most recently in Williams (p. 1035) and Rogers (p. 300).

7   *poor Sheelah.* Obviously an Irish maid-servant. A "Shela" in Peter
     Murray's poem below, "A Receipt to Frighten Away the Dean," is
     identified as Sheridan's cook at Quilca.

Quilca House to the Dean (Brooke)

If Henry Brooke wrote this effective piece shortly after Swift wrote "To Quilca" in the summer of 1725, then Brooke would have been a rather young man. However, Henry Wilson in *Brookiana* prints several accomplished pieces of both poetry and prose, which Brooke is supposed to have written even earlier as a schoolboy under Sheridan. Of this poem, Wilson writes:

> Mr. Brooke was not a little nettled at the verses which Dean Swift wrote, on the old family mansion of the Sheridans in Quilca, in which he (Mr. Brooke) had so often partook of the hospitality of his master's table, and enjoyed the pleasures of his conversation, which, on some occasions, was a high treat, indeed. He conceived, perhaps, that it would be presumptuous in him to enter the lists openly with a writer that kept even Pope in awe. He knew, besides, that nothing hurt Swift so much as a shaft of wit, when winged by a blockhead, or one that was deemed so; in consequence of which, Mr. Brooke wrote the following lines, which were readily fathered by one Peter Murray, a dancing-master in the neighbourhood, who had attempted some rhimes, which furnished the dean with a quantum of sarcastic pleasantry, at the expence of the author. . . .
> These verses spread like wild-fire; almost every one in the parish had them

by rote, nor did the majority scruple to say, that the dean was paid off in his own coin.

The above quotation, as well as apparently the first publication of the poem, appeared in Wilson's *Brookiana,* Vol. I (pp. 41–43). Some doubt has occasionally been expressed about the authenticity of the material in *Brookiana,* but whether this poem is really by Brooke is rather beside the point, as it is definitely about Swift and Sheridan.

40 *Poddle.* "A muddy river that runs near the deanry-house of St. Patrick's, Dublin." Wilson's note.
51 *Polyhymny.* Polyhymnia, the Muse of the mimic arts.
59 This quotation is a slight variation of Swift's line "And pick my Chicken to the Bone." The line occurs in the poem "The Author's Manner of Living" (Williams, p. 954; Rogers, p. 187), which Rogers tentatively assigns to 1718.

A Receipt to Frighten Away the Dean (Murray)

The only previous publication that I have discovered of this piece is in Wilson's *Brookiana,* Vol. I (pp. 44–46). There Wilson describes how Brooke attributed his poem "Quilca House to the Dean" (see previous note) to Murray, a neighborhood dancing-master, and then continues:

The supposed author received presents, and, what was still more, fine compliments, which pleased him better than all. Peter, however, did not wish to shine in borrowed plumes; he was determined to resort to his own talents, and from the following specimen it will be found that they did not lie entirely in his heels.

1 *Kate and Rose and sleepy Ned.* "Doctor Sheridan's servants." Wilson's note.
3 *Shela.* "The cook." Wilson's note.
8 *praties.* "Potatoes." Wilson's note.
16 *farden.* "Farthing." Wilson's note.
29 *bands.* "*Clerical bands* are a relic of the ancient *amice,* a square linen tippet tied about the neck of priests during the administration of mass. (Discontinued by the parochial clergy the latter part of the 19th century, but still used by clerics on the Continent.)" Brewer.

40 *Mullingar.* "A fine corn country." Wilson's note.

To His Excellency Our Lord Carteret . . .

The first publication of this poem was an unsigned Dublin broadside of 1725 (BL, Huntington, Penn); it was reprinted in *JIL,* Vol. XVI, No. 3 (p. 28). Although nominally written by Sheridan's scholars, and apparently chiefly by young Lord Mountcashel, the piece is undoubtedly by Sheridan himself. (See, nevertheless, the remarks on Lord Mountcashel in the note below to "A Poem Delivered to the Reverend Doctor Swift. . . .") As in several of the prologues and epilogues to the school plays, the nominal schoolboy twice pokes gentle fun at an allegedly tyrannical master, but the thrust of the poem is to portray Sheridan as most conscientious.

The poem would appear to have been written in early August of 1725, after Sheridan's debacle in Cork with his "Sufficient unto the day" sermon. That sermon was preached on August 1, and "Bart'lomy-tide" mentioned in line 4 was August 24, St. Bartholomew's Day. An alternative dating, however, might be the middle of September, and the British Library copy does have a contemporary manuscript date of "7bre 13th 1725." In that case, the boys would be speaking after St. Bartholomew's Day, and saying that, having missed their usual two weeks' vacation, they would now settle for one.

In any event, Sheridan would now have been out of favor with Dublin Castle, and this poem might be seen as a joking attempt to regain lost ground. One problem with this reading, however, is that lines 15–20 would suggest that Sheridan at the time of writing was still in favor with Dublin Castle, but that may have been part of his strategy.

29 *Great patron and lover of scholars.* Carteret had a deserved reputation as an able classicist, and in his Life of Swift the younger Sheridan remarked:

Lord Carteret, who was himself an excellent scholar, soon distinguished the Doctor's merit in that line, nor was he less pleased with him as a companion, often inviting him to his private parties, and sometimes, laying his state aside, he would steal out from the castle in a Hackneychair, to pass the evening at Sheridan's with Swift, and the select set which used to meet there. By the desire of the Lord Lieutenant, the Doctor had one of the tragedies of Sophocles performed by his scholars for his entertainment. Before the day of exhibition Lord Carteret appointed a morning to pass with him in reading the play together, in order to refresh his memory after so long an absence from his Greek studies. The Doctor was astonished at the facility and accuracy with which he translated this difficult Author, having scarce any opportunity of giving him assistance through the whole play. While he was expressing his surprise at this, and admiration at the wonderful knowledge which his Lordship shewed of the Greek language, Lord Carteret, with great candour, told him he would let him into the secret how he came to be so far master of this particular Author. He said that when he was Envoy in Denmark, he had been for a long time confined to his chamber, partly by illness, and partly by the severity of the weather; and having but few books with him, he had read Sophocles over and over so often, as to be able almost to repeat the whole verbatim, which impressed it ever after indelibly on his memory.

34   Te Carteret amamus. We love you, Carteret.

To the Honorable Mr. D. T.

The first printing of this poem, upon which this present printing is based, seems to have been in a Dublin broadside published by S. Harding on the Blind-Key, 1725 (NLI). There is a "Note" at the bottom of the broadside that remarks, "This paper will be continued weekly, if due Encouragement be given." Ball reprinted the poem in *Swift's Verse* (pp. 349–51) and attributed it to Swift, but Williams rejected the attribution and mentioned a copy once in the possession of Messrs. Pickering & Chatto with a contemporary manuscript attribution to "T. Sheridon, D.D." Sheridan's disappointment and frustration and anger against Dick Tighe make the attribution very plausible; for, according to all accounts, it was Tighe who reported Sheridan's "Sufficient unto the day" sermon to Carteret and thereby caused Sheridan to lose a valuable living and his favor with Dublin Castle. Certainly both Sheridan and Swift wrote some other vicious and amusing pieces against Tighe.

If the poem be Sheridan's, its composition may be tentatively assigned to late September or early October 1725; for on September 25 Swift wrote to Sheridan from Quilca, and parts of one paragraph may well have suggested some of the imagery of this poem and of its sequel, "The Sick Lion and the Ass":

. . . All Animals fight with the Weapons natural to them . . . and the Devil take that Animal, who will not offend his Enemy, when he is provoked, with his proper Weapon; and though your old dull Horse little values the Blows I give him with the Butt-end of my Stick, yet I strike on and make him wince in Spight of his Dulness; and he shall not fail of them while I am here; and I hope you will do so too to the Beast who has kick'd against you, and try how far his Insensibility will protect him, and you shall have Help, and he will be vexed, for so I found your Horse this Day, though he would not move the faster. I will kill that Flea or Louse which bites me, though I get no Honour by it. (Williams, *Correspondence,* Vol. III, p. 101)

There is also some similarity in the image of lines 65–82 to lines 25–32 in the 1718 poem "Sheridan to Dan Jackson." The poem's most recent appearance was in *JIL,* Vol. XVI, No. 3 (pp. 28–30).

Ex Despauterio "Joannes Despauterius (1460–1520), grammarian. The line, a fragment of Ennius, is quoted by Despauterius in his treatise 'De Figuris,' *Commentarii,* 1537, p. 613." Ball's note. The line, fragment 60 from Book I of Ennius' *Annals,* may be translated as "O Titus Tatius the tyrant, you brought on such troubles yourself." However, part of the point of the quotation would seem to lie in the "ti" sounds which occur only in the italicised words and which would have been a pointer to the name "Tighe." Mark Amsler notes that "The connection of alliteration and rage or scorn is something of a classical convention (cp. Sophocles, *Oedipus Rex,* 1. 371)."
19 Not indented by Ball.
21 Not indented by Ball.
25 Not indented by Ball.
31 Not indented by Ball.

The Sick Lion and the Ass

This printing is based upon the poem's original appearance as a broadside printed in Dublin by Sarah Harding in 1725 (NLI, BL). It was reprinted without the dedication and the epigraph in *Poems Written Occasionally by the Late John Winstanley . . . ,* Vol. II (pp. 44–46). The poem was also reprinted by Ball (pp. 352–53), who attributed it to Swift, an attribution dismissed by Williams. The piece was attributed to Sheridan in its most recent printing in *JIL,* Vol. XVI, No. 3 (pp. 30–31) where it was noted that the form—the dedication, the epigraph, the fable, and the iambic tetrameter couplets—is precisely the same as that of "To the Honourable Mr. D. T.," and must strongly suggest the same author.
Written in ink on the back of a copy of the broadside in the British Library are these lines which Ball printed:

D—— T—— the greatest of the great
D—— T—— the pillar of the state
D—— T—— the ablest politician
D—— T—— the skilfulest physician

Of all the hero's of antiquity
There never yet was one like D——y T——.

5 Not indented by Ball.
9 Not indented by Ball.
15 Not indented by Ball.
19 Not indented by Ball.
32 *these.* Winstanley prints "them."

A Poem Delivered to the Reverend Doctor Swift . . .

The first publication of this piece is in a Dublin broadside (TCD, Camb, Penn), of which Foxon writes: "Ms. ascribed to Mountcashel in the C[ambridge] copy and index to the DT [Trinity College, Dublin] volume; wrongly ascribed to Lord Orrery in PU [University of Pennsylvania, Philadelphia]." Orrery is, of course, wrong because this poem was written several years before he met Swift. However, despite lines 79–86 being written in the character of Edward Davys, Third Viscount of Mountcashel, that attribution seems equally unlikely. At the time of writing, Mountcashel was only a boy of fourteen years, and, although this is not a great poem, it is in places extremely fluent and graceful and quite beyond the capabilities of a fourteen year old unless he were a considerable prodigy like Alexander Pope. There is little evidence to indicate that Mountcashel was anything more than a promising youth. The poem most likely to have been Mountcashel's own production when he was a student at Sheridan's school was "To the honourable Master Henry Barry, son of the right honourable the Lord Santry, on his birth-day. By one of his school-fellows" (BL); and it is considerably less technically able than either "To His Excellency Our Lord Carteret . . ." or this poem to Swift. It might also be noted that, although the speaker of this poem to Swift is "a Young Nobleman," the title of the poem does not say that it was "written," but that it was "Delivered" by him.

There are, however, several points about the poem that point to Sheridan as its author. It was his custom in the prologues and epilogues of his school plays to adopt the persona of one of his students, and "The Epilogue to *Julius Caesar*" of 1718 was written in the persona of a young student and delivered by Mountcashel. Further, only a couple of months earlier, about the middle of August perhaps, Sheridan seems to have written just another such piece in "To his Excellency Our Lord Carteret, Lord Lieutenant of Ireland: The Humble Petition of Lord Viscount Mont-Cashel, and the Rest of His School-Fellows." Like that piece, this birthday poem to Swift may be partly seen as an attempt to retrieve the lost ground his "Sufficient unto the day" sermon had occasioned, and to regain favor with the Lord Lieutenant. See the graceful allusion to Carteret in the last line.

At the same time, thhe poem seems to allude to Swift's continued friendship for him and defense of him after the debacle of the Cork sermon. See particularly lines 70–74. Also, the poem shows a certain intimate knowledge of Swift's peculiarities that the young Mountcashel would scarcely have had. For instance, Swift, like Yeats, had no ear for music while Sheridan was an able violinist, and this matter seems distinctly alluded to in the section about Apollo, particularly in lines 26–34. Finally, the poem in its classical conceit resembles a number of Sheridan's other poems, particularly his 1737 "Birthday Poem on the Anniversary of the Birth of the Rev. Dr. Swift." So, although there is no one totally determining piece of evidence for attributing the poem to Sheridan, all of these matters together strongly point to his authorship.

The poem was reprinted in *JIL,* Vol. XVI, No. 3 (pp. 31–32).

15   *a woman.* Possibly Helen of Troy.
55   My indentation.
     Jove's daughter. Athena, the goddess of wisdom.
67   My indentation.

From A Satyr (Smedley)

Jonathan Smedley's attack against Swift was first printed in a broadside of 1725 (BL) and has been reprinted by Ball in *Swift's Verse* (pp. 340–42), by Williams (pp. 369–71) and by Davis (pp. 288–90).

2   *Hel——m's Sleight of Hand.* For Richard Helsham, see Biographical Index. If *Sleight of Hand* is a title, I have failed to identify it.

From A Letter from D. S——t to D. S——y (Swift)

Swift's retort to Smedley was first printed in a broadside in 1725 (BL) and has been reprinted by Ball (pp. 343–45), Williams (pp. 371–73), Davis (pp. 290–92), Rogers (pp. 284–85), and others.

1 Hel—am. Richard Helsham. See Biographical Index.
4 idem The same.

Tom Punsibi's Farewell to the Muses (Anon.)

The first publication of this fluent and effective attack was apparently in a Dublin broadside of 1725 (BL). It was reprinted with but trifling variations in *Whartoniana* (pp. 61–63). This printing is based mainly on the broadside.

Epigraph Lo, Crispinus again! H. Rushton Fairclough remarks in his edition of Horace that "Crispinus, according to the scholiasts, was an aretalogus, one who babbled about virtue. He wrote, we are told, in verse."

3 antic. Spelled in *Whartoniana* "antick"; the broadside has "Antique."

7 Ogilby, Hobbes or Sylvester. John Ogilby (1600–1676) published verse translations of Aesop, Virgil, and Homer. Thomas Hobbes (1588–1679), the great political thinker, was probably included in this trio for his translation of Thucydides and Homer. Joshua Sylvester (1563–1618) translated Du Bartas.

15 thy. *Whartoniana* has "the."

17 Punchinello. Punch in the Punch and Judy show is a shortening of Punchinello.

18 prunello. Or prunella. "A strong stuff, originally silk, afterwards worsted, formerly used for graduates', clergymen's, and barristers' gowns; later, for the uppers of women's shoes." *OED.*

21 Xantippe. *Whartoniana* adds the footnote "Socrates' wife, a noted Scold."

22 Aganippe. "A fountain of Boeotia at the foot of Mount Helicon, dedicated to the Muses, because it had the virtue of imparting poetic inspiration." Brewer.

34 exegi . . . monumentum. I have raised a monument. See Horace, *Odes,* 3. 30. 1.

39 Jonathan. Probably Swift.

42 Lilly. William Lilly, or Lily, or Lyly, notable sixteenth-century grammarian.

46 tenters. Tenterhooks.

52 C-ffey, Jet Black, or the journalist Daniel. Charles Coffey (ca. 1700–1745), Irish dramatist, author of the very popular *The Devil to Pay* and other plays. Jet Black is a name applied to William

Tisdall. See Biographical Index. For "the journalist Daniel," *Whar-toniana* adds the footnote "Arbucle." See Biographical Index.

53   *Balaam.* Spelled "Baalam" in the broadside.

A New Jingle on Tom Dingle (Anon.)

This jingle seems to have been first published in an undated Dublin broadsheet (TCD) that Foxon suggests may be from about 1726. The Trinity copy is gathered together with other material from the years 1725–26. Several of the allusions make it clear that the author knew Sheridan and Swift well—particularly the lines (16ff.) about Swift's will, and so possibly Helsham, who was one of Swift's executors, could be a candidate for its authorship.

9   *vill.* Farm, country house or even village.
14   *Jill.* Dr. Johnson defines Jill, which was more frequently spelled "Gill," as a malt-liquor medicated with ground-ivy. *OED* cites *Miller's Gardener's and Botanist's Dictionary* of 1807 as remarking that "The leaves [of Ground Ivy] were formerly thrown into vat with ale to clarify it, and to give it a flavour. This was called Gill-ale."]
30   *Tom Lill.* In *Alumni Dublinenses,* Burtchaell and Sadleir note that a Thomas Lill, who is described as "Generosus" or gentleman, sent three sons to Trinity College in the early 1730s.

A True and Faithful Inventory . . .

There is some problem about dating the composition of this much published poem. In his Life of Swift, the younger Sheridan notes that Swift's verse on Quilca prompted his father to write "A True and Faithful Inventory" (pp. 402–5). Williams, however, writes:

> . . . the story does not appear probable. Sheridan's "Inventory" belongs to 1724; and it has, on the face of it, no direct relationship to Swift's verses. At the end of May and beginning of June, 1724, Swift was in Trim, or the neighbourhood, in the company of Henry Downe, who had just been transferred from the bishopric of Killala to that of Meath (*Corresp.* III, 193 n.). It is probable that it was at this time that Swift offered to lend the Bishop his house at Laracor until his own could be built. Sheridan's "Inventory" may be regarded as having preceded Swift's lines on Quilca by about a Year. (pp. 1034–35)

Scott notes, "This poem was written by Sheridan, who had it presented to the Bishop by a beggar, in the form of a petition, to Swift's great surprise, who was in the carriage with his Lordship at the time." (Vol. XV, pp. 149–50).

If Williams rather than the younger Sheridan is correct, the poem may have been written around June 1724. A 1726 dating, however, should not at all be ruled out. In addition to its three previously known first printings in 1726, I have discovered a fourth in *The Dublin Weekly Journal* for July 2, 1726 (p. 256), and Sheridan's usual habit with these *jeux d'esprit* was to print them soon after he had written them. The other notable printings are in *Cadenus and Vanessa,* Blandford's 4th edition in 1726; *The London Journal,* June 25, 1726; a Dublin broadside of 1726 (TCD), upon which this printing was based; *The Drapier's Miscellany,*r 1733; *Ladies Magazine,* Vol. I, November 18, 1749; Cogan's *Supplement to the Works of Dr. Swift,* 1752; Faulkner's *Works,* Vol. VIII, 1762 (p. 168); Faulkner's *Works,* Vol. XI, 1763 (p. 424); *Gentleman's Magazine,* October 1773; *Additions to the Works of Alexander Pope,* Vol. I, 1776 (p. 89); Sheridan's *Life of Swift,* 1784 (pp. 402–5); *The New Foundling Hospital for Wit,* Vol. V, 1784 (p. 87); Scott, Vol. XV, 1814 (pp. 149–50); Scott, Vol. XV, 1824 (pp. 155–56); *Cheltenham Journal,* Monday, January 28, 1828; Williams (pp. 1044–45). The Cheltenham printing is reprinted in *Notes and Queries,* Vol. CXCIII, 7 February 1948 (pp. 56–57), and appears to be rather faulty. The most recent printing is in *JIL,* Vol. XVI, No. 3 (pp. 32–33).

1   *elbow-chair.* Armchair.
2   *caudle-cup.* A small, two-handled cup with a bulbous body, a contracted neck and often a top made of silver. Caudle is a drink made of warm ale or wine, with eggs, sugar and spice.
19 *save-all.* A device to hold a candle and allow it to burn to the very end.

To the Dean, When in England, in 1726

This poem appeared in April 1767, in *The Gentleman's Magazine,* Vol. XXXVII (p. 183), and also in Faulkner's *Works,* 1767, Vol. XVI, 1767 (Appendix, p. 17). It has been reprinted by Scott, Roscoe, Browning, Williams (pp. 1042–44), and most recently by *JIL,* Vol. XVI, No. 3 (pp. 33–34) and in *The Field Day Anthology of Irish Writing* (Derry, 1991), I (pp. 459–60). This printing is based on Faulkner.

9   *elbow-chair.* Armchair.
15 *Faustina.* Faustina Bordoni, famous Italian singer of the day, who made her London debut in Handel's *Alessandro* on May 5, 1726.

16 *Sheelina.* Unidentified, but a variant of Sheila, or Shelagh.

23 Williams omits "dear."

34 *Ireland's Eye.* An island off Howth.

37 *McFadden's horny brothers.* This might suggest that Sheridan had playfully given his bull the name of his in-laws.

41 *quicks.* This could mean either a young thorn tree and go with line 39, or green fodder and go with "famished beeves," also in line 41.

53 Scott has "now come."

58 *sturks.* Obsolete form of stirk, which is a young bullock or heifer.

63–64 Possibly a reference to Sheridan's wife.

fn Possibly Faulkner's, although its jokey tone sounds like Sheridan who a couple of times elsewhere did refer to Cavan servants as thieves.

From An Epistle in Behalf of Our Irish Poets . . . (Anon.)

This excerpt is from a poem written on the occasion of Lady Carteret, the wife of the Lord Lieutenant, leaving Ireland, and it suggests that all of the Irish poets will leave when she does. Apparently its only previous appearance was as a Dublin broadside, printed by E. Needham in 1726 (TCD).

General St-rl-ng. Undoubtedly James Sterling (fl. 1718–55), playwright, journalist, and friend of Mathew Concanen, who wrote a play acted in Dublin called *The Rival Generals.*

The Humble Petition of Stella's Friends

The manuscript of this poem is in Sheridan's hand. After the last line and in the same hand is the line "Signed by the following Persons." Then follow the signatures of John and Mary Worrall, of Delany and of Rebecca Dingley. Then there is a space, and at the bottom of the page is Sheridan's signature. This would suggest that Sheridan copied out the poem, signing his name at the very bottom and leaving room for the other signatures above. As Sheridan acted as scribe, and as neither the Worralls nor Mrs. Dingley is known to have attempted verse, it is possible that most of the composition is his.

The paper was folded in half three times, and on the outside Sheridan wrote "The Humble Petition of Stella's friends written June the eleventh, 1727." Following in another hand is the note "at 14 Beaufort building Strand."

Stella had been very ill for a couple of years. In 1725, Swift and Mrs. Dingley had spent several months with her at Quilca, probably in an attempt to build her up. When Swift was in England in 1726, her friends thought that she was very near death. On July 1, 1727, Swift wrote to Sheridan from Twickenham, "I was in a Fright about your Verses about *Stella's* Sickness, but glad when they were a Month Old." She died on January 28, 1728.

All of the signatories were close companions of both Stella and Swift. Worrall was the choirmaster of St. Patrick's, and Swift often dined with him and his wife. Delany described him as "a man of sense, and a great deal of humour," and described his wife as "remarkably cleanly, and elegant in her person, in her house, and at her table, where she entertained her friends with singular cheerfulness, hospitality and good humour."

This printing is based on the manuscript in the British Library. The poem was printed in *TLS*, by Williams in *Correspondence*, Vol. V (pp. 239–40), and by *JIL*, Vol. XVIII, No. 1 (p. 46).

An Invitation to Dinner . . .

This printing is based upon the poem's first appearance in Faulkner's edition of the *Works* edited by Deane Swift (1765, 4to, Vol. VIII, p. 174; 8vo, Vol. XVI, p. 290). It also appears in Scott, Roscoe, Browning, Williams (pp. 1048–49), and *JIL*, Vol. XVIII, No. 1 (pp. 46–47).

1   *ladies.* "Mrs. Johnson [Stella] and her friend Mrs. Dingley." Deane Swift's note.

2   *Rathfarnham.* "A village near Dublin, where Dr. Sheridan had a country-house." Deane Swift's note. For Dean Swift's account of this "rotten house at Rathfarnham," see his "The History of the Second Solomon."

4   *leanship.* "Stella was at this time in a very declining state of health. She died the January following." Deane Swift's note.

5   *bret.* "Or 'burt.' Turbot." Williams's note.

8   *sippets.* Small pieces of toast soaked in milk or broth. Also small pieces of toast or fried bread used as a garnish.

11 *Narcissus.* "The youth who died for love of his own image reflected in a fountain, and was changed into a flower of the same name. Ovid, 'Metam.,' iii, 407." Browning's note.

16 *she.* "He means Stella, who was certainly one of the most amiable women in the world." Deane Swift's note.

20 *Durfey, or Smedley, or Tisdall.* Thomas D'Urfey (1653–1723);

dramatist and song writer, best known for his collection of ballads and songs called *Wit and Mirth, or Pills to Purge Melancholy.* Jonathan Smedley (ca. 1671–ca. 1729). See Biographical Index. William Tisdall (1669–1735). See Biographical Index.

To the Right Honorable the Lord Viscount Mont-Cassel

This poem's previous appearance was as an eight-page pamphlet printed in Dublin by S. Harding in 1727 (BL). For Mont-Cassel, who was one of Sheridan's favorite students, see Biographical Index under the more usual spelling of Mountcashel.

57–58 Unidentified.
 70 *choused.* Swindled, cheated.
 92 *fights.* Possibly a misprint for "frights."
131–42 This passage utilizes part of the well-known story of Daedalus, the famous smith, craftsman, and inventor of the ancient world. When he and his son Icarus were imprisoned in Crete by King Minos, Daedalus devised a pair of wings for himself and another for Icarus. However, the wings were held together partly by wax, and so Daedalus advised Icarus to follow him closely and not to soar too near to the sun. Icarus, however, ignored the advice, and flew too high. When the wax melted, he fell into the sea and drowned. See Ovid, *Metamorphoses,* viii, 182–235.

Prologue Spoken at Mr. Sheridan's School

The first printing of this piece that I have found is in *Whartoniana,* Vol. I (pp. 6–7). It was reprinted in Nichols's *Supplement* (pp. 540–41). The poem is unsigned, but the usual jokes directed against himself as the tyrannic schoolmaster would indicate that this is Sheridan's production. This printing is based on *Whartoniana,* save one exception noted below.

Title *Mr.* Nichols has "Dr."
 2 *younkers.* Youths. Nichols has "yonkers."
 7 *Adelphi.* A Latin play by Terence.
 16 This line is an allusion to the proverb "Set a beggar on horseback, and he'll ride to the Devil."
 18 *Pegasus.* The winged horse of Greek mythology, sometimes used as an emblem of poetic inspiration.
 26 *beaver.* Possibly a tall hat for men.

28 *Sir Fopling.* The main comic character in Sir George Etherege's play, *The Man of Mode or Sir Fopling Flutter* (1676).

30 *true.* This word is not printed in *Whartoniana,* but seems necessary for the meter and does appear in Nichols.

34 *scandalum magistri.* Scandal of the master.

35 *mitches.* The word in both *Whartoniana* and Nichols is "witches," which does not seem to make sense, and which I suspect is a misprint. "Mitches" or "miches" means being absent without leave from school.

From Tim and the Fables

This printing is based on the first appearance of the lines in the tenth *Intelligencer,* which James Woolley convincingly argues was published circa 13–16 July, 1728. They were reprinted in A. Moor's collected edition of *The Intelligencer* of 1729 (p. 100), in Francis Cogan's second edition of 1730 (p. 114), and in James Woolley's edition of 1992, as well as in Williams (pp. 782–83), Rogers (pp. 343–44), and elsewhere. In a letter to Pope of June 12, 1732, Swift described what parts of *The Intelligencer* he had written, and of the tenth number he said that he had written "only the verses, and of those not the four last slovenly lines." If Swift is correct, the lines then have to have been added by Sheridan who was, of course, quite capable of the vulgarity.

Ballyspellin

This poem may be dated by a letter of Swift, of September 28, 1728, in which he wrote:

> We have a design upon Sheridan. He sent us in print a ballad upon Ballyspelling, in which he has employed all the rhymes he could find to that word; but we have found fifteen more, and employed them in abusing his ballad, and Ballyspelling too. I here send you a copy, and desire you will get it printed privately, and published.

A typical stanza of Swift's fifteen stanza answer reads:

> But Tom will prate
> At any rate
> All other nymphs expelling:
> Because he gets

A few grisettes
At lousy Ballyspellin.

Sir Walter Scott notes:

> This answer was resented by Dr. Sheridan as an affront to himself and the
> lady he attended to the Spa; and Swift, very unjustly, in the opinion of the
> present Editor, has recorded his doing so as an offence against "all the rules
> of reason, taste, good-nature, judgment, gratitude, or common manners." The
> answer seems to have been written during Swift's residence with Sir Arthur
> Acheson. (1814, Vol. XV, p. 131)

Williams remarks that "Ballyspellin, not far from Kilkenny, has a chaly-
beate spring which was, in Swift's day, greatly in favour for its radical
properties." An advertisement in J. Carson's *The Dublin Intelligence* of
July 30, 1723, describes "The Farm of Ballyspellan, containing 750 Acres,
with a good Dwelling House fit for a Gentleman, a large Barn, Stable,
Pigeon-House, also a good Inn and Stable, a large Padock wall'd with
Lime and Stone, and the famous Spaw thereon."

Sheridan's 1728 publication has not survived, and the first extant print-
ing of the ballad is in Concanen's *The Flower-Piece* (1731 and 1733, p. 36).
It was also printed in Cogan's *Supplement to the Works of Dr. Swift*
(pp. 121–23); in Faulkner's *Works* (Vol. VIII, 1762, pp. 163–67; Vol. XI,
1763, pp. 420–26); in the London trade editions of 1762 and 1764; in Scott,
Roscoe, Browning, Williams, Horrell, and Davis. This reprinting is based
on Concanen. Swift's "Answer" has been most recently printed by Wil-
liams (pp. 440–43), Horrell, Davis, and Rogers (pp. 356–58).

2   *Llewellyn.* Rogers suggests Llwelyn ab Gruffydd (d. 1282), "but, as
    Swift says, the name is just there for the rhyme." Rogers alludes to
    the fourth stanza of Swift's "Answer," which reads:

> Llewellyn! why,
> As well may I
> Name honest Doctor Pelling;
> So hard sometimes
> You tug for rhymes
> To bring in Ballyspellin.

5   *skin. Works,* 1762, has "Skins."
18 *Ross ... Dunkelling.* These seem more like placenames than
    names of people; however, Dunkelling is not listed in Joyce's *Irish
    Names of Places.* Ros in Irish is a promontory or peninsula, and
    there are various places in Ireland with Ros or Ross contained in

their names, such as New Ross in Wexford or Roscrea in Tipperary. Adrian Room in *Bloomsbury Dictionary of Place-Names in the British Isles* (London: Bloomsbury, 1988) writes, "Today the name of Ross is familiar from the administrative district of Ross and CROMARTY, while formerly it was well known as that of the county of Ross-shire. The basic name is also found in the two districts of Easter Ross and Wester Ross, respectively in the eastern and western regions of the territory." Roscoe and Browning print "Rose" for "Ross."

26 *way. Works,* 1762, has "Pow'r."
45 *Though. Works,* 1762, has "If."
59 *transported. Works,* 1762, has "transporteth."
65 *There. Works,* 1762, has "Here."

You That Would Read the Bible . . .

Number XI of *The Intelligencer,* the paper written by Sheridan and Swift, contains a letter from "A. B." that purports to send along some proposals to the editor of the *London Journal.* This letter also promises to send along "A. B's" poetic version of the proposals, which he admires as much as he admires their author, "the Great and Learned S——d——l——y." The prose proposal is signed by Jonathan Smedley, the longtime foe of both Sheridan and Swift, and advertises a two-volume work to be called *An Universal View of all the Eminent Writers on the Holy Scriptures* which is to be an anthology of "the chief Sentiments of the best Authors, in most Languages, on those Subjects." Sheridan's verse version closely follows the sense of the proposal but derisively changes the tone to make the original look portentous and absurd.

The individual numbers of *The Intelligencer* were printed in Dublin by Sarah Harding in 1728 and 1729, and James Woolley suggests ca. 8–12 October, 1728 for Number XI. The first collected edition was printed in London by A. Moor in 1729, and a second edition was printed by Francis Cogan in 1730. The poem's most recent appearance is in Woolley's edition of *The Intelligencer* (pp. 141–44). This printing is based on Harding.

24 *Kinsale.* A town in Co. Cork.
37 *Profecto legi plus quam satis.* Actually I have collected more than enough.
38 *Mithridates.* Or more correctly Mithradates. Probably Mithradates VI, called the Great, a king of Pontus who opposed the Romans in Asia Minor in the first century B.C. Despite his tendency to murder people, a patron of letters and learning.

62   *Pool, Petavius and Calmet.* Matthew Poole (1624–79), English non-
      conformist theologian whose *Synopsis Criticorum biblicorum*
      (1669–76) summarizes the views of 150 biblical critics. Denys Petau
      (1583–1652), better known as Dionysius Petavius, a Jesuit and emi-
      nent biblical scholar. Antoine Augustin Calmet (1672–1757), French
      Benedictine who wrote the nine-volume *Commentaire litterale sur
      tous les livres de L'Ancien et du nouveau testament.*

82   *of.* Sarah Harding's edition erroneously has "if."
      Hammond. Henry Hammond (1605–60), English divine, who wrote
      *A Paraphrase, and Annotations upon All the Books of the New
      Testament: Briefly Explaining All the Difficult Places Thereof* (Lon-
      don: Flesher, 1653).

83–84 Compare these lines from "A True and Faithful Inventory of
      1726:

          A dish, which might good meat afford once;
          An Ovid, and an old Concordance. . . .

105–6 *Popery . . . rope awry.* Moor's English edition has "Pop'ry" and
      "rope 'wry." Harding's early Dublin edition spells "awry" as "a
      wry."

124   *Doctor Innis.* "Alexander Innes's ΑΡΕΤΗ-ΛΟΓΙΑ, *or, An Enquiry
      into the Original of Moral Virtue* (Westminster, 1728) was published
      the day Smedley wrote his letter. . . . Innes, a fellow-traveller of
      the hoaxer George Psalmanazer, stole the work from Archibald
      Campbell. See Boswell, *Life of Johnson,* under 1761; *DNB* under
      Archibald Campbell (1691–1756); and Bernard Mandeville, *The Fa-
      ble of the Bees,* ed. F. B. Kaye (Oxford, 1924), ii, 25–26." James
      Woolley's note in his edition of *The Intelligencer.*

The Tale of the T——d

This adroit and noxious piece appeared in the fourteenth *Intelligencer,*
for which Woolley suggests a dating of "probably 29 October–2 November
1728." The printing here is based on the first collected edition (London:
A. Moor, 1729, pp. 153–55). The poem's most recent appearance is in
Woolley's 1992 edition of *The Intelligencer.*

20   *Shrovetide . . . the pliant cake.* Shrovetide is the season just before
      Lent, and the name is derived from "to shrive" or to hear confes-
      sion. Shrove Tuesday precedes Ash Wednesday, and is sometimes

called Pancake Tuesday in England from the custom of eating pancakes on the last day before Lent.

Prologue Spoken Before a Greek Play . . .

The previous printing of this poem was as a broadside (TCD), Dublin: Printed and Sold at the Pamphlet-Shop opposite the Tholsel in Skinner-Row, 1729. The same broadside also prints an epilogue that Sheridan had apparently written a decade earlier, and that had appeared in *WM* as "The Epilogue to *Julius Caesar.*" Sheridan used the epilogue first for his 1718 school play, and then may have used it again for a new generation of students in 1728 when he printed it.

The Five Ladies' Answer to the Beau . . .

In 1727 and 1728, an officer in Dublin became a general butt of ridicule under the name of the Little Beau, and occasioned a spate of satiric poems. Swift wrote a poem in the character of the Little Beau, titled "On the five Ladies at *Sots*-Hole, with the Doctor at their Head." According to Faulkner, Sots-Hole was "A famous Ale-house in Dublin for beef-stakes," and Sir John Gilbert in his *History of the City of Dublin,* Vol. II, pp. 23–25, adds that it was between Essex Bridge and the Custom House. Swift's poem twits Sheridan for keeping low company, and begins:

> Fair Ladies, Number five,
> Who in your merry Freaks,
> With little *Tom* contrive
> To feast on Ales and Steaks.
> While he sits by a grinning,
> To see you safe in *Sots-Hole,*
> Set up with greasy Linnen,
> And neither Muggs nor Pots whole. . . .

Sheridan's reply was first printed by Deane Swift in 1765 (4to, Vol. VIII, p. 197; 8vo, Vol. XVI, p. 319), and reprinted by Faulkner in the same year (Vol. XIII, p. 327). A manuscript, which Williams and James Woolley think is not in Sheridan's hand, is in the Huntington Library in the Theophilus Swift papers, and this printing is based upon it. The manuscript also contains Swift's "The Beau's Reply . . ." in his own hand and two endorsements by him, the fuller of which reads, "Sheridan's answer to the Beau, and the Beau's reply."

In his answer, "The Beau's reply to the five Ladyes answer," Swift retorted directly to Sheridan:

> Why, how now dapper black
> I smell your gown and cassock
> As strong upon your back
> As Tisdel smells of a sock. . . .

He then went on to deny that ladies could write such "scurvy stuff," as appeared in Sheridan's poem, and concluded:

> But, Satan never saw
> Such haggard lines as these
> They stick athwart my maw
> As bad as Suffolk cheese.

The exchange has been reprinted in various Swift collections such as Scott, Roscoe, Browning, Williams (pp. 424–29), Horrell, and Davis (pp. 335–37).

Title *Wings.* Wings can be a pair of lateral projecting pieces of a garment on or near the shoulders. However, James Woolley also suggests "perhaps the enormous bow of ribbon at the nape of the neck on some then-fashionable wigs."

15 *clocks.* Sir Walter Scott, apparently thinking it made more sense, changed this word to "cloaks." However, a clock can also be an ornamental figure or figured work on the ankle or the side of a sock or stocking, and this is assuredly Sheridan's meaning.

To My Worthy Friend Tom Sheridan, D. D. . . . (Anon.)

This gently mocking gibe at Sheridan's abilities as a translator and also at his pedantry appeared as a Dublin broadside (TCD) in undoubtedly the year 1728 when Sheridan's translation of Persius was published.

Epigraph Persius's lines in the Prologue to the first Satyr actually read:

> Quis expedivit psittaco suum Xaĩpe,
> Picasque docuit verba nostra conari?

Dryden translates the lines as:

> Who taught the Parrot Human Notes to try,
> Or with a Voice endu'd the chatt'ring Pye?

And Sheridan translates them as:

> Who taught the Parrot its usual Complement of Xaῑpe? and
> Pyes to endeavour at Human Speech?

And he footnotes Xaῑpe as "a Word which they taught their Parrots."

2 *the Sacred Nine.* The nine Muses.

7 *Stapleton.* Sir Robert Stapleton (d. 1669), dramatic poet and translator.

10 *Latian.* Latin.

11 *Your first attempt.* An allusion to Sheridan's Grammar. See the poems published here as "Figures of Speech."

16 *Dunster.* Samuel Dunster (1675–1754), clergyman and translator, whose dull version of Horace evoked this couplet:

> O'er Tibur's swan the Muses wept in vain,
> And mourn'd their Bard by cruel Dunster slain.

29 *did'st.* The broadside has "diddilst."

fn. 4 In Satire I of Persius, lines 99–102 read:

> Torva Mimalloneis implerunt cornua bombis;
> Et raptum vitulo capat ablatura superbo
> Bassaris, & Lyncem Manas flexura Corymbis,
> Evion ingeminat: reparabilis adsonat Echo.

Sheridan translates these lines as:

> Grim Horns they fill'd with Mimallonian Sounds,
> From the proud Calf the ravish'd Head, with Wounds
> The Mother tears; The spotted *Lynx* who draws
> The *Maenad* mad, the brandish'd *Thyrsus* aws.
> *Evion* with loud Acclaim these Furies roar,
> And Echo joins to make the Tumult more.

fn. 6 Sheridan translates the first lines of Persius's Prologue as, "Do not remember I took a hearty Draught of the *Pegasean* Fountain, or that I dreamed like *Ennius* on the two headed *Parnassus,* that all of a sudden I should commence a Poet."

fn. 7 Sheridan translates Persius's "quorum imagines lambunt / Hederae sequaces" as "whose images, on account of their fine Performances, are covered with Ivy." In his footnote, Sheridan calls this "A very proper *Metaphor,* because the Ivy Leaf is in the shape of a tongue."

fn. 8   adionat. Misquoted. Persius wrote "adsonat."

An Ode to Be Performed at the Castle of Dublin . . .

This seems to be the song that Swift wrote about in "The History of the Second Solomon" (1729):

> Having lain many years under the obloquy of a high Tory and Jacobite, upon the present queen's birth-day he writ a song, to be performed before the government and those who attended them, in praise of the queen and king, on the common topics of her beauty, wit, family, love of England, and all other virtues, wherein the king and the royal children were sharers. It was very hard to avoid the common topics. A young collegian who had done the same job the year before, got some reputation on account of his wit. Solomon would needs vie with him, by which he lost all the esteem of his old friends the Tories, and got not the least interest with the Whigs; for they are now too strong to want advocates of that kind; and therefore one of the lords justices, reading the verses in some company, said, "Ah, doctor! this shall not do." His name was at length in the title-page; and he did this without the knowledge or advice of one living soul, as he himself confesseth.

And, in truth, even making allowance for this piece being meant to be sung rather than merely read, one must admit that it is not one of Sheridan's successful productions.

The only previous printing that I have discovered is a broadside, printed in Dublin, 1728/29 (TCD). However, see "An Ode to be Performed at the Castle of Dublin" of 1729/30 (Appendix III), which uses the first twenty-two lines of the 1728/29 poem and then adds thirty-five new ones.

From The Critical Minute (Tracey)

In 1731, James Hoey of Dublin published *The Critical Minute: A Poem of the Epick Kind in Two Books* by Michael Tracey. It was "Inscribed to the Rev. Dr. S," and contained these familiar, joshing lines.

1–5   These lines are a pastiche of lines 17–21 in Book I of *The Dunciad Variorum:*

> O thou! whatever Title please thine ear,
> Dean, Drapier, Bickerstaff, or Gulliver!

> Whether thou chuse Cervantes' serious air,
> Or laugh and shake in Rab'lais' easy Chair,
> Or praise the Court, or magnify Mankind. . . .

4 *Busby's easy chair.* Possibly a reference to Richard Busby (1606–95), who was for many years the headmaster of Westminster School. According to the *DNB*, "Busby's name has become proverbial as a type of the severest of severe pedagogues; and though this character of him only rests upon general tradition, there appears to be little doubt that during his extraordinarily long reign at Westminster he ruled the school with a rod of iron, or rather of birch. But it is also clear that his rule was as successful as it was severe. He gained the veneration and even love of his pupils, among whom were numbered a vast majority of the most distinguished men in a distinguished era." Such men included Dryden and Locke. The *DNB* description, incidentally, rather resembles Swift's description of Sheridan as a schoolmaster.

A New Simile for the Ladies

Sheridan's poem appeared first in a small octavo pamphlet of eight pages, in Dublin in 1732 (NLI, Forster, Illinois, Texas), and next in *The Gentleman's Magazine* of August 1732. The poem occasioned Swift's witty "An Answer to a Scandalous Poem," and both were printed together in a small octavo pamphlet of sixteen pages, in Dublin, in 1733. Notable subsequent appearances were in Faulkner, Vol. VI, 1738 (pp. 173–78); in *Miscellanies in Prose and Verse,* Vol. VIII, London: T. Cooper, 1742 (pp. 334–48); *Miscellanies,* Vol. IX, 1745 (pp. 268–71); in *The Muse in Good Humour,* 6th ed., 1751 (p. 321); in Scott, in Roscoe without the footnotes, in Browning, in Williams (pp. 612–28), and in Davis (pp. 547–50).

Sheridan's sixth footnote, with its anecdotes about Xantippe, reflects his preoccupation with the topic of shrewish wives, and the three stories of the footnote are all contained in his collection of Apothegms.

1 A London publication of the poem by W. Owen in 1748, under the title of "The simile: or, woman a cloud" (BL) has a slightly different first line: "In vain I oft have try'd to find."

A Prologue to *Julius Caesar* . . .

The only previous printing I have discovered of this prologue is the broadside printed by S. Hyde in Dame Street, Dublin, undoubtedly around the time of the production (Folger). Earlier, probably in 1718, Sheridan had also produced *Julius Caesar,* and the epilogue for that production appears in *WM* and in a broadside of 1728 or 1728/29. Had this amusing prologue been written before its 1732 production, I am inclined to think it would have appeared in the broadside together with the epilogue.

Title   Madam Violante. Madam Violante had for a few years in Dublin a Lilliputian troupe of child players, among whom was the subsequently celebrated Peg Woffington.

Now to Lampoon Myself for My Presumption

This previously unpublished quatrain occurred in a letter of January 5, 1734, to Jane Oughton (Yale), and was a comment on his translation of "Pere Bouhours' Fountain" (see App. I) contained in the same letter. The title printed here appears indented and immediately above the poem in the Oughton letter.

The pun on human feet and metrical feet had been made earlier by Sheridan in his poem to Swift of ca. September 21, 1718, where he wrote:

> Thy verse, which ran both smooth and sweet,
> Now limp upon their gouty feet. . . .

I Ritu a Verse o Na Molli o Mi Ne

This Anglo-Latin jape appeared in a letter from Sheridan to Swift, dated June 28, 1734. The copy-text is its first printing by Deane Swift in 1768. Its modern reprintings occur in Ball's *Correspondence,* Vol. V (p. 75), and in Williams's, Vol. IV (p. 239). Sir Walter Scott translated it as:

> I write you a verse on a Molly o' mine,
> As tall as a May-pole, a lady so fine,
> I never knew any so neat in mine eyes;
> A man at a glance, or a sight of her, dies;
> Dear Molly's a beauty, whose face and whose nose is
> As fair as a lilly, as red as a rose is.
> A kiss o' my Molly is all my delight;
> I love her by day, and I love her by night.

1 Williams mistranscribes this line as "I ritu a verse of na Molli o mi ne."

His Modest Apology . . .

In 1731, Charles Carthy published a translation of Horace, and its awkward verses occasioned a spate of satirical epigrams by Swift and his friends. Some were published in *An Account of a Strange and Wonderful Apparition Lately seen in Trinity-College, Dublin,* and some others collected in *Mezentius on the Rack,* both published in 1734. None of the poems was so far signed; however, three selections of them appeared in *The Gentleman's Magazine,* in October and November 1734 and in January 1735. In the 1735 selection (p. 48), there appeared this quatrain which was there titled "Mr. Carthy's Apology for Knocking out a Newsboy's Teeth, who told him his Works would not sell." It was signed "T. S——an." This printing is based on the piece's previous appearance in *Mezentius* (p. 21). The group has also been printed by Scott and Williams (pp. 665–72).

As Ball writes, when this clash took place in 1734, "Carthy, who was the son of an innkeeper in Longford, was a man of thirty years of age and a master of arts of Dublin University, where he had been distinguished as a sizar and scholar, earning his bread as a schoolmaster in Dublin" (*Swift's Verse,* p. 289).

Tanti Vi Sed I Tanti Vi

This bit of Anglo-Latin doggerel is contained in a letter from Sheridan to Swift on July 15, 1735. It was first printed in Deane Swift's edition of 1768, Vol. III (p. 12), and appears in the modern collections of Swift's letters: Ball, Vol. V (p. 208); Williams, Vol. IV (p. 364). This printing is based on Deane Swift. Sir Walter Scott, who printed it also, translated it as:

> Tantivy, said I, tantivy,
> Hy! for a Dick in a privy.

Dick is Richard Tighe, a *bête noir* of both Sheridan and Swift.

A Letter of Advice to the Right Hon. John Earl of Orrery

This printing is based on that in *The Gentleman's Magazine,* V, July 1735 (p. 378). The poem was also printed in the *American Magazine and*

Historical Chronicle, November 1744 (p. 658), and in a broadside edition of about twelve copies ("Dublin: Printed by George Faulkner in Essex-street, 1735") by Herbert Davis's bibliography students at Oxford, 1951.

Title   *Orrery.* See Biographical Index.
16 *dean D——l and dean C——.* Richard Daniel (1680/81–1739). Daniel was from 1731 Dean of Down, and Rogers notes that he was "held in low esteem by Swift, both as a man and a poet." The only name in Leslie's *Biographical Index to the Clergy of the Church of Ireland* (NLI) that would seem to fit "dean C——" is William Cross, Dean of Leighlin from 1723 to 1749, and that, of course, rhymes with "loss."
17 *dean I——r and dean S——ne.* I can find in Leslie no plausible possibility for "dean I——r"; however, James Woolley plausibly notes that, as none of the 1735 deans had a name beginning with "I" or "J" and only one 1735 name ended with "r," the "I" could be a misprint for "T." In which case, Robert Taylor or Taylour, Dean of Clonfert, might well have been meant. The "dean S——ne" is probably Louis Saurin, Dean of Ardagh from 1727 to 1749.
34 *solitair, toupee, and snake.* Solitair is possibly a loose neck-tie of black silk or broad ribbon worn by men in the eighteenth century; toupee is a curl or artificial lock of hair, or sometimes the top of a periwig, or even a small wig; snake is a long curl formerly worn with a wig.

While Footman-like He Waits in Every Hall

This quatrain is contained in a letter of Sheridan to Swift of April 3, 1736. The copy-text is its first printing by Deane Swift, Vol. III (p. 73). Its modern reprintings occur in Ball, Vol. V (p. 318), and in Williams, Vol. IV (p. 474).

Upon a Certain Bookseller, or Printer, in Utopia

The subject of this fragment is Samuel Fairbrother who had irritated both Swift and Sheridan by printing some of their poems in the fourth volume of his *Miscellanies in Prose and Verse* in 1735. In a letter of April 3, 1736, Sheridan wrote to Swift that "I am . . . writing a satire upon Mr. Fairbrother, whom I style Fowlbrother, the parish boy." He then included the opening and ending couplets, printed here, and remarked, "If you can think of any hints of a softer kind, I beg you may send them by the next post; for I am in haste to whip the rascal through Dublin." This letter was first printed by Deane Swift, 1768, Vol. III (p. 317), and reprinted in the editions of Swift's *Correspondence* by Ball, Vol. V (pp. 317–18), and Williams, Vol. IV (p. 474). The copy-text is Deane Swift.

In a letter of May 12, Sheridan enclosed the Fowlbrother "encomium," and in a letter of May 15 Swift promised to try and have the poem printed and also suggested the present title. I have not discovered a printing of the complete poem.

My Hens Are Hatching

This piece of doggerel appeared in a letter from Sheridan to Swift. The vague Sheridan apparently considerably misdated his letter, but Swift's reply of June 5 notes that Sheridan's letter had been written twelve days earlier. The letter was first printed by Deane Swift in 1768, Vol. III (p. 81), who printed only the last two lines as verse. Recent appearances are in the editions of Swift's *Correspondence* by Ball, Vol. V (pp. 340–41) and Williams, Vol. IV (pp. 495–96); I have followed their lead in printing the entire piece as verse.

20   *Busy as Kouly Kan against the Turk.* This refers to Tahmasp Quli Khan (1688–1747) who was born Nadr Quli Beg in Northern Kursan, and as Nadir Shah ruled Persia from 1736 to 1747. He was very busy indeed and was constantly at war, driving the Turks out of Persia, threatening Russia, conquering Oman, and occupying Delhi. Of him, the *Encyclopedia Britannica* remarks, "Although so brilliantly successful as a soldier, Nadir was no statesman; his only thoughts were for war." Once, when informed that there was no warfare in paradise, he remarked, "How then can there be any delights there?" In a letter of June 3, 1736, to Swift, Sheridan had also referred to the Persian chief, remarking, "I hear that the czarina, *Kouli Kan,* and the emperor will overrun *Turkey.*" Ball in his edition of the letters has "Kuli Khan."

My Walk It Is Finished and You Shall Want Nothing Fit for Mortal Man

These two pieces of doggerel appeared in a letter to Swift from Quilca, dated June 3, 1736. They were originally printed by Deane Swift in 1768, Vol. III (p. 79 and 80). Recent printings are in the editions of Swift's

Correspondence by Ball, Vol. V (pp. 342 and 343) and Williams, Vol. IV (pp. 497 and 498). This printing is based on Deane Swift.

Grouse Pouts Are Come In

This piece of doggerel originally appeared in a letter from Sheridan to Swift, dated June 23, 1736. It was first printed by Deane Swift in 1768, Vol. III (p. 83); recent appearances are in the editions of Swift's *Correspondence* by Ball, Vol. V (p. 354) and Williams, Vol. IV (pp. 507–8). This printing is based on Deane Swift.

1   *grouse pouts.* A game bird.
6   *We'll.* Deane Swift incorrectly has "Wo'll."

I Wish Your Reverence Were Here to *Hear* the Trumpets

These lines appeared also in the June 23 letter cited above, and are reprinted by Ball and Williams.

1   here . . . *hear.* Ball italicizes neither word; Williams italicizes both.

Our River Is Dry

These lines first appeared in a letter to Swift, dated July 6, 1736. They were first printed by Deane Swift in 1768, Vol. III (pp. 84–85); recent printings are in the editions of Swift's *Correspondence* by Ball, Vol. V (p. 361) and Williams, Vol. IV (p. 513). This printing is based on Deane Swift.

Grouse Pouts

These lines first appeared in a letter to Swift, dated July 20, 1736. They were first printed by Deane Swift in 1768, Vol. III (pp. 89–90); recent printings are in the editions of Swift's *Correspondence* by Ball, Vol. V (p. 367) and Williams, Vol. IV, (p. 520). This printing is based on Deane Swift.

1 Grouse pouts. A game bird.

To the Rev. Doctor Swift, Dean of St. Patrick's. A Birthday Poem . . .

Williams remarks, "This birthday offering by Sheridan is mentioned by him in a letter to Mrs. Whiteway, 21 Nov., 1736, *Corresp.* V. 394–5. He intended it 'for Faulkner to publish.' This publication has not been traced; and the poem is reprinted from *Miscellaneous Pieces in Prose and Verse,* 1789, p. 210."

Actually, Faulkner did publish the poem, and its first appearance was in *The Dublin Journal,* November 27–November 30, 1736, No. 1113. It was then reprinted in *The London Magazine,* December 1736 (p. 696). Its appearance in *Miscellaneous Pieces* of 1789 was on pp. 210–12, and this reprinting is vitually identical with Faulkner's. In Williams, the poem appears on pp. 1050–52.

17–18 These lines doubtless refer to Pope's tribute to Swift in *The Dunciad,* Book I, lines 19–26.
  19 *those by you to Oxford writ.* Probably a reference to Swift's "To the Earl of Oxford, Late Lord Treasurer" and "Horace, Epistle VII, Book I: Imitated and Addressed to the Earl of Oxford."

A Birthday Poem on the Anniversary of the Birth of the Rev. Dr. Swift . . .

The only previous printing of this poem is in George Faulkner's *The Dublin Journal,* No. 1194, Dec. 13–Dec. 17, 1737. The poem is unsigned, but the promise in the previous year's birthday poem, which was also printed in *The Dublin Journal,* to contribute a new poem each year on Swift's birthday, surely makes this poem Sheridan's, as also do the remarks upon Stella and the many musical details. Another corroboration is Sheridan's remarks to Mrs. Whiteway that he was working on a St. Andrew's Day poem, and St. Andrew's Day was also the day of Swift's birth.

Epigraph The quotation is from an Ode of Horace, Liber Secundus, Carmen II, lines 7–8. In Faulkner's printing, "solvi" was misspelled "salvi." W. E. Gladstone translates the lines as:

Borne up, by fame that shall endure,
On wings from melting ray secure.

That is, his desire to gain fame with his pen will lead his pen to
take no account of disaster.

34   *the dark invader, Wood.* For William Wood, see Biographical Index.
This line and the next few refer to Swift's opposition, especially in
The Drapier's Letters, to Wood's halfpence.

41   *Lydian airs.* Milton has the phrase "soft Lydian airs" in "L'Alle-
gro," line 136. The Lydian was one of the modes of Greek music,
and was relaxing, languishing, and sensual, unlike the chaste Do-
rian, the wild Phrygian, or the brisk Ionian.

O Would That Enemy I Dread, My Fate

Previously unpublished. Contained in Sheridan's holograph *Apo-
thegms,* Vol. 3, Greek and Latin, the Gilbert Collection, MS. 125, no
pagination. This poem and the five immediately following were jotted
down on occasional free leaves of the *Apothegms,* and, although the fly-
leaf of the volume contains a class list dating from possibly 1725, the
poems may be more plausibly assigned to the early or middle 1730s.
Indeed, the "Joshua Battus" poem was most probably written in 1730
around the time of Swift's quarrel with Joshua Allen.

The first allusion to the *Apothegms* was in Swift's letter to Sheridan of
March 27, 1733. However, the project was such a large one that Sheridan
may have been working on it for a considerable time before that date. In
any event, on July 31, 1736, Sheridan wrote to Swift that, "My collection
of witty sayings, &c. is finished." It was not, however, until nearly eleven
months later that Sheridan wrote to Swift, on June 22, 1737, saying:

Ego habeo tres libros sapientum dictorum transcripto pro te in pulchra et
magna manu, quas mittam ad te per primam opportunitatem, ante ut meus
dominus Orrery vadit pro Anglia: nam promisit capere illos cum se, et facere
pactum pro me cum praelatore.

Which I translate as:

I have three books of wise words transcribed for you in a beautiful and large
hand, which I will send to you at the first opportunity, before my lord Orrery
goes to England, for he promised to carry them with him, and to make an
agreement for me with someone who will put it forward (i.e., a printer or
publisher).

As this sonnet and the five following poems contain Sheridan's revisions, these volumes of *Apothegms* would seem to be the originals to which Sheridan referred in 1736 and from which he made Orrery a transcription "in pulchra et magna manu" to take to England. In any event, it is impossible to date this group of poems with any more precision than assigning them probably to the period of 1730 to 1736.

The sonnet in manuscript is untitled.

3 Sheridan originally started to write this line with the words "Of Sacred Silence."
5 *soft.* Sheridan originally wrote "dear."
6 *great Love.* Sheridan originally wrote "myself."
11 For this line, Sheridan originally wrote "And leave me those cares to discompose my breast."
14 *but you.* These are my words; what Sheridan wrote is illegible.

When G——le Has Her Mind at Ease

Previously unpublished. Contained in Sheridan's holograph *Apothegms,* Vol. 3, Greek and Latin, in the Gilbert Collection, MS. 125.

This poem is much more worked over than any of the other occasional pieces in *Apothegms* as Sheridan was trying out various lines and interpolating revised ones. The version here is probably close to his final intention, but the stages by which he reached it, although intriguing, are impossible to reproduce in print. The original conclusion of the poem, starting with line 21 was, however, somewhat longer:

> But in a moment all is over;
> Again revived by smiles, you love her;
> Again you see that heav'nly grace
> Which youth and mirth had in her face.
> Thus April days give joy or pain,
> Just as they please to shine and rain.
> Thus as she's better, as she's worse,
> She is my blessing or my curse.

The poem has some slight similarity to Swift's "Daphne" about Lady Acheson, which begins:

> Daphne knows, with equal ease,
> How to vex and how to please. . . .

The poem in manuscript is untitled.

Joshua Battus's Spepeech to the Paparliament

The subject of this poem is Joshua Allen, the second Viscount Allen. His father, although a Whig, had opposed the ministry over Wood's coinage, and the younger Allen was also friendly with Swift. However, the younger Allen spoke out in the Privy Council against the award of a small gold box and the freedom of the city of Dublin to Swift. At the same time, he let it be known to Swift that he was not at all ill-disposed to him. From this incident came two of Swift's most vicious poems, "Traulus, Parts I and II," in which he flayed not only Allen, but, in traditional Irish fashion, the low professions of Allen's ancestors. These poems were published in 1730, and it is probable that Sheridan's poem was written about the same time. Lines 3–16 of Sheridan's poem seem a clear reference to Swift's fierce attack on politicians in the 1730 poem "A Libel on D—— D——. and a Certain Great Lord" and to Allen's attack on Swift in the Privy Council where, according to Swift, he said, "My Lord, you and your city can squander away the public money in giving a gold box to a fellow who has libelled the government!" The humor of Sheridan's poem derives from Allen's speech impediment and his cowardice, and may have been suggested by such lines from "Traulus" as:

> And though you hear him stut-tut-tut-ter,
> He barks as fast as he can utter.

And:

> Fierce in tongue, in heart a coward.

The poem is previously unpublished and is contained in *Apothegms,* Vol. 3.

Title Battus. Stammerer, from the Greek "battos" to the Latin "battus."
After line 16 Sheridan struck out this couplet:

We'll strike the MuMuMuses dumb,
And DuDuDulness shall o'ercome.

20 *nennannaked sword.* Sheridan did not cross out these words, but
    he did write above them "sword, I give my word."

So on the Stream the Silver Swan

Previously unpublished, but contained in *Apothegms,* Vol. 3. This and
the two following poems may possibly have been intended as one poem.
The form of each is identical, and the content is similar. James Woolley
has, in fact, suggested that perhaps they are not to be read in the order
in which they appear in *Apothegms,* and that "So on the Stream the
Silver Swan" might be meant to follow "Some Nymphs May Boast Ex-
ternal Grace." The poem in manuscript is untitled, and is possibly a
translation.

4 *flying.* This is my word. Sheridan's is illegible, but is in two sylla-
   bles, and the second syllable is probably "ing."

Be Still, Thou Busy Foolish Thing

Previously unpublished, but contained in *Apothegms,* Vol. 3. The poem
in manuscript is untitled.

 3 *causèd.* This word is my substitution. The original is illegible.
 5 *flame.* This word is my substitution. The original is illegible.
 8 *dear.* Sheridan originally wrote "sweet."
13ff This entire stanza is crossed out in the manuscript.

Some Nymphs May Boast External Grace

Previously unpublished, but contained in *Apothegms,* Vol. 3. The poem
in manuscript is untitled.

10 *the barren.* Sheridan originally wrote "th' uncomely."
19 *mortal.* Sheridan originally wrote "outward."
20 *a celestial.* Sheridan did not cross "a celestial" out, but he did write
    "an aetherial" above the line.

29–30.   Sheridan did not cross these lines out, but on the facing page he wrote these alternative lines:

> But by her rosy hue revealed
> Is seen by every eye.

36   *A mild though piercing.* Sheridan originally wrote "A calm and piercing."
37   Sheridan originally wrote and then crossed out "So when we view some stream."

From Some Critical Annotations . . . (Whyte)

Laurence Whyte's poem appeared in his collection titled *Poems on Various Subjects, Serious and Diverting, Never before Published* (Dublin: S. Powell, 1740). The ten lines devoted to Sheridan appear on pp. 150–51. The poem, like several others in the book, was probably composed in the 1720s or early 1730s, but is impossible to date more precisely. Little, in fact, is known about this interesting and able poet. Bryan Coleborne, who reprints some Whyte pieces in *The Field Day Anthology,* writes that "He was born in County Westmeath, perhaps around 1700, and lived in Dublin where he became a teacher of mathematics. He was associated with John and William Neal, father and son, leading publishers of music in Dublin in Swift's day. Whyte appears to have been active in writing poetry between the mid-1720s and the early 1740s. He died in 1755." Patrick Fagan, who reprints more of Whyte in *A Georgian Celebration* (pp. 32–42), thinks that he was born in the early 1680s and died in 1752 or early in 1753.

70   *in the tenters.* To be in a position of strain, uneasiness, or anxious suspense.

Appendix I: Verse Translations

AFTER LUCRETIUS

From the "Preface" to *Ars Pun-ica* . . . (Dublin: James Carson, 1719). This is a translation of:

> Omnia enim lepidi magis admirantur, amantque,
> Germanis quae sub verbis latitantia cernunt:

> Verbaque constituunt simili fucata sonore,
> Nec simili sensu, set quae mentita placerent.

These lines, however, are Sheridan's adaptation of lines 641–44 from Book I of Lucretius' *De Rerum Natura*:

> omnia enim stolidi magis admirantur amantque
> inversis quae sub verbis latitantia cernunt,
> veraque constituunt quae belle tangere possunt
> auris et lepido quae sunt fucata sonore.

W.H.D. Rouse and Martin Ferguson Smith translate these lines as:

For dolts admire and love everything more which they see hidden amid distorted words, and set down as true whatever can prettily tickle the ears, and all that is varnished over with fine-sounding phrases.

AFTER CLAUDIAN

From the "Preface: to *Ars Pun-ica*. This is a nominal translation of:

> Vocibus alternant sensus, fraudisque jocosae,
> Vim duplicem rident, lacrymosaque gaudia miscent.

AFTER MARTIAL?

The "Preface" to *Ars Pun-ica* assigns the following lines to Martial:

> Sit mihi, Cinna, comes, salibus dictisque facetus,
> Qui sapit ambiguos fundere ab ore sonos.

However, Edgar Siedschlag's *Martial-Konkordanz* (Hildesheim and New York: Georg Olms Verlag, 1979) shows no such lines in Martial, and they are probably Sheridan's own.

AFTER PETRONIUS

From the "Preface" to *Ars Pun-ica*. This is a nominal translation of:

> Dicta, sales, risus, urbana crepundia vocum,
> Ingenii facilis quae documenta dabunt.

The only line I can find resembling this in Petronius occurs in Poem 16:

Dicta, sales, lusus, sermonis gratia, risus vincunt naturae candidioris
   opus.

See the Loeb Classical Library edition (London: William Heinemann,
1913), p. 352. Michael Heseltine translates the line as "Words, wit, play,
sweet talk and laughter, surpass the work of too simple nature."

AFTER LUCAN?

From the "Preface" to *Ars Pun-ica*. This is a nominal translation of:

> Ille est imperium risus, qui fraude leporis
> Ambigua fallens, humeros quatit usque solutis
> Nexibus, ac tremuli trepidant curvamina dorsi,
> Et jecur, et cordis fibras, et pandit anhelas
> Pulmonis latebras. . . .

However, *A Concordance of Lucan* by Deferrari, Fanning, and Sullivan
(Washington: The Catholic University of America Press, 1940) cites no
such lines in the *Pharsalia*, and I suspect that these are Sheridan's own.

AFTER HORACE

From the "Preface" to *Ars Pun-ica*. This is a nominal translation of:

> . . . Si quid novisti rectius istis,
> Candidus imperti; si non, his utere mecum.

> (Hor. I. Ep. vi. 67)

H. Rushton Fairclough translates more literally: "If you know something
better than these precepts, pass it on, my good fellow. If not, join me in
following these."

AFTER MARTIAL?

In *Ars Pun-ica*, p. 8, the following lines are attributed to Martial:

> Qui studet alterius risum captare lepore,
> Imprimus rictum contrahat ipse suum.

Again, Siedschlag's *Martial-Konkordenz* shows no such lines in Martial,
and they are probably Sheridan's own.

CHORUS FROM SOPHOCLES' *PHILOCTETES*

Sheridan's *The Philoctetes of Sophocles* was published in Dublin in
1725, printed by J. Hyde and E. Dodson, for R. Owen, Bookseller in

Skinner-Row. The chorus occurs on pp. 25–26. Antistrophe II is here omitted, for it concerns the plot of the play and also seems of lesser merit.

2 *Ixion.* "After he had murther'd his Father-in-law Deioneus being much rack'd on that Account, Jupiter in Compassion translated him to Heaven, where he basely attempted Juno; for which, Jupiter had him fix'd to a Wheel in Hell, which was to turn round for ever." Sheridan's note.

CHORAL SONG FROM *PHILOCTETES*

The Philoctetes of Sophocles (p. 31).

AFTER HORACE

This printing of this loose translation is based on its first publication in *The Intelligencer*, No. 4, probably on June 1, 1728. It is based on Book II, Satire VI, ll. 70–76 of the Satires:

> . . . ergo
> sermo oritur, non de villis domibusve alienis,
> nec male necne Lepos saltet; sed quod magis ad nos
> pertinet, et nescire malum est agitamus: utrumne
> divitiis homines an sint virtute beati;
> quidve ad amicitias, usus, rectumne, trahat nos;
> et quae sit natura boni, summumque quid eius.

H. Rushton Fairclough translates the passage as:

And so begins a chat, not about other men's homes and estates, nor whether Lepos dances well or ill; but we discuss matters which concern us more, and of which it is harmful to be in ignorance—whether wealth or virtue makes men happy, whether self-interest or uprightness leads us to friendship, what is the nature of the good and what is its highest form.

TASSO'S *AMORE FUGGITIVO*

The text of this translation is in Volume 3 of Sheridan's manuscript collection of *Apothegms* (Gilbert). It was published as an appendix to *The Faithful Shepherd, A Translation of Battista Guarini's* Il Pastor Fido *by Dr. Thomas Sheridan* (Newark: University of Delaware Press, 1989). There is no indication of when Sheridan wrote it, but it appears among work he was doing in the early and mid 1730s.

1   *realms of light.* Sheridan originally wrote "bright abodes."
3   *to find my.* Sheridan originally wrote "of a stray."
4   For this line, Sheridan originally wrote "Who has himself and me undone." He next tried "The cruel Brat from me has run."
8   For this line, Sheridan originally wrote "And almost pierc'd me to the heart."
11   *saw.* Sheridan originally wrote "found."
31   *Yet he.* Sheridan originally wrote "But oft."
40   This line was originally "Shall be rewarded by a kiss."
43   This line was originally "Whoever sends him back to me."
44   In the manuscript, there are two illegible, crossed-out versions of this line.
50   This line was originally "I plainly see, that I'm beguil'd."
59–60   These lines were originally "But I shall mark him so, no doubt, / At first sight you'll find him out." In the revision, the word "know" was at first "find."
63   *by.* Sheridan originally wrote "with."
78   This line is crossed out in the manuscript, but not revised.
86   *a dancing.* Sheridan originally wrote "the brightest."
110   *love.* Sheridan originally wrote "like."
123   *hide.* Sheridan originally wrote "strive."
132   *shall not.* Sheridan originally wrote "ne'er shall."
138   *a.* Sheridan originally wrote "some."

PERE BOUHOURS' FOUNTAIN MADE MUDDY BY THE TRANSLATOR

This translation appeared in a letter to Jane Oughton, dated January 5, 1734, where Sheridan gave it this title and where it was followed by the original quatrain "Now to Lampoon Myself for My Presumption." A slight variation titled "The Fountain" is contained in Vol. 7 of *Apothegms* (Gilbert, MS. 129). This printing is based on the version in the letter (Yale).

Pere Bouhours is Dominique Bouhours, a French Jesuit who was born in 1628 and died in 1702. He wrote theological and polemical work, but was best known as a literary critic. His *La manière de bien penser* of 1687 was his most ambitious critical work and was anonymously translated into English in 1705 under the title of *The Art of Criticism: or, the Method of making a Right Judgment upon Subjects of Wit and Learning*, and was known and admired by Addison, Dryden, Pope, Johnson, Chesterfield, and others.

"The Fountain" is quoted in Dialogue III of *The Art of Criticism*, and is not by Bouhours, but I have been unable to trace the author. The French version reads:

C'est-la par un chaos agréable & nouveau
Que la terre & le ciel se rencontrent dans l'eau;
C'est-la que l'oeil souffrant de douces impostures,
Confond tous les objets avec leurs figures;
C'est-la que sur un arbre il croit voir les poissons,
Qu'il trouve des roseaux auprès des hameçons,
Et que le sens charme d'une trompeuse idole,
Doute si l'oiseau nage, ou si le poisson vole.

3   In the *Apothegms* volume, Sheridan crossed out the original line, which read "Thy sweet imposture strikes the wond'ring eye."
6   *And.* In *Apothegms*, Sheridan wrote "There."
7   *deluding.* In *Apothegms*, Sheridan wrote "delusive."
8   *While.* In *Apothegms*, Sheridan wote "That." However, he then struck out "That birds," but the new words are illegible.

FROM LUCAN

This translation occurs in *Apothegms*, Vol. 9, pp. 74–75 (Gilbert, MS. 131). Sheridan is translating lines 4 to 6 and lines 14 and 15 from Book II of Lucan's *Belli Civilis*:

Cur hanc, tibi, rector Olympi,
Sollicitis visum mortalibus addere curam,
noscant Venturas ut dira per omnia clades? . . .
Sit subitum, quodcumque paras; sit caeca futuri
mens hominum fati; liceat sperare timenti.

Appendix II: Educational Verses upon Latin Grammar, Prosody, and Rhetoric

THUS CACUS-LIKE, HIS CALVES HE BACKWARDS PULLS

The previous publication of these untitled lines was in the Preface to Sheridan's *An Easy Introduction of Grammar in English for the Understanding of the Latin Tongue* (p. v). They illustrate the point Sheridan was just making about the difficulty young students had in learning Latin by memorizing the many rules in the Colet-Lily *A Short Introduction of Grammar.*

1   *Cacus.* Lewis and Short in *A Latin Dictionary* describe Cacus as a "son of Vulcan, contemporary with Evander, a giant of immense physical strength, who dwelt in a cave on Mount Aventinus, and troubled the whole region around by his robberies; he robbed even

ᅟᅠᅠ

Hercules of the cattle of Geryon, and was on that account slain by him." See Ovid's *Fasti*, Book I, line 550: ". . . traxerat aversos Cacus in antra ferox." Sir James George Frazer translates the line as "Fierce Cacus had dragged the bulls backward into his cave."

2 *Lily's.* William Lily (1468?–1522), English grammarian, whose rules Sheridan adapted for his own grammar.

OF THE GENDERS OF NOUNS

The previous publication of these verses was in Sheridan's *An Easy Introduction of Grammar* (pp. 36–40). Sheridan considerably expands Lily's rules into verse, and then discusses them in prose. Thus Sheridan's General Rule 1 is an expansion of Lily's "The Masculine Gender is declined with this Article; Hic; as, Hic vir, *A Man*." And Sheridan's General Rules 2 and 3 expand Lily's "The Feminine Gender is declined with this Article Haec; as, Haec mulier, *A Woman*." I have omitted Sheridan's examples of Latin words following each rule, even when he arranges them in meter and rhyme.

1 *haec virago.* This example might well reflect Sheridan's feelings about his unhappy marriage.

FROM OF KNOWING THE GENDER OF NOUNS BY TERMINATION

Sheridan's rules for the five declensions, of which only the first is printed here, first appeared on pp. 41–42 of *An Easy Introduction*.

FROM OF PROSODY

Sheridan's verses on Latin prosody, of which only one seems of sufficient interest to print here, first appeared on pp. 185–89 of *An Easy Introduction*.

OF QUANTITY WHICH DEPENDS UPON THE AUTHORITY OF THE POETS

These lines first appeared on p. 196 of *An Easy Introduction*.

OF FIGURES PECULIAR TO PROSODY

These lines first appeared on pp. 241–44 of *An Easy Introduction*.

FIGURES OF SPEECH

The only previous printing of these lines was in "A Method to Improve the Fancy. In which is a Choice Collection of Images and Descriptions.

With Various *Figurative* Beauties, gather'd from the Best *Latin* and *English* Poets, both *Ancient* and *Modern*" (Dublin: Printed by Daniel Tompson, in Cole's-Alley, Castle-street, [1714]). Although "A Method to Improve the Fancy" is a separate work and has its own title page, it was published with Sheridan's *An Easy Introduction of Grammar in English for the Understanding of the Latin Tongue*, and its pagination continues directly on from that of the *Easy Introduction*. About the poem, Sheridan notes:

> I have not here Comprehended all the several sorts of Figures that are to be met with in the *Poets*, nor did I think it necessary; since my Design was only to chuse such as were chiefly Ornamental, and as might be sufficient to *improve* the *Fancy*, and *refine* the Taste. Whatever Figures there are besides in Poets, they seem rather to be the Production of Chance than Choice; and are such too as the common Current of Language leads us naturally to, so that I, for that very Reason, thought it needless to lay down any Rules for what might be understood without 'em. (p. 326)

In the original printing, the piece is broken up into small verses with their title on each topic, and each small verse is then followed by illustrations from various classical or English authors. However, the various small verses really constitute one verse essay, and there are enough connectives and transitions between verse paragraphs to warrant considering them so.

The illustrative quotations are typographically set off from the verses themselves, and most of them are attributed to some particular author. A handful, however, are not, and I have included them in the body of the poem as they resemble several illustrations in the poem itself and I have discovered no other author and hence have concluded that they may be by Sheridan himself. They are, however, identified in the notes.

John Greer in *Bathyllus Redivivus* demonstrates that Sheridan's verse rules in *An Easy Introduction of Grammar* are but slightly varied cribs from Lily. However, as Greer scrutinized Sheridan's volume very closely but made no charges about these Figures of Speech verses, and as I have discovered no source myself, I assign them to Sheridan as original work. The title is the present editor's.

28 *Antonomasia.* Identification of a person by an epithet or appellative that is not his name, as "his lordship."
29 *Molo.* A teacher of rhetoric at Rhodes in the first century B.C.
30 *Catachresis.* Misuse or strained use of words.
36 *Metonymia.* Metonymy is the use of one object or concept for another to which it is related, or of which it is a part, as in "crown" for "sovereign."

42–45   In the original printing, these lines are typographically indicated as an illustration. As they are attributed to no author and as I have not been able to ascribe them to one, I include them in the body of the poem as possibly being either Sheridan's own composition or his translation from a classical source.

50   *I've lived some autumns.* Italicized in the original to indicate that the clause is itself an illustration of synecdoche.

52–53   These two illustrative lines from Horace are probably Sheridan's translation.

72   This line is unpunctuated in the original printing, but "much" and "little" are italicized.

74–75   In the original printing, these are unattributed illustrative lines.

123–124   In the original printing, these are unattributed illustrative lines.

125   *Prosopopoeia.* Personification.

Title   *Aposiopesis.* ". . . a rhetorical artifice, in which the speaker comes to a sudden halt, as if unable or unwilling to proceed." *OED.*

133   *Asyndeton.*   The omission of conjunctions.

OF EPIGRAM

This verse first appeared in Sheridan's "A Method to Improve the Fancy" (p. 326).

Appendix III: Poems of Doubtful Attribution

A HUNTING SONG

This conventional piece was first published in Charles Henry Wilson's *The Polyanthea: or, A Collection of Interesting Fragments, in Prose and Verse: Consisting of Original Anecdotes, Biographical Sketches, Dialogues, Letters, Characters, &c. &c.*, Vol. I (London: J. Budd, 1804, pp. 6–7). There, the author describes an interview, presumably at some time in the late eighteenth century, with a Mr. Con. Sheridan of Uaghteraghy, Co. Cavan, who says that he grew up with Dr. Sheridan and was, indeed, his cousin. Con. Sheridan is quoted as saying of the young Sheridan and of this poem:

His father kept a pack of hounds, and if he had not parted with them in time, he would have shared the fate of Actaeon. The son, to the great mortification of the old man, preferred the dog-kennel to the school; the sound of the horn would have roused him from his bed, the coldest morning in winter; and as the chase was all the rage in the part of the country where he lived, I am really astonished that a line of Lily ever stuck to his memory. He was not insensible, however, to the charms of learning; he was fond of listening to the conversation of those who had made any progress in letters, and would treasure up their remarks; and sometimes he would make such observations on them as evinced, that the seeds of genius were sown in his mind, and that a little cultivation would call them into a plentiful harvest. The father saw this, and made use of every argument in his power, to draw his favourite son from those pursuits and amusements that are so congenial (if I may use the expression) to the youthful mind. I recollect a hunting song he wrote, when he was twelve years old; and if it does not exhibit strong marks of poetical powers, it will at least tend to confirm what I have said, that the chase was his favourite amusement. This is the song; as it is the copy of a copy, perhaps the original has lost as much by transcription, as some originals have lost by translation. (pp. 5–6)

The title is taken from Con. Sheridan's remarks above.

VERSES ON A WOODEN LEG

The only previous printing of this poem is in Wilson's *The Polyanthea*, Vol. I (pp. 7–9). There, Wilson reports that Sheridan's cousin, Mr. Con. Sheridan, called this piece "a bud of the same spring" in which "The Hunting Song" was written. If Sheridan did write the piece, it is a surprisingly smooth and humorous work for a boy of twelve, but the various sardonic references to marriage, which he well might have made a dozen years later, seem curious for a youth.

6   *Richard Roe.* The party to legal proceedings whose true name is unknown, especially the second such party when two are unknown, the first being called John Doe.

7   *Old Nick.* The devil.

29   Although the original printing contains no quotation marks, line 28 would indicate that the following remarks have been spoken by Jerry Cross.

40   *a Tartar.* A savage, intractable person.

44   *tare . . . tret.* The author seems to be attempting a semipun utilizing the cliché "wear and tear"; however, tare and tret are the two ordinary deductions made in calculating the net weight of goods to be sold by retail. Tare refers to the weight of the wrapping, receptacle, or conveyance of the goods, which is deducted from the gross weight; tret (spelled "trett" in *The Polyanthea*) is the allowance of $\frac{1}{26}$ allowed for wastage during transportation.

52   *trice.* There may be something of a false pun here, relating back to the "one-third price" of the previous line, and depending upon the similarity of sound of "trice" and "thrice."

66   Although no punctuation is used in the original publication, line 67
      begins with the words "Now, reader," and so possibly Jerry Cross's
      remarks end with line 66.

THE ENIGMA IN THE LAST *MERCURY* EXPLAINED

This verse first appeared in *The Muses Mercury* of May 1707 (p. 116)
where it was described as "By Mr. S. W." It was an answer to a riddle
in the previous month's issue, which has been sometimes attributed to
Swift and which reads:

> From India's burning Clime I'm brought,
> With cooling Gales, like Zephirs fraught;
> Not Iris, when she paints the Sky,
> Can shew more different Hues than I;
> Nor can she change her Form so fast,
> I'm now a Sail, and now a Mast;
> I here am Red, and there am Green,
> A Begger there, and here a Queen.
> I sometimes live in House of Hair,
> And oft in Hand of Lady Fair;
> I please the Young, I grace the Old,
> And am at once both Hot and Cold:
> Say what I am, then if you can
> But find the Rhime, and you're the Man.

Both verses were reprinted in an undated Dublin broadside of the 1720s
(TCD), when the first was attributed to "Dr, S——t, to My Lady Cart-
eret," and the answer to "Dr, S——g." They were next printed by Faulk-
ner in Vol. VIII of Swift's *Works* (1762, p. 17) and Vol. XI (1763, p. 428),
and also in the London trade editions of Swift's *Works* (Vol. XIV, 1762,
p. 144; 4to, Vol. VII: 2, 1764, p. 136; 8vo, vol. XIV, pp. 242–43). In these
editions the riddle was attributed to Swift and the answer to Sheridan.
Williams in reprinting them (p. 912) remarks that, although the original
riddle might have been by Swift, the explanation could not have been by
Sheridan. Certainly Sheridan's authorship seems highly improbable, but
the verse is printed here for completeness. Both poems are reprinted by
Davis (p. 613) in the section called "Riddles by Swift and his Friends";
Rogers does not include them.
    Immediately following "The Aenigma in the last *Mercury* Explained"
in *The Muses Mercury* of May 1707 is the editor's note that "The Author
of the Explanation of the last *Aenigma*, has sent us another, which he
tells us is general, though it seems to be particular." This riddle ("I'm

wealthy and poor," see Davis, p. 614) could not be by Sheridan as it makes reference to two English women whom he could not have known.

PADDY'S CHOICE

The only previous printing of this poem is in Wilson's *The Polyanthea*, Vol. I (pp. 17–21). If we credit the account of Con. Sheridan there, these verses were written about his brother's marriage. Wilson quotes him as saying:

> Well, Sir, as I see you have a good stock of patience, I'll read you some lines which are connected with the subject we have touched upon [the relations of young men and women], which I did not think time had spared; they were written by my cousin, on an occasion that will be long remembered in this part of the island; and as poets succeed best in fiction, perhaps in addition to his youth, the best apology will be to assure you, that they are founded in truth. They were written on my brother, a very worthy man; who had the happiness of living and dying in the bosom of a fine family of children, five sons and six daughters; blessed with common sense, and an education that every day improves. (p. 16)

The suggested dating of the poem is pure conjecture. However, Paddy Sheridan's age at his marriage is given in the poem as twenty-four; if Thomas Sheridan were a few years younger, the poem might have been written in his very early twenties.

For the most part, the poem is merely conventionally graceful; however, it is worth preserving for the effective and homely details of Shela's speech at the end.

AN IMPROMPTU ON PARTING FROM ELIZABETH MACFADDEN

This quatrain first appeared in *The Polyanthea*, Vol. I (p. 28). There Wilson quotes Con. Sheridan as saying:

> The Doctor and I called one morning on Miss Mac Faden, in order to take his leave of her for a few days, as he was to set out on a journey, I forget where. The young lady asked in a tone that well expressed more than the words that accompanied it, how long he intended to stay away? to which he immediately answered . . . .

Sheridan married Elizabeth MacFadden probably shortly after he received his B.A., on February 9, 1710/11, and so this piece might be dated sometime fairly shortly before that date.

Although he was no doubt sufficiently ardent in his courtship to have composed such lines to her, we have it clearly stated several times by him and his friends and acquaintances that his marriage was almost instantly to be unbearably unhappy. The point, then, that makes the authenticity of the four poems attributed to him in *The Polyanthea* so suspicious is Con. Sheridan's account therein of the marriage:

I knew her very well, a woman of spotless character, Miss Mac Faden; she was descended of a Scottish family of respectability; she was agreeable in conversation, pleasing in her manner; in short, she was a good girl and an affectionate wife: I cannot say that she was handsome; she had beauty sufficient, however, to captivate the Doctor; and the truth is, he rejoiced through life in his captivity, for it was a gentle one. (p. 26)

AMPLISSIMO DOCTISSIMOQUE VIRO RICARDO BULSTRODE . . .

This previously unpublished poem appears in A Collection of Latin Poems Addressed to Sir Richard Bulstrode and is in the collection of the Beinecke Rare Book and Manuscript Library at Yale. Following the poem is the attribution to "Mr. Sheridan" in another hand than that of the poem itself. The handwriting of the poem has some points of resemblance to Sheridan's, but I would by no means assert that it is his.

Sir Richard Bulstrode (1610–1711) was the very long-lived soldier, diplomatist, and author who followed the fortunes of the Stuarts. At the outbreak of the Civil War, he joined the army on Charles's side and was subsequently promoted to adjutant-general of horse and then to quartermaster-general. After the Restoration, he was appointed agent at the court of Brussels, and in 1675 he was knighted. After the accession of James II, he was given the higher title of envoy to Brussels. After the revolution, he followed King James to the court at St. Germains, where he died on October 3, 1711. According to the *DNB*, "He is said to have 'enjoyed a wonderful firmness of mind and strength of body to the very last,' and to have died, not of old age, but of an indigestion which in all probability would not have ended fatally had his own physician not been out of the way."

Save for one early poem printed when he was at Cambridge, all of Bulstrode's literary works were posthumously published. In 1712 there appeared his *Original Letters written to the Earl of Arlington* (London: R. Sare, 1712). This volume also contained a selection from the 185 Latin verse elegies and epigrams, chiefly on divine subjects, which Bulstrode

had written when he was in his eighties. It is these poems that are cele-
brated in "amplissimo Doctissimoque viro Ricardo Bulstrode."

LINES WRITTEN ON A WINDOW IN THE EPISCOPAL PALACE AT
KILMORE

The first publication of this poem that I have discovered was in the
Armenian Magazine, Vol. VIII (1785, p. 536). It was printed as a riposte
to the poem quoted below in Wilson that begins "Resolve me this, ye
happy dead," and both pieces were attributed to Sheridan. Both pieces
were republished in Wilson's *Swiftiana*, Vol. I (pp. 198–200), and only the
reposte was attributed to Sheridan. Wilson wrote:

> Soon after Swift's acquaintance with Dr. Sheridan they passed some days
> together at the episcopal palace in the diocese of Kilmore: when Swift was
> gone, it was discovered that he had written the following lines on one of the
> windows, which looks into the church-yard:

> Resolve me this, ye happy dead,
> Who've lain some hundred years in bed;
> From every persecution free
> That in this wretched life we see;
> Would ye resume a second birth,
> And choose once more to live on earth?

Wilson's further remarks have a persuasive circumstantiality: "In the year
1780, the late Archdeacon Caulfield wrote some lines in answer to both.
The pane was taken down by Dr. Jones, Bishop of Kilmore, but it has
been since restored." The present episcopal palace in Cavan is a mod-
ern building.

Bishop William Bedell (1571–1642) is most known for his translation of
the Old Testament into Irish, a task in which he was assisted by his
protégé, Denis Sheridan, who was possibly Dr. Sheridan's ancestor.

Both poems were reprinted by Scott and later editors. Williams in-
cluded them only in his section "Poems Attributed to Swift" (pp. 1099–
1100), and suggested a possible date of 1717 or 1718.

    1 Bedell. "Bishop Bedell's tomb lies within view of the window."
       Scott's note.

ASSIST ME, MY MUSE, WHILST I LABOR TO LIMN HIM

This poem first appeared in *WM* (pp. 335–36). It was first printed by
Fairbrother, Vol. IV (pp. 201–202), as well as by Scott, Williams (pp.

997–98), and others. There is some uncertainty about its authorship. Although untitled in *WM*, Fairbrother assigns it the title of "Sh——n to D-n J——n," while Williams gives it the title of "Answer by Dr. D——ny." There is some evidence in the poem to support both views, but the ending would seem to tilt the evidence in favor of Delany. So also would the fact that Sheridan also wrote a reply to Swift's "In Vindication of Dan **Jack**son's picture," to which this poem is itself a reply. In *WM*, the "In Vindication" poem occurs immediately before this one (on pp. 333–35), and reads:

> Three merry Lads with Envy stung,
> Because Dan's face is better hung,
> Combin'd in Verse to run it down,
> And in its Place set up their Own;
> As if they'd run it down much better   5
> By Number of their Feet in Metre.
> Or that it's Red did cause their Spight
> Which made them Draw in Black and White:
> Be that as 'twill, this is most True,
> They were inspir'd by what they Drew.   10
> Let then such Criticks know my Face
> Gives them their Comliness and Grace,
> Whilst ev'ry Line of Face does bring
> A Line of Grace to what they Sing.
> But yet methinks, tho' with disgrace   15
> Both to the Picture and the Face
> I shou'd name the Men who do Rehearse
> The Story of the Picture Farce.
> The Squire in French as hard as stone,
> Or Strong as Rock, that's all as One,   20
> Or Face on Cards is very brisk, Sirs,
> Because on them you Play at whisk, Sirs;
> But much I wonder why my Crany
> Shou'd envy'd be by De'el-any
> And yet much more that my half namesake   25
> Shou'd joyn as Party in the Freak,
> For sure I am it was not Safe
> Thus to abuse his better half,
> As I shall prove you, Dan, to be
> Divisim and Conjunctively;   30
> For if Dan love not Sherry, can
> Sherry be any thing to Dan?
> This is the fate from whence you see
> That Dan: makes nothing of Sherri.
> Or Shou'd Dan be by Sherry ore ta'en   35
> Then Dan wou'd be poor Sheridan.

'Tis hard then Dan shou'd be decry'd
By Dan with Sherry by his Side
But if the Case must be so hard
That Faces suffer by a card;   40
Let Criticks Censure, what care I? ⎫
Back biters only We defy,   ⎬
Faces are free from Injury. ⎭
  Merry Dan, as 'tis fitting
  To Sheridan Sendeth greeting.   45

(This poem I have transcribed from *WM* without modernizing the spelling or capitalization, although I have inserted a mark or two of punctuation when it seemed that the sense might otherwise be confused.)

This poem seems possibly by Swift, just as several later pieces in the exchange were written by him in Dan Jackson's name. The cleverness of the word play about names is quite in Swift's vein.

Williams notes that the last two lines of "In Vindication" are the incorrect heading of "Assist Me, My Muse." The two lines in *WM* are between the two poems, and their position on the page makes it difficult to see with which poem they belong. In content, however, they appropriately conclude "In Vindication," and make no sense at all appended to "Assist Me, My Muse."

  2   *Credite, Pisones, isti tabulae persimilem.* This line is quoted a little inaccurately from l. 6–7 of Horace's *Ars Poetica.* Philip Francis translates it as "Would you not laugh such Pictures to behold?"
  4   Williams, following *Miscellanies. The Tenth Volume* of 1745, has "That I envy your Verse, tho' I didn't your Face."
 10   I have followed Fairbrother, 1745 and Williams in using the word "Monstership's," although *WM* appears to say "Mastership's."
 14   *greatly.* Fairbrother, 1745 and Williams have "justly."
 15   *well.* 1745 and Williams have "right."
     and by. Fairbrother, 1745 and Williams have only "and."
 19   *your.* Fairbrother has "the."
 22   *the.* Fairbrother has "your."
 27   *that.* Fairbrother has "but."
 31   *Consort.* Fairbrother and Williams have "Concert."

ENIGMA *AND* DIRECTIONS FOR LAUGHING

These two poems occur toward the end of Vol. III (p. 372) of *WM*, and they immediately follow the section of poems by Sheridan, Swift, and their friends. Other than that fact, and also that Sheridan, Swift, and their friends did write a number of unsigned riddles to each other, there is no reason for attributing the poems to them. Nevertheless, the adroitness of the poems, their appropriate content, and their obscurity have persuaded me to include them here.

SHERIDAN'S MASTERPIECE . . .

This minuscule dramatic parody is in several ways a puzzle. The anonymous author of "A Letter to Tom Punsibi" (se l. 51 and fn. 6) seems definitely to attribute it to Sheridan; Foxon, however, describes it as a satire on Sheridan's play, which probably it is, as its subtitle, "Tom Pun-Sibi's Folly Complete," would hardly have reflected Sheridan's own sentiments. Certainly also, on its own, it is much too short to be a play, unless, indeed, the very shortness is part of the parody of the heroic tragedy's length and afflatus, just as Fielding's Tom Thumb is a parody of the superhuman Drawcansirs and Tamarlanes. However, whether this be Sheridan's own parody or someone else's of a serious or even burlesque heroic tragedy by Sheridan, the piece is quite clever.

The other principal parody, which Sheridan might have known, of heroic tragedy was Buckingham's *The Rehearsal* of 1671. Fielding's brilliant *The Tragedy of Tragedies* did not appear until 1731, ten years after Sheridan's piece. Curiously, though, Fielding's parody seems very close. For instance, in the broadside printing of "Sheridan's Masterpiece," lines 9, 10, 16, 36, and 46 are asterisked, indicating that footnotes, in the manner of Fielding, were to follow (although for some reason they do not).

Apparently the only previous printing was a Dublin broadside of 1721 or 1721/22 (Cambridge, Rothschild).

Title Sheridan's. The broadside prints "S——s."
Epigraph Scriptis Patet Scriptor. The writer is laid bare in what he writes.
 14 beggar's bullets. According to Brewer, stones.
24 & 29 Xerxes. Spelled "Zerxes" in the original.
 50 Jackadandy. According to Brewer, "a term of endearment for a smart, bright little fellow."

VERSES WRITTEN ON ONE OF THE WINDOWS AT DELVILLE

Concanen included this piece in his *Miscellaneous Poems* of 1724 (p. 242), and Nichols in his *Supplement* of 1776 (pp. 536–37) reprinted it. In both instances, it was unsigned, but followed "A Description of Dr. Delany's Villa," which is usually attributed to Sheridan. Williams discussed the poem in his section of "Poems Attributed to Swift" without coming to any conclusion, and Rogers did not include it as Swift's. Part of the

joke in the poem, however, is also the basis of the joke in "A Description
of Dr. Delany's Villa"—that this largish estate is assumed by the writer
to be diminutive. The possible date of composition, in 1722 or 1723, is
suggested by Williams. This printing is based on Concanen.

9–10   Delany frequently entertained at Delville such poets as Sheridan,
         Swift, and Helsham.

PUNCH'S PETITION TO THE LADIES

This poem was first collected by Scott who remarked:

> This poem partly relates to Wood's halfpence, but resembles the stile of
> Sheridan rather than of Swift. The latter would not have used such frequent
> elisions, or left so many bad rhymes; though some of the last may be the errors
> of the transcriber. It is copied from a manuscript occurring in a thick volume
> of broadsides and loose tracts, chiefly printed, containing several of the Dean's.
> In the same hand and volume I find a manuscript of the Dean's version of
> Horace, Book I, Ode XIV, and Mr. Hartstonge inclines to think the hand-
> writing of both corresponds with that of the Lanesborough MS [*The Whimsical
> Medley*]. Hoppy or Hopkins, here mentioned, seems to be the same rapacious
> master of the revels satirized in Vol. XIV, p. 156. He was secretary to the Duke
> of Grafton, when Lord-Lieutenant. (Vol. X, 1814, pp. 587–90)

Stretch was a puppet-master who came to Ireland from England and
played in Capel Street. Although the poem has some droll allusions to
Wood's coinage, as when Punch suggests that puppets being false people
should pay in false coins, its principal target is Edward Hopkins,
Grafton's secretary and also Master of the Revels who refused to allow
the puppet show to proceed without a large payment.

The poem was first printed in two very slightly different Dublin broad-
sides of 1724 (Huntington). There are two or three differences in punctua-
tion and spelling, and in line 24 one broadside mistakenly prints "And" for
"An." Also one broadside has no spaces between the verse paragraphs.
Nevertheless, the broadsides are basically the same version of the poem,
and that version is fairly close to Scott's printing. Both the broadsides
and Scott differ considerably from a manuscript copy once owned by
Barry Brown, dated January 1723 (Huntington). The Brown version con-
tains about eighteen lines more, and also seems metrically more correct.
The present printing is based mainly on the Brown version, and the differ-
ences between it and the broadsides and Scott are noted below.

Williams thinks that there is no evidence for Swift's authorship. There
is also no certainty that the piece is by Sheridan; however, in 1721, Sheri-
dan did produce a play entitled *Punch Turned Schoolmaster*, in which the

actors, to combat the success of the puppets, themselves played puppets. Sheridan's prologue to that play, also spoken by Punch, appears above.

Epigraph   *Quid non mortalia pectora cogis, / Auri sacra fames? Virgil, Aeneid*, III, l. 56. Translated by Covington as "Fell lust of gold! abhorred, accurst! / What will not men to slake such thirst?" The epigraph is not printed by the broadsides.

1 Scott has "Fair ones who do all hearts command. . . ."

5 *you'd.* The broadsides and Scott print "you'll."

6 *Vander hop.* Printed as "Vanderhop" by the broadsides. An allusion to Edward Hopkins (1675–1736), Master of the Revels in Ireland in 1722. Beneath the title, one of the broadsides has, in a contemporary hand, "Written upon Secretary Hopkins refusing to let Stretch act without a large Sum of money."

14 This line is the version of the broadsides and Scott. Brown more awkwardly has, "Has forced our George away and Dragon."

16 *or.* Scott has "nor."

17 *E'en.* The broadsides have "Even," which harms the meter.
    me. Scott has "us."
    fell. The broadsides and Scott have "full."

19 The broadsides indent this line.

23 *we'd.* Scott has, less metrically, "we had." The broadsides indent this line.

25 *Bannameer.* Spelled "Bandimere" by the broadsides and "Banamiere" by Scott. Neither the broadsides nor Scott indent the line.

28 *the Chancellor.* "Lord-chancellor Middleton, against whom a vote of censure passed in the house of lords for delay of justice occasioned by his absence in England. It was instigated by Grafton, then Lord-Lieutenant, who had a violent quarrel at this time with Middleton." Scott's note.

30 The broadsides have "To Rochford, on the Meath Election." Scott has "To Rochford or the Meath election." As David Hayton remarks, "the disputed By-Election for County Westmeath in 1723 briefly achieved, the status of a *cause célèbre* when the two giants of the Irish Parliament, Speaker William Conolly and Lord Chancellor Middleton . . . patronized opposing candidates." The Speaker supported Richard Levinge and the Chancellor Rochfort. When the returning officer closed the poll prematurely and declared Levinge elected, Rochfort protested; and, after investigation, the ultimate vote in the House of Commons went against him by 89 to 88. See David Hayton, "Two Ballads on the County Westmeath By-Election of 1723," *Eighteenth-Century Ireland*, Vol. 4 (1989), pp. 7–30.

31 Scott's version reads "Nor did we sing,—'Machugh he means.'"

The Brown version and the broadsides more plausibly suggest that the last three words are spoken by Hopkins not Bannameer. The Westmeath By-Election occasioned a number of songs and poems. The poem "Sir Owen MacHugh," printed by Hayton, lampooned Speaker Conolly and almost caused a riot when played during the intervals at the theater. Punch's meaning in lines 26–31, then, is that the puppets did not take sides in political matters.

32   *The.* The broadsides print "ye" and Scott prints "You."
      his. The broadsides and Scott print "your."

34   *nor.* Scott has "or."

35   *I'm.* The broadsides have "I."

38   The broadsides and Scott have "till fifty pounds to me paid down."

39   *dev'lish.* The broadsides and Scott have, less metrically, "devilish." The broadside does not indent this line.

40   *new half-pence.* The broadsides and Scott have "brass farthings."

42   *stews.* The broadsides have "Hews."

43   *to you then be.* The broadsides have "then be to you."

45–50   These six lines are replaced in the broadsides by these two:

> Quoth he! thou Vile Mishapen Beast,
> Thou Knave, am I become thy Jest.

One broadside indents the first line. These lines also replace ll. 45–48 in Scott. Lines 45–48 in both the broadsides and Scott are used later and slightly changed: in the broadsides they are lines 64–67, and in Scott they are lines 65–68.

46   *could'st.* The broadsides have "could" in line 65.

47   *I have.* The broadsides have "that I've" in line 66.

48   *fuer le temps.* Pass the time. In line 67 the broadsides' version is "But to stand prating here with you." In line 68 Scott prints "But to stand prating thus with you?"

49   *Or.* Scott has "And."

52   *were.* Scott has "are."

56   The broadsides' and Scott's version. Brown awkwardly omits the second "for."

60   The broadsides have "I in sober sadness tell ye?" Scott has "I do in sober sadness tell you."

61   *think . . . is.* the Broadsides and Scott have "thought" and "was."

62   The broadsides have "In us fictitious men to bring." Scott has "For us fictitious men to bring."

63-65   The broadsides have:

> Brass counters made by William Wood,
> Which might as well be Understood,   }
> Intrinsick as we Flesh and Blood.

Scott has only two lines:

> Brass counters made by William Wood
> Intrinsic, as we flesh and blood . . . .

66   *And.* The broadsides and Scott have "Then."
68–85   These lines do not appear in the broadsides or in Scott.
86–91   The equivalent lines of the broadsides read:

> Quoth he, thou lovest PUNCH to prate,
> And could for ever hold Debate,
> But think'st thou that I've naught to do;
> But to stand prating here with you,
> Therefore to stop your noisy Parly
> I at once assure you fairly,
> That not a Puppet of you all,
> Shall stir a step without this Wall,
> Nor Merry Andrew beat his Drum,
> Untill you've paid the aforesaid Sum.

88   *Now.* Scott has "that." Also in Scott this line is preceded by the couplet "Therefore to stop your noisy parly, / I do at once assure you fairly . . . ."
90   *Merry Andrew.* Clown, buffoon, mountebank.
91   *th' aforesaid.* Scott has "the foresaid."
92   *solemn pace.* The broadsides have "swiftest pace." Scott has "swiftest race," and does not indent the line.
93   *his Grace.* The Duke of Grafton, the Lord Lieutenant, to whom Hopkins was secretary.
96   *fair ones.* The broadsides have "Ladies."
     I e'er.   Scott has "e'er I."
97   *if.* The broadsides have "that."
98   *the Sec.* Scott has "your sec."
100   Scott has "And tho' he thinks as much of gold . . . ."
103   The broadsides have "your's must Influence, must prevail. . . ."
104   *command.* The broadsides have "Request."
107   The broadsides have "And we in Duty Bound will Pray." Scott has "And we'll in duty ever pray." After this last line of the poem proper,

the broadsides print "PUNCH Cum Sociis," which might be translated as "Punch with his comrades."

A FAITHFUL INVENTORY . . .

This version of this poem was first published by Scott, Vol. XIV (1814, pp. 120–210), who remarked, "this description of a scholar's room in Trinity College, Dublin, was found among Mr. Smith's papers. It is not in the Dean's hand, but seems to have been the production of Sheridan." To support Scott's attribution, one might adduce the flipness of the rhymes and also two somewhat similar poems by Sheridan, "A True and Faithful Inventory of the Goods Belonging to Dr. Swift" of 1724, and "Tom Punsibi's Letter to Dean Swift," possibly of the same year. This version of the poem also appeared in Scott's second edition, in Roscoe and in Browning.

Another considerably different and, I suspect, earlier version appeared in the first volume of *Poems Written occasionally by John Winstanley . . , Interspers'd with many Others by Several Ingenious Hands* (Dublin: Printed by S. Powell, for the Author, 1742, pp. 86–87). That version, under the title of "An Inventory of the Furniture of a Collegian's Chamber" and without its Horatian epigraph, was reprinted by Fagan in *The Second City* (Dublin: Branar, 1986, pp. 107–8), and by Bryan Coleborne in *The Field Day Anthology* (Derry: Field Day, 1991, I, p. 406), and attributed to Winstanley. Many of its lines are the same as those of "A Faithful Inventory," but the lines are differently arranged. There are also lines not in "A Faithful Inventory," and the poem is four lines shorter. Probably the easiest way to show the difference between the two versions is to print the Winstanley version in its entirety:

> Persicos odit puer apparatus. Hor.
>
> Imprimis, there's a table blotted;
> a tattered hanging all besnotted;
> a bed of flocks as one may rank it,
> reduced to rug and half a blanket;
> a tinder box, as people tell us,
> a broken-winded pair of bellows.
> A pair of tongs, bought from a broker,
> a fender and a rusty poker.
> A penny pot and basin, this
> designed for water, that for piss.
> A trencher and a College bottle
> riding on Locke or Aristotle;
> a smutty ballad, musty libel,

a Burgersdiscius and a bible;
a prayer book he seldom handles;
item, a pound of farthing candles.
A rusty fork, a blunted whittle,
to cut his table and his vittle.
There is likewise a pair of britches,
but patched and fallen in the stitches.
Item, a surplice, not unmeeting,
either for chapel or for sheeting,
hung up in study very little,
plaistered with cobwebs, ink and spittle,
with lofty prospect, all so pleasing,
and skylight window without glazing.
Item, if I am not mistaken,
a mouse trap with a bit of bacon,
A candle stick without a snuffer,
whereby his fingers often suffer;
and chairs a couple (I forgot 'em)
but each of them without a bottom;
A bottle standish, pen unmended,
his inventory thus is ended.

Epigraph   Quaeque ipse miserrima vidi.   Scenes of misery which I my-
self witnessed. Virgil, *Aeneid*, Book II, l. 5.

 3   *flocks.* Wool stuffing for a mattress.
21   *trencher.* A platter on which food is cut.
     college bottle. A wine bottle with the college seal on it.
24   *save-all.* A device to hold a candle and allow it to burn to the
     very end.
26   *Burgursdicius.* "Francis Burgursdicius, author of 'An Argument to
     prove that the 39th section of the Lth chapter of the Statutes given
     by Queen Elizabeth to the University of Cambridge includes the
     whole Statutes of that University, with an answer to the Argument
     and the author's Reply,' London, 1727. He was one of those logi-
     cians that Swift disliked." Browning's note. Browning may be cor-
     rect about the author, but is not about the particular book, for the
     one he cites was published two years after the composition of this
     poem. In fact, the reference is probably to Franco Burgersdijck
     (1590–1635), who wrote rather prolifically in Latin under the name
     of Franciscus Burgersdicius, and possibly the volume referred to is
     his *Idea philosophiae moralis, sive Compendiosia institutio* of 1623.
     Scott and Roscoe incorrectly print "A Burger's dicius."
27–28   *C——.* "Illegible. John Overton, 1640–1708, a dealer in mezzo-
     tints." Browning's note. Scott adds, "John Overton's prints are

often mentioned as the furniture of mean apartments." See also
DNB.

THE LINNET AND THE JAY

This poem was published by Nichols in *A Supplement*, Vol. XXIV
(1776, p. 534). In a footnote, Nichols quotes Delany on the poem:

> I have often heard a man of credit, and a competent judge, declare, that he
> never passed one day in *Stella's* society, wherein he did not hear her say
> something, which he would wish to remember, to the last day of his life.—An
> humorous, but wrong-judging, gentleman of her acquaintance, took it into his
> head to set up the character of another lady in rivalship to hers; and raised
> some awkward mirth to himself, from *Stella's* sitting silent, at a visit where
> that lady displayed her talents. On which occasion the above verses were sent
> to her the next morning, probably from some friend of Stella's, for more than
> one of her friends were then present.

Nichols then concludes, "To Dr. Delany himself, the verses may confi-
dently be ascribed." This is certainly possible, and certainly also the
"humorous, but wrong-judging, gentleman" is an apt description of Sheri-
dan. Indeed, the "Poll" of line 9 is a name sometimes applied to Sheridan.
On the other hand, Sheridan was so fond of Stella that it is unlikely he
would have planned a joke at her expense, and this sympathetic poem
might as easily be his as Delany's.

ON FABRICIUS

This piece appears in Henry Brooke's "A Dialogue between Boiled
Beef and Cabbage," which is printed in *Brookiana*, Vol. I (p. 70). It is not
quite apparent from the context whether this poem is meant to be by
Sheridan. Cabbage remarks, ". . . witness the famed Fabricius; how often
have I heard the Doctor run out in his praises. I remember some lines
he repeated the other day on that gallant leader." As I have discovered
the lines nowhere else, I have included them here.
Gaius Fabricius Luscinus was a Roman general of the third century
B.C. He was the hero of the war with Pyrrhus and was noted, as the
poem indicates, for this austere and incorruptible character. Indeed, Cic-
ero often cites him as a typical specimen of Roman virtue.

8   *coleworts.* Any plant of the cabbage kind, such as kale or greens, which does not have a heart.

ON POTATOES

In Henry Wilson's *Brookiana*, Vol. I, there occurs the following account:

> As Mrs. Sheridan was one evening descanting on the beauties of her pansies and tulips, the doctor happened to say, that he preferred a good cabbage to all the "infants of the spring." Nay, even to the rose itself. The lady thought herself bound to defend those flowers to which her cheeks had been so often compared. It hurt her very much to think the offspring of a kitchen-garden should be put in competition with the pride of a flower-garden. The doctor would not yield, in colour, taste, or smell; and, as the company seemed to take part with him, Mrs. Sheridan, at length, in a tone of warmth, which was not natural to her, declared that, in future, the subject of the doctor's panegyric, should give up a certain portion of the garden to carrots and parsnips; and that even boiled beef should be accompanied by these, instead of its wonted companion. (pp. 67–68)

Wilson then relates how Brooke wrote "A Dialogue between Boiled Beef and Cabbage," and left it on the table where it was discovered and read to the company by one of the students. In this amusing dialogue, the present Latin couplet is attributed to Sheridan by the two disputants:

> Cabbage: As the Doctor says.
> Potatoes: The Doctor is fond of punning on my name.
>
> (p. 72)

The title is the present editor's, as is the loose doggerel translation. The suggested dating is utterly a guess.

WONDERFUL MAN, PART THE THIRD

This poem appeared in a Dublin broadside of about 1725 to 1727 (TCD). According to the title, two earlier parts had been published. Possibly the target of the satire is Marmaduke Coghill, an ecclesiastical judge and member of the Irish parliament; see Biographical Index. The connection to Sheridan is the authorial footnote about "some Papers upon the Wooden Man in Essex-Street"; for, according to Tisdall in "Tom Pun-Sibi Metamorphos'd," Sheridan had written on the Wooden Man.

Epigraph: Difficile est proprie communia dicere.   From Horace's *Ars*

Poetica, l. 128. Philip Frances translates it as "'Tis hard a new-form'd Fable to express, / And make it seem your own."

THE BLUNDER OF ALL BLUNDERS . . .

This defense of *Gulliver's Travels* first appeared as a Dublin broadside in 1726 (TCD). A note at the end remarks that "The Publisher hereof will shortly publish a pamphlet, discovering the Ignorance and Stupidity of the Decypherers and Commentators on *Gulliver.*"

A good discussion of the authorship of the poem is by Jeanne K. Welcher and George E. Bush, Jr. in their "Introduction" to *Gulliveriana VI* (Delmar, New York: Scholars' Facsimiles & Reprints, 1976, pp. xxviii–xxxi). They remark, "Sheridan's candidacy as author of *The Blunder of All Blunders* is very possible, but probably unprovable." After noting how Swiftian is the technique, they also note that "The one disordant [sic] note is the high frequency here of feminine rhymes, a feature relatively rare in Swift's work, but very characteristic of the verse of Swift's friend Thomas Sheridan."

The poem's most recent publication is in *JIL*, Vol. XVIII, No. 1 (pp. 44–45).

Epigraph   These lines from "Cadenus and Vanessa" are slightly mis-quoted. The true form is:

> So Stars beyond a certain Height
> Give Mortals neither Heat nor Light.

6 *Newton.* Sir Isaac Newton (1642–1727). English philosopher and mathematician.

     Gassendus. Pierre Gassendi (1592–1655). French philosopher, scientist, and mathematician. Like Bacon he urged the importance of experimental research and was well aware of the discoveries of Galileo and Kepler. The author may have called him Gassendus by assuming that Gassendi was the genitive form.

8 *John O'Noke or John O'Style.* According to the *OED*, John O'Noke was "A fictitious name for one of the parties in a legal action (usually coupled with John-A-Stiles as the name of the other); hence sometimes used indefinitely for any individual person." Like John Doe and Richard Roe.

20 *Don Arbuckle.* Undoubtedly James Arbuckle, editor of *The Dublin Weekly Journal.* He was sometimes called Dan or Daniel Arbuckle, as in the poem "Tom Punsibi's Farewell to the Muses" or in the

broadside "The Last and Dying Words of D-n A——rb——kle, author of 'The Weekly Journal.'" See Biographical Index.

48   This line is a well known saying of the day. The *OED* cites "I know your meaning by your mumping" from James Kelly's *A Complete Collection of Scottish Proverbs* of 1721. "Mumping" would mean foolish tricks or apish pranks.

60   *stuff.* Worthless ideas or discourse, nonsense, rubbish.

81   *Per pauca Desunt.* Probably "Perpauca desunt," a very few are wanting.

EPILOGUE DESIGNED TO BE SPOKEN BY ALONZO . . .

The first printing of this poem is apparently a broadside printed in Dublin about 1726. The TCD copy is contained in *Irish Pamphlets, 1725–1726*. Foxon suggests that the early MS. numeration of the British Library copy suggests 1726. He also remarks that Sheridan possibly wrote it for his school. As there is no record of any other Dublin school producing plays, Foxon's supposition seems likely, even though the subject is uncharacteristically serious. Further, printed on the verso of this broadside are two other poems, one of which is attributed to "T-M PUN——I" in its title; see "A Riddle . . ." below. The "Epilogue" most recently appeared in *JIL*, Vol. XVIII, No. 1 (pp. 45–46).

Title   Alonzo . . . The Revenge.   Alonzo is the hero of Edward Young's very popular tragedy *The Revenge* which was first performed at Drury Lane on April 18, 1721. This is the only instance that has come to light of Sheridan possibly producing a contemporary play.

15   *Southampton.* Henry Wriothesley, 3rd Earl of Southampton (1573–1624). A munificient patron of poets, including Shakespeare.

16   *Dorset.* Probably Charles Sackville, 6th Earl of Dorset (1638–1706). Poet, wit, rake, and patron of letters.

A RIDDLE BY T-M PUN——I, ADDRESSED TO D——H

This riddle is printed on the verso of "Epilogue Design'd to be Spoken by Alonzo . . ." (TCD). The riddle is printed below another piece, "A riddle by the Reverend Dean S——y, to the Countess of N——g." Foxon remarks, "Smedley and Sheridan are clearly intended as the authors, but it is impossible to tell whether the attributions are correct." Given Sheridan's and Swift's dislike for Smedley, it is improbable that Sheridan would have authorized a poem of his to be printed with one by Smedley. I have been unable to solve the riddle, but it sounds like some sort of laxative. If so, it is the sort of riddle that Sheridan might have concocted. Its most recent printing was in *JIL*, Vol. XVIII, No. 1 (p. 46).

ON PADDY'S CHARACTER OF "THE INTELLIGENCER"

This poem was first published as a Dublin broadside of 1728 or 1729 (TCD). It is an answer to William Tisdall's broadside of 1728, "The True Character of the Intelligencer," written under the pseudonym of "Pady Drogheda." This identification was made by Rogers and convincingly refutes Williams's assertion that the poem is a reply to Delany's criticism of Sheridan and Swift's journal. Williams includes the poem as Swift's (pp. 457–58), but Foxon believes that "There seems to be no strong authority for Swift's authorship, plausible though it is." And Rogers adds, "I am not at all certain it is by Swift; it could easily be Sheridan's."

Teerink notes that the poem was reprinted in Cogan's *The Entertainer*, Vol. I (1746); it also appeared in Cogan's *A Supplement to the Works of the Most Celebrated Minor Poets . . .*, vol. III (1750) and his *A Supplement to the Works of Dr. Swift* of 1732, and in many later editions of Swift's poems.

14   *Tom*. Sheridan.
23   *S——'s*. Dean Jonathan Smedley, a frequent literary opponent of both Swift and Sheridan. See Biographical Index.

DEAN SMEDLEY GONE TO SEEK HIS FORTUNE

This poem first appeared as a belated *Intelligencer* in May 1729. It was reprinted in Francis Cogan's second collected edition of *The Intelligencer* in 1730. The most recent editors of Swift's poems, Williams (pp. 454–56), Davis and Rogers (pp. 373–74), have accepted the piece as his, but James Woolley's earlier view, that "there is little evidence as to which of the two authors was responsible," has, nevertheless, still some force.

The occasion for the poem was an account in a London newspaper that Smedley was sailing for India.

Epigraph   Per varios casus, per tot discrimina rerum.   "Through various hazards and events." Dryden's translation.
26   *sped*. Flourished.
28   *cog the dice*. Cheat.
30   *à quatre trois*. In Anglicised pronunciation, "catertrey," meaning to charge that the game is rigged or the dice are loaded.

48   Fort St. George. Madras in India

AN ANSWER TO THE CHRISTMAS-BOX

Toward the end of 1729, Delany, finding his improvements at Delville
had led him into considerable expense, published a poem called "An
Epistle to his Excellency John Lord Carteret," in which he solicited addi-
tional preferment. This occasioned a poem by Swift, "An Epistle upon
an Epistle from a certain Doctor to a certain great Lord: Being a
Christmas-Box for D. D——ny" (Williams, pp. 475–79; Rogers, pp.
400–4), in which he gently ridiculed Delany. There followed a spate of
other attacks and defenses, some by Swift himself. "An Answer to the
Christmas-Box" is nominally ascribed to Rupert Barber, the husband of
the poetess Mary Barber. (A reason for the poem being jokingly attrib-
uted to Barber is that Delany had apparently let Delville, or part of it, to
him. See Swift's "An Epistle Upon an Epistle," where he wrote, "And
set the House to R-p-t B-b-r.") Elrington Ball, however, in *Swift's Verse*
assigns the piece to Sheridan. Williams, in his edition of Swift's poems,
says on p. 487 that the poem may be Sheridan's, and on p. 499 definitely
assigns it to him. Foxon notes that the evidence is wanting for any certain
attribution. Nevertheless, we know that Sheridan did enter into the con-
troversy; for Delany, in his poetic defense called "The Pheasant and the
Lark," described some of his attackers and remarked:

> *Jack-Daw* was seconded by *Tit*
> Tom-*tit* cou'd write, and so he writ.

Sheridan, because of his small size, had previously been called Tom-tit.
There is also a bit of evidence in "An Answer" itself, in line 70, where
the author refers to Delville as "a very small garden." The "smallness"
of Delville was, of course, the central joke in Sheridan's "A Description
of Dr. Delany's Villa." Also, the allusions to Geryon (line 50) and to
Priscian (line 58) had been used by Sheridan before, and Sheridan had
once or twice quoted from Ennius as the author of "An Answer" does in
his epigraph. Further, the familiar and gibing lines at Swift (lines 31–32)
suggest a knowledgeable friend like Sheridan. However, some case—
although not, I think, as circumstantial a one—might also be made for
Sheridan's authorship of another poem in the controversy, "A Letter of
Advice to the Reverend Dr. D-la-y . . ." (see below).
   This printing is based on a Dublin octavo leaflet dated 1729. The TCD
copy is cropped at the bottom, and so the words "reading may sleep" in
the last line may be incorrect.

Epigraph   I have been unable to locate the quotation in Ennius, but a translation might read, "If Troy could be saved with a right hand, it would have been saved by mine."

1   *criblers.* Possibly a misprint for "scribblers."

3   *may go whistle.* Two definitions in Brewer seem relevant: "*You may whistle for that.* You must not expect it. The reference is to sailors whistling for the wind" and also "*Whistle Down the Wind* . . . To defame a person. The cognate phrase 'blown upon' is more familiar. The idea is to whistle down the wind that the reputation of the person may be blown upon."

14   *Sir Ralph.* In "An Epistle to Lord Carteret," Delany had written:

> What fine Cascades, what Vistos might I make,
> Fixt in Centre of th' *Iernian* Lake!
> There might I sail delighted, smooth, and safe,
> Beneath the Conduct of my good Sir Ralph. . . .

His original footnote read "Sir Ralph Gore, who has a Villa in the Lake of Erin." Gore (b. ca.1675) was Speaker of the Irish House of Commons, as Sheridan notes in line 17.

43   *tittle.* A very small bit.

48   *quicker.* Possibly allied to the description of Delany as "planter" in the same line, and therefore meaning one who gives life to or restores to vigor.

50   *Geryon.* In Greek mythology, Geryon is represented as a monster with three heads and sometimes three bodies. It was one of the labors of Hercules to drive off his cattle.

52   *Fermanagh.* Spelled in the original "Farmanagh." Delany had a living in Co. Fermanagh, and had written in his original poem:

> My Horses founder'd on Fermanagh Ways;
> Ways of well-polish'd, and well-pointed Stone,
> Where every step endangers every Bone . . . .

58   *Priscian.* Priscian was a celebrated Roman grammarian, ca. 500–530 A.D.

61   *Charley.* In "An Epistle to Lord Carteret," Delany had written:

> But that the World would think I plaid the Fool,
> I'd Change with Charley Grattan for his School. . . .

Williams notes that "Charles Grattan, seventh son of Rev. Patrick Grattan, of Belcamp, was master of Portora School."

83   Delany had razed the house that was already on his estate and built a new one.

88   *hatched.* The TCD leaflet has, probably incorrectly, "katched."
90   *Swift to his Harley.* Probably the reference is to Swift's poem of
     about 1716, "To the Earl of Oxford, Late Lord Treasurer."

A LETTER OF ADVICE TO THE REVEREND DR. D-LA-Y . . .

We know from Delany's "The Pheasant and the Lark" that Sheridan
entered the verse warfare occasioned by Delany's appeal to Carteret for
patronage. We do not know what Sheridan wrote. "An Answer to the
Christmas Box" is probably his, but "A Letter of Advice," although a
more phlegmatic piece, could plausibly—in knowledge, content, and
style—be his also. The poem refutes a number of Delany's points, such
as his various offices not bringing in sufficient money to allow him to
garden, to buy new books or to contribute to charity.

The text is based on what was probably the first printing, the Dublin
broadside of 1730 (BL, Camb, Rothschild, Yale). It was reprinted by
Scott.

12   *his Gaulstown friend.* This would appear to refer to Swift's poem,
     variously called "The Journal," "The Country Life," or "The Part
     of a Summer at the House of George Rochfort, Esq." Swift was
     accused of ingratitude for having written it.
20–21 These lines might refer to Delany's landscape improvements at
     Delville. See also lines 55–56 of Delany's "Epistle" where he wrote
     "What fine Cascades, what Vistos might I make, / Fixt in Centre of
     th' IERNIAN Lake."
30   *double vicar, double rector.* Quoted from line 30 of Delany's
     "Epistle."
42   *Rupert Barber.* "An Answer to the Christmas Box," which Ball
     attributed to Sheridan, was nominally written by Rupert Barber, a
     Dublin tailor married to the poet Mary Barber whom Swift assisted.

FROM AN ODE (1729/30)

This ode is a revision of the one performed a year earlier in Dublin
Castle. Its first twenty-two lines are identical with those of Sheridan's
1728/29 Ode, except for line 11 which omits the words "at once." The
final thirty-five lines are entirely new.

The only previous printing which I have discovered is an octavo
pamphlet, printed in Dublin for George Ewing in 1730 (BL). The title
page again lists Matthew Dubourg as the composer but, unlike the previ-
ous year's version, does not mention Sheridan. Indeed, his authorship of
the new lines must be considered uncertain. As Swift relates in "The

History of the Second Solomon," Sheridan had come in for considerable criticism for his original effort, and such disapprobation might suggest that Sheridan would have been hesitant about repeating the experiment.

On the other hand, the following gibing comment from the *Dublin Journal* of March 7, 1729/30, with its suggestion of plagiarism, might well suggest that Sheridan did write the second Ode:

Monday last being her Majesty's Birth-Day, was here celebrated with great Solemnity, on which Occasion there was a Song sung, gather'd out of the very Loyal Writings of the Revd. *D——*, and Mr. *Rowe*, late Poet Laureat, *Defunct*. It begun in this or the like Manner,

> *Early Queen of Light arise,*
> *Grind your Colours, Paint the Skies.*

It seem'd like a Magical Incantation to the Goddess *Aurora*, but being perform'd so late, she had got too far of her Journey to be call'd back, and so we have not yet receiv'd any Advices of her returning to Compliment the Poet, who, 'tis believ'd, will not fail to Resent it in his next Poeticks.

A FABLE OF THE LION AND OTHER BEASTS

This verse fable first appeared in *The Dublin Weekly Journal* on November 7, 1730 (pp. 188–89). It was reprinted by Scott who incorrectly says that it first appeared on November 17, but goes on to say:

Many fugitive pieces by Swift and his friends occur in this paper, and, from internal evidence, one is strongly tempted to ascribe the following fables either to the Dean himself, or Sheridan or Delany, under his auspices.

The poem was definitely attributed to Swift by Ball, but Williams more soundly remarks:

It is possible, to judge by internal evidence, that the poem may have come from Swift, but equally possible that it may have been written by Sheridan, Dunkin, or another. After Scott included it the poem was needlessly incorporated in later editions of the *Works*. (p. 1134)

In *The Dublin Weekly Journal*, the poem was introduced by a note to the publisher:

Sir,

Be pleas'd to insert the following FABLE in your paper, and you will oblige some of your constant Readers, but in particular,

Your humble Servant,

Z.

2 sylvester. Inhabiting the woods, wild.

27 Not indented by Scott.

35 Not indented by Scott.

50 Nemine contradicente. Unanimously.

51 Not indented by Scott.

67 These. Scott erroneously prints "such." Also he does not indent this line.

A TRIP TO TEMPLE-OGE, STEPHEN'S GREEN AND THE
BASON . . .

This Dublin broadside was printed in 1730 (BL) and described as "By Thom. Pun-sibi, D.D." Foxon, however, remarks, "The implied attribution to Thomas Sheridan does not seem plausible." One reason for agreeing with Foxon would be that, although Sheridan might still have signed himself Pun-sibi, he would hardly have committed the flippancy of adding "D.D." particularly when the poem was as vulgar as this one occasionally is.

Templeogue is a suburb of Dublin, and in 1730 it had a rather Bath-like spa which featured a weekly ball, morning drives, and promenades. St. Stephen's Green is a public park south of the Liffey, and in 1730 was a place for the fashionable to promenade. Of the Bason, Sir John Gilbert remarks:

A reservoir or "Bason," capable of containing five hundred thousand hogsheads of water, was excavated at the west end of Dublin in 1722.

The grounds surrounding the "Bason" were made attractive by handsome green walks with trees, shrubs and flowers. The place soon became a fashionable resort for the Dublin people, and musical performances were frequently held there.

These remarks appeared in *Calendar of the Ancient Records of Dublin, in the Possession of the Municipal Corporation of That City*, Vol. VII (Dublin: Joseph Dollard, 1878, p. vii). Charles Brooking's 1728 map contained in the volume shows the Bason on the south side of the city, near St. James Street. See also Illustration IX at the end of the volume. The site is presently a park and playground for some nearby corporation flats.

Although it is far from water nowadays, a nearby Harbour Bar suggests its past.

36 *C——t.* Probably Carteret.
49 *B——ly . . . C——s.* The first is unidentified, but possibly "Bailey." The second by the rhyme is undoubtedly "Coxes."
51 *T——h . . . M——C——l.* The first is unidentified. The second is probably "Mountcashel."
57 *Monikee Gaul.* Apparently a well-known prostitute. She was also the subject of "An Excellent New Ballad in Praise of Monaky Gall; in Imitation of Molly Mogg," a Dublin broadside of around 1726, which reads in part:

> Tho' Fortune the Gods have deny'd her,
> Is Wealth to good Judges a Call,
> There's a Fortune (if ever you try'd her)
> In the Arms of dear *Monaky Gall.*

60 *——.* Undoubtedly "pricks."

ON THE REVD. DR. SWIFT, D.S.P.D. LEAVING HIS FORTUNE . . . AND ON THE SAME

These two couplets were first printed by Faulkner in *The Dublin Journal*, No. 920 (Jan. 21–25, 1734). They were unsigned, and there is no reason to attribute them to Sheridan, other than that he did publish anonymously in Faulkner's *Journal*, and that they are quite the kind of squibs he would have written. In any event, they are worth reviving. They were reprinted in *A Supplement*, Vol. XXIV (1776, pp. 583 and 676). When Roscoe reprinted them, the following couplet, which could hardly have been written by Sheridan, had become attached to the second poem:

> Great wits to madness nearly are allied,
> This makes the dean for kindred *thus* provide!

TO THE EDITOR OF *The Dublin Journal*

This unsigned piece was printed by George Faulkner in *The Dublin Journal*, No. 922 (Feb. 1–Feb. 4, 1734). Sheridan published several unsigned pieces in Faulkner's paper, and this one could have been his because of the criticism of Samuel Fairbrother's *Miscellany*, which had contained without authorization some poems by Sheridan and Swift. In a letter to Swift, Sheridan had described Fairbrother as "Foulbrother." See also his fragment, "Upon a Certain Bookseller, or Printer, in Utopia."

PEG RATCLIFF THE HOSTESS'S INVITATION TO DEAN SWIFT

The first known appearance of this piece was in the *London and Dublin Magazine* for June 1735. It was reprinted by Scott, Roscoe, Browning, and Williams (pp. 1049–50). A manuscript copy, upon which this printing is based, is in the Theophilus Swift papers in the Huntington Library. The bracketed words in the text are taken from Scott, as some words are missing from the frayed Huntington manuscript. Scott surmised that the piece was by Delany or Sheridan, but Williams thought that the content quite suggested Delany. The poem does refer to Delany in the third person, but in his *Observations* Delany did refer to himself in the third person.

If the poem were written about the time of publication, Sheridan would not be the likely author, for he was living in Cavan. However, there is some internal evidence to suggest that the poem was written some years before publication. The reference in line 10 to Madam Violante's rope-dancing would suggest that the poem was written in 1729 or 1730. Madam Violante was an Italian rope-dancer and tumbler who appeared in Dublin in December 1729. After some months her popularity waned, and her performance was even attacked as "shockingly indecent." She then organized a company of child actors that may have included Peg Woffington, and her competition to the theater in Smock Alley became so formidable that she was finally forbidden to produce. She left Dublin in 1732 (see LaTourette Stockwell, *Dublin Theatres and Theatre Customs* (Kingsport, Tennessee, 1938, pp. 66–68). If the poem had been written at the beginning of the decade, Sheridan would be a much more likely candidate for its authorship. The poem has, of course, his signature of a farfetched pun, the one on Glasnevin, and has also some general similarity to a few other Sheridan poems such as "An Invitation to Dine."

Title *Ratcliffe.* Scott has "Radcliffe."
   3 *A glass and no wine.* "A pun on Glasnevin—Glass-*ne*, no, and *vin* wine." Scott's note.
  14 *week your.* Scott has "week Sir, your," which helps the meter of one iamb and three anapests.
  16 *Ratcliff's.* Scott has "Radcliffe's."
  21 *or a chair.* Scott has "or chair," which hurts the meter.

24   many. Scott has "any."

WHILE FAME IS YOUNG, TOO WEAK TO FLY AWAY

This poem is contained in *Apothegms*, Vol. 8, p. 55 (Gilbert, MS. 130).
It is impossible to tell if this is an original poem or Sheridan's translation
from an unknown source. It has a thematic connection to the immediately
preceding anecdote in the collection.

   9   china. The thick fleshy root-stock of a shrubby climbing plant
   closely akin to Sarsaparilla, and once supposed to have great me-
   dicinal virtues.

NOW IN THIS THANKLESS WORLD THE GIVERS

This poem is contained in *Apothegms*, Vol. 8, pp. 75–76 (Gilbert, MS.
130). It is impossible to tell if this is an original poem or a translation of
some unidentified piece. It has a thematic connection to the immediately
preceding anecdote.

HOW ARE THEY BANDIED UP AND DOWN BY FATE

This quatrain appears in *Apothegms*, Vol. 8, p. 84 (Gilbert, MS. 130).
It may be a quotation from Otway, but, if so, I have failed to locate it.

LOVE THE MOST GEN'ROUS PASSION OF THE MIND

This poem is included in *Apothegms*, Vol. 9, p. 22 (Gilbert, MS. 131). It
may not be an original poem, but I have not been able to locate the lines.

HE THAT IMPOSES AN OATH

This quatrain appears in *Apothegms*, Vol. 9, p. 99 (Gilbert, MS. 131).
It may not be original.

Biographical Index

ALLEN, JOSHUA, SECOND VISCOUNT (1685–1742). Politician. At one time friendly with Swift, Allen enraged the Dean by speaking out in the Privy Council against the award of an inscribed box and the freedom of the city of Dublin to him. Swift then wrote his two "Traulus" poems against Allen, and Sheridan contributed the probably previously unpublished "Joshua Battus's Spepeech to the Paparliament," one of his most effective pieces of ridicule.

ARBUCKLE, JAMES (d. 1742). Journalist and essayist. A native of Belfast, he published in 1717 a poem called *Snuff*, and was a friend of the Scottish poet Allan Ramsay. In Dublin, as "Hibernicus," he contributed to and for a couple of years edited James Carson's *Dublin Weekly Journal*. A Dublin broadside poem of ca. 1725–26 titled "The Printers Petition to the Poetical Senate assembled in Grub-Street" (TCD) describes his work as editor thusly:

> Arbuckle writes in's *Wee[k]ly Journal*
> How *Phoebus* rose and set diurnal,
> A motto takes from *Rome* or *Greece*,
> A venerable Frontispiece,
> He tells how forty Thousand Men
> Arose, and went to Bed again,
> And mixes true News with what's Spurious,
> To please the Ignorant and the Curious.
> Yet after all this Stir and Pother,
> The *Journal* soon became BumFodder:
> And Elegies their Lordships mourning,
> Keep *Christmas* Pies and Tarts from burning.

He ceased to be editor on March 25, 1727, but his "Hibernicus" papers were published in two volumes in London in 1729 under the title of *Letters and Essays on Several Subjects published in the Dublin Journal*. Robert Munter in *The History of the Irish Newspaper, 1685–1760* remarked that they "were written in a vigorous but unsubtle style, his obvious aim being to teach virtue in a way that the public could not possibly misunderstand .... Arbuckle's writings leaned toward aesthetics." He also wrote the short-lived periodical, *The Tribune* in 1729, the authorship of which has occasionally been mistakenly attributed to Patrick Delany. He was sometimes referred to as Daniel or Dan or Don Arbuckle as in the poem "Tom Punsibi's Farewell to the Muses" or in the broadside "The Last and Dying Words of D-n A-rb-kle, author of 'The Weekly Journal.'" According to a report of a talk given to the Bibliographical Society of Ireland and contained in *The Irish Book Lover*, Vol. XXVI, No. 5 (May, 1939, pp. 103-4), he died intestate on January 16, 1742, and was then described in contemporary papers as a clerk in the Custom House and the Quit Rent Office. See also John F. Woznak, "James Arbuckle and the *Dublin Weekly Journal*," *JIL*, Vol. XXII, 2 (May 1993, pp. 46–52).

BROOKE, HENRY (1703?–1783). Novelist and dramatist. According to Burtchaell and Sadleir, Brooke was born in Co. Cavan, educated by Dr. Jones of Dublin, and admitted to Trinity College as a pensioner on February 6, 1720/21, aged 17. He is said by Henry Wilson in *Brookiana* to have been a pupil of Sheridan before entering Trinity, but there is no hard evidence for the supposition. Nevertheless, as a promising young Cavan neighbor, it is possible that he knew Sheridan fairly well. The poem Wilson attributes to Brooke, "Quilca House to the Dean," is a defense of Sheridan's hospitality against Swift's hard words. In 1739, his *Gustavus Vasa* was proscribed from production at Drury Lane, probably by Walpole. However, it was very successful when issued by subscription and when produced in Dublin as *The Patriot*. His *Jack the Giant-Queller* was produced in Dublin, and also proscribed by the government. His tragedy, *The Earl of Essex*, was produced in 1749 in Dublin and then in London. It contained the passage, "Who rule o'er freemen should themselves be free," which Dr. Johnson lampooned with the line "Who drives fat oxen should himself be fat." Brooke is most remembered for his long novel *The Fool of Quality* in five volumes, which began to appear in 1766. Garrick is said to have so admired his work that he offered Brooke a shilling a line for whatever he would write, an offer haughtily refused. Brooke returned to Cavan where he finally sunk into mental depression and debility, and was tended by his daughter Charlotte, the sole survivor of a family of twenty-one. He died in Dublin on October 10, 1783. Charlotte Brooke is most known for her significant collection, *Reliques of Irish Poetry* (1789).

CARTERET, JOHN, SECOND BARON (1690–1763). Statesman. Nichols's note in *A Supplement*, 1776, remains full and exact: "John lord Carteret was born April 22, 1690, and succeeded his father in the barony September 22, 1695. He was introduced into the House of Lords, May 25, 1711; was appointed a Lord of the Bedchamber in 1714; Bailiff of Jersey, July

20, 1715; Lord Lieutenant of Devon, July 6, 1716; Ambassador Extraordinary and Plenipotentiary to the Queen of Sweden, January 25, 1718/19; and had the honour of mediating the peace between Sweden and Denmark, and between Sweden and the Czar of Muscovy. He was appointed Secretary of State, March 4, 1720/21, and sworn of the Privy Council; constituted Lord Lieutenant of Ireland April 3, arrived at Dublin October 24, 1724; and continued in that high station until May, 1730. He had no other public employment till February 12, 1741/42, when he was again declared Principal Secretary of State. On the death of his mother. . . . his lordship succeeded to the titles of Earl Granville and Viscount Carteret, October 18, 1744; and resigned his office, November 24. On the memorable resignation of the Duke of Newcastle and Lord Harrington, he was once more declared Principal Secretary of State, February 10, 1745/46, but continued only five days in that employment; he was honoured with the Garter, June 22, 1749; and opted Lord President of the Council, June 17, 1751; in which station he died, January 2, 1763." The relations of Carteret and his wife with Swift were cordial, as they were also with Sheridan until the unfortunate sermon in Cork made it politically necessary to terminate them. Carteret was admired for his learning, and on the occasion of a visit to Sheridan's school when a play in Greek was being presented, Carteret familiarized himself with the text beforehand.

COGHILL, DR. MARMADUKE (1670–1738). Judge and politician. He was the son of Sir John Coghill, Master in Chancery, who died in 1699. Coghill received a B.A. from TCD in 1691 and an LL.D. in 1695. In *A History of the City of Dublin*, Sir John Gilbert writes that Coghill "became Judge of the Prerogative Court, Chancellor of the Exchequer, and Member of Parliament for Trinity College, Dublin.

"In his capacity of Judge of the Prerogative Court, Coghill was called on to decide a question between a wife and her husband, who had given her a good beating. The doctor delivered a grave opinion, that moderate chastisement, with such a switch as he held in his hand, was within the husband's matrimonial privilege. This decision so alarmed a lady to whom he had paid his addresses with a prospect of success that she dismissed the assertor of so ungallant a doctrine. Coghill died, unmarried, in 1738." (Vol. II, Dublin: McGlashan and Gill, 1859, pp. 151-52).

CUMPSTY (or CUMSTY), ANDREW (d. 1713). Almanac maker, schoolmaster, and self-styled "master gunner of Ireland." In the late seventeenth century, he and John McComb established a school on Wood Quay, specializing in mathematics, astronomy, navigation, gunnery, and allied subjects. In 1694, he began issuing his *Dublin Almanac* which appeared until 1714. He once had the misfortune to fall out with his fellow almanac maker, the formidable John Whalley who accused him of plagiarizing the cover of Whalley's own almanac, and abused him in prose, poetry, and engraving as "my sheeps-face antagonist" and "a Mathemaggotty Monster," whose almanacs were "yearly nonsense." A Whalley poem on Cumpsty read in part:

> Draw near, you Painters, who your art would grace,
> View here a monster with a sheeplike face:
> A monster in figure, a monster by nature too,
> A monster in arts, all monstrous things can do,
> None e'er did more pretend, or less e'er knew,
> No baboon else, so monstrously divine,
> No ape or monkey ever half so fine;
> And yet in temper ruder than a swine . . .

DELANY, PATRICK (ca. 1685–1768). Clergyman and teacher. Born at Rathkrea, Queen's County, the son of a small farmer, Delany was admitted to Trinity on September 13, 1701, aged 17. He received a B.A. in 1706, became a Fellow in 1709, received an M.A. in 1709, and a B.D. and D.D. in 1722. An extremely popular tutor and lecturer, he was appointed Archbishop King's Lecturer in 1722 and Professor of Oratory and History in 1724. An early friend of Sheridan and highly valued by Swift, he was also an able poet. Several of his pieces about Sheridan appear here, as also do certain others, such as the droll "To My Worthy Friend Tom Sheridan, D.D. on his Incomparable Translation of and Notes on Persius," which may well be his. His estate, Delville, in Glasnevin was, despite its distance from the city, a frequent meeting place for Swift's circle. Delany's extensive improvements to the estate proved a drain on his purse, and he wrote a poem to Carteret seeking further preferment. As he had several church positions in additions to his professorship at Trinity, he came in for several gibing poems from Swift and at least one from Sheridan. Apparently in later years, Sheridan and Delany fell out. The situation was that, at Swift's instigation, Sheridan had been offered a lucrative school at Armagh; however, he took the advice of Delany and other Trinity friends and declined the position, deciding to retain his school in Capel Street. Subsequently, Delany and his friends sponsored a new school in Dublin that seriously harmed Sheridan's. In 1736, when Sheridan had retreated to a school in Cavan, he seemed to refer to this matter when he wrote to Swift, "As for my *quondam* friends, as you style them, *quondam* them all." According to Swift, who had retained his friendship for Delany, Delany had intended Sheridan no harm. In his *Observations upon Lord Orrery's Remarks*, Delany agrees that Orrery's description of Sheridan is generally just, but adds: "He had a faculty, and indeed, a felicity of throwing out hints, and materials of mirth and humour, beyond any man I ever knew. If he were not the stanchest hound in the pack, he was at least the best starter." In May 1744, Delany was appointed Dean of Down. His later years were harried by a lawsuit arising out of his disposal of the property of his first wife, and he died in Bath on May 6, 1768. He wrote much on ecclesiastical matters, volumes of sermons and treatises on transubstantiation, polygamy, and King David. His great talent, however, was as a fluent and able poet, and it is a pity that his productions were only the casual byproducts of his pen. He has never had a collected edition of his poems, but some have been reprinted in various editions of Swift. Of Delany, the *DNB* concludes: "Delany was clearly a man of great talent and vivacity, rather flighty in his speculations, and apparently not very steady in his politics. He was warm-hearted and impetuous, and hospitable beyond his means, leaving nothing but his books and furniture." His second wife, Mary Pendarves (1700–1788) was a notable needleworker and a friend of the royal family and of various literary ladies such as Mrs. Montague and Fanny Burney. Her autobiography and correspondence are of considerable interest.

FAULKNER, GEORGE (1699–1775). Dublin printer, publisher, and bookseller. Called by Swift "the Prince of Dublin printers," he published Swift's works in 1735, and by 1769 there were twenty volumes of them. He also published *The Dublin Journal*, in the pages of which are various items by Sheridan as well as by Swift. For further information, see Robert E. Ward's *Prince of Dublin Printers, The Letters of George Faulkner* (Lexington: University Press of Kentucky, 1972).

GRATTAN FAMILY. A notable Dublin family who lived near Howth. Ehrenpreis writes of them and their relations with Swift:

> But the family that meant most to him was the Grattans. The father [Rev. Patrick Grattan, Fellow of Trinity], now dead, had been chaplain to the first Duke of Ormonde and Prebendary of Howth in the chapter of St. Patrick's. The seven sons all distinguished themselves, the eldest (Henry) being the ancestor of the great patriot. James was one of the leading physicians of Dublin. Richard, a merchant, became Lord Mayor. The youngest, Charles, was master of Portora School, a royal foundation in the north. Three were priests, and of these, two were favourites of Swift: Robert, the fourth son, and John, the fifth. Both were eventually among the executors of Swift's will.

Sheridan was equally their friend, and his song, "My time, O ye Grattans, was happily spent," was written after a convivial visit to their home, Belcamp.

HELSHAM, RICHARD (1682–1738). Physician and scientist. Born at Leggatsrath, Co. Kilkenny, Helsham was educated at Kilkenny College and entered Trinity on July 18, 1697. He obtained a scholarship in 1700, received a B.A. in 1702, and was elected Fellow in 1704 and Senior Fellow in 1714. He was also Lecturer in Mathematics at Trinity from 1723 to 1730, the first to hold the Professorship of Natural Philosophy from 1724 to 1738, and was Regius Professor of Physic from 1733 to 1738. Swift called him "the most eminent physician in this city and kingdom." He was the friend of both Sheridan and Swift and also their personal physician. After his death, his *Lectures on Natural Philosophy* were edited by Bryan Robinson and published in 1739. His will charged his executors that "before his coffin should be nailed up his head was to be severed from his body." He was an able versifier, and on one occasion, perhaps assisted by Swift, played a notable trick on Sheridan (see "Prologue to *Hippolytus*, Spoken by a Boy of Six Years Old"). Swift summed Helsham up in a letter to Pope of February 13, 1728/29:

> Here is an ingenious good-humoured physician, a fine gentleman, an excellent scholar, easy in his fortunes, kind to everybody, has abundance of friends, entertains them often and liberally. They pass the evening with him at cards, with plenty of good meat and wine, eight or a dozen together. He loves them all, and they him. He has twenty of these at command. If one of them dies, it is no more than "poor Tom"! He gets another, or takes up with the rest, and is no more moved than at the loss of his cat. He offends nobody, is easy with everybody. Is not this the true happy man?

For further information, see Brocard M. Mansfield, "Dr. Richard Helsham," *Old Kilkenny Review*, Vol. 3, No. 4, Second Series (1987), pp. 399–405.

JACKSON, DANIEL (1686/87–?). Clergyman. Born in Co. Dublin, he entered Trinity on November 6, 1701, aged 14, and received a B.A. in 1706 and an M.A. in 1709. A member of Swift's Irish circle, and apparently a tolerant one, for suffering the many jokes and poems about his long nose. How extensive his participation was in the sequence of nose poems is uncertain, for both Swift and Sheridan wrote poems in his name. He was a cousin of Sheridan's friends, the Grattans.

JOHNSON, ESTHER (1681–1728). Stella, Swift's protégé, perhaps his wife. Moved to Ireland around 1701, and was much admired by Swift's circle. Sheridan was greatly devoted to her and constantly in attendance at her bedside during her final illness. Sheridan's son in his life of Swift relates that Sheridan was present when Stella in her last illness begged the Dean to acknowledge their marriage. Swift abruptly left, and "it was a long time before [Sheridan] could be thoroughly reconciled to him." This story has generally not been given great credence by Swift's biographers, but it has some points of plausibility. Sheridan was one of Stella's executors.

MOUNTCASHEL, EDWARD DAVYS, THIRD VISCOUNT (1711–1736). As a boy, a student of Sheridan. Entered TCD on December 1, 1727, aged 16, and received a B.A. in 1730. Took his seat in the House of Lords on October 4, 1733, and died unmarried on July 30, 1736, aged twenty-five, at St. Catherine's, the family seat in Co. Dublin. Upon the youth's entering Trinity, Sheridan published an eight-page pamphlet of advice about the future conduct of his life, titled "To the Right Honourable the Lord Viscount Mont-Cassel," and in 1728 Sheridan dedicated his translation of Persius to him, noting that Persius offered appropriate "Systems of Morality" for a young man.

ORRERY, JOHN BOYLE, FIFTH EARL (1707-1762). Became acquainted with Swift and Sheridan in the early 1730s and initially impressed both of them. In 1733, Sheridan dedicated his edition of Sir John Davis to Orrery, and in 1735 published a genially joshing poem called "A Letter of Advice to the Right Hon. John Earl of Orrery." After Swift's death, Orrery published his *Remarks on the Life and Writings of Dr. Jonathan Swift*. This was the first memoir of Swift, but its "rancorous and grudging criticism" offended many of Swift's friends. Rebuttals were published by Delany and Deane Swift, and the younger Sheridan wrote, "I appeal to the Reader whether he ever met in the most stupid, or malicious Commentator, such a total perversion of the meaning of words." In the *Remarks*, Orrery wrote that the elder Sheridan possessed

> . . . the *cacoethes scribendi* [the itch of writing] to the greatest degree, and was continually letting off squibs, rockets, and all sorts of little fireworks from the press, by which means he offended many, particularly persons, who, although they stood in awe of Swift, held Sheridan at defiance. The truth is, the poor Doctor, by nature the most peaceable, inoffensive man alive, was in a continual state of warfare with the minor poets, and they revenged themselves . . .
>
> Dr. Sheridan was a schoolmaster, and, in many instances, perfectly well adapted for that station. He was deeply versed in the Greek and Roman languages; and in their customs and antiquities. He had that kind of good-nature, which absence of mind, indolence of body, and carelessness of fortune produce; and although not over strict in his own conduct, yet he took care of the morality of his scholars, whom he sent to the University remarkably well founded in all classical learning, and not ill instructed in the social duties of life. He was slovenly, indigent, and cheerful. He knew books better than men: and he knew the value of money least of all. In this situation, and with this disposition, Swift

fastened upon him, as upon a prey with which he intended to regale himself, whenever his appetite should prompt him. Sheridan therefore was kept constantly within his reach . . . . But still he remained a punster, a quibbler, a fiddler, and a wit. Not a day passed without a rebus, an anagram, or a madrigal. His pen and his fiddlestick were in constant motion; and yet to little or no purpose . . . .

Orrery later became a friend of Pope and of Johnson, and published a translation of the letters of Pliny the Younger. Dr. Johnson, however, regarded his literary aspirations as exceeding his abilities.

POPE, ALEXANDER (1688–1744). Poet. Through his friendship with Swift, Sheridan came to Pope's notice, and occasionally Sheridan corresponded with Pope, and once or possibly twice sent manuscripts to Pope for comment. When Sheridan's son was sent to Westminster School, Swift wrote to Pope to be kind to him should be the boy present himself. In his poems to Swift, Sheridan frequently alluded to Pope and also to John Gay as models of poetic excellence.

ROCHFORT, GEORGE (ca. 1682–1730). Irish M.P. Son of Robert Rochfort who was Attorney-General for Ireland, Speaker of the Irish House of Commons, and Chief Baron of the Irish Exchequer. His son George, says Nichols, "married Elizabeth Moore, youngest daughter of Henry Earl of Drogheda. He was appointed Chief Chamberlain of the Court of Exchequer, which he held till his death, July 8, 1730. He represented the county of Westmeath in parliament and was of the Privy Council." Swift and his friends were often entertained at Gaulstown House, near Duleek in Co. Meath, the country seat of the Rochfort family. From the handful of verses by Rochfort that have survived, it is clear that he was well able to hold his own in the banter, badinage, and poetic games of Swift and his circle.

SMEDLEY, JONATHAN (1671–?). Clergyman. Born in Dublin and educated at TCD, receiving a B.A. in 1695 and an M.A. in 1698. Took orders and received the living of Rincurran, Co. Cork. He lived, however, mainly in Dublin and was an outspoken Whig. According to the *DNB*, he wrote "some rasping verses affixed to the portal of St. Patrick's upon the announcement of Swift's appointment as Dean." In September 1718, he was presented the Deanery of Killala. His *Poems on Several Occasions* appeared anonymously in 1721, and some of his verses appeared in Concanen's *Miscellaneous Poems by Several Hands* in 1724. In the same year, he resigned from Killala but was instituted as Dean of Clogher in June 1724. There he was visited by Thomas Birch, the future historian and antiquarian, with whom he planned *An Universal View of All the Eminent Writers in the Holy Scriptures*, a plan ridiculed by Sheridan in his "Proposal in Verse for Dean Smedley's *An Universal View.*" Smedley wrote various facile verses, hoping for preferment, and also some attacks against Swift and Pope, particularly in *Gulliveriana* of 1728. Swift referred to him as "that rascal Smedley," and in *The Dunciad* Pope wrote that he was "a person dipped in scandal, and deeply immersed in dirty work." In 1727, he resigned his impoverished deanery of Clogher, and in 1729 he sailed for India, after which nothing is known of him. For further information, see James Woolley's edition of *The Intelligencer* (Oxford, 1991), pp. 135–36.

TIGHE, RICHARD (ca. 1678–1736). Politician. Born in Dublin, admitted to TCD on March 21, 1692/93, aged fifteen, and received a B.A. in 1696. Was a member of the Irish Parliament for Belturbet in 1703, for Newtown in 1715, and for Augher in 1727. An embattled Whig and a member of the Irish Privy Council. It was Tighe who reported to Dublin Castle Sheridan's ill-starred "Sufficient unto the day" sermon, thereby seriously harming Sheridan's career. Swift and Sheridan both vented their spleen on Tighe in various ferocious essays, poems, and squibs, such as Sheridan's "Dick in a Privy" and "To Mr. D.T." or Swift's "Mad Mullinix and Timothy," "Dick, a Maggot" and "Clad All in Brown," a typical stanza of which reads:

> Foulest Brute that stinks below
>> Why in this Brown dost thou appear?
> For, would'st thou make a fouler Show,
>> Thou must go naked all the Year.
> Fresh from the Mud a wallowing Sow
> Would then be not so brown as thou.

Tighe was supposed to have been descended from a contractor who supplied Cromwell's army with bread, and also was said to have beaten his wife—matters duly noted and relished by Swift and Sheridan. For further information, see James Woolley's edition of *The Intelligencer* (Oxford, 1992), pp. 101–3.

TISDALL, WILLIAM (1669–1735). Clergyman. born in Dublin. Entered TCD on April 8, 1688; became Scholar in 1692, received a B.A. in 1693, became a Fellow in 1696, and received a B.D. in 1703 and a D.D. in 1707. Swift was friendly with him from about 1695, but when Tisdall made known his desire to marry Stella, Swift reacted with cold rage. After Stella's death, their relations seem to have improved, and Tisdall was a witness of Swift's will. Tisdall became a notable controversialist, publishing in 1709 "A Sample of True-Blew Presbyterian Loyalty, in all Changes and Turns of Government," and in 1712 "Conduct of the Dissenters in Ireland." The first brought a retort from John McBride entitled "A Sample of Jet-black Prelatic Calumny—hence the name "Jet Black" was occasionally attached to Tisdall. In 1724, Tisdall made his notable verse attack on Sheridan as Swift's fawning sycophant, "Tom Pun-Sibi Metamorphosed: Or, the Giber Gibed." This poem occasioned Sheridan's reply in prose and verse titled "A Letter from a Dissenting Teacher to Jet Black," and also the anonymous "The Rivals," in which Tisdall's poem is attributed to spleen for being excluded from Swift's circle. Denis Johnston used Tisdall as the embodiment of Gluttony in his Swift play, *The Dreaming Dust*.

WHALLEY, JOHN (1653–ca. 1724–29). Newspaper editor, astrological almanac maker, printer, and purveyor of nostrums. His *News Letter* appeared in 1714, and R. R. Madden in *Irish Periodical Literature* writes, "The proprietor, editor and publisher of this newspaper, a *quondam* shoemaker, an astrologer, a quack doctor, an almanack maker, a no Popery firebrand, a champion of Protestant principles, a celebrated empiric, was called 'Dr. Whalley.'" Sir John Gilbert adds that he settled in Dublin in 1682 and was placed in the pillory in 1688. John O'Donovan in *Life by the Liffey* (Dublin: Gill and Macmillan, 1986) calls him "a nasty customer who fulfilled a promise to provide in his *News Letter* 'a full and particular account of foreign and domestic news, by packing its pages with scandals, reckless libels on prominent citizens, fake prophecies and lickspittle support of the government.'" He was certainly abrasive, combative, and abusive, and a poem about him called "A full account of Dr. John Whalley's forced Confession and Entertainment in H-11" concludes with this Epitaph:

> Under this stone doth lie secure
> A man in heart, that of no wife, was wooer,
> The D[evil']s pride, and the world's wonder,
> For perjury and vice doth here lye under.
> A cobbler, doctor, and star gazer, too,
> Methinks he gave the D——l enough to do.
> I beg the favour of you, pond'rous stone,
> To keep secure this wretched dolt and drone.

Whalley's last almanac was published in 1724, and his mantle descended on a Munster astrologer and almanac maker, John Coats or Coates, whose *Vox Stellarum* Madden calls one of the most remarkable almanacs published in Ireland.

WOOD, WILLIAM (1671–1730). Aptly described by Rogers as a Projector. In 1721, he received a patent from Walpole's government to coin half-pence for Ireland. This plan was hotly contested by Swift in "The Drapier's Letters" and other works, and made the Dean an Irish national hero. In this contest, Swift was apparently aided and abetted by Sheridan, although all of what Sheridan himself wrote is not known. See, however, his "The Drapier's Ballad." In his life of Swift, the younger Sheridan wrote:

> During the publication of the Drapier's Letters, Swift took great pains to conceal himself from being known as the Author. The only persons in the secret were Robert Blakely, his butler, whom he employed as his Amanuensis; and Dr. Sheridan. As Robert was not the most accurate transcriber, the copies were always delivered by him to the Doctor, in order to their being corrected, and fitted for the press; by whom they were conveyed to the printer in such a way, as to prevent a possibility of discovery.

Index of Titles

The notes to the poems are indicated by the number in parentheses.

Index of First Lines

General Index

Italicized numbers indicate where a poem appears in the book. The following numbers in parentheses indicate where the notes to the poems appear in the book.

422